CHRISTOPHER SMART

SCHOLAR OF THE UNIVERSITY

CHRISTOPHER SMART
Christopher Smart, 1722-1771, from the portrait in
Pembroke College Hall, Cambridge. Reproduced
through the courtesy of the Master and Fellows of
Pembroke College.

CHRISTOPHER SMART

SCHOLAR
OF THE
UNIVERSITY

by
ARTHUR SHERBO

Michigan State University Press
1967

★
 ★
★
 ★
 ★

*For the Master and Fellows
of Pembroke College,
Cambridge*

CONTENTS

ACKNOWLEDGMENTS

Some indication of the kind, but not necessarily the amount, of help I have received from various people and institutions can be had or guessed at from my footnotes. Other help, specifically that help which makes it possible to do research at all, or which expedites research enormously, is not discernible in the work itself. I willingly catalogue the former, insofar as I can recollect it, and even more willingly and gratefully record the latter. My sincere thanks go to the late Donald Hyde and to Mary Hyde of Somerville, New Jersey, and to James M. Osborn of New Haven, Connecticut, who graciously allowed me to examine and quote materials from their collections. Mr. Herman W. Liebert of New Haven, Connecticut, loaned me his copy of the very scarce *Universal Visiter*. I have received every cooperation from a number of libraries, chiefly those of the British Museum, Pembroke College (Cambridge), Cambridge University, Yale University, and Durham Cathedral. To these should be added the New York Public Library and the Bethnal Green Public Library. The staff of the Public Records Office, the Guildhall Library, of Somerset House, and of the Cambridge University Archives made a number of scholarly chores pleasant and, I must admit, much easier for me. I owe outstanding debts of gratitude to Lord Barnard of Raby Castle, Staindrop; to Dr. Ian Doyle of the Durham University Library; to Dr. Felix Hull, Kent County Archivist; to Drs. Robert Hunter and Ida McAlpine of Bayswater Road, London; to Mr. Stanley Horrocks, Borough Librarian of Reading, Herts; and to Professor Bruce Dickens of Christ's College, Cambridge. Dr. William Bond of the Houghton Library, Harvard University, and Professor Donald Creene of the University of California at Riverside, read parts of my manuscript and suggested changes, almost all of which have been incorporated into my final version. Professor Cecil Price, now of the University College of Wales in Swansea, made available to me information on Smart's letters to Paul Panton. Others, scholars and non-scholars, have contributed in one way or another, and I should like to make a blanket acknowledgment of gratitude to those, their names now lost to me, who answered my letters on this person or that detail.

The Michigan State University All-University Research Board has been kind to me in the years in which I have pursued Smart. Without its aid and that of the John Simon Guggenheim Founda-

ACKNOWLEDGMENTS

tion, which made my original research in England possible, my biography of Smart might conceivably never have come into being.

My greatest debt is to those to whom this book is dedicated. They opened up the resources of their college to me, assisted me in every way possible, put up patiently with my ignorance, and offered me their gracious hospitality.

East Lansing, Michigan   A.S.

September 1966

I.

KENT AND DURHAM, 1722-1739

During May of 1633 Charles I was entertained at Raby Castle, county Durham, by Sir Henry Vane the elder, courtier and later parliamentarian. Vane, starting life with modest holdings in land in Kent, had by a judicious marriage and an eye for the main chance become a rich and important personage. Born in 1589 and described by Clarendon as "of very ordinary parts by nature" and "very illiterate," although of a "stirring and boisterous disposition, very industrious and very bold," he was able shortly after 1614 to buy the estate of Fairlawn near Shipbourne, Kent, at a cost of four thousand pounds. As part of this same expansion of his holdings he also spent eighteen thousand pounds in acquiring the seignories of Raby, Barnard Castle, and Long Newton in Durham. At about the same time that Sir Henry was entertaining his monarch at Raby Castle, Peter Smart, one-time prebendary of Durham Cathedral, was waging a temporarily unsuccessful battle to be released from the King's Bench Prison where he had been confined for views expressed in a sermon entitled "The Vanitie and Downefall of Superstitious Popish Ceremonies," delivered and published in 1628. On the first of March, 1629, he deeded the farmhold known as Snotterton, located near Raby Castle in the parish of Staindrop, to his brother John in consideration of four hundred pounds. Smart had acted with speed to get rid of his estate and procure some ready money, the proceedings against him rising from his sermon having been transferred to another court or commission on January 29, 1629. The small estate was handed down in the family, eventually coming into the possession of John Smart, Christopher Smart's uncle, in March, 1692.[1] Peter Smart of Durham, "Clark" and protomartyr, was Christopher Smart's great-great-uncle. His name has been linked with that of Sir Henry Vane by conjecture alone, but, whatever the worth of such conjecture, the destinies of the Vane family and its neighbors, the Smarts of Snotterton, were to be joined in the next century.[2]

Sir Henry Vane's grandson Christopher inherited Raby Castle when his father was beheaded on Tower Hill in 1662; in 1699 William III created him Baron Barnard of Barnard Castle, and it was he who owned the family's land in Kent. Peter Smart, Christopher Smart's father, was baptized in Snotterton on July 19, 1687 and as a very young man moved south to the Kentish estates of the Vane family where he soon won the confidence of his master. As early as January, 1707, when Peter was but nineteen years old, Christopher Vane conveyed to him and to a certain John Bazire all his lands and holdings in Kent and Durham to be held in trust "for the use of the said Lord Barnard and his heirs forever," evidently anticipating litigation among his heirs after his death. Later events show him to have been prophetic in his fears, for Peter, described fifteen years later as "of Fair Lawne in Wrotham Kent gentleman," was again called upon to lend his name to help Lord Barnard.[3] And when Lord Barnard died on October 28, 1723, it was found that his will, dated September 27, 1715, contained a codicil, added in May of the following year, directing Lady Barnard to pay out of his present estate the sum of forty pounds a year "to my servant Peter Smart during his natural life by four quarterly payments."[4] Smart, as Lord Barnard's steward, would be invested with authority to collect rents, arrange leases, adjudicate problems, and be generally responsible for the estate in the absence of his master.[5] A steward was, then, a person of considerable importance and authority, commanding an annual salary of some fifty to sixty pounds at a time when a laborer in the country earned about thirteen pounds a year.

Not only was Peter Smart well off financially, but it is also clear from a description of his duties that he was a man of some abilities. In addition he was evidently capable of considerable tact, for Lord Barnard possessed a violent temper. On one occasion Barnard became so incensed at his son Gilbert, who had had Raby Castle settled upon him, that he ordered some two hundred workmen to strip the castle of all its lead, iron, glass, doors, and boards.[6] And he, like other members of the Vane family, seems also not to have had the least aversion to litigation. Peter Smart, according to his son Christopher's biographer and nephew, Christopher Hunter, "having been originally intended for Holy Orders, had a better taste for literature than is commonly found in a country gentleman; a taste which he transmitted to his son."[7] Whatever the accuracy of this last statement, Peter was a trusted and respected gentleman occupying the highest position in the management of Fairlawn, a beautiful estate located in one extremity of the parish of Wrotham with part of its stables in the neighboring parish of Shipbourne.[8] There Christopher Smart was baptized on May 11, 1722. Hunter says Smart was born on April 11, and that "in the beginning of his life our Author was of a delicate constitution, having been born earlier than the natural period" (p. vi), causing one to wonder why the baptismal day was delayed for a whole month.

Christopher was not the first child to be born to Peter and his wife Winifred, about whom all that is known is that her family name was Griffiths and that she came from the sparsely populated and hilly county of Radnorshire in Wales. Her granddaughter, Elizabeth LeNoir, wrote of her that "her family had an estate of which I have forgotten the name. She had I think two brothers, and a sister married to Colonel Webb."[9] Colonel Richmond Webb, who married Winifred's sister Sarah, was a kinsman of the famous General John Richmond Webb; it is apparent that the Griffiths were people of position and consequence.[10] Winifred Smart had already given birth to two daughters, Mary Anne, baptized on October 11, 1720, and Margaret, her first born. Although the date of Margaret's birth is not known, the latest possible date of Winifred's marriage to Peter is easily calculable. By 1718 Peter was solidly established, a gentleman in a responsible position enjoying a very comfortable annual wage; he would of course have married in his own class rather than below it. Since the state of education in Wales was fairly primitive at that time—the whole country could not boast of a single established bookseller, only of itinerant book peddlers—the chances are that Christopher's mother was not able to contribute much to her son's formal education. His only references to her occur in the *Jubilate Agno* where he writes that he "made over" his inheritance to her "in consideration of her infirmities" and of her age and poverty (B1, 46–8), and where he exclaims defensively, "For I am the seed of the WELCH WOMAN, and speak the truth from my heart" (B1, 91). At some unknown time, after the period of his last confinement for madness, Smart broke with his mother and probably with the rest of his family, for a letter written by Margaret on the occasion of their mother's death implies that he would not go to the trouble of attending the burying. The letter, written on May 8 from Margate, is to Smart's wife and bears testimony of the "tender respect" Margaret felt for her sister-in-law. The reference to Smart reads, "this days post carries a Letter to my Brother to tell him if he thinks of coming to the Burying he must be at Margate by next Tuesday night."[11] In 1764, after many years of separation, he did not so much as ask a single question about his mother of a friend who had recently visited her. Whatever his feelings for her as a child and a young man, and whatever her early influence on him, the two pursued different paths, she eventually going to Margate to live with Margaret who had married a Mr. William Hunter, a surgeon originally of Ramsgate, he spending the years after he left Cambridge in London.

The parish of Shipbourne where Smart was born lies for the most part below the sand hills in that part of Kent called the Weald. The village itself is at a small distance south of the hill around Shipbourne green with its church on the west side. The mansion of Fairlawn was on the slope of the hill, the offices and some of the grounds lying within the parish. Much of the country thereabouts was unpleasant, very often deeply mired and difficult of passage.[12] It was here that the boy Christopher spent the first four years of his life, his actual residence during this time being on the Fairlawn estate. Again, as so often, it was in *Jubilate Agno* that he recalled the scenes of his early years: "For I bless God in SHIPBOURNE FAIRLAWN the meadows the brooks and the hills" (B1, 119) and "Let Mary rejoice with the Carp—the ponds of Fairlawn and the garden bless the master" (B1, 168). Christopher played in the grounds at Fairlawn with his sisters, occupying an enviable position as the only male child of the family. Considering the importance of his father as steward, the greater age of the Vane children, and the subsequent warm treatment accorded him by the Vane family in Durham, Christopher must have been the pride of Fairlawn as infant and child. His name was doubtless given him by his father as a mark of respect for his employer. When Christopher, Lord Barnard, died in 1723, Peter Smart decided to try his luck as his own master and purchased an estate called Hall-Place in East Barming in 1726, undertaking a mortgage of approximately thirteen hundred pounds, no inconsiderable sum at this time. The property included the mansion house Hall-Place, hopfields, orchards, land in tillage, gardens, woodland, buildings, etc., all to the extent of forty-eight acres largely in the parish of Maidstone, a very respectable piece of land upon which to start a new life.[13] Peter Smart, it is evident, was setting up as an independent landowner and landlord.

East Barming, unlike miry Shipbourne, inspired one antiquarian to lyric terms; it "lies on high ground", he wrote, declining southward to the valley, through which the river Medway flows, being its southern boundary. It is situated opposite to East Farleigh, than which it has a far less rustic and more ornamented appearance. The soil like that is fertile loam, slightly covering the quarry rock, from under which several small springs gush out, and run precipitately in trinkling rills into the Medway; it is enriched too with frequent hop and fruit plantations; the fields are in general larger, and surrounded with continued rows of lofty elms and large spreading oaks, which contribute greatly to the pleasantness of the place. The situation of it, as well as of the neighboring parishes, from Maidstone as far as Mereworth, is exceedingly beautiful, the river Medway meandering its silver stream in the valley beneath, throughout the greatest part of the extent of them; the fertility of soil, the healthiness of air, the rich variety of prospect, adornd by a continued range of capital seats, with their parks and plantations, form altogether an assemblage of objects, in which nature and art appear to have lavished their choicest endeavours, to form a scene teeming with whatever can make it desirable both for pleasure and profit.

The high road from Maidstone to Tunbridge, crosses the upper part of the parish of East Barming, over a beautiful, though small plain, called Barmingheath, part of which is in Maidstone parish. Hence the ground rises to the coppice woods, part of which lie within this parish, and adjoin to a much larger tract northward. About a quarter of a mile on the other side of the road is the church, standing by itself among a grove of elms, the slight delicate white spire of which rising above the foliage of the grove, affords a pleasing prospect to the neighbouring country.

The same writer also says that the sale of Hall-Place near the village of Barming "to Mr. Peter Smart, who bore for his arms, *Argent, a chevron between three pheons sable*" reveals the family arms of which Christopher Smart was so proud.[14]

In due course Christopher was sent to school in the town of Maidstone, situated centrally in the county in a pleasant location, "happily screened by the surrounding hills, arising from the beautiful vale, through which the Medway runs beneath." In the vicinity of the town "the banks of the river continue highly ornamented with spreading oaks, while the country round wears an appearance equal to that of a garden, in its highest state of cultivation," with a soil "remarkably kind for hops, orchards of fruit, and plantations of filberds." The officials and citizens of Maidstone had long enjoyed the "privilege of keeping and preserving swans and signets," normally reserved for royalty, and it is hence no accident that glimpses of these beautiful birds, rarely encountered in English poetry up to this time, appear more than once in Smart's poetry. As the chief town in the county it was alive with activity; barges and small vessels of up to fifty and sixty tons made their way up the Medway as far as the town, which was renowned for its fine paper and linen thread manufactures. A flourishing trade in animals, timber, fruit, hops, and fine white sand for glasshouses and stationers was centered in the town; there the assizes were held; and there four annual fairs were "resorted to by the country for many miles around." There was a free grammar school and two boarding schools "for the education of young ladies, all three schools enjoying good repute."[15] The *London Magazine* of November, 1749, reported that "there are abundance of gentry in and near this town, which renders it very polite," adding, in September, 1750, that it "is an ancient, large, fair, sweet, populous, and well-frequented borough town." Samuel Pepys had visited Maidstone on March 24, 1669, and his description parallels that of later accounts:

> Thence to Maydstone, which I had a mighty mind to see, having never been there; and walked all up and down the town, and up to the top of the steeple, and had a noble view, and then down again: and in the town did see an old man beating of flax, and did step into the barn and give him money, and saw that piece of husbandry which I never saw, and it is very pretty: in the street also I did buy and send to our inne, the Bell, a dish of fresh fish. And so having walked all round the town, and found it very pretty as most towns I ever saw, though not very big, and people of good fashion in it, we to our inne to dinner . . .

Within a few miles of one another, then, or even blending the one into the other, young Smart could enjoy the beauties of nature in no inconsiderable abundance and still thrill to all the hustle and bustle of a thriving town—as well as take whatever advantages might be derived from the polite society made possible by the number of gentry resident in it. Among those who contributed to the air of gentility in Maidstone were the Kingsleys whose old house on Stone Street, one of the four principal streets, Smart doubtless passed many times. Other great families were the Finches, the Marshams, the Colepeppers, and the Riders, all of whose members represented Maidstone in Parliament at one time or another. Years later Smart wrote a poem on a member of the Kingsley family who had distinguished himself in the Battle of Minden in 1759. And he remembered this same Kingsley or another of his family in a collective wish that "God be gracious to Smith, Cousins, Austin, Cam & Kingsley & Kinleside" (*Jubilate Agno*, D, 224). Even more inclusive was the wish that "God be gracious to the people of Maidstone" (D, 197). The fondness with which he recalls his early years in Kent bespeaks a happy childhood.

For Smart school was the free grammar school with instruction under Charles Walwyn. Walwyn had been a scholar at Eton from whence he was admitted to King's College, Cambridge, in 1688, proceeding to a Master of Arts degree in 1696. That same year he became Master of Maidstone school and remained in that capacity for the next forty-four years. Walwyn and the other teachers of his school introduced Smart and his schoolmates to the Latin language in the same way and using the same texts that had been used in the preceding decade in Lichfield Grammar School, where a seven-year-old named Samuel Johnson had similarly made the acquaintance of Latin. Johnson, and Smart no doubt, went to school six days of the week and was examined on what he learned every Thursday and Saturday. Recalcitrance and simple lack of comprehension led to corporal punishment, many schools having a three-legged flogging stool prominently in evidence in the classroom. Johnson's headmaster, Johnson himself is the authority, was inordinately severe, even downright cruel and perverse in his demands, but no record of Walwyn's disposition or of Smart's progress survives, although the latter may be surmised. Johnson, and Smart, once they had mastered declensions and conjugations, went on to syntax and some simple translating. They would almost surely have used a text by John Clarke, his "Corderius," and then would have progressed to such writers as Erasmus, Eutropius, Cornelius Nepos, Ovid, Justin, Caesar, Virgil, and Horace. Greek would come toward the end of their time at the grammar school; by then they would already have been writing themes and verses in English and Latin and translating them from one language into the other.[16] The curriculum of grammar schools varied little, it is clear, and Smart made his way through *Propria quae Maribus, Quae Genus,* and *As in praesenti,* in one or another edition, just as generations of schoolboys before him had. Unlike most of those boys, he turned in later life to some of the authors he had been forced to translate as a youngster and translated them for publication, this time because of pressures of a different kind.

More significant for Smart's development as a poet was the fertile richness and exuberant growth of the East Barming countryside in which he passed the impressionable years from four to eleven. The extent to which he observed his natural surroundings in these years is seen, of course, in his poetry, where time and again he refers to the Medway or to the flora and fauna of his native Kent. Central to it all is the river, "sweetest daughter of the ocean," "silver Medway" whose breast "views the reflected landscape." It was from the "bent oaks" that line the river that the wood nymphs of *The Hop-Garden* looked down and wondered "at silver bleak and prickly pearch,/ That swiftly thro' their floating forests glide." There, too, in a boat with a book in his hand he saw "the silverlings and crusions glide." It was on its banks that Smart promised himself in *The Hop-Garden* that he would muse on his dead friend Theophilus Wheeler, while her streams "shall flow/ In sullen silence silverly along/ The weeping shores." And it was in the Medway that Smart, who was to bid "God be gracious to Mr. Fletcher who has my tackling" in 1759, went fishing as a boy and probably later when he visited his sister Margaret in Maidstone. One of the pleasures he promised a young lady in *"A Noon-Piece"* was the opportunity with "well-disguised hook" to "cheat the tenants of the brook," and he was entranced by the sudden leap of fish from out of the water as well as by glimpses of them as they glided along well below the surface. The long catalogue of fish in *Jubilate Agno* owes much to books but some part of the knowledge displayed there was from first-hand experience. Swans sailed along the river, catching the eyes of all who had even the least appreciation of beauty; they caught young Smart's eyes and he later remembered their appearance as they silently moved along and "laved." The feeling they produced in him he caught in a line in *Jubilate Agno*, "Let Shelumiel rejoice with Olor, who is of a goodly savour, and the very look of him harmonizes the mind" (B1, 5). His eye for the colors and unique features of various flowers was keen. One of the loveliest passages on flowers in his poetry occurs in his Hymn XIII, "St. Philip and St. James,"

> Tansy, calaminth and daisies,
>   On the rivers margin thrive;
> And accompany the mazes
>   Of the stream that leaps alive[17]

combining flowers on the river bank with the leaping fish that seem to make the stream a living thing. In the same poem he describes other flowers with an eye to detail,

> Couslips seize upon the fallow,
>   And the cardamine in white
> Where the corn-flow'rs join the mallow.

His loveliest poem on flowers is *On a Bed of Guernsey Lilies*, written in the month of September, 1763.

> Ye beauties! O how great the sum
>   Of sweetness that ye bring;
> On what a charity ye come
>   To bless the latter spring!
> How kind the visit that ye pay,
> Like strangers on a rainy day,
>   When heartiness despair'd of guests:
> No neighbour's praise your pride alarms,
> No rival flow'r surveys your charms,
>   Or heightens, or contests!
>
> Lo, thro' her works gay nature grieves
>   How brief she is and frail,
> As ever o'er the falling leaves
>   Autumnal winds prevail.
> Yet still the philosophic mind
> Consolatory food can find,
>   And hope her anchorage maintain:
> We never are deserted quite;
> 'Tis by succession of delight
>   That love supports his reign.

Elsewhere he writes of the "tulip and auricula's spotted pride," and in other poems throughout his life he shows that he had taken more than a mere superficial notice of flowers and their names. "For the right names of flowers are yet in heaven. God make gardners better nomenclators," he states in a passage on flowers in *Jubilate Agno* (B2, 492–510) which contains such provocative lines as "For flowers are peculiarly the poetry of Christ" and "For flowers are musical in ocular harmony." He was himself a gardener and he knew the popular and learned names of flowers and plants, however little he thought of the merit of their nomenclature. Even in confinement he worked in the garden and, as he did on every occasion, turned to

God, to ask this time, that his "pink borders" succeed. His joy in God's creatures extended to birds and to animals. References to a number of the former are frequent in his poetry, and he noticed and recalled in the poetry at least three times how the coney made his home in rocks, and quarries, and caves. And when he congratulated himself in *Jubilate Agno*, "For I was a Viper-catcher in my youth and the Lord delivered me from his venom" (B1, 96), he was doubtless recalling a real pastime of his youth.

Smart was not, as some would make him out to have been, a rather withdrawn, somewhat sickly youth who was constantly thrown into the company of females, with whatever blight that is supposed to have cast over the rest of his life. Highly gregarious as a man, enjoying good fellowship or what he may sometimes have mistaken for that, as a boy and youth the pattern of his life in rural Kent and in Maidstone was a normal one. He did what other boys of his age and situation did; the difference between him and most of his fellows was that he was gifted with the perceptiveness and sensitivity that turned him to poetry and enabled him to record in memorable lines a great deal of what he had seen and experienced. After all, for a number of years he was thrown into the company of boys of his own age at Maidstone school; their interests were his interests; he shared in their games and pastimes; and the larger part of his time for six days each week of the school year was spent with them.

One anecdote survives that deals with this period. Smart, at about four years of age, reports Mrs. LeNoir, "was very fond of a lady of about three times his own age, who used to notice and caress him. A gentleman old enough to be her father to tease the child would pretend to be in love with his favourite and threatened to take her for his wife—'You are too old,' said little Smart; the rival answered, if that was an objection he would send his son, he answered in verse as follows, addressing the lady.

> Madam if you please
> To hear such things as these
> Madam, I have a rival sad
> And if you don't take my part it will make me mad;
> He says he will send his son;
> But if he does I will get me a gun.
> Madam if you please to pity,
> O poor Kitty, O poor Kitty.

The anecdote dates from about one hundred years after the facts it records, but a precocious four-year-old could write such verses, or better, and the sentiments expressed, such as they are, would not be impossible to reconcile with Smart's later efforts.[18]

On the third of February, 1732/33, Christopher's father died, and Winifred Smart, left with three children and having no relatives in Kent, decided to send Christopher and Margaret north to Durham where they would at the very least have the benefits of association with other members of a not inconsiderable Smart family. She thought that Christopher would find a change of air helpful and she may have counted upon the continued or renewed advantages to be derived from the Vane family whose northern seat was Raby Castle in Staindrop, Darlington. She herself remained at Hall-Place with Mary Anne, being joined there later by Margaret. Since Peter had died intestate the property was entirely hers, and it was not until 1746 that she was forced to sell it. By that time Margaret had married William Hunter, for the Barming parish register records the birth of a son to them on September 24, 1745, and his death on November 10 of the same year. In 1748 Christopher Hunter, their eldest son of four, was born in Maidstone; later the family moved to Margate, taking Winifred Smart with them. In Durham in 1733 Peter Smart's brother John and his wife were alive and had two sons, Francis and Thomas, both older than Christopher. Peter's sisters Jane and Margaret had both married Durham men and still lived in the county. And there were other, more remote members of the family in the vicinity. Smart may have lived with John Smart, his uncle, or with another relative, or he may have boarded with his school master. The city of Durham where he went to school exhibited, as did other English cities at this time, a curious combination of vestigial medievalism and refined cultural and social activity. Although one could attend a cock fight or see a bull being baited and although he would be confronted with the sight of animals being butchered in the streets, if he were of the right class he would be privileged to hear much good music and move in a polite society which set great store by entertainment. Indeed, the Dean and the Canons of the Cathedral were expected to entertain during their residence, and Dean Spencer Cowper writes of dinner parties which he gave for up to one hundred people at a time.[19] One anxious father, vacillating between sending his son to Eton or to Durham Grammar School, considered the former only because he was afraid of his "son's getting a taste for company and dress by too frequent attending the Assembly and Concerts in Durham."[20] It is entirely probable that Smart, whose love of music is attested by a number of his poems, was taken to concerts and to the assembly by the Vanes, thereby also "getting a taste for company and dress."

The city itself was physically unprepossessing. To Tobias Smollett's splenetic Matthew Bramble, writing to his friend Dr. Lewis, it appeared "like a confused heap of stones and brick, accumulated so as to cover a mountain, round which a river winds its brawling course. The streets are generally narrow, dark, and unpleasant, and many of them almost impassable in consequence of their declivity. . . . the country, when viewed from the top of Gateshead Fell, which extends to Newcastle, exhibits the highest scene of cultivation that ever I beheld." And Spencer Cowper, Dean of the Cathedral for almost thirty years, describing the city and its environs in 1746, the year he was elevated to the Deanery, saw them with almost identical eyes. "The country about the town vastly romantic and beautiful, the hills being mostly covered with fine woods. The town itself nasty and disagreeable, the streets narrow and wretchedly paved, and the houses dirty and black, as if they had no inhabitants but colliers."[21] But it was the Cathedral that dominated the city; "a huge gloomy pile," Matthew Bramble described it, hastening to add, "but the clergy are well lodged." Dr. Johnson, passing through Durham in 1773, was almost equally unimpressed. After commenting that the Bishop's palace had "the appearance of an old feudal Castle, built upon an eminence and looking down upon the river upon which was formerly thrown a draw-bridge," he proceeded to the Cathedral, which "has a massiness and solidity such as I have seen in no other place; It rather awes than pleases, as it strikes with a kind of gigantick dignity, and aspires to no other praise than that of rocky solidity, and indeterminate duration." Inside, all he could find to say was that the "Library is mean and scanty."[22] All in all, the city and the Cathedral failed to elicit the admiration of these viewers; whatever their effect on Smart, he never mentioned them in his poetry.

Raby Castle does, however, figure in Smart's poetry for it was there that he and his sister spent much of their school vacations. But it, too, seems to have inspired a kind of grudging respect rather than any deep-seated feeling of admiration. Again Dean Spencer Cowper is a vocal witness; the castle, he wrote in 1753, is "fine

rather than agreeable" with a "sullen Grandeur [which] runs thro
the whole within and without," adding a few years later, that on
great occasions there was much formality with "the Flag flying on
the Great Tower, [and] Cannon firing every half hour on the
Ramparts."[23] Somewhat later, another writer describes its setting:
"The situation, in a part, beautifully admitting a view of the deer,
is rather pastoral than romantic, being on the side of a vast amphi-
theatre of country, which affords a prospect of a rich cultivation,
terminated by west and east by distant hills, and to the south by an
extended plain."[24] The castle was enormous, with nine great towers
and a vast entrance place containing a fireplace about twelve feet
wide, an inordinately long Baron's Hall, and enough room to house
seven hundred retainers. Smart's grateful recollection of the castle
and its lord was expressed in the ode he wrote when the latter
became Lord Barnard in 1754:

> Was it not he, whose pious cares
> Upheld me in my earliest years,
>   And chear'd me from his ample store,
> Who animated my designs,
> In *Roman* and *Athenian* mines,
>   To search for learning's ore?
> . . . .
> Can I forget fair *Raby's* tow'rs,
>   How awfull and how great!
> Can I forget such blissful bow'rs,
>   Such splendour in retreat!
> Where me, ev'n me, an infant bard,
> *Cleveland* and *Hope* indulgent heard.

Something undoubtedly must be put down to the flattery usual in
such occasional poems; something, equally surely, must be put
down to sincere gratitude, a virtue much hymned in Smart's poetry.
There was, however, no ulterior motive when he prayed, "Lord
have mercy on the soul of Lord Vane" (D, 22). What he had in
mind when he wrote in *Jubilate Agno* "For my grounds in New
Canaan shall infinitely compensate for the flats & maynes of Staindrop Moor" (B1, 23) is less certain, unless he is referring to the
Snotterton estate of the Smarts.

The master of Raby Castle was Henry Vane, eldest son of Gilbert,
second Baron Barnard, to which title he succeeded in 1753. Except
for some electioneering in and around Durham for the Duke of

Newcastle, he was little in the public eye. But Harry Vane enjoyed his position as grand lord, his predilection being for great drunken bouts preceded by magnificent suppers accompanied by fireworks. Often the suppers took place at midnight and were followed by gambling into the small hours of the morning. Another of Harry Vane's diversions was playing practical jokes and he could be quite rude to those of his guests who did not share in his merriment.[25] In an age of heavy drinking he managed to acquire a reputation for frequent and deep exercise with the bottle, prompting Horace Walpole's remark that Harry Vane "whenever he was drunk told all he knew, and when he was sober more than he knew."[26] What is more Harry Vane was evidently not above making free with money other than his own, so extravagant must he have been. "What share Harry will give his Daughter [Lady Mary] of the £20,000 settled on younger children I have not heard," wrote Dean Spencer Cowper in 1752, "but a Captn Forth of Darlington died some years ago, and left her 8,000£. About 1,500 of this Harry has had the fingering of, but the rest, by the Lady Grace's [his wife's] advice, she has not suffer'd him to touch, tho' he fought very hard once to pay his Eldest Daughter's [Lady Anne's] Fortune with it."[27] If the young Smart had already acquired a taste for strong drink, because of the cordials he is supposed to have been administered as a child, he would certainly not have been discouraged in his fondness for it by Harry Vane. And it is more than merely probable that he would have got, or have further nurtured, his liking for living well at Raby Castle.

Harry Vane married Grace, daughter of the first Duke and Duchess of Cleveland, and by the time Christopher Smart came to Durham to live she had borne him four children, Henry and Frederick, born in 1726 and 1732, respectively, and Anne, also born in 1726, and Mary. Two other children, Raby and Henrietta, their last, were born while Smart was still in Durham. But it was with Henry and Anne that Christopher and his sister spent most of their time while at Raby Castle during the school vacations. Several anecdotes of these happy days at the castle have been recorded by Mrs. LeNoir and their total effect is suggestive of a free and easy intimacy among the children. As children will, they paired off, both for friendly and hostile purposes. Nothing is said in these anecdotes about Frederick Vane, presumably because he was too young; Christopher and Anne formed one alliance while Henry and Peggy, the eldest of the Smart children, paired off in reciprocal dislike. For Mrs. LeNoir wrote of the latter pair: "The young Lord a little superior in years was not so in understanding; he had been so often twitted with the quicker progress of learning of Peggy Smart that he once made a desperate attempt at putting an end to it in a huge water tub that was in the stable yard. Her cries brought the servants to her assistance or it is probable that she would never have eclipsed him again."[28] The worth of this anecdote is somewhat diminished by the fact that Mrs. LeNoir makes Henry Vane older than Peggy Smart; she was about six years his senior. She may, however, have erred only in detail.

Anne Vane was Christopher's first love. When he came to Durham from Kent he was eleven years old and she was seven; when he left he was seventeen, a young man about to enter the university, and she was thirteen, seven years away from her first marriage. At some time in those six years Christopher was stricken by that mysterious ailment called puppy love and he never entirely recovered from it. Proof of the fact lies in the *Jubilate Agno*, one of the most artless and naive documents in English literature, despite its method and its learning and its antecedents. For there, and at a time when self-revelation was given full scope, he wrote of Anne Vane,

> For I saw a blush in Staindrop Church, which
>   was of God's own colouring.
> For it was the benevolence of a virgin shewn
>   to me before the whole congregation. (B2, 668—9)

And again, without apparent bitterness at her marriage, "God be gracious to Anne Hope" (B2, 534) and "I bless God for two visions of Anne Hope's being in charity with me" (D, 186). Still again, but reverting to her maiden name, "God be gracious to the house of Vane especially Anne" (C, 104). Somewhat less valuable as evidence of this attachment is Mrs. LeNoir's story that Smart's poem "To Ethelinda, on Her Doing My Verses the Honour of Wearing Them in Her Bosom" was addressed to little Anne Vane. "Oft thro' my eyes my soul has flown,/ And wanton'd on that ivory throne," the poet wrote, and finally, after having expressed the wish that his body might follow where his eyes have been, he implores the girl to dislodge the verses: "Then throw them down from that downy bed,/ And take the poet in their stead." Since the poem as printed bears the further information, "Written at Thirteen," it not only demands some literary and amatory precocity in Smart but also a perceptible degree of physical precocity in nine-year-old Anne. Mrs. LeNoir's story ends with the remarkable aftermath to the writing and presumptive presentation of the poem; "this very spirited ode," she wrote, "had taken such effect that these young lovers had actually set off on a runaway match together; they were however timely prevented and saved as opportunely from sinister accident as Peggy Smart had been from drowning."[29] No more should be made of this affair, almost a paradigm, of the boy of somewhat humbler estate aspiring to the love of the child of the castle. Such marriages were not unknown in the worlds of eighteenth-century fiction and fact—in 1745 the nineteenth Earl of Salisbury married his steward's niece, "daughter to a barber and shewer of tombs at Canterbury"[30]—but they were rare.

Lady Anne married Charles Hope Weir, Esq., brother to the Earl of Hopetown in 1746; eleven years later she married George Monson, but by that time she had already been separated from her first husband for at least five years. Again the retailer of gossip is Dean Spencer Cowper. "They," he is referring to Harry Vane and his wife Grace, "have at last managed matters so, that Mr and Mrs Hope are quite separated, and she, who married for Love, now gravely complains whenever her husband, tho' in her absence, comes nigh the house to see his own children, 'he spoils them so'. I wonder what Idea they can have at Raby of a spoil'd child. I fancy it is a sort of child that in other families would pass for a tolerable good one. I am certain I never saw any of their own that it was in the Power of Lucifer himself to hurt after it reached 15." This was in 1752; in 1756 the Dean wrote of the "horrid stories that go about of his [Harry Vane's] Daughter," not specifying which daughter.[31] By this time Anne's sister Mary had been married for about four years to Ralph Carr; six years later, in 1762, "Lady Mary Carr returned from London to Cocken with her husband Ra. Carr. The report was, he was to allow her 500£ as a separate maintenance, and to give 1,000£ to buy furniture for a house."[32] Others of Harry Vane's progeny lend truth to the Dean's remarks; Frederick was involved in a disgraceful episode that led to a near riot at Cambridge in 1751 and his elder brother Henry fathered an illegitimate child with the assistance of Lady Caroline Petersham.[33] Anne, however, made George Monson a fine wife, achieved some reputation as a very superior whist player and was loved and respected in Calcutta; her husband's grief upon her death was described as "inexpressibly distressing."[34] While it is only idle speculation, Smart might have been happy with Anne Vane if the disparity in their stations had not made a marriage virtually impossible and if, indeed, the thought had ever entered Smart's mind. When his second daughter was born, Lady Anne Hope was her godmother and gave the child her middle name.[35]

Despite, or even possibly because of, the cordial reception her children, particularly Christopher, were accorded at Raby Castle, Winifred Smart knew that the future well-being of her family lay in her son's hands. Although her husband's estate was originally supposed to be worth about three hundred pounds a year, a sum sufficient to keep them all quite handsomely, his sudden death "in embarrassed circumstances" had compelled her "to sell the largest portion of the estate at considerable loss." Christopher, the only male child in the family, had already demonstrated an aptitude for learning and some knack for versification by the time he had gone to Durham to live, and sometime between 1733 and 1739, if the thought had not crystallized earlier, she determined to send him to the university. A young man of bookish leanings, incapacitated by a generally weak constitution and of too proud a family to enter upon an apprenticeship, could most painlessly make his way by getting his Master of Arts at the university and either settling down as a Fellow or accepting a living in the church. Smart's promise at school in Durham attracted the notice of the Duchess of Cleveland, Harry Vane's mother-in-law, who very generously allowed him forty pounds a year, a sum which her husband continued to him after her death in 1742. His gratitude to his benefactress took the external form of an *Epitaph on Henrietta, Late Duchess of Cleveland*, probably written shortly after her death but not published until 1764. With forty pounds a year a young man could attend the university very comfortably, if he did not throw his money around.

Certainly Smart's schoolmaster at the Durham Grammar School, where old Peter Smart had once been headmaster, impressed by the boy's abilities, would have urged Winifred Smart to send her son to the university. The Reverend Mr. Richard Dongworth had, like Charles Walwyn, Smart's teacher at Maidstone, gone to Eton as a King's scholar; he was admitted to Magdalene College as a sizar in

1722, obtaining his Bachelor of Arts, a Fellowship, and then his Master of Arts by 1730. During his years at Magdalene he was successively a Gooch Fellow and a King's Fellow in 1728 and 1729. Two years after taking his Master of Arts he became Master of Durham Grammar School, a position he kept until he died in 1761. Hunter described him as "an Etonian, and so eminent a scholar, that in the judgement of one, who was himself in that station, he would have obtained the Mastership of that celebrated Seminary, had it been accessible to simple merit" (p. viii). And an entry in a diary kept by Thomas Gyll, a lawyer of Barton, Yorkshire, recorded his opinion that Dongworth was "a learned and polite gentleman. Some few years agoe he was offered the Headmastership of Eaton School, but declined it."[36] Whether or not he was offered the very desirable head mastership at Eton and declined it, Dongworth was recognized as a man of learning and a good teacher. A Mr. Carr of Whitworth, writing in 1754, attested to his reputation: "instead of sending my son Ralphy from hence [a private school] to Eton, I have let him go back with my nephew to Durham. As to the point of learning I think he can be nowhere so well as under Mr. Dongworth." Fearing, however, that Durham offered Ralphy too many opportunities to forget his studies, Mr. Carr went to see Mr. Dongworth and "upon a little conversation with him, he in a great measure dissipated our fears and he is so much of a man and so good a scholar that I thought it too late to remove him to another school." But maturer reflection and another day caused Mr. Carr to change his mind again. "I think Ralphy too young to be trusted to the management of himself there," he wrote, and accordingly sent his boy to Eton where he could be "under much greater restraint than at Durham."[37]

Smart, while he may have succumbed to some of the temptations of Durham, continued to distinguish himself as a student during the years he spent with Dongworth, cultivating among other things his gift for Latin versification; "and a very learned and eminent Divine, now living," wrote Hunter in 1791, "has expressed obligations to our Author for his own first successful essays in Latin Versification" (p. viii). As he was a provident person as far as his poetical efforts were concerned and never seems to have thrown anything away which might some day be impressed into emergency service, he probably used some of these exercises in Latin versification of his Durham days, wholly or in part, in his later years. His "Fanny

Blooming Fair, Translated into Latin," was written while he was still at Durham, if the "C.S. Aetat., 16" that serves as signature to the piece's publication in the *Gentleman's Magazine* for April, 1754, can be believed. And if the Latin translation of the poem was written in 1738, then the English original, also by Smart, was written then or shortly before. The poem is astonishingly good of its kind, considering Smart's tender years. It begins,

> When Fanny, blooming fair
>   First caught my ravish'd sight,
> Pleas'd with her shape and air,
>   I felt a strange delight:
> Whilst eagerly I gaz'd
>   Admiring ev'ry part,
> And ev'ry feature prais'd
>   She stole into my heart.

It ends, rather passionately albeit with recourse to mythology,

> Venus round Fanny's waist
>   Has her own cestus bound,
> These guardian Cupids grace
>   And dance the circle round.
> How happy must he be,
>   Who shall her zone unloose!
> That bliss to all but me,
>   May heav'n and she refuse.

Apparently written even earlier, some Latin verses entitled "Arion, By a Boy of Fourteen" appeared in the first number of the *Universal Visiter* of January, 1756.

At Maidstone Smart had been taught to read and write his own language with fluency, a process that took him to his seventh or eighth year, after which he was put to Latin. Under Walwyn at Maidstone he had studied Latin for some three years when he left to go to Durham. There, as in all grammar schools in England in that time and for some hundreds of years past, the curriculum centered upon the Latin and Greek languages. Indeed, the deed of foundation of the Durham Grammar School specified that it "was designed for instructing boys in the rudiments of learning, unto the Latin and Greek grammar," and those in Durham who were not interested in such a course of study could enter another school devoted to teaching boys "in the art of writing and plain songs."[38] The two schools faced each other across the palace green, with the grammar school being the nearest building to the cathedral on the west side and having its back windows looking down upon a beautiful prospect of the River Wear. It was under the shadows of the Cathedral and the Castle that Smart studied his texts. The typical day at a grammar school was long and hard with nine or more hours of work. The boys read Ovid, Cicero's Letters, Caesar's Commentaries, Aesop's Fables, Livy, Virgil, Horace, Juvenal, Pliny, Plautus, Terence, and others in Latin, and such Greek authors as Isocrates, Demosthenes, Homer, and Hesiod. They wrote themes and exercises, epistles and dialogues, and verses in Latin, and they memorized much Latin verse. They translated from Latin into English and from English into Latin. They read in the Greek Testament and wrote Latin verses on scriptural subjects. In addition they received instruction in logic, in the Christian religion, and sometimes in the Hebrew language. The slow to learn and the mischievous could look forward to the rod or a box on the ear or a slap in the face, sometimes even to confinement. There was much to learn and little time for idleness, but for Smart to whom all this learning came easily there was time to indulge his taste for independent composition both in English and in Latin. He remembered both his master and his school with gratitude and fondness during the years in which he was writing his *Jubilate Agno*, for in one of those seemingly mad associations he wrote "Let Josiphiah rejoice with Tower-Mustard. God be gracious to Durham School" (C, 55), remembering "Durham mustard" a condiment with which he tempted a friend to come and dine with him in a poem of his later years. [*Epistle to Dr. Nares.*] As for Dongworth, Smart prayed "God be gracious to the immortal soul of Richard Dongworth" (D, 28). And he may have remembered Thomas Randall, submaster under Dongworth, for "God give Randall success" occurs in the line following that on his former master.

Thus, after six years in Durham, where Smart had acquired a solid grounding in Latin and Greek as well as a reputation as a ready versifier in at least two languages, he set out for Cambridge and Pembroke College, with the assurance of a very substantial forty pounds to hearten him. Behind him he left his mother and two sisters, by that time together again in Kent; in Durham he said his farewells to the thirteen-year-old Anne Vane who was not for him. She was the first of a number of young women to capture his heart and command his pen.

II.

CAMBRIDGE, 1739-1749

Cambridge, where Smart was to spend the next nine years of his life, was described to Horace Walpole by Thomas Gray in 1734 as "a great old Town, shaped like a Spider, with a nasty lump in the middle of it, & half a dozen scrambling long legs,"[1] the nasty lump being Market Hill. A survey in the year 1749, the year Smart left for London, numbered 1792 houses in the borough of Cambridge and 6131 inhabitants, with almost one inn or public house (156) for every ten houses in the borough; Smart and his friends helped to keep them solvent. The amusements afforded by the town, other than drinking, were somewhat limited. Loose women were available at Castle End, an area situated at one extremity of the town, while a greater degree of privacy was afforded by the places of amorous resort in Barnwell, a small nearby village. Toward the end of Smart's residence at Cambridge he could, if he were so minded, see performances of plays by Shakespeare, Vanbrugh, Mrs. Behn, and others put on by troupes of actors performing in nearby Royston or in Stamford. Balls and musical entertainments were within easy reach; sometimes there were elegant fireworks. And those whose predilections were of a different bent could betake themselves to the famous horse matches at Newmarket. But the great event of any year was the three-week long "Sturbridge Fair" held in September, ceremonially announced by the highest University officials and, after 1745, much advertised in the pages of the *Cambridge Journal*. For a shilling one could be transported the mile and a half from Cambridge to one of the most famous fairs in all England. Plays were performed there as late as 1748 despite the protests of the University, but less refined tastes could be regaled with conjurors, rope-dancers, tumblers, giants, dwarfs, and wild beasts. Again Gray was on the scene: "I am coming away all so fast, and leaving behind me . . . all the beauties of Sturbridge Fair," he wrote to West in September, 1738. "Its white bears may roar, its apes wring their hands, and crocodiles cry their eyes out," he continued, and then told of the edict against "schismatical congregations" created to prevent Orator Henley from preaching. And while the fair was described as an occasion for vice and debaucheries, it was also a gathering place for booksellers who sometimes sold whole libraries at auction. Proctors from the University patrolled the fairgrounds in a vain attempt to keep discipline among the younger students. During the rest of the year, with the exception of Pot Fair for a fortnight, entertainment was largely of one's own making. Some indication, other than in Smart's own poetry, of the possibilities of extracurricular diversion, is had from Gray as an undergraduate. He wrote to Walpole on November 17, 1734, "do but imagine me pent up in a room hired for the purpose, & none of the largest, from 7 a-clock at night, till 4 in the morning! 'midst hogs heads of Liquor & quantities of Tobacco, surrounded by 30 of these creatures [fellow students], infinitely below the meanest People you could even form an Idea off, toasting bawdy healths & deafned with their un-meaning Roar." Of course students were not allowed to run wild and they were not really supposed to be in taverns or public houses except under supervision or with the permission of their master. But college regulations have always existed to be broken. Very occasionally, singers or musicians from London put on performances; more occasionally the Fellow-Commoners took tea with the ladies. Most often, however, those students who could afford to, gamed, rode, and otherwise amused themselves. Sometimes the bucks went cock-shying at Market Hill, a pastime that consisted of throwing sticks to see who could knock down or kill a cock tied to a post. And, since the streets of Cambridge were not lighted at night, there was ample opportunity for the exercise of ingenious mischief. When all else failed coaches to London left Cambridge on Monday, Tuesday, Thursday, or Friday mornings and returned Tuesday, Wednesday, Friday, and Saturday evenings, taking ten to twelve hours one way. There, in London, one could really dissipate.

The Pembroke College Admissions Book, under date of October 20, 1739, records the fact that Christopher Smart, son of the late Peter Smart, gentleman of Kent, born in that same place and being seventeen years of age, was admitted as a sizar under the tutelage of Mr. Addison. Since neither the members of the Vane family nor Dong-worth, his master at Durham Grammar School, had attended Pembroke, no reason for the choice of college has survived. It could not have been dictated by the presence there of a former school friend or by the desire to be with some other friend who had just left Durham school with him, for no admissions from Durham are recorded in 1739 or for a number of years before that date. Admission as sizar did not carry any particular opprobrium, for many sizars came from respectable but not especially opulent families. They were not too much distinguished at this time from the pensioners with whom they often fraternized, although they were sometimes required to do menial tasks, Smart referring humorously in one of his Tripos poems to the old custom of their waiting on the Fellows' table. Sometimes when there were not enough scholars, that is, students on scholarships, to wait on the Fellows' table or to toll the bell to chapel and act as bible-clerks, some of the sizars were impressed into service. Such a situation was recorded under the date of October 23, 1740, when four sizars, Smart possibly among them, were obliged to undertake scholars' duties and were paid four pounds each for the ensuing year.[2] The Fellow-Commoner was the aristocrat of the student body, paying higher fees, wearing rich and ornamented clothes —for ceremonial occasions he wore a gown trimmed with gold or silver lace, and a velvet cap with a gold or silver tassle—and, in general, taking great advantage of the relaxed rules of study and discipline to which he was subject. Thomas Gray wrote to Thomas Wharton in March, 1747, that "the Fellow-Commoners (the Bucks) are run mad, they set Women upon their Heads in the Streets at noonday, break open Shops, game in the Coffee-houses on Sundays," and other contemporary accounts of their behavior described them as a hard-drinking, high-living, lubricious lot. While they, like Smart, were under tutors, very often the relationship was that of a wealthy youngster and a toadying academic. And yet the reputation of a tutor could make one college a success or ruin another, for it was the tutor, acting as guardian as well as instructor, who enforced discipline, corrected misdemeanors, and even supervised his pupils' finances. Samuel Johnson, while at Oxford, told his friend Taylor that "he could not, in conscience, suffer him to enter [Pembroke Hall] where he knew he could not have an able tutor" and consequently had him enter the college that had the ablest tutor.[3] Leonard Addison, Smart's tutor, did what he could to curb his pupil's extravagances and his often outlandish behavior, even after Smart had become a Fellow of Pembroke, but his remonstrances had little enduring effect. Addison at one time or another was Praelector of Philosophy, Greek and Hebrew, Rhetoric, and Algebra, Pembroke being one of nine colleges to introduce this last subject into their regular curriculum in 1706. Besides Smart, Addison was tutor to twelve other boys admitted in 1739 and 1740. Of these, only two were admitted *secundam mensam*, that is, as pensioners, the others were admitted as sizars. Since a nobleman, as Fellow-Commoner, paid at least three pounds per term for tuition while a pensioner paid approximately half that sum and a sizar one fourth, the reason for Smart's decision to enter as a sizar is apparent. With the forty pounds yearly given him by the Duchess of Cleveland and some help from his mother plus whatever he was given for services rendered as a sizar and an additional six pounds yearly as a scholar on the Dr. Watts's Foundation, he should not have had to worry about money. The Watts scholarship was awarded him on July 12, 1740; under its conditions he was to receive the six pounds annually until he became a Bachelor of Arts or until the vacancy he had been chosen to fill was filled by a regular Watts scholar. For this, if called upon, he would carry out the tasks expected of the Watts scholars.[4] Presumably he kept the scholarship until he proceeded to his Bachelor of Arts. At about the same time another young man, one who read the holy scriptures on his knees while at college but had little else in common with Smart as an undergraduate, maintained himself for three years as a servitor at Oxford without having "to put all [his] Relations together to above 24l Expence." But George Whitefield did not indulge himself as Smart did.[5] Of course if Smart tried to emulate the style of living of the Fellow-Commoners, he could not possibly have done so on his limited means, for an extant college bill for Francis Scobell for the first term of his admittance to Pembroke in 1732 amounted to some one hundred and seventeen pounds.[6] Thomas Gray, at Peterhouse in 1736, paid about fifteen pounds for all his college expenses in that year with the exception of his rent and certain other annual charges, but he, unlike Smart, was of an abstemious nature.

As an undergraduate, then, Smart devoted himself to his studies under the supervision of Leonard Addison. His academic successes lead to the belief that he applied himself conscientiously or that he had already achieved a knowledge of Latin and Greek that made the university curriculum rather easy for him. Thomas Sheridan could write contemptuously of education in England that "when a boy can read English with tolerable fluency, which is generally about the age of seven or eight years, he is put to school to learn Latin and Greek, where seven years are employed in acquiring but a moderate skill in those languages. At the age of fifteen or thereabouts, he is removed to one of the universities, where he passes four years more in procuring a more competent knowledge of Greek and Latin, in learning the rudiments of logick, natural philosophy, astronomy, metaphysicks, and the heathen morality. At the age of nineteen or twenty a degree in the arts is taken, and here ends the education of a gentleman."[7] Hunter wrote that "though the favorite studies of this Seat of Learning were not congenial with his mind, yet his classical attainments and poetical powers were so eminent, as to attract the notice of persons, not very strongly prejudiced in favor of such accomplishments" (p. viii). Evidence for Smart's dislike of the favorite studies of Cambridge and for his classical attainments is seen in his selection to write the Latin Tripos verses for three successive years, his first printed publications. In these, given the dubious honor of translation into English by Francis Fawkes of Jesus College, a contemporary and friend of Smart's, there is no mistaking the poet's extreme dislike for mathematics, sophistry, natural sciences, and atheism. Years later, when he wrote in *Jubilate Agno*, "God be gracious to the soul of HOBBES, who was no atheist, but a servant of Christ, and died in the Lord—I wronged him God forgive me" (B1, 227), he was recalling his having branded Hobbes an atheist in the second of these Tripos poems. Whatever his professed aversion to the sciences and their preeminence at Cambridge, he acquired a store of scientific knowledge which remained with him, or was to be revived later by reference to some of the very texts he had used at the University. Nowhere is this more remarkable than in *Jubilate Agno*.

Smart's coevals at Pembroke among the sizars were William Turner, James Neale, Thomas Knowles, James Burslem, Thomas Robinson, James Trevillian, John Bedford, William Fawconer, and Michael Dorsett, men whose names mean little now except to those few who are interested in Cambridge and more particularly Pembroke in mid-eighteenth century. But it was with these young men as well as with young men from other colleges that Smart studied, drank, feasted, and compared verses. The names of most of these men appear in the list of Bachelors of Arts from Pembroke on January 13, 1743/44, Smart being third in the *ordo* behind

27

Knowles and Burslem. Two weeks later, Knowles, Smart, and Dorsett were chosen Latin scholars, adding something to their annual income.[8] And when Smart became a Fellow and then a Master of Arts some of the freshmen who had matriculated with him also became Fellows and Masters of Arts, and it was they who helped in the education of the undergraduates at Pembroke.

"Such was the force of his genius, and such the vivacity of his disposition," wrote Hunter of Smart at Pembroke, "that his company was very earnestly solicited; and to suppress or withhold our talents, when the display of them is repaid by admiration, is commonly too great an effort for human prudence. He was therefore quickly involved in habits and expences, of which he felt the consequences during the rest of his life" (p. viii). With his ready wit and flair for extempory composition he was sure of the admiration and the envy of the less gifted. His best-remembered display of wit was occasioned by the coincidence of the three university bedells all being fat men. "Pinguia tergeminorum abdomina Bedellorum," he extemporized, and thought well enough of his effort to include it, virtually unchanged, in his Tripos poem, *Materies Gaudet Vi Inertiae*. He is supposed to have said of Thomas Gray that he walked as though he had fouled his small-clothes and looked as though he was aware of the fact, a remark which would hardly have endeared him to Gray, if it ever came to the latter's ears.

One of his friends at this time was Samuel Saunders of King's College to whom he wrote a Latin poem inviting him to dine.

> Phoebus and Bacchus—it is Hermes' vow—
> The Graces too, tonight feast at my side.
> But surely will they spurn our cups, if thou
> wilt not preside.
>
> Come, rich in wit thou learned from Athens' land,
> Come, full of laughter, of thy heart a sign.
> In open countenance let humour bland
> happily shine.
>
> And Georgius I wait on, keen wit's true
> Constructor, full of art enough. Let be
> Now, as there was before, between you two
> fair rivalry.

Until kind night, through all the season cold
 In labour spent, on tender young lads looks,
 Who taking rest from printed page unrolled
     close up their books.

For shame! The young, whose heart for lucre quests,
 (which maidens fair and old men too have sought)
 Pale to stay sleepless at the long-drawn jests
     of our hard sport.

Turn you away, come, (for your mind so rare
 Minerva fills) from trifles, pedantry,
 Useless and hard; and bitterness of care
     cast out with me.

The earth is hard with frost these wintry weeks,
 Yet let your laurel flourish, and long may
 The sweet rose of your health upon your cheeks
     not fade away.[9]

Another friend was Thomas Comber of Jesus College, referred to in the preface to Smart's "Ode for Musick on St. Cecilia's Day" as suggesting "David's playing to King Saul when he was troubled with the evil spirit" as a fine subject for an ode on St. Cecilia's Day.* Still another friend was the unfortunate Theophilus Wheeler who matriculated at Christ's College on January 11, 1741–2, and died in Cambridge almost exactly a year later and whose death is mourned in Smart's *The Hop-Garden*. And from Caius College there were Edward and Jermyn Pratt, one of whom introduced Smart to their sister Harriot and thus paved the way for some excellent love poetry in a light vein.

However much or little time a student spent in extracurricular activities of one kind or another, the majority of his waking hours were taken up with the academic life of his College and of the University—in that order. Once Smart was put under the guidance of Leonard Addison, the formal part of his education for the next three years was determined by the kind of man and teacher his tutor was, for some tutors ignored their students completely while others conscientiously strove to shape the minds and characters of their charges. While the extent of Addison's influence on Smart's

*William Cole, the antiquarian, wrote that Smart "was much pleased with it at first, but was deterred from pursuing it by the greatness of the subject." BM Add MSS 5865 fol. 21 (verso).

development is a matter for conjecture, he remained his friend for some eight years, being the last to be alienated by Smart's irresponsible behavior as a Fellow. The Professors, depending upon their knowledge or complete ignorance of their subject, gave or omitted to give lectures. Joseph Spence, for example, held the Professorship of Modern History at Oxford from 1742 to his death in 1768 without lecturing or even residing there. Others made tremendous efforts to prepare themselves in subjects about which they knew nothing so that they might at least fulfill their obligations. The extent and kind of learning one acquired was then, as well as now, in almost direct proportion to one's desire for knowledge. At Cambridge, mathematics and science, fostered by a number of Newtonians, were held in greater esteem than classical studies; both Gray and Walpole have attested to their dislike of this imbalance. Gray wrote to West in December, 1736, that he had "endured lectures daily and hourly" hoping soon to be free to devote himself to "his friends and classical companions, who, poor souls! though I see them fallen into great contempt with most people here, yet I cannot help sticking to them." Indeed, the Craven scholarship and later the Dr. Battie scholarship, founded in 1747, were the only channels for recognition open to classical scholars.

The Master of Pembroke in 1739 was Dr. Roger Long, who was admitted to that College in 1697 as a sizar, elected to a Fellowship in 1703, resigned it in 1716, returned to Pembroke as a Fellow-Commoner in 1728, and was elected Master in 1733. He was widely known as a lecturer in astronomy and he was something of an inventor. He built an engine for a cold bath which he devised himself and had set up in the Fellows' garden, charging a subscription fee for its use. Smart, either because he wanted to or felt he ought to, subscribed to it in 1745-6 but did not pay the two-pounds, two-shillings fee; he subscribed once more the following year and paid that fee, but whether the first was ever paid is doubtful.[10] The number of Fellowships at Pembroke at this time was fourteen, with another two vacant, and a number of these same Fellows who were in residence in 1739 were still there when Smart himself became a Fellow. The names of one or more of them were to crop up at different times during his later life. The real stalwart among the Fellows at Pembroke throughout Smart's time was James Brown, who held or was to hold most of the positions of importance in the College and in the University, and whose courage and shortness of stature caused Gray to write of him that he wanted nothing but "a Foot in height & his own Hair, to make him a little old Roman." He was sometimes aided by Samuel May and "gentle Mr. Peele (who never acts but in Conjunction),"[11] most notably in the prolonged battle with the Master over the election of Tuthill, a Peterhouse Bachelor of Arts who migrated to Pembroke and was backed for a Fellowship by Wharton and Gray. It is enough to say that Dr. Long lost the battle, thanks to Brown's persistence. Smart, then a Fellow, was present at two College meetings, October 27, 1747, and November 9, 1748, when the battle was nearing its climax, and he adhered with the other Fellows present in unanimously opposing Long.[12]

From the poem to Samuel Saunders, from the one hundred and nineteen lines of the first canto of Butler's *Hudibras* "translated into Latin doggerel" when he was still a freshman, and from the poem "The Pretty Bar-Keeper of the Mitre," written in 1741, it is evident that Smart did not have to devote all his energies to his studies. Some of the studies he enjoyed and they cost him little effort; but he also acquired enough mathematics, moral philosophy and metaphysics, and the sciences to meet his requirements. Success smiled on his effort throughout the undergraduate years. Not only was he chosen to write the Tripos verses three years running and made a Dr. Watts scholar, but he also won the highly coveted Craven scholarship on June 10, 1742, earning the right to call himself "Scholar of the University." For the Craven scholarship, competitive in nature although political influence sometimes came into play, was open to anybody in the University under the degree of Master of Arts. The annuity of twenty-five pounds was good for fourteen years or until the scholar got "a preferment of a double value," another significant and welcome addition to Smart's annual income as well as a legitimate source of real pride. The candidates underwent an examination, sometimes *viva voce*, in Greek and Latin, and then the Vice-Chancellor, the five Regius Professors, and the Public Orator voted to decide the winner. The award and the procedures that led to it were such, therefore, as to constitute a memorable milestone in his academic career. Smart eventually lost the benefits of the scholarship on June 25, 1750, because of nonresidence at Cambridge, but he never forgot the honor that had been conferred upon him, as the title pages of some of his publications in the 1760's attest. The Craven scholarship was followed in the very next year with publication by the Cambridge University Press of Smart's translation of Pope's *Ode on St. Cecilia's Day*; on the title page he is described as of Pembroke College and Scholar of the University. What is more, the book was published at his own expense—"impensis authoris." Translation of Pope's poem into Latin was no novelty; Samuel Johnson translated his *Messiah* while at Oxford and William Whitehead had translated the first epistle of the *Essay on Man*. But Smart found in William Murray, Pope's friend, a champion who suggested that he broach the subject of a Latin translation of the entire *Essay on Man* to Pope himself. It is probable that Murray, who married Lady Elizabeth Finch, one of seven daughters of Daniel, sixth Earl of Winchilsea, in a ceremony at Raby Castle in September or November of 1738, met young Smart about that time or at least learned about him from the Vanes. In any event, Smart wrote to Pope from Pembroke on November 6, 1743,

> Sir,
> Mr. Murray having told me that it would, he thought, be agreeable to you to see a good Latin version of your Essay on Man, and advised me to undertake it, though I know myself vastly unfit for such a task, I will attempt to render any number of lines that you shall be pleased to select from any part of the work, and as you approve, or dislike them, will pursue or drop the undertaking.
> I am, Sir, with the utmost respect, yours,
C. Smart.
> To
> Alexander Pope, Esq.
> I should not have presumed to have given you this trouble had not Mr Murray assured me that I might safely venture. I have made bold likewise to send you a specimen of a translation of your Essay on Criticism, verse the 339th.

Pope answered from Twickenham on the 18th,

> Sir,
> I thank you for the favour of yours I would not give you the trouble of translating the whole Essay you mention; the two first Epistles are already well done, & if you try, I could wish it were on the last, which is less abstracted, & more easily falls into Poetry & Commonplace. A few lines, at the beginning & the Conclusion will be sufficient for a Trial, whether you yourself can like the task, or not: I believe the Essay on Criticism will in general be the more agreeable, both to a young writer, & to the Majority of Readers. What made me wish the

other well done, was the want of a right Understanding of the Subject, which appears in the foreign Versions in 2 Italian 2 French & 1 German. There is one indeed in Latin Verse printed at Wirtembergh, very faithful, but inelegant, & another in French prose; but in these the Spirit of Poetry is as much lost, as the Sense & System itself in the others. I ought to take this Opportunity of acknowledging the Latin Translation of my Ode, which you sent me, & in which I could see little or Nothing to alter, it is so exact. Believe me Sir, equally desirous of doing you any Service, & afraid of engaging you in an Art so little profitable, tho' so well deserving, as good Poetry.

I am
Your most oblig'd
& Sincere humble Servant
A. Pope.

Smart preserved and cherished Pope's letter for a long time, causing it to be legibly displayed when he sat for a portrait some years later. There is even the possibility that Pope invited the young poet to visit him at Twickenham.

Smart was at work on other poems at this time. When his georgic poem *The Hop-Garden* was published in the 1752 *Poems on Several Occasions* it bore these lines, soon after the opening of the second Book,

> THEOPHILUS, thou dear departed soul,
> What flattering tales thou told'st me? How thou'dst hail
> My Muse, and took'st imaginary walks
> All in my hopland groves! Stay yet, oh stay!
> Thou dear deluder, thou hast seen but half—
> He's gone!

Smart's note on this reads, "Mr. Theophilus Wheeler, of Christ-College, Cambridge." Wheeler died in December, 1743, in Cambridge, by which time he had seen about half of the georgic Smart was writing; as a native of Kent himself he was in a fine position to compare notes with Smart on the hops industry. At the same time that Smart was engaged on *The Hop-Garden* and on other poems, a memorable event at Pembroke elicited still another poem from him. The occasion was the Jubilee at Pembroke, probably held on New Year's day 1743–4, celebrating the foundation of the college four hundred years earlier; the poem was "A Secular Ode on the Jubilee

33

at Pembroke-College, Cambridge, in 1743." Little, if anything, in the poem bears quotation; it was adequate for the occasion, said most of the appropriate and expected things about the College, and marked another degree in the rising reputation Smart was gaining as a poet. On January 13, soon after the declamation of the Jubilee ode, Smart and most of those who matriculated with him received their B.A. degrees. Since this was another occasion that called for some kind of commemoration, Smart wrote an "Ode on taking a Bachelor's Degree," taking his point of departure from Horace's Book III, Ode 30. And, since the poem awaited publication until 1750, he probably handed it about or read it to his fellow graduates; its theme was the joys of freedom. About this time, too, inspired by the sight of an eagle chained in one of the courts of Trinity College,[13] he mourned the noble bird's loss of freedom and its imprisonment in the University in an ode that showed what he could do in the humorous vein. As in the poem on taking his degree and others of his undergraduate poems he hymns the joys of freedom, either actually or facetiously identifying himself with the captive. The lines from Virgil and Horace which he prefixed to the poem are a scholarly flourish; the first asks "who chose to wreak a penalty so cruel, who had power so to deal with thee?" and the second speaks of fastening "to earth a fragment of the divine spirit."[14] At no time was Smart at a loss for an apposite quotation.

To an EAGLE confin'd in a COLLEGE-COURT.

Quis tam crudeles optavit sumere poenas,
Cui tantum de te licuit? —VIRG.

Atque affigit humi divinae particulam aurae.—HOR.

Imperial bird, who wont to soar
   High o'er the rolling cloud,
Where *Hyperborean* mountains hoar
   Their heads in Ether shroud;—
Thou servant of almighty JOVE,
Who, free and swift as thought, could'st rove
   To the bleak north's extremest goal;—
Thou, who magnanimous could'st bear
The sovereign thund'rer's arms in air,
   And shake thy native pole!—

Oh cruel fate! what barbarous hand,
   What more than *Gothic* ire,
At some fierce tyrant's dread command,
   To check thy daring fire,
Has plac'd thee in this servile cell,
Where Discipline and Dulness dwell,
   Where Genius ne'er was seen to roam;
Where ev'ry selfish soul's at rest,
Nor ever quits the carnal breast,
   But lurks and sneaks at home!

Tho' dim'd thine eye, and clipt thy wing,
   So grov'ling! once so great!
The grief-inspired Muse shall sing
   In tend'rest lays thy fate.
What time by thee scholastic Pride
Takes his precise, pedantic stride,
   Nor on thy mis'ry casts a care,
The stream of love ne'er from his heart
Flows out, to act fair pity's part;
   But stinks, and stagnates there.

Yet useful still, hold to the throng—
   Hold the reflecting glass,—
That not untutor'd at thy wrong
   The passenger may pass:
Thou type of wit and sense confin'd,
Cramp'd by th' oppressors of the mind;
   Born to look downward on the ground;
Type of the fall of *Greece* and *Rome*;
While more than mathematic gloom,
   Envelopes all around!

The mathematic gloom that enveloped all around, distantly reminiscent of the end of Pope's *Dunciad*, must have driven Smart down to London on occasion, for he was running up quite a tailor's bill in that city at least as early as 1744; what else he did on these visits can be guessed at with varying degrees of certainty. Charles Burney, many years later, wrote to a friend: "I c^d give you a long hist^y of my acquaintance, intimacy, and correspondence w^th . . . Kit Smart, wch began as early as the year 1744 on my first arrival in London," evidence that Smart was making friends in the city.[15] He must also, among other things, have been trying to establish literary connections, a belief that is strengthened by the appearance in the May, 1745 *Gentleman's Magazine*, the leading London periodical, of his poem "To Idleness," set to music by William Boyce. And he was probably making the acquaintance of writers, booksellers, musicians, and others who would not only represent a welcome change from his academic colleagues but might also some day help him in a career far different from that of the cloistered Fellow of a college. For it was on July 3, only a short time after he had the great satisfaction of seeing a poem of his in Cave's *Gentleman's Magazine*, that he was elected a Fellow of Pembroke College. At the October, 1745 election of college officers for the following year Smart was made Praelector in Philosophy and, with Peele and Smyth, one of the three Keepers of the Common Chest. As Praelector of Philosophy he received one pound annually and had to lecture on philosophy and logic and act on the disputations; as a Keeper of the Common Chest he was responsible for the sum of four hundred and twenty pounds from which the Fellows of Pembroke could and did borrow. Indeed, the one year that Smart acted as Keeper—the entries for loans are in his hand—there was only seventy-three pounds, eleven shillings, "Left in the Bag" after deep inroads by May and Peele. And it was in December of this year, 1745, that he moved from room forty-three to a more expensive room, number thirty-eight, belonging to the Master. Clearly Smart was not one to live below his means. He was able to afford the better room and other comforts by the simple expedient of forgetting to pay some of his bills. For example, he was expected to give an "Entertainment" as a Fellow and he was supposed, by regulation, to pay three pounds for his "first problem." The treasury accounts of the College reveal that on three successive years he was billed eight pounds for each of his entertainments; he did not pay in 1744–5 or in 1745–6, but did in 1746–7.[16] No record exists that he ever paid in the sixteen pounds due the College for those first two years.

With election to two college offices Smart would seem to have been settling down to the secure if somewhat monotonous routine of university life. Such a life had its many advantages, however. Expenses were small, and one's annual income as a Fellow more than sufficed to keep one in comfort. The duties of a Fellow were not strenuous and there was ample time for scholarship, if that is what one desired to do, or for the writing of poetry. Thomas Gray's life at Peterhouse and then at Pembroke, very similar to Smart's in certain external happenings, affords an almost perfect example of the kind of quiet life one could have. Gray, like Smart, his junior by six years, was distinguished by being chosen to write Tripos verses and a contribution to a Cambridge *Gratulatio*; his was on the marriage of the Prince of Wales. He was awarded a scholarship, as was Smart. Both men were poets; both suffered from extreme sensitivity of one kind or another. Gray spent all his life at Cambridge and found some lasting content; Smart left and found some content, too, but it was ephemeral. True, few men in the university attained to fame except on a very limited scale, but there was always the possible satisfaction of being a large frog in a small puddle. True, too, polite feminine society in Cambridge left much to be desired—Gray wrote to Wharton in October of 1751 that "the women are few here, squeezy & formal, and little skill'd in amusing themselves or other People"—but there were always women whose favors could be had. A Fellow had to be a bachelor but he did not have to be chaste. Above all, academic society, the society of the Fellows of one's own college as well as of other colleges, was a restricted one, with its own traditions, customs, jokes, and predictable way of life. One could remain at the University for the rest of his life, free from the fierce competition of the outside world, lecturing and supervising students, taking his turn at the various college and university offices, maybe even becoming Master of his college, surely the crowning felicity of academic existence. Or one might, in due course of time, be presented with one or more of the livings that the college had periodically at its disposal. Sometimes a wealthy or high-born student, after making his way in public service, would remember his tutor and offer him a sinecure in London at an enticing salary. The eighteenth-century Fellow was often the butt of satirists who depicted him as usually of comparatively low origin, innocent of the amenities of the polite world, overbearing to his inferiors and servile toward his superiors, lazy, gluttonous, bibulous, opportunistic. Although true of many university Fellows, many others were conscientious, hard-working, sober, and, above all, possessing a love for and deep sense of loyalty to their colleges. The decision to spend the rest of one's days at the university, whether consciously reached or the result of the avoidance of decision itself, was not a difficult one. Such a life was one that Smart could have had and one in which he might have found a measure of content. That he did not choose to stay was owing to a temperament that saw security as confinement and that yearned for a greater share of the material rewards of life. Coupled with these factors was a growing desire to occupy a more prominent place in the eyes of the world.

Some suggestion of what Cambridge may have looked like to Smart can be had from a poem first published in *The Midwife*, entitled "A Description of the Vacation, to a Friend in the Country." There is every possible reason to think the poem is Smart's; almost equally probable, the recipient of the poem when originally written was Charles Burney.

> A Description of the Vacation, to a Friend in the Country.
> Dear CHARLES,   Camb. July 9, 1745.
>
> At length arrives the dull Vacation,
> And all around is Desolation;
> At Noon one meets unapron'd Cooks,
> And leisure Gyps with downcast Looks.
> The Barber's Coat from white is turning,
> And blacken's by Degrees to Mourning;
> The Cobler's Hands so clean are grown,
> He does not know them for his own;
> The Sciences neglected snore,
> And all our Bogs are cobweb'd o'er;
> The Whores crawl home with Limbs infirm
> To salivate against the Term;
> Each Coffee-house, left in the Lurch,
> Is *full* as *empty*—as a Church—
> The Widow cleans her unus'd Delph,
> And's forc'd to read the News herself;
> Now Boys for bitten Apples squabble,
> Where Geese sophistic us'd to gabble;
> Of hoary Owls a reverend Band
> Have at *St. Mary's* took their Stand,
> Where each in solemn Gibberish howls,
> And gentle *Athens* owns her Fowls.
> To *Johnian* Hogs observe, succeed
> Hogs that are real Hogs indeed;
> And pretty Master *Pert* of *Trinity*,
> Who in lac'd Waistcoat woos Divinity,
> Revisits, having doft his Gown,
> His gay Acquaintance in the Town:
> The Barbers, Butlers, Taylors, Panders,
> Are press'd and gone to serve in *Flanders*;
> Or to the Realms of *Ireland* sail,
> Or else (for Cheapness) go to Gaol.—
> Alone the pensive Black-Gowns stray
> Like Ravens on a rainy Day.
> Some saunter on the drowsy Dam,

CAMBRIDGE, 1739-1749

Surrounded by the Hum-drum CAM,
Who ever and anon awakes,
And grumbles at the Mud he makes,
Oh how much finer than the Mall
At Night to traverse thro' *Clare-Hall*!
And view our Nymphs, like beauteous Geese,
Cackling and waddling on the Piece;
Or near the Gutters, Lakes and Ponds
That stagnate round serene St. *John's*,
Under the Trees to take my Station,
And envy them their Vegetation.

Caetera desiderantur.

Not only was Cambridge a deadly dull place to be stuck in during the vacations, but also during term, the poem more than strongly implies, it was far from an earthly utopia.

Smart's jaundiced eye saw little to admire in academic life, if his essays in *The Student*, written soon after he had established himself in London, can be credited. Writing as the "Female Student" he traces the progress of a university student from his admission to his rise to power.

He was originally a sizer, and when he was first sent to college, wore his own lank greasy hair, and in his dress and manners was as meer a rustick as ever came from the plough-tail. By dint of plodding and perseverance he at length obtained a scholarship, from whence he gradually rose to be a fellow. After this, by conversing with his betters, he so far improv'd in good behaviour, as by an affected gentility and studied grimace to pass off for well-bred; tho' he knew too little of the world to deserve that character. At the time I first knew him, he fill'd the important office of proctor with all the significancy imaginable. He was, besides, the ruling magistrate of his college (under the head) and a most furious disciplinarian. He carried it with a very high hand towards his inferiours; and heap'd punishment on punishment for the slightest offences. In his nature he was morose, sullen, and imperious; but as he cloak'd his temper with the veil of dissimulation, to us women (who are but ill judges of human nature) he appear'd affable, obliging, and meek. One of his society justly compar'd him to bottled small-beer, which smiles in your face, and cuts your throat. . . . After a while, he was presented to a living of not less that 400 *l.* per annum, by the father of a young gentleman, whom he had the care of, and with whom he had ingratiated himself by the meanest flatteries. (II, 189—90)

Another essay by the "Female Student" gives a more general, although no less biased, view of students and teachers, as well as of life in Cambridge as a whole.

> A young fellow, on putting on the gown, is by that badge of learning mark'd for a scholar; and tho' his ignorance be really beyond the art of a tutor to cure, yet does he imagine the world will certainly mistake him for a man of knowledge, and therefore he prizes himself vastly beyond the rest of mankind. His conceit habitually improves in him, as he advances *in degrees*: but the first time that he begins to assume a more than ordinary importance, is upon being dubb'd A.M. A magisterial strut, a wise gravity of countenance, and a general stiffness in all his actions denote him for a man of consequence. He is taught to entertain a sovereign contempt for undergraduates, and, forsooth, scorns to demean himself by conversing with his inferiors. Hence the whole scene of his life is confin'd to those of his own standing: and the college-hall, the common-room, the coffee-house, and now and then a ride on Gogmagog-hills, is all the variety he has a taste for enjoying. One half of the human creation, (which men have complaisantly term'd the *Fair*) he is an utter stranger to; and that softness, that delicacy, that *je ne scai quoy* elegance of address, which our company imperceptibly inspires, is in his eyes a foolish impertinent affectation. Thus does he gradually degenerate into a mere—what I don't care to name; 'till at last he has liv'd so long at college, that he is not fit to live anywhere else. (I, 311)

And in still another essay by the same pen more rancor is displayed: "even the old senior fellows (who, forgetting their juniors) would cringe, and fawn, and stoop to the meanest offices, for the sake of a present dinner, or the prospect of a future preferment" from a titled student (II, 107).

Others besides Smart were disgusted at the abysmal pass matters had come to in the University. On June 26, 1750, eighteen new orders and regulations were approved by the Senate; their plain intent was to curb all manner of student abuses or excesses, ranging from overly elaborate clothes to the keeping of servants and horses and including prohibitions against gambling, drinking after eleven in the evening, and keeping evil company.

A test case was not long in coming: on November 17 James Brown, Fellow of Pembroke and at that time a Proctor, came upon a large group, members of the Westminster Club, drinking a final toast, shortly after eleven, at the Tuns Tavern. Brown's presence as

Proctor was resented; the offenders were later summoned before the Vice-Chancellor's court, found guilty, and reprimanded; and a number of pamphlets made their appearance as a result. One of these, the anonymous *Free Thoughts on University Education; Occasioned by the Present Debates at Cambridge*, 1751, stresses the evil influence of bad tutors, their servility before rich students, and their injustice to poor students. It suggests that the Fellows themselves set the students an example of good living and reports that "some years since" a proposal originating from Pembroke Hall had suggested the institution of a body of four Fellows, "remarkable for sound Learning, Purity of Morals, and a genteel Address," to "direct and assist students in their studies." Each was to give a course of lectures; one was to examine and correct English compositions, "such as themes and declamations"; another was to "show the Reasonableness and Truth of Christianity." While Smart may have had cause to be proud of these Pembroke proposals, in which he could conceivably have had a part, it is easy to see why he turned his back on a university career. Studies and morals had degenerated to a very low level indeed.

Smart could not, however, have stayed as long as he did at Cambridge if he had not had any kindly feeling for the University and for a number of his contemporaries there. Although he could write in *Jubilate Agno*, "For I pray God for the professors of the University of Cambridge to attend & to mend" (B1, 69), he could later in the same poem reverse his stand, "For the two Universities are the Eyes of England," "For Cambridge is the right and the brightest," "For Pembroke Hall was founded more in the Lord than any College in Cambridge" (B2, 617–19). And within ten lines of section B1 he asked for blessings upon seven Cambridge men, among them three geologists (279–88). *Jubilate Agno* is studded with the names of the men of Pembroke and the other colleges of Cambridge. He mentions the River Cam twice, once to ask God to bless it (B1, 66, For) and once to ask Him to be gracious to it (B1, 162, Let). He even remembered the "society" of Royston crows at Trumpington and Cambridge (B1, 46, Let), linking them in the corresponding For line in the words "For I bless the Lord Jesus from the bottom of Royston Cave to the top of King's Chapel." There are also other direct and some indirect references to the people, buildings, societies, and environs of Cambridge in this same poem. Toward the end of his confinement he wrote, "The Lord magnify the idea of Smart singing hymns on this day in the eyes of the whole University of Cambridge. Nov.ʳ 5ᵗʰ 1762. N.S." (D, 148), the only time he mentions himself by name in the poem. All this seems to breathe a nostalgia for those days when, restricted as he may have thought his life was, he was far, far better off than he now found himself.

The barest chronicle of Smart's life at Pembroke in the next four years resolves itself into a list of the College offices to which he was elected. He became a Master of Arts with Bedford, Jr., and Tuthill, on February 11, 1746. On October 10, 1746 he was reelected to the Praelectorship in Philosophy; he was elected Praelector of Rhetoric; and he was again one of the Keepers of the Common Chest. As Praelector of Rhetoric he received another two pounds annually; things were going well. On May 21, 1746, prior to the October election of officers, a scheme of studies which gave the duties of the lecturers had been drawn up and signed by the Master and seven Fellows, among them Smart. The new curriculum provided for a weekly lecture in the Greek Testament, for various other lectures and readings for the different classes, and for certain translations, orations, and exercises. Among the authors represented were Quintilian, Xenophon, Plato, Cicero, Aristotle, Euripides, Demosthenes, and, of course, Horace.[17]

How great a share Smart had in the new scheme of studies is not known but can be arrived at with some degree of certainty. Records exist of his borrowings from the Pembroke College library, and, while they do not make him out a prodigy so far as the number and variety of withdrawals are concerned, they show that he was reading steadily. Not only was he preparing himself in the works mentioned in the new scheme of studies, but he was also supplementing this fare with books in many different fields. As well as books in English and Latin and Greek, he was taking out an occasional volume in French and Italian. At least once he took out a Hebrew Lexicon. In Italian he read *Viaggi di Pietro Della Valle*; in French, Theophrastus, Homer, and la Fontaine. His readings in English literature included Chaucer, Randolph, Shakespeare, Beaumont and Fletcher, Milton, and Locke. He withdrew and presumably read the sermons of Newcome, Atterbury, Calamy, Wharton, and Père Bourdaloue. He read much in the Latin and Greek classical authors, but he also ranged from a "musick book" to two volumes on delphinium planting. He withdrew Delany's *Life of King David* and much has been made of this fact; others at Pembroke, including students, were reading the same book. Indeed, the records show a great deal of releasing of books from one borrower to another, Smart, for example, giving up books to Dorsett, Gaskarth, Acton, and a number of others of Pembroke as well as to men of other colleges. The same records also show that while some Fellows were given a page in the book for their withdrawals the page remained blank. Smart's pages, in addition to the books already mentioned, show him turning to various scientific works, to Thuanus, Camden, Newton, Rapin, to "Hugenii Opuscula," Corpus Juris Civilis, "Grotii. Op. Theol. vol. 1," and to "Medicina Gymnastica" among others. But other borrowers, notably Brown, Bedford, Jr., May, and Peele, were withdrawing more books, representing a similar range of interests, at this same period. Smart's release of books to Pembroke undergraduate students suggests that he may have been their tutor, but at no time anywhere in the College records is he called that. He may have been a private tutor to one or more of the Fellow-Commoners, his name being linked in that capacity with John Blake Delaval's, but again there is no documentary evidence to this effect. Whatever his association with students, as revealed by these library records, he was evidently conscientiously at work at his books, settling down to his academic tasks.

But it was only on the surface that things were going well. Smart's conviviality had exceeded all bounds during this period, and Gray, now of Pembroke Hall himself, wrote in November, 1747, to his friend Wharton at length about the sad predicament in which Smart found himself.

> your Mention of M[r] Vane, reminds me of poor Smart (not that I, or any other Mortal, pity him) about three weeks ago he was arrested here at the Suit of a Taylor in London for a Debt of about 50£ of three Years standing. the College had about 28£ due to him in their Hands, the rest (to hinder him from going to the Castle, for he could not raise a Shilling) Brown, May, & Peele, lent him upon his Note. upon this he remain'd confined to his Room, lest his Creditors here should snap him; & the Fellows went round to make out a List of his Debts, w[ch] amount in Cambridge to above 350£. that they might come the readier to some Composition, he was advised to go off in the Night, & lie hid somewhere or other. he has done so, & this has made the Creditors agree to an Assignment of 50£ per ann: out of his Income, w[ch] is above 140£, if he lives at Cambridge (not else). but I am apprehensive, if this come to the Ears of M[r] Vane he may take away the 40£

hitherto allowed him by the Duke of Cleveland; for before all this (last summer) I know they talk'd of doing so, as Mr Smart (they said) was settled in the World. if you found an Opportunity, possibly you might hinder this (wch would totally ruin him now) by representing his Absurdity in the best Light it will bear: but at the same Time they should make this a Condition of its Continuance; that he live in the College, soberly, & within Bounds, for that upon any Information to the Contrary it shall be absolutely stop'd. this would be doing him a real Service, tho' against the Grain: yet I must own, if you heard all his Lies, Impertinence, & Ingratitude in this Affair, it would perhaps quite set you against him, as it has his only Friend (Mr Addison) totally. & yet one would try to save him, for Drunkenness is one great Source of all this, & he may change it. I would not tell this Matter in the North, were I you, till I found it was known by other Means.[18]

Wharton lived fairly close to Raby Castle, "in the North," and Gray was concerned lest news of Smart's disgrace reach the ears of Harry Vane. How Smart, with a total income of more than one hundred and forty pounds a year could have managed to run up bills of over three hundred and fifty pounds in Cambridge alone defies solution. There are limits to the amount one can drink, although the practice of standing friends to drinks would account for some of the outlay. Smart enjoyed being popular and he had had a taste, or at least a glimpse, of high living while staying at Raby Castle. Hobnobbing with the Fellow-Commoners, buying drink for drink and dressing up to their standards, undoubtedly contributed largely to his downfall. "While he was the pride of Cambridge," wrote Dr. Charles Burney in 1792, reviewing Hunter's edition of Smart's poems for the *Monthly Review*, "and the chief poetical ornament of that university, he ruined himself by returning the tavern-treats of strangers, who had invited him as a wit, and an extraordinary personage, in order to boast of his acquaintance. This social spirit of retaliation, involving him in debt with vintners and college cooks, occasioned his fellowship to be sequestered, obliged him to quit the university, and crippled him for the rest of his life." Since Smart's fellowship was sequestered in 1753, Burney is not completely accurate, but as one of Smart's earliest London friends the core of his account has the merit of extreme plausibility.

At the October, 1747, election of officers Smart was not re-elected to either of the Praelectorships he had held the previous year; his only college office was Keeper of the Common Chest with Smyth and

Bedford, Jr., and it was not he who kept the accounts. But he was chosen "Concionatori Coram Praetore oppidano," for which he received thirteen shillings, four pence. As Preacher before the Mayor of Cambridge Smart had to deliver a sermon on Michaelmas Day "in such a place as the Mayor elect shall appoint," the Masters and Fellows of Pembroke in 1668 having covenanted with the Corporation of Cambridge to "procure an able orthodox divine" for this purpose in consideration of a gift of land from that body.[19] Smart, in 1747, was hence considered "an able orthodox divine" by Dr. Long and the Fellows of Pembroke and he was thought worthy to represent them in that capacity at a public function of some importance. He must have made a favorable impression on the occasion of this, his first sermon, for next year the University had him prepare and deliver the annual speech on January 30 in observance of the martyrdom of King Charles I. For this he received the very handsome sum of four guineas.[20] To his position as Preacher before the Mayor in 1747 may be added his post as one of "Tribus Comemoratoribus," bringing him twelve shillings.[21] An absence from October 9 to 25, 1747, may be put down to his fear of being taken up for debt. Indications are, however, that he behaved himself discreetly for a while, as he was not only again chosen one of the Keepers of the Common Chest on October 10, 1748, and Praelector in Philosophy but he was also given the comparatively lucrative office of catechist, the money deriving from a gift of Robert Mapletoft, a former Master of Pembroke, and varying in amount from year to year. Addison, Smart's tutor, had been catechist, a post which entailed giving religious instruction to the younger students, for some years. The position brought Smart eighteen pounds, ten shillings, for the year, much preferable to the two pounds he would have got for re-election to the lectureship in rhetoric. There is no knowing how much religious instruction Smart was either expected or prepared to give; up to this point in his life he had not distinguished himself for depth of religious feeling. But, although no record of his ordination survives, his preaching before the Mayor of Cambridge and his election to the post of catechist make it plausible that he had taken minor orders and point to the confidence reposed in his orthodox divinity by his college. Had he not been ordained, he would not have been elected to preach before the Mayor; had his religious views been at all suspect, he would not have been elected to give religious instruction.[22] Probably his colleagues, concerned

45

about his physical, spiritual, and financial well-being, had concerted to elect him to the position as catechist, hoping that his duties and the extra income might help him to straighten out his affairs and himself. Smart retrenched to the extent of moving into less expensive quarters, but this slight saving could not contribute perceptibly to his revised economy. Nor did the effort of the Fellows bear fruit either; at the annual election of officers for the academic year 1749–50 he was elected to no offices. He did not appear at any of the College meetings and he was not at hand for the choosing of plate. The explanation lies in an entry in the College records: "Nov. 9, 1749 at the same time it was ordered that, Mr. Smart, being obliged to be absent, be allow'd, in consideration of his circumstances, the sum of 12 pound; half to be paid by the treasurer and half by the bursar, for the year ensuing ended Oct. the 10th 1750."[23] Smart was no longer in Cambridge.

Smart's activities in the last four years of his academic life in Cambridge were much more varied and exciting, of course, than a simple listing of his duties as a Fellow can possibly suggest. He fell in love, he saw his name in print a number of times, he wrote and acted in a play, he established connections in the London publishing world, he continued to write poetry and dream of freedom from his academic prison, he absented himself from the University more than once, and he read many books.

Edward Pratt of Ryston Hall, Market Downham, Norfolk, had been admitted to Caius College as a pensioner in 1734–5, proceeded to a Bachelor of Arts in 1739–40, and became a Master of Arts in 1743. He was Smart's senior at Cambridge by three years. His brother Jermyn matriculated at Caius in 1742 and was ordained a deacon in 1746 and a priest in 1749. At some time between 1740 and mid-1746, at the earliest and latest, either Edward or Jermyn introduced their sister Harriot to Christopher Smart, who promptly fell in love with her and remained in that condition for some years. All that is known of Harriot Pratt is what Smart reveals in his poems to her. The earliest of these is "On seeing Miss H---P--t in an Apothecary's Shop"; it was printed without signature in Robert Dodsley's *Museum* for September 27, 1746. Earlier in this year, in March, Anne Vane, his childhood love, had married Charles Hope Weir, Esq.; if Smart had continued to harbor thoughts of her, the marriage would have ended them, and he was all the readier to write love poems to another. Playfully conventional in vein, the first

Harriot poem elaborates on the slight conceit that the "Fallacious Nymph," present "by Stealth" in the shop, "Would seem to be the Goddess HEALTH," whereas she is actually studying to "learn infallibly to kill." Much livelier, much more delightful and ingenious, is the crambo ballad, "Lovely Harriote," where the trick was to fashion a number of rhymes for "Harriote." After such variations as "chariot," "Marriot," "carry aught," and others, the poet ends with

> I swear by *Hymen* and the Pow'rs
> That haunt Love's ever-blushing Bow'rs,
> So sweet a Nymph to marry ought:
> Then may I hug her silken Yoke,
> And give the last, the final Stroke,
> T'accomplish lovely *Harriote*.

Written in the stanza he was to use for *A Song to David*, the poem reveals that lovely Harriot was, at least to Smart's ears, an accomplished singer and instrumentalist. Another poem, "To Miss H---, with some Musick, written by a Poet outragiously in love," identifies the instrument as of the keyboard variety and lauds the girl's mind and temper as well as her more obvious charms. A note of seriousness creeps in in the lines

> May all the pow'rs that on fair virgin's wait,
> Heap on thee all that's happy, good and great,
> All that of earthly bliss you can conceive,
> Your hopes can image, or your faith believe.

At least two more poems were inspired by Miss Pratt, an "Ode to Lady Harriot" and the birthday poem, "On the Fifth of December." And it is she, by name, not the "Delia" of the 1748 version of the poem printed in the *London Magazine*, whom Smart addresses in *A Noon-Piece*, printed in *The Student* in 1750. There he could still call her "sovereign mistress of my heart." The end of the passion inspired by this young lady is proclaimed in a poem to another young woman, "The Lass with the Golden Locks"; the poet declares roundly, "No more of my Harriot, of Polly no more,/ Nor all the bright beauties that charm'd me before." This last poem appeared in the 1752 *Poems on Several Occasions*; among the many subscribers was the Reverend Jermyn Pratt, and both he and Roger

47

Pratt, Esq., of Ryston Hall, his father, subscribed to Smart's translation of the Psalms of David, published in 1765. Evidently the Pratts were willing to overlook the poet's public abjuration of Harriot.

The Pratts were of an old Norfolk family who had lived on their Ryston estate for at least two hundred years; they were well-to-do landed gentry, marrying in their own class. Smart was received by the family on at least one occasion. He wrote to Charles Burney from Market Downham, Norfolk, on July 29, 1749, having probably silently taken his leave of the University.

> My Dear Charles.
> I have left your last unanswered so long that I am under some apprehension; lest it shou'd be now too late. You must know I am situated within a mile of my Harriote & Love has robd Friendship of her just dues; but you know the force of the passion too well to be angry at its effects. I condole with you heartily for the loss of your Father, who (I hope) has left behind the cole, which is the most effectual means of consolation. I am as much a stranger as you to what is going on at Vaux Hall, for we are so wrapt up in our own snugness at this part of the kingdom, that we know little what's doing in the rest of the world. There was a great musical crash at Cambridge, which was greatly admired, but I was not there, being much better pleased with hearing my Harriote on her spinnet & organ at her ancient mansion.--- If you are still in the Kingdom I beg the favour of an immediate line or two, but if you are not, I hope even the Ocean will not, nay, he shall not cut off our correspondence & friendship----Yrs most inseparably   C. Smart.[24]

Some notes on this letter in Fanny Burney's hand contain other references to her father's early friendship with Smart.

> The letter of the most ancient date that remains in the manuscript epistolary collection of Dr. Burney is from Kit Smart who, facile alike in Poetry Learning & Humour, excited an admiration in young Burney that was soon raised to intimacy, by reciprocated confidence in their juvenile distresses of the Heart. Kit Smart here opens upon his own, with extreme nay boyish simplicity that seems so little to appertain to a lover of the Parnassian breed as to render it curious.
> Smart had so long delayed answering some previous letter that in the interval of his silence the Int. to which he alluded had been broken off & the intended Tourist was become the happiest of married men.[25]

The picture Smart paints of his stay at Market Downham is an idyllic one; there is even the strong suggestion that his love for Harriot was returned. The poems "Lovely Harriote" and "Ode to Lady Harriot" appeared in *The Midwife* for 1751; "On the Fifth of December" was published a year earlier in *The Student*; and "To Miss H---, with some Musick, Written by a Poet outragiously in love" was first printed in the *Gentleman's Magazine* in 1754, two years after Smart had written, in "The Lass with the Golden Locks," that he was done with Harriot and Polly and an indeterminate number of other "bright beauties." Publication of the poem in 1754 was dictated by necessity, no doubt, but it betrays a sensibility distasteful to modern minds. Again, at a critical juncture in his life, Smart was either unfortunate or somehow spoiled his chances for happiness. Life with the lovely and accomplished Harriot Pratt, a peaceful, secure life as a country gentleman, writing poetry, possibly with a living in Norfolk, might have been his.

While he was laying seige to Harriot and writing delightful poems to her, he was also busy with other poems and plans for publication. A second edition of the Latin translation of Pope's St. Cecilia Ode, accompanied this time by a poem by Smart, "Ode for Musick on St. Cecilia's Day," appeared in 1746. In his Preface to his own *Ode* Smart made his first appearance in print as a critic of poetry. After justifying himself for having written a St. Cecilia's Day ode despite the existence of those by Dryden and Pope, he went on to assess their merits and shortcomings.

> There is in them both an exact unity of design, which though in compositions of another nature a beauty, is an impropriety in the *Pindaric*, which should consist in the vehemence of sudden and unlook'd-for transitions: hence chiefly it derives that enthusiastic fire and wildness, which greatly distinguish it from other species of Poesy. In the first stanza of *Dryden* and in the fifth of *Pope* there is an air, which is so far from being adapted to the majesty of an Ode, that it would make no considerable figure in a Ballad. And lastly, they both conclude with a turn which has something too epigrammatical in it. Bating these trifles, they are incomparably beautiful and great; neither is there to be found two more finish'd pieces of Lyric Poetry in our language, *L'allegro* and *Il penseroso* of *Milton* excepted, which are the finest in any. *Dryden's* is the more sublime and magnificent; but *Pope's* is the more elegant and correct; *Dryden* has the fire and spirit of *Pindar*, the more elevated performance of the two, but by no means so much so as people in general will have it. There are few that will allow any sort of comparison to be

made between them. This is in some measure owing to that prevailing but absurd custom which has obtain'd from *Horace's* time even to this day, viz. of preferring Authors to the Bays by seniority. Had Mr. *Pope* wrote first, the mob, that judge by this rule, would have given him the preference; and the rather, because in this piece he does not deserve it.

Two Greek quotations in a footnote, one from Homer and the other from Pindar, six lines from Du Fresnoy's *De Arte Graphica* in the Preface, and a quotation from Lilius Gyraldus in a footnote to the *Ode* itself reveal the author's consciousness of his scholarly erudition. The volume was printed by J. Bentham, Printer to the University, but it, unlike the first edition, was for sale at a London bookseller's, R. Dodsley's. Robert Dodsley, a one-time footman, became a successful publisher, playwright, patron of literature, and friend of most of the writers of his time. Samuel Johnson said of Dodsley's evening gatherings of men of letters that "the true Noctes Atticae are revived at honest Dodsley's house." A notice in this second edition of the Pope translation announced that "There is preparing for the Press, by the same hand, a Latin Version of Pope's Essay on Criticism, and of the L'Allegro and Il Penseroso of Milton." Smart had taken Pope's suggestion to heart and was getting a Latin translation of the *Essay on Criticism* ready. Whether he was merely hoping for literary fame alone or was trying to escape from Cambridge to London by means of his poetry, there is no doubt that he was busy with more than his routine academic chores. Since his mother was forced to sell Hall-Place in East Barming in this same year, there was the additional pressure of knowing that even the possible, if distasteful, alternative of retreat into the country was denied him. Smart's concern about the new edition of the Pope translation is obvious from a letter to Dodsley, dated August 6, 1746, and written from Pembroke.

Sir
    I sent you this morning, by the coach, an hundred copies of my affair, which, I suppose, will be as many as you will be able to dispose of. I won't have it advertised but for three days, & only in one paper each day. The price of 'em is two shillings apiece. I beg the favor the advertisement may be carefully copied from the title page, because there were two unlucky mistakes in the latin parts of the former three advertisements. If you find they go off tolerably let me know.—

    I am yours etc.   C. Smart[26]

At least one place in which Dodsley advertised is known; the *General Evening Post*, 14–16 August, 1746, carried a "This day was published" notice of the work.

Two weeks after the publication of his book Smart was absent from Cambridge for at least fifteen days beginning on August 29. The strong presumption is that he journeyed to London to see Dodsley, either about the St. Cecilia translation or about his poems in the *Museum*; the first of these poems, the last two stanzas of his own ode on St. Cecilia's day, appeared on September 13. Smart continued his campaign to establish himself firmly with Dodsley by a letter dated January 30, 1746–7, in which he informed the bookseller that he had "imitated a Satyr of Horace in the manner of Pope," referring to the "Horatian Canons of Friendship," which was not to be published for another six years.[27] A year later he wrote again to Dodsley, on January 7, 1747–8, in words expressive of both uncertainty and pride,

> Sir,—I beg the favour you'll advertise my Proposals six or seven times in the Papers you think best and make the following addition viz: There will be [no] more copies printed, than what are subscribed for, and if there shou'd ever be occasion for a second impression nothing will.be abated from the original price. yrs etc.
>
> C. Smart.[28]
>
> Please to advertise immediately on the receipt of this.

On January 9, 1748, there appeared, in at least three London newspapers, proposals for printing by subscription "A Collection of Original Poems, By Christopher Smart, M.A., Fellow of Pembroke Hall, in the University of Cambridge," which was to include "The Hop-Garden," various odes, "The Judgment of Midas, a Masque," and some translations into Latin as well as some original poems in that language. The conditions were rather grandiose, with the subcriptions to be taken by C. Bathurst and R. Dodsley in London, J. Fletcher in Oxford, J. Richardson in Durham, and by W. Thurlbourn, "and the Author, in Cambridge." Thomas Gray was referring to this, in a letter dated March 17, 1747, when he wrote of Smart's "Collection of Odes." The collection, under still another entirely different name, was not to be published until 1752.

Another letter, undated and with no recipient's name, is also undoubtedly to Dodsley:

I beg the favour you'd send me by the Maidstone-stage Littleton's Persian Letters, & Bruyere's characters in English—& if you possibly can get me Dalton's alteration of Comus you will do me great service, because I am writing a Masque myself—I am afraid you gave me wrong directions to Will Whitehead for I received no answer to a letter about business—

Yrs. etc. C. Smart

And in a postscript:

send another copy of *Musaeus* and another Prospect of Eton.[29]

Dodsley published William Mason's *Musaeus* on April 17, 1747, and Gray's Eton ode on May 30 of the same year; Smart's letter would have been dated some time after May 30 therefore. Nothing is known about the "business," probably literary, he wanted to discuss with William Whitehead, almost all of whose work was being published and was to be published by Dodsley. Whitehead's career at Clare College, Cambridge, which he entered as a sizar in 1735, somewhat paralleled Smart's at Pembroke. He received his Bachelor of Arts degree in 1739, the year Smart entered Cambridge, was elected a Fellow in 1742, received his Master of Arts in 1743, and then moved to London two years later to make his living largely by writing. He early won a reputation as a poet in Cambridge and was the kind of man, both by temperament and literary interests, who would attract the attention of young aspiring poets. Indeed, in 1748 both he and Smart wrote poems in *Gratulatio Academiae Cantabrigiensis* on the return of George II from Europe, and some years later Smart remembered to ask "God be gracious to William Whitehead" in *Jubilate Agno*. Whitehead, for his part, subscribed for two copies of Smart's *Poems On Several Occasions* in 1752, and for one copy of the version of the Psalms in 1765. The masque Smart was working on was *The Judgment of Midas*, published in 1752, of which the less is said the better. Possibly the letter that mentions Whitehead was written very late in the year and, Dodsley not sending the books as requested, was followed by this next letter, written on February 9, 1748; again there is no direct clue to the recipient:

Sr
I sent to you about a month ago for some books, & should be glad to know whether you have forgot, or not received the letter—

My service to Mason when you see him, & tell him if he stay'd much longer in Town, I should expect to hear from him.

Yrs.

C. Smart[30]

William Mason, a graduate of St. John's College, was nominated to a Fellowship in Pembroke in 1747, but Dr. Long opposed his election until 1749. He, like Whitehead and Smart and others, doubtless went to London to see Dodsley about publication of his work. None of Dodsley's answers survives, but however warmly Smart courted the bookseller no firm alliance was reached between the two.

Pembroke in the 1740's was not a beehive of activity; there was a dearth of students, and of the average seventy-five or so Bachelor of Arts awarded annually in Cambridge at this period, Pembroke turned out three or four. Gray commented on the situation in two letters of 1749, in the latter of which he told Wharton that "there is no making Bricks without Straw. they have no Boys at all."[31] The college records show only one pensioner admitted in 1748 and two sizars in 1749; a number of the rooms stood empty. Such a situation might have appealed to some of the Fellows; for Smart, bursting with energy and with something always going forward, it must have been boring. Some of this energy, according to Hunter who had it from one of Smart's fellow students, was channeled into walking, an exercise of which he was so fond that he wore a path "on the pavement under the Cloisters of his College" (p. xxvii). To escape being bored and to take the center of the stage, both figuratively and literally, he wrote, directed, and acted in a play. Thomas Gray's, as usual, is the best account; the date is March, 1747, and he is writing to Wharton:

as to Sm:, he must necessarily be abîmé, in a very short Time. his Debts daily increase (you remember the State they were in, when you left us) Addison, I know, wrote smartly to him last Week; but it has had no Effect, that signifies. only I observe he takes Hartshorn from Morning to Night lately: in the mean time he is amuseing himself with a Comedy of his own riteing, wch he makes all the Boys of his Acquaintance act, & intends to borrow the Zodiak Room, & have it performed publickly. our Friend Lawman, the mad Attorney, is his Copyist; & truly the Author himself is to the full as mad as he. his Piece (he says) is inimitable, true Sterling

53

Wit, & Humour by God; & he can't hear the Prologue without being ready to die with Laughter. he acts five Parts himself, & is only sorry, he can't do all the rest. he has also advertised a Collection of Odes; and for his Vanity & Faculty of Lyeing, they are come to their full Maturity. all this, you see, must come to a Jayl, or Bedlam, & that without any help, almost without Pity.[32]

The play, *A Trip to Cambridge*, or *The Grateful Fair*, was put on in April in Pembroke College-Hall, with the parlor serving as green room. Smart acted only one part, the others beings taken by boys from Trinity, Clare, St. John's Emmanuel, and Pembroke. Richard Stonhewer was prompter and it was probably he who gave Christopher Hunter a written account of the play and the actors in it. What little remains of the play, the prologue and one soliloquy, as well as the plot outline, indicates that its humour was not of the most subtle kind. *The Cambridge Journal & Weekly Flying-Post* got hold of the text of the prologue, probably from the *Gentleman's Magazine*, and printed it on September 19, 1747, with the statement that the play was acted "with Universal Applause." The newspaper text has a couplet, "Swift to the Soul the piercing Image flies,/ More swift than *Celia's* Wit or *Celia's* Eyes," which is changed at some later date so that the Wit and the Eyes become Harriot's, another compliment to lovely Miss Pratt. Some of those who acted in Smart's play remembered him in later years and helped him; he, for his part, remembered some of them and invoked God's blessings on them in *Jubilate Agno*.

Smart had seen one of his poems printed in the *Gentleman's Magazine* in 1745 and three in Dodsley's *Museum* in 1746. This periodical, subtitled *Literary and Historical Register*, was edited by Mark Akenside and was publishing poems by the two Wartons and their friend Collins, William Whitehead, James Merrick, and others. Smart sent a pair of companion poems, "The Talkative Fair" and "The Silent Fair," to Dodsley in 1747 and had the satisfaction of seeing them in the September 12 issue of the *Museum*. His ode *To Idleness* was reprinted in the *London Magazine* in January, 1748, and the three poems, "A Morning Piece," "Noon Piece," and "Night Piece," all unsigned, graced the pages of the December, 1748 issue of the same periodical. And the prologue to his play was printed in the *Gentleman's Magazine* for August, 1747. With publication in two of London's leading monthly periodicals and in the prestigious *Museum*, Smart could justifiably consider himself well on the way to recognition as a poet of some abilities. About his ability, even at this early stage of his career, there can be no doubt. He could write humorous verse with the best of his contemporaries, but he could also, like many of them, turn to more serious subjects, and he was already at ease in a variety of stanzaic forms. The three pieces printed in the *London Magazine* show him to good advantage; it is typical of him that each poem should have an epigraph, one from Lucretius and two from Horace. Smart was always conscious of his position as Scholar of the University and all that the title he had won implied. The first of these pieces, *A Morning Piece, Or An Hymn for the Hay-Makers*, contains the stanza so much admired by Goldsmith,

> Strong Labour got up, with his pipe in his mouth,
>   And stoutly strode over the dale,
> He lent new perfumes to the breath of the south,
>   On his back hung his wallet and flail.
> Behind him came Health from her cottage of thatch,
> Where never physician had lifted the latch.

A Noon-Piece, Or The Mowers at Dinner, while the latter half constitutes a conventional, if somewhat warm, love poem to Harriot Pratt, has a stanza which shows how Smart could paint a picture with words.

> Their scythes upon the adverse bank
>   Glitter 'mongst th' entangled trees,
> Where the hazles form a rank,
>   And court'sy to the courting breeze.

Surely it was no accident that Smart had his friend Thomas Worlidge paint just this scene for engraving and inclusion in his *Poems on Several Occasions*; he knew that he had written some charming lines. The third of these companion poems *A Night-Piece, Or Modern Philosophy*, is more consistently all of a piece than its fellow poems, and, although it is in a tradition of "night" poems, it is a poem with a difference.

> 'Twas when bright Cynthia with her silver car,
>   Soft stealing from Endymion's bed,
> Had call'd forth ev'ry glit'ring star,
>   And up th' ascent of heav'n her brilliant host had led.

Night with all her negroe train,
Took possession of the plain;
In an hearse she rode reclin'd,
Drawn by screech-owls slow and blind:
Close to her with printless feet,
Crept Stillness in a winding sheet.

Next to her deaf Silence was seen,
Treading on tip-toes over the green;
Softly, lightly, gently she trips,
Still holding her finger seal'd to her lips.

Then came Sleep serene and bland,
Bearing a death watch in his hand;
In fluid air around him swims
A tribe grotesque of mimic dreams.

You could not see a sight,
    You could not hear a sound,
But all confess'd the night,
    And horrour deepen'd round.

Beneath a plantain's melancholy shade,
SOPHRON the wise was laid:
And to the answ'ring wood these sounds convey'd:
While others toil within the town,
And to fortune smile or frown,
Fond of trifles, fond of toys,
And married to that woman, Noise;
Sacred Wisdom be my care,
And fairest Virtue, Wisdom's heir.

His speculations thus the sage begun,
    When lo! the neighbouring bell
In solemn sound struck one:-
    He starts—and recollects—he was engag'd to Nell.
Then up he sprang nimble and light,
    And rapp'd at fair Elenor's door;
He laid aside Virtue that night,
    And next morn por'd in Plato for more.

The reader expects, at least through the end of the third stanza, that the poem is to sustain the note upon which it began, only to be brought up short with the satiric ending. Smart's opinion of his poetic abilities or of the scope of their recognition was not lessened when he was included among the contributors to the *Gratulatio* celebrating George II's return to England after the peace of Aix-la-Chapelle in 1748. The list of contributors bristles with "Honourables" and even the Vice-Chancellor, Dr. Thomas Chapman, exercised his pen on this occasion. Smart, with Mason, Whitehead and two or three others, must have been flattered to have his services enlisted even though he later sneered at the whole business in *The Student*, writing of "a late *gratulating* occasion, when our very worthy the Vice-Chancellor deign'd to tag a rhyme, and our learned Professors play'd at crambo in Hebrew, Arabic, and—WELCH" (II, 225). While Smart's poem is occasional, with the sins of most occasional poems upon its head, it is a harbinger of worthier efforts yet to come. Smart's habit of linking words in triads, often alliteratively, a habit that is seen in the poetry of his later years, crops up in " 'Tis this confirms, compleats, and nobly crowns the whole." And his question "Was it thy fleet that smoak'd the depth along/Swift as the eagle, as the lion strong" anticipates, in its latter half, the *Song to David*. When officials of Cambridge University went to St. James's Palace on December 10 to welcome the King in person they were accompanied by a number of Masters of Arts; Smart, as a contributor to the *Gratulatio*, must surely have been one of the latter.

Next year, 1749, Smart left Cambridge in the summer, by June 5 according to the "Liber Absentiae," and spent some time at Market Downham, Norfolk, near Harriot Pratt. From there he went to London or back to Cambridge to pack his belongings, if he had not already done so, the Master and Fellows of Pembroke allowing him twelve pounds in lieu of commons for the year from Michaelmas term, 1749 to Michaelmas term, 1750. On October 24, 1750, whether actually present in Cambridge at that time or not, he, with three other Fellows, was granted permission to be absent "usque ad comitia Major."[33] Despite his absence from Pembroke his name was continued in the records, being charged rent for a room, sharing in the yearly dividends and in the money due to the Fellows "on all Bursary accounts," getting his proportionate part of the benefits from Mr. Crossinge's Benefaction, and being carried on the Sizing book. He was even elected again to be one of the three commemorators for the academic year 1750–1 and at least three entries, to November, 1752, are given over to his absences.[34] And in successive years, in October, 1751 and 1752, the records show orders for Smart to be allowed ten pounds and six pounds, respectively, in lieu of commons for the past year.[35] But all this was on paper; Smart was in London.

III.

LONDON, 1749-1759

Smart's removal to London in the latter part of 1749 was dictated by his desire for fame and for the freedom to have and savor new experiences. He had every reason to believe, as he eagerly wished to believe, that fame would be his for the asking; his pen had won him local fame at the University and it, and his wits, would do the same on a larger scale in the literary jungle of London. After all, it was not every Fellow of a college who could come to London with a commendatory letter from the great Alexander Pope in his pocket. Nor was the fact of publication of his poems in the *Gentleman's Magazine* and the *London Magazine*, as well as in the prestigious *Museum*, entirely without its comforting aspects. And London, the bustling center of English life, with one tenth the entire population of England and Wales milling about in it, with its booksellers and theaters, with its great figures from the worlds of art and music and literature, with its pleasure gardens and resorts, and with its endless variety afforded every opportunity for new experiences, every opportunity to make a new life vastly different from the enervating routine of Pembroke and Cambridge town. But with all the exhilaration incident upon being comparatively young, quite unmarried, and unmitigatedly free of all obligations, Smart, like many others who came to London intent upon conquest with their pens, had to find some way in which to begin to earn money by his writing. Although he was by no means destitute when he arrived in London, he had never learned to deny himself when he wanted something, and every day in London thrust new objects of desire across his path. A man who loved the good things in life, fine clothes, good drink, and good fellowship, had to have the money with which these things could be bought or enjoyed. Smart was not unacquainted with Grub Street, if only at second or third remove, and he knew that a beginning writer, even with some published work behind him, had to join forces with or subordinate himself to some extent to a bookseller. His first task, once he had settled himself in respectable lodgings near St. James's Park, was, therefore, to establish such a connection.

Although Smart had courted the favors of Robert Dodsley, having him in mind as the publisher of the collection of poems upon which he had worked off and on for about six years by the time he went to London to stay, he early formed an alliance with another bookseller, John Newbery. One of Smart's earliest friends was Charles Burney, to whom he had written from Market Downham in July, 1749, and with whom, in Burney's own words he "reciprocated confidence[s] in their juvenile distresses of the heart." Smart's love of music and of good company had at some time taken him to Vauxhall Gardens where, as early as 1745, Thomas Arne had been appointed composer, being helped in various capacities by Burney, by that time his apprentice of one year's standing. Burney introduced Smart to Newbery "who was then engaged in the publication of a magazine entitled the Midwife or Old Woman's Magazine and looking out for an assistant competent to the undertaking," and thus began a business and personal relationship that lasted for more than a decade.[1] In 1750 Newbery, a man thirty-seven years old, had already achieved considerable success and fortune. He had started work as a printer's helper in Reading in his native Berkshire and by dint of application and a keen nose for a profitable deal had become publisher and owner of the local newspaper, the *Reading Mercury, or Weekly Post*. Upon the death of his employer, William Carnan, Newbery inherited the newspaper by Carnan's expressed desire; he also married Mrs. Carnan and thus acquired three children. Newbery expanded the sale of books and quack medicines which had been a side line with Carnan, and in 1743 he and four associates bought the exclusive right to vend certain medicines, among them the famous Dr. James's Fever Powders. He moved to London in 1744, established himself at the Bible and Sun in St. Paul's Churchyard in 1745, and began a flourishing trade in children's books, publishing a number of widely different works at the same time. At one time or another he employed as writers Oliver Goldsmith, Samuel Johnson, Griffith and Giles Jones, Hugh Kelly, William Guthrie, Benjamin Martin, and others. He was a master of and firm believer in advertising his products, books as well as quack medicines, and he used the *Reading Mercury*, which he held on to until 1762, and other newspapers as the best means for puffing his wares. Indeed, Smart may have become aware of Newbery's existence as early as 1745, for in that year the *Cambridge Journal and Weekly Flying Post* had begun, and it was not long thereafter that Newbery advertised regularly and for years in its columns. He had part interest in the *Public Ledger*, the *Gentleman's Magazine*, and other periodicals at one time or another in his career, and his whole life was one constant whirl of activity. Johnson, who had reasons enough to be grateful to him, characterized him in *Idler 19* as Jack Whirler, "whose business keeps him in perpetual motion," also saying of him that "his disposition is kind, and he has many friends" and that "Jack's cheerfulness and civility rank him among those whose presence never gives pain, and whom all receive with fondness and caresses." Goldsmith, who had even more cause to be grateful to Newbery, inserted a little sketch of him in *The Vicar of Wakefield*, stressing his incessant activity but also commenting on his good nature and his philanthropy. Newbery may have had a hand in one or more of the periodicals that appeared under his imprint, for Johnson, probably confusing him in his dual role of publisher and sometime author, said of him that he was "an extraordinary man, for I know not whether he has read, or written, most books."

Smart made friends easily; according to Hunter, he was "friendly, affectionate, and liberal to excess; so as often to give that to others, of which he was in the utmost want himself; he was also particularly engaging in conversation, when his first shyness was won away" (p. xxviii). While Smart met many figures of the literary and subliterary world through Newbery, he was by no means dependent upon him for his wide circle of acquaintances. In the summer of 1749 he had written to Burney, "I am as much a stranger as you to what is going on at Vaux Hall," good evidence that he was not unfamiliar with that place or its habitués. His signature is one of four witnessing a transaction between a Mr. Henry Chitty and Mr. Jonathan Tyers, lessee and soon to be proprietor of Vauxhall Gardens, on June 1, 1750.[2] By mid-1750, at the latest, then, Smart was on fairly intimate terms with the members of the Vauxhall group; again it may have been through young Charles Burney that he gained entrée into that circle. References to various people associated with the Gardens appear in Smart's poems and prose pieces and there is mention, in this connection, of William Hogarth, who designed the silver admission tickets; of Francis Hayman, who painted the supper boxes; of Louis Francois Roubiliac, whose statue of Handel graced the gardens; and of the singers and musicians who performed there nightly.* At Vauxhall Smart made the acquaintance of Richard Rolt and others who composed the lyrics that were set to music for performance by Tyers' singers and musicians. There, a favorite place of recreation for him, Smart saw Frederick, Prince of Wales, later the subject of one of his poems. There, too, if he had somehow not already met him, Smart would have become acquainted with the composer William Boyce, who had in 1745 set his song *To Idleness* to music. Thomas Arne he would already have known through Burney. And through Burney, according to Burney's daughter, Fanny, he met still other famous men and women. As Madame d'Arblay, in 1832, Fanny edited her father's *Memoirs* and wrote that "With a different set [that is, with Garrick, James Thomson, Mrs. Cibber, and Arne], and at a different part of town, young Burney formed an acquaintance with Kit Smart the poet; a man then in equal possession of those finest ingredients for the higher call of his art, fire and fancy, and, for its comic call, of sport and waggery. No indication, however, of such possession was granted to his appearance; not a grace was bestowed on his person or manners; and his physiognomy was of that round and stubbed form that seemed appertaining to a common dealer behind a common counter, rather than to a votary of the Muses. But his intellects, unhappily, were more brilliant than sound; and his poetic turn, though it never warped his sentiments or his heart, was little calculated to fortify his judgement" (I, 17—18). Smart described himself pseudonymously in 1750 in *The Student*; "my stature is so very low . . . My eyes, which are extremely small and hollow, may truly be styl'd of the *amorous* kind, for they are always looking at one another. In the rest of my person there is nothing very singular, saving that when I take the air, having neither horse nor vehicle, I am obliged to do it on a pair of bandy legs" (I, 249). Another friend of the bandy-legged poet was Arthur Murphy with whom he became acquainted before the end of 1751.[3] John Hawkesworth, the miscellaneous writer and friend of Johnson's early London years, was still another whom Smart probably met through Burney. Thus, through Burney or through one friend or another, Smart was speed-

*Smart would seem to have been particularly friendly with Hayman, praising him in *The Midwife* (II, 279), calling him "my friend" in *The Student* (I, 249), and again praising him in *The Blockhead and Beehive*.

ily accepted into the literary, musical, and artistic circles of mid-eighteenth-century London.

Newbery's willingness to employ Smart soon after the latter came to live in London may have been due to the reputation his poetry had already made for him; it may have resulted from Burney's recommendation, as Mrs. LeNoir stated;[4] and it may simply have been a matter of chance, Newbery needing somebody with a lighter touch to give new life to *The Midwife* and to *The Student* and Smart needing gainful literary employment. When it became known on March 25, 1750, that Smart was the first winner of the Seatonian prize with his poem *On the Eternity of the Supreme Being*, the publisher must have been impressed and decided, if he had not already, to enlist him in his group of writers. Thomas Seaton, an ex-Fellow of Clare College, had given an estate to the University of Cambridge by a clause in his will, dated October 8, 1738, which reads,

> I give my Kislingbury Estate to the University of Cambridge for ever: the Rents of which shall be disposed of yearly by the Vice-Chancellor for the time being, as he the Vice-Chancellor, the Master of Clare-Hall, and the Greek Professor for the time being, or any two of them shall agree. Which three persons aforesaid shall give out a Subject, which Subject shall for the first Year be one or other of the Perfections or Attributes of the Supreme Being, and so the succeeding Years, till the Subject is exhausted; and afterwards the Subject shall be either Death, Judgment, Heaven, Hell, Purity of Heart, &c. or whatever else may be judged by the Vice-Chancellor, Master of Clare-Hall, and Greek Professor to be most conducive to the honour of the Supreme Being and recommendation of Virtue. And they shall yearly dispose of the Rent of the above Estate to that Master of Arts, whose Poem on the Subject given shall be best approved by them. Which poem I ordain to be always in English, and to be printed; the expense of which shall be deducted out of the product of the Estate, and the residue given as a reward for the Composer of the Poem, or Ode, or Copy of Verses.

Although Seaton died in 1741, the first competition for the prize did not take place until 1750, the executors of his will contesting the clause but finally losing their case. Smart was living in London at the time he was awarded the prize, but he was still a Fellow of Pembroke and as such entitled to compete. Even after rumors of his marriage reached the Master and Fellows of his college in November, 1753, and it was ordered "that the dividend assigned to Mr.

Smart be deposited in the treasury till the society be satisfied that he has a right to the same," pride in Smart's success caused the same Master and Fellows to order, on January 16, 1754, that "Mr. Smart have leave to keep his name on the College books without any expense, so long as he continues to write for the premium left by Mr. Seaton."[5] By January, 1754, Smart had won the premium four years running with poems on the *Immensity* (1751), *Omniscience* (1752), and *Power* (1753) of the Supreme Being, as well as the *Eternity* poem of 1750. He did not submit a poem in 1754 and just managed to meet the deadline in 1755 with a poem on the *Goodness* of the Supreme Being which was also awarded the prize. Thereafter he competed no more. The poems achieved a surprising popularity; the *Eternity* and *Immensity* poems reaching three editions by 1756 and the others each being printed in a second edition. Dodsley and Bathurst were the London booksellers who sold the first Seatonian poem, *On the Eternity of the Supreme Being*; thereafter, in addition to other booksellers, one finds Newbery's name in the imprint to the other four Seatonian poems in their first and subsequent editions, with the exception of the first edition of *On the Power of the Supreme Being* in 1754, a possible though by no means certain indication of a temporary rift.

Smart's pride in his continued success with the Seatonian poems was great and he came to depend upon the prize money and upon the lift to his spirits that he got from the yearly public recognition of his abilities. He must have derived some consolation in 1754, the year he did not submit a poem, when the *Gentleman's Magazine*, reporting on the results of the competition, felt constrained to explain that the "ingenious Mr. Christopher Smart . . . was not this year among the competitors." Smart's gratitude to Seaton expressed itself at some later date by a poem, admirably entitled *On Gratitude, To the Memory of Mr. Seaton*, which praises that worthy's benevolence and concludes that Paradise would never have been lost "had heavenly Gratitude remain'd."[6]

Thomas Seaton had specified only that a subject be determined by three officials of the University and that the poems submitted be in English. Smart chose to write his Seatonian poems in blank verse and he also chose to imitate or emulate Milton as closely as possible. The results of these decisions are for the most part unfortunate, for Smart's poetic bent was not for blank verse and the influence of Milton led him, and many of his contemporaries, into absurdities.

The infelicities in the poems are all too easily discerned; the occasional lines and passages that are intrinsically good or foreshadow the other religious poetry to come, the poetry printed after 1763, have sometimes been overlooked. To be stressed initially is the emergence of the great themes of Smart's religious verse, gratitude, praise of the Lord, and charity. Hunter's statement that his uncle wrote "particular passages" of his religious poems "on his knees" (p. xxviii) gives evidence of the mood in which Smart approached these poems. In 1756, the year in which the last Seatonian poem, written late in 1755, was published, Smart also published a *Hymn to the Supreme Being, on Recovery from a dangerous Fit of Illness.* Taking his cue from James Thomson's *Hymn to the Seasons,* he used his *Hymn* in part to recapitulate some of the themes and preoccupations of the Seatonian poems, and the *Hymn* is to be considered as rising, although only in part, from those poems. The *Hymn* is to the "Supreme Being," the words used to describe the Lord in Seaton's will and in Smart's prize poems, and Smart himself as much as states the connection explicitly in the tenth stanza of the *Hymn,* there mentioning the titles of the Seatonian poems almost in the order of their publication:

> All glory to th' ETERNAL, to th' IMMENSE,
> All glory to th' OMNISCIENT and GOOD,
> Whose power's uncircumscrib'd, whose love's intense.

Where the Seatonian poems, when they extol the virtue of gratitude and exhort creation to praise the Lord and to be thankful to him, are general or all-encompassing in their utterances, the *Hymn* is personal, the poet is himself praising God and thanking Him for the mercy shown to him. Where, in the *Omniscience* poem, both at the beginning and at the very end, the identical lines are used to describe the cherub Gratitude, enshrined as the chief virtue,

> And thou, cherubic Gratitude, whose voice
> To pious ears sounds silverly so sweet,
> Come with thy precious incense, bring thy gift,
> And with thy choicest stores the altar crown.

in the *Hymn* the gratitude is present but largely implicit, and it is charity that occupies the highest rank. Smart, in one of the few passages in his poetry where he speaks of the great chain of being, lists the terrestrial primates and then goes on to say

> Thus in high heaven charity is great,
>   Faith, hope, devotion hold a lower place;
> On her the cherubs and the seraphs wait,
>   Her, every virtue courts, and every grace;
> See! on the right, close by the Almighty's throne,
>   In him she shines confest, who came to make her known

One other similarity links the *Hymn* and the Seatonian poems. In the latter Smart revealed for the first time the fascination he felt for the tiniest as well as the hugest of God's creatures. The ant is described in detail as it makes provision for the winter in the *Omniscience* poem; in the *Immensity* poem the whale swims above the rest of the "finny race"

> While high above their heads Leviathan
> The terror and the glory of the main
> His pastime takes with transport, proud to see
> The ocean's vast dominion all his own.

Leviathan is described in much the same words in the *Hymn,*

> What can with great Leviathan compare,
>   Who takes his pastime in the mighty main?

Nearest in time to the *Hymn* and the best of the Seatonian efforts is the *Goodness* poem, composed hurriedly and rushed to Cambridge just in time to be considered in the competition—possibly the pressure on Smart was responsible for its superior merits. Much of what bears quotation from the five prize poems is concentrated in this poem, the last of them. The poem begins with a plea to "Israel's sweet psalmist," Smart asking that "in this breast/ Some portion of thy genuine spirit breathe,/ And lift me from myself," thus continuing the preoccupation with David, "the poet of my God," that marks the opening of the *Immensity* poem. Without the aid of the sun, Smart writes,

> Lost were the garnet's lustre, lost the lilly,
> The tulip and auricula's spotted pride;
> Lost were the peacock's plumage, to the sight

So pleasing in its pomp and glossy glow.
O thrice-illustrious! Were it not for thee
Those pansies, that reclining from the bank,
View through th' immaculate, pellucid stream
Their portraiture in the inverted heaven,
Might as well change their triple boast, the white,
The purple, and the gold, that far outvie
The Eastern monarch's garb, ev'n with the dock,
Ev'n with the baneful hemlock's irksome green.

While two or three of these lines might easily be spared, the rest of
the passage shows what Smart could do and would before very long
do better. When Smart turned to describe the birds' praise of their
Creator he did not forget one of the unloveliest of their kind,

Th' invoking ravens in the greenwood wide;
And tho' their coarse throats ruttling hurt the ear,
They mean it all for music, thanks and praise
They mean, and leave ingratitude to man—

And as he invites various areas of the world to come and bear gifts
as tokens of their gratitude to God he turns to Arabia,

Approach and bring from Araby the blest
The fragrant cassia, frankincense and myrrh,
And meekly kneeling at the altar's foot
Lay all the tributary incense down.

Dr. James Grainger, reviewing the poem for the *Monthly Review* in
June, 1756, pronounced it "certainly inferior to his former productions" and censured his handling of blank verse. He deprecated the
fact that Smart missed the fine opportunities offered by his subject,
found it ungrammatical in places, and objected to the use of "low
and trifling expressions." But Grainger, author of *The Sugar Cane*,
was hardly a competent judge.

These six poems, the five Seatonian poems and the *Hymn*, written over a period of six years, represent Smart's religious verse of the
period before his confinement for madness. They are prophetic of
the religious poetry of the years during and after the confinement
and they contain the themes that Smart was later to develop with
greater precision and beauty. Even some of the words he was to
favor in his later poetry are to be found here. Here, too, are a few
verbal coinages and a few epithets that find their counterparts in

the later religious poetry, the "dust-directed" thought and "heav'n-directed" hands of the *Eternity* poem being paralleled by the "heart-directed" vows of a *Song to David*, the "heav'n-directed" shower of the *Psalms*, and the "hope-retarded" death of the *Hymns and Spiritual Songs*. A few alliterative doublets such as "want and woe" and "miracles and might"; some triplets, "low, imperfect, incorrect," and one or two more; a good deal of alliteration; and a number of anticipations of phrases in the later poetry link these poems with Smart's great religious poetry of the 1760's. The "orphans mite" of the *Immensity* poem prepares for the "widow's mite" of the *Song*, and the "out-stretch'd arm," the "still profound," and the "pensile house" of these early poems are echoed in the later. While the Seatonian prize poems and the *Hymn* are apprentice work, they contain in them virtually all the elements that give the *Song*, the *Psalms*, and the *Hymns and Spiritual Songs* their distinctive character. Once Smart had shed the blank verse in which he was never at ease, and once he had had to suffer and turn in on himself, as he did in the asylum and the mad house, he was ready to write the kind of poetry of which he had allowed glimpses now and again.

Unfortunately, the rents of Mr. Seaton's estate were small, amounting to seventeen pounds a year, and, when the cost of publishing five hundred copies of each poem was added to the taxes to be paid, Smart was left with only between nine and ten pounds, not the generous thirty or forty that he is believed to have received.[7] Hence he was more than glad to enter into some sort of working arrangement with Newbery. The first fruit of this association was "The Horatian Canons of Friendship," an imitation of the third satire of the first book of Horace's *Satires*, published in June, 1750. In one dedication Smart sought to goad the Rev. William Warburton, Shakespeare's editor and Pope's literary executor, into answering him and thus precipitating him into public attention; in a second he inserted a compliment to Henry Fielding, possibly trying to attract the favorable notice of one of the leading writers of the time. This piece, the first of Smart's to be separately published in London, is a workmanlike but otherwise undistinguished imitation of Horace in heroic couplets. One example will give something of the quality of the poem and point up Smart's practice of borrowing from himself.

> The sire, whose son squints forty thousand ways,
> Finds in his features mighty room for praise:
> 'Ah! born' (he cries) 'to make the ladies sigh,
> Jacky, thou hast an amorous cast o' the eye.'

Smart used this "amorous cast" of the eyes in his description of himself in *The Student* and, possibly for the first time, in what has been described as an extempore epigram on John Wilkes.

> His eyes are surely of the *am'rous* kind,
> For to *each other* they are *still inclin'd*.[8]

Another bid for attention and a promise of things to come was an appended advertisement announcing the imminent publication of *The History of Jack the Giant Killer*, "with a Commentary and Notes . . . by Master Billy Pentweazle, a child of nine years old," presumably Smart himself who had taken on the pseudonym of Ebenezer Pentweazle for the *Horatian Canons*.*

At this same time Smart was contributing to *The Student, or Oxford and Cambridge Monthly Miscellany* (the *Cambridge* of the title being added with No. 6, June 30, 1750 when he joined forces with the other editor). His work in this periodical, unlike *The Horation Canons*, shows Smart off to advantage, for he was at his humorous best in those essays and poems which asked of him only that he relax and enjoy himself while entertaining his readers. *The Student*, published monthly from January 31, 1750, to about July, 1751, was evidently edited by somebody then at, or recently from, Oxford.[9] The periodical had been largely composed of serious essays and poems, translations and imitations, critical essays, a few poems in a lighter vein, and some not very convincing attempts at humor. Much of the sixth number was the same, but Smart's hand was discernible in an "Introduction to a new system of Castle-Building" under one of his eye-catching pseudonyms, Chimaericus Cantabrigiensis. The same number contained two of Smart's poems. And beginning with the second number of Volume 2 he also contributed a series of six essays by "The Female Student"; "and to tell

---

*Some learned nonsense in the form of mottoes in nine languages in the advertisement suggests that Newbery may have been thinking of getting together a projected collection of curious "Mottos from Greek, Latin, French, and English Authors, for the use of Poets and Puppeys, by Lawrence Likelihood, Esq.," for which he would doubtless have called upon Smart. See Charles Welsh, *A Bookseller of the Last Century* (London, 1885), p. 14.

you a secret," she writes in one of these essays, "I am that very same MIDWIFE, who publishes the *Old Woman's* Magazine" (II, 52). Eventually fifteen of his essays appeared in the two volumes of the periodical. He also appended three numbers of a humorous news report entitled "The Inspector" to the second volume. In these, as in almost everything else he wrote around this time, he puffed his own work and those of his friends—or those writers with whom he would have liked to be acquainted. Among these were Fielding, Johnson, Akenside, Armstrong, Collins, the Wartons, Smollett, Mason, Lowth, and Brown. Johnson's life of Dr. Francis Cheynel was reprinted, making up part of three successive numbers; and a minor poet named Ben Sedgly, who was more remarkable for his ability to drain "half a tankard at a single draught" (II, 217) than for his verses, may have been the author of three letters by Timothy Beck, the Happy Cobler of Portugal Street.[10] But the majority of the poems in *The Student* were Smart's, at least fourteen of them being printed there for the first time. Although they appeared in print for the first time in *The Student*, one, a Latin translation of some lines from the first canto of *Hudibras*, had been written as long ago as 1740 when Smart was a freshman at the University, and another, the Latin poem to Samuel Saunders of King's College, also dated from his university days. So, too, impressed into hasty service were "The Pretty Bar-Keeper of the Mitre, written at College, 1741" and the Prologue to *A Trip to Cambridge*, Smart's play put on at Pembroke in 1747. Thus early in his career Smart was already reaching into his reserve to provide materials for the many and diverse undertakings into which his need for recognition and later his extravagance led him. Newbery saw to it by judicious advertising that *The Student* was never out of the public eye, using the *Cambridge Journal and Weekly Flying-Post* as one very logical place in which to accomplish this end. Significantly enough, one finds at least two essays from *The Student* reprinted in the *Cambridge Journal*; one is from the Castle-Building series, the other is from the series by "The Female Student," some evidence of their popularity.* Both the essays are by Smart; they, with his poems,

---

The Cambridge Journal, in its issue for August 11, 1750, notified its readers that the eighth number of *The Student* would be published on the sixteenth of that month and thereafter rather than on the last day of each month in order to prevent its being robbed (more evidence of popularity) by "the Authors of a late despicable Monthly Medley," possibly the *Royal Magazine, or Quarterly Bee.*

make *The Student* memorable and would have been enough by themselves to assure him a place in the second rank of English humorists. While engaged on *The Student* Smart also undertook the virtually singlehanded authorship of the monthly periodical called *The Midwife, or The Old Woman's Magazine,* employing as pseudonym "Mrs. Mary Midnight," a "Mrs. Midnight" being a "midwife" in underworld slang. The first number of this three-penny production came out on October 16, 1751, and it ran to approximately April, 1753, for a total of sixteen numbers. By the time of the appearance of the first number Smart had been contributing to *The Student* for about five months and was to do so for another eight or nine, initiating the practice which marked his Grub-Street career of juggling two or more literary enterprises at the same time. He used the two periodicals as vantage points for reciprocal compliments and advertising as well as for praise of the character and accomplishment of his friends. To the roll of those he noticed favorably in *The Student* can be added Newbery, Murphy, Garrick, Rolt, and Burney; and having reprinted a biography by Johnson in *The Student* he went even further and reprinted one *Rambler* in each number of *The Midwife* for a number of issues.*
While there are a few poems by other writers, some of them identified and others not, and while material was reprinted from *The Student* and from Mrs. Midnight's Oratory, still another enterprise upon which Smart was engaged, again he provided the lion's share of the prose and poetry in *The Midwife.*† Nor did he write all fresh material for his periodical; although there were at least seventeen poems printed for the first time in its pages, many of them were of earlier composition. *The Midwife* contains much excellent humor, but there are also some serious essays and there is some parade of learning, albeit cloaked in facetiousness. Evidence of its contemporary popularity can be seen in the fact that at least two magazines, the *Royal Magazine, or Quarterly Bee* and the *Ladies Magazine,* reprinted a considerable number of pieces from it and a few from *The Student* in their early volumes. Smart protested in a footnote

---

*Smart was an early admirer of the *Rambler* essays; Burney writes that "Smart, the poet, first mentioned them to me as excellent papers, before I had heard any one else speak of them" (Boswell, *Life,* I, 208, n.).

†Although Hunter thought that "Mr. Newbery and himself [Smart] were the chief, if not only contributors" (p. xix), nothing has been claimed for Newbery with any certainty. And neither Bonnell Thorton nor Richard Rolt, both of whom have been mentioned in this connection, has been conclusively shown to be a contributor.

in *The Midwife*, but there was really nothing he could do; indeed, he was probably pleased at the opportunity to call attention to his own popularity. *The Midwife*, like most other eighteenth-century periodicals, was published in collected form, appearing in three volumes in 1753; to it was added *An Index to Mankind*, a collection of maxims that had originally been printed in 1751.

The Midwife, and *The Student* to a lesser extent, is partly in the tradition of learned humor exemplified by Rabelais, Fielding, and Sterne. There is a certain amount of wit and word play which demands a knowledge of languages other than English as well as the terminologies of the professions. Also present are rather farfetched and ridiculous conceits, that is, that a mill exists for grinding old people down into young or that it is possible to devise and operate an organ whose music is provided by cats. Elaborate fun is made of such pretenders to learning as the Robin Hood Society, antiquaries and virtuosi, university students and fellows, writers of pseudo-odes and pseudo-elegies, and even specific individuals such as John Hill and William Kenrick. None of all this, however, is acidulous; all is conceived and carried out in a spirit of good clean fun, with the author enjoying his own wit and humor as much as anybody else. What is most remarkable, perhaps, in *The Midwife*, and to a lesser degree in *The Student*, is the whirlwind variety of fantastic ideas and subjects for humorous treatment that succeed one another in kaleidoscopic sequence. This even extends to "The Midwife's Politicks: Or, Gossip's Chronicle of the Affairs of Europe," a concluding part to each issue clearly modeled on the "Historical Register" or "Foreign Intelligence" of other periodicals. Clearly Smart was enjoying himself, allowing his bent for broad comedy full sway, mentioning in terms of intimacy the names of the great and near-great, writing steadily in a variety of forms, gaining the recognition he so desired, and making money.

Late in 1750 Smart fell under the lash of William Kenrick, one of the more virulent controversialists of Grub Street. Smart's "Night Piece," originally published in the *London Magazine* had been used again in *The Student*, Smart protesting in a note that the *London Magazine* had printed an "imperfect copy . . . without the knowledge or consent of the author." Kenrick poked fun at the poem in an epigram, part of his *Kapelion, or Poetical Ordinary*, and added a surprisingly mild note suggesting that Smart not be so quick to condemn faults in others when he was "liable to such gross

Failures himself." Since the *Kapelion* was sold by Newbery, and since Kenrick subscribed to Smart's *Poems on Several Occasions,* 1752, and years later subscribed for the extraordinary number of six copies of Smart's version of the Psalms, there is ample warrant to suspect complicity. Smart, as a virtual newcomer to the London literary scene, was to be given his baptism of fire by Kenrick, one of Newbery's stable of writers, and thus gain greater publicity for his literary endeavors, also under Newbery's aegis. In any event, Kenrick or somebody else allied with him or with Newbery, continued the attack with a three-penny pamphlet entitled "The Magazines Blown Up," which employed most of its barbs in a satiric treatment of Smart under his Pentweazle pseudonym. Actually annoyed, or as part of a prearranged scheme, Smart made it publicly known in *The Midwife* for December, 1750, that he would take his revenge in an *Old Woman's Dunciad,* then ostensibly being prepared for the press. The work was never published, however, if indeed it ever progressed beyond the title itself, for Kenrick usurped the title and published his satire on Smart in January, 1751. The speed with which Kenrick's *Old Woman's Dunciad,* printed actually or only nominally by Carnan, whom Smart, as Mrs. Midnight, had designated as his sole printer in the future, got into print makes it all the more probable that the whole controversy was a put-up affair. The blank verse text of this *Dunciad,* the Interpretation in octosyllabics, and the sometimes long, pseudo-learned notes must have taken some time to put together, however dismal their quality. In his preface, Kenrick, writing as Margelina Scribelinda Macularia, stated that Mrs. Midnight, the ostensible author of *The Old Woman's Dunciad,* had been approached by several authors wishing to bribe her to omit their names from the work. "Among which came the celebrated *Pentweazle,*" she writes, knowing that Smart would be recognized under this pseudonym, "and meanly offer'd her *five Guineas* in part, on Subscription to her Miscellany of Poems, to be publish'd some Time in *February* next." Under the guise of an insult it seems that Kenrick, acting under instructions from Newbery, was directing attention to Smart's poems to whose probable date of publication he alluded. As a last feeble attempt to hit back Smart did what he could in the April, 1751, number of *The Midwife,* among other things exposing the many faults of Kenrick's *Monody* on the death of the Prince of Wales.

Smart had seen the Prince of Wales many times at Vauxhall

Gardens and he, too, with a host of others, did not omit to mourn his death in verse. It is possible that Smart, self-revealed as a Freemason in *Jubilate Agno*, may have met the Prince of Wales in Masonic circles. Smart could have joined the Freemasons by the last year of his stay in Cambridge, or he might have joined soon after coming to London; many prominent men of the groups he moved in were of the Society.[11] His *Solemn Dirge, Sacred to the Memory of his Royal Highness Frederic Prince of Wales* was sung, appropriately enough, at Vauxhall by Mr. Lowe, Miss Burchell, and others, to music composed by Thomas Worgan; the printed *Dirge*, dedicated to young Prince George, went into three editions in the year of its publication. John Hill, soon to be Smart's bitter enemy, in one of his *Inspector* essays on the "Elegies, Monodies, Threnodies, and Elegiac Pastorals" occasioned by the Prince's death, seems to except Smart's *Solemn Dirge* from his satire. But by the time Smart wrote his *Solemn Dirge* he had already been publishing a variety of pieces, some of which were to be fair game for his satirists. Chief among these was a collection of jests, epigrams, and epitaphs called *The Nutcracker*, edited by Ferdinando Foot, Esq., and dedicated to "my very good Friend, His Imperial Excellency, The Publick." It was this same public, or at least one section of it, for which Smart wrote a prologue and epilogue to an amateur performance of *Othello* put on at Drury Lane on March 7.* Francis Blake Delaval and his brother John Blake Delaval were the moving spirits in this production, playing Othello and Iago, respectively. John Blake Delaval had been all too briefly a student at Pembroke, his stay being brought to an end when the Captain Hargraves "whom he had carried all about to see Chappels & Libraries, & make Visits in the Face of Day" was found out to be a woman, and it was he who asked Smart to write the prologue for *Othello*.[12] The performance was a tremendous success and made a considerable stir in the periodicals. The actors had been coached by Spranger Barry and Charles Macklin, and the Delavals, a third brother taking the role of Cassio, were greatly praised for their abilities. One thousand selected persons, among them members of the royal family, had

*Although the play was originally intended for presentation at the Little Theatre in the Haymarket, the actors, according to the *General Advertiser* for March 6, were so "much importuned by their friends and acquaintances for tickets" that it was shifted to the larger Drury Lane Theatre when David Mallet, author of the masque *Alfred*, then being performed at that theater, agreed to interrupt the run for two days.

tickets, and the periodicals commented on the brilliance and splendor of their dress as well as the rich costuming of the play. Even the House of Commons adjourned early to allow those fortunate members who had tickets to attend. While some aspects of the performance may have raised eyebrows, Miss Elizabeth La Roche, Francis Blake Delaval's mistress, being cast as Emilia and her sister Deodata, also no better than she should be as far as morals went, performing Desdemona, it was something of an honor for Smart to be associated with it. His prologue and epilogue, dedicated to Francis and John Delaval, were published in three editions in the same year, reprinted, imitated, and attacked. One attack came in the form of a letter signed B.C. in the March *Gentleman's Magazine*. After criticizing the performance and the toadying praise lavished upon it solely because the performers were rich, B.C. turned to Smart's share. "I wish," he wrote, "the world had not known that this prologue and epilogue were written by a gentleman, who has hitherto been esteem'd a genius and a scholar; for nothing but a publication of them with his name, would have convinced the world that he was the author; and it is to be hoped that he will consider before it is too late, that even genius and learning, prostituted to such service, must at length lose their dignity, and be regarded only as the tools of those who hire them for their use." B.C. may have been incensed that Smart designated himself, as he still had every right to, "Fellow of Pembroke-Hall, in the University of Cambridge" on the title page of the published poems. Smart, for his part, was too busy puffing the performance in *The Student* and *The Midwife* and warning the unscrupulous against pirating his prologue and epilogue to pay any attention to the letter in the *Gentleman's Magazine*. Characteristically, he used the last inch of space at the end of the published prologue and epilogue to put in a word for *The Midwife*, assuring readers that the "Sixth number of the Midwife, or the *Old Woman's Magazine*, will certainly be published the 16th of this Instant *March*; and will compleat the First Volume of that elaborate Undertaking, so necessary for all Families, and for Gentlemen and Ladies pockets—The price is only *Three Pence* a Number."

Whoever B.C. was, he must have felt some annoyance and chagrin in the very next month, for on April 20 Smart was again awarded the Seatonian prize, this time for his poem *On the Immensity of the Supreme Being*. Not only could he turn his hand to occasional verse whenever asked but here was added assurance of his talent for poetry of a higher order. Not only was he Kit Smart, already friend or acquaintance of half of literary and musical London; he was also Christopher Smart, Master of Arts, Fellow of Pembroke College in the University of Cambridge. But it was in the former capacity that he made his next appearance, or at least in one of the aspects of the former, for in June he took on a new role with the second number of Newbery's publication for little children, *The Lilliputian Magazine*. For this he wrote a *Morning Hymn* and possibly a very few other poems.[13] Here Smart, as he was to do more than once again, was forced to descend from the level of serious composition to put together rhymes and display his wit for the entertainment of little masters and misses. Perhaps he and Newbery were casting about for another enterprise for him, since *The Student* ceased publication in July and the *Gentleman's Magazine* for 1751 reported in its Preface that the "poor Old Woman [*The Midwife*] has already had several fainting fits, from which she has with great difficulty recover'd."

One would expect from all this literary activity that Smart was enjoying a period of relative prosperity, but that this was not true is revealed by his promise to pay Jonathan Tyers "on Order Ten Pounds on Demand Value," dated June 11, 1751.[14] Not earning enough, clearly, to satisfy his need for the luxuries of life Smart, possibly financed by Newbery and helped by Richard Rolt, embarked on a new and evidently most congenial venture.* He had already learned the art of puffing, both before and after an event, from that consummate master, Newbery, and hence used *The Midwife* of January, 1752, as a logical place in which to reprint "The Inauguration Speech of Mrs. Mary Midnight, at the opening of her oratory." For on December 3, 1751, "in the Guest Room at the Castle Tavern in Paternoster-Row" there had been "A Grand Concert of Vocal and Instrumental Musick, By several Eminent Hands." Given gratis at the same time was "The Old Woman's Oratory; or Henley in Petticoats . . . conducted by Mrs. Midnight, Author of the Midwife, and her Family." The program of this premiere performance consisted of four orations, Signor Antonio

*Mrs. LeNoir, in a letter to Sharp, August 22, 1831, wrote that "at this period [when *The Midwife* was being published] the same conductors [Newbery and Smart] had an Oratory (as they called it) somewhere in the Haymarket where some things from the Magazine and drolleries of various kinds were exhibited" (p. 9).

Ambrosiano playing a concerto on the Salt-Box, some more orthodox musical pieces, and one or two more items, the whole concluding with the singing of a song to the tune of *Roast Beef of Old
England*. John "Orator" Henley, the eccentric preacher of Clare
Market, a man of some learning and abilities, delivered sermons
and orations in a breathless staccato style from a gaudily decorated
pulpit; needless to say he was for twenty-odd years fair game for the
satirists. In his inaugural oration Smart's ridicule of Orator Henley
took the form of a parody of that worthy's style.

Henley hit back, accusing "the old woman," Smart in female
attire, of being a man, only to be counterattacked in the pages of
The Midwife to the effect that he was in love with Mary Midnight,
but that she was convinced that he was *himself* an old woman and
would not "repeal this Sentence, till he by a Jury of Matrons shall
convince the publick of the contrary." The *Gentleman's Magazine*
for January, 1752, announced that among "other diversions and
amusements which increase upon us, the town has been lately entertained with a kind of farcical performance called *The Old Woman's
Oratory*, conducted by Mrs *Mary Midnight* and her family; intended as a banter on *Henley's* Oratory, and a puff to the Old
Woman's Magazine—*Henley's* Oratory they call the slaughter house
of wit, morals, and divinity." Newbery used the *Reading Mercury*
for December 30, 1751, to advertise and vindicate the Oratory, reprinting one of Smart's light poems used therein:

> Yesterday Noon was performed at the New Theatre in the Hay-
> Market, Mrs. MIDNIGHT'S ORATORY, which was conducted
> with the utmost Decency, and received with the most extraordinary
> Applause, notwithstanding the many Articles made Use of to de-
> preciate it in the Eyes of the Publick; and we are informed that the
> same will again be exhibited at the above Place, at Twelve o'Clock
> on Monday next.

> N.B. There was a most excellent Band of Musick, consisting of
> thirty Hands, among them were several Persons of Fortune and
> Distinction, on whose Account all the Performers were dressed in
> Masquerade, and it was universally acknowledged that there was
> more *real casuistry* in the Jew's Harp, and more *Sterling Sense* in
> the Salt Box, than ever came from the Tub, at the Slaughter House
> of Sense, Wit and Reason, near Clare Market. As Mrs. Midnight's
> voice is greatly impaired by Age, She begs the Favour of her
> Friends to join her in the Chorus of the Song as it was sung
> Yesterday at the New Theatre in the Hay-Market.

To the Tune of the Roast Beef of Old England:
If Virtue's in Vogue and if Honesty thrives.[15]

Whereupon Henley took to the pages of the *Public Advertiser* on March 21, 1752, to proclaim definitely that "One Time with another, my Oratory is as full as ever, when I please, and my Service to Mr Smart, Mrs Warner, Mr Newbery, etc." Exactly a week later the *Daily Advertiser* carried a rejoinder from Mrs. Midnight, "The last time this Entertainment was performed, the House was crowded, that many Hundreds could not get admittance, and persons of Quality and Distinction found Satisfaction . . . My Service to Sister Henley."[16] Whatever Henley's further fulminations, Smart had hit upon a new source of revenue, one that was to be tapped again and again intermittently up to 1761.

Giving his venture a variety of different names, associated with different and mostly fantastically pseudonymous performers, with all kinds of specialty acts designed to attract the eyes and ears of the none too discriminating man in the street, Smart supplemented the income he earned by his pen by donning the robes of an old woman, speaking orations and occasional verse of all kinds, playing on the kettle-drums, and, in general, clowning before the throngs who came to the Castle Tavern, and then to the Haymarket Theatre, and even to Southwark Fair, when the Lord Mayor forbade the use of the unlicensed Castle Tavern a scant two months after the Oratory opened. Smart was not entirely without experience of the stage, as he had written, directed, and acted in his comedy *A Trip to Cambridge, or The Grateful Fair*, less than four years ago while at Cambridge. Further evidence of his interest in the stage and acting can be found scattered in *The Midwife*. What is more, an anecdote in the London *Morning Herald* for January 20, 1783, published well after Smart's death, told of Garrick's asking to meet Mrs. Midnight after reading and enjoying an article in *The Midwife*, almost surely the "letter from Mrs. Midnight to David Garrick, Esq." (I, 87–8), which contained some strictures on him. Smart, "dressed as an ancient lady of the last age," met Garrick in the presence of another lady. While arguing about the stage and poetry Smart let out an oath that shocked the real lady and "stung the two gentlemen into violent fits of laughter." His daughter Elizabeth wrote that Newbery introduced Smart "dressed in formal attire to Mrs. Garrick under the name of Mrs. Midnight: as he was

77

of low stature and had delicate arms and hands the joke succeeded until the gentlemen thought fit to reveal it, when Mrs. Garrick observed that she thought Mrs. Midnight in saluting her kissed very close."[17] Evidently Smart could take off an old woman with some skill. Whether he advertised his efforts as The Old Woman's Oratory, Mrs. Midnight's Grand Concert, Mrs. Midnight's New Carnival Concert, The British Roratory, Sack Posset, or one of at least a half-dozen more such titles, Smart must have continued to derive profit from these ventures. His best season, on the evidence of playbills and newspaper advertisements, was that of 1752–1753 with at least sixty-eight performances of the Oratory. Indeed, it was in this season that he advertised for performers, stating that "any Person of whatever Party, Perswasion, Countenance, or Country, who is able to entertain the Publick in a singular and agreeable Manner, may enter into present Pay and Good Quarters, with Mrs. Midnight's Band of Originals, by applying to her at the Theatre in the Haymarket, any evening at five o'clock." Up to the time of this advertisement, late December, 1752, Smart could number among his "Band of Originals" only the pseudonymous Signors Ambrosiano, Bombasto, Bombazino, and Molipitano; the nine-year-old violincellist Benjamin Hallet; and some unnamed musicians. Doubling must have been the order of the day. Subsequently, however, the announcements and advertisements fairly bristled with the eye-catching inventions of Smart's mind; Italian singers and dancers named Bambaregines, Rerriminonies, Piantofugo, Signor and Signora Balletino, and many more were promised and appeared. As the theatrical seasons progressed Smart was able to present animal pantomime, a company of Lilliputians, a dancer with a wooden leg, an assortment of pieces on such unlikely instruments as wooden spoons, Jew's-harps, slippers, hurdy-gurdies, and almost anything that would produce noise, and a number of singers and musicians with believable names such as Lauder, Warner, and Noell. The Old Woman even gave birth to a daughter, who first appeared, as just having "arrived from Padua" for the first time on March 21, 1752, playing a humorous solo on the French horn. Whoever she, or he, was, her appearances in the following seasons were numerous. At least one of these performers was remembered in *Jubilate Agno* where Smart prays "bless the Lord Jesus BENJAMIN HALLET" (B1, 243).

Extracts from playbills and newspaper advertisements best recreate the kind of entertainment with which Mrs. Midnight's public was regaled. Thus, the *Public Advertiser* for March 13, 1753, carried an ad announcing

> *The Old Woman's Concert.* Principal parts by Mrs. Midnight; her daughter Dorothy; Sig Bombasto, just arrived from Padua; Sig Bombazeeno, also arrived from Italy; Signora Spoonatissima, dug out of the ruins of Herculaneum; Sig Ambrosiano, alias Sig Salt-Box; Sig Twangdilo, the Casuist; Sig Piantafugocalo; Sig Gapatoono, first cousin to Farinelli; Mynheer Puffupandyke; Mlle Rompereau; Mme Hophye; the two Mlle Broileau; Miss Merit, an English Lady of an ancient Family, almost extinct, with Dancing in the Old British Taste and a Hornpipe by Mr. Timbertoe.

At another time the master of the animal pantomimists used in the Oratory wrote, or presumably somebody wrote for him,

> As my Monkeys and me and my Dogs am promised to go to L'Haye and Vienna after some Days more, the grand Noblemans and Gentlemans of this Nation England do desire me to perform every Night, and so me shall do with Mrs. Midnight at the Haymarket Playhouse this Thursday Night. Ballard Mango, my big Monkey, will talk the *Prologue*.

Mrs. Midnight's concern for her patrons' comfort was tender indeed and made unashamedly public. She spared no expense for wax candles to illuminate the Large Room, Swan Yard, or West Smithfield during the short time of Bartholmew Fair and she hoisted a flag over the passage leading to her Room, lest prospective viewers became confused in the Fair and not find their way to her. On another occasion, for a performance in the same place, she decorated the Room "in an elegant Manner, for the better reception of the Nobility and Gentry," adding "There is a back door to Hosier Lane for the conveniency of those who don't chose to be Crowded . . . The passages will be elegantly illuminated." Mrs. Midnight was justifiably proud of the variety of entertainment she could offer. Now it was the Lilliputians' performance of *Gli Amanti Gelosi, or The Birth of Harlequin*; at another time it was *The Adventures of Fribble*, a play or dialogue for two actors, Miss Midnight and "a choice Spirit." Or it might be dancing by "an Extraordinary Original who will not touch the Ground either with his hands or feet." There were many concerts of vocal and "instrumental" music, solemn processions, pantomimes, prologues and epilogues spoken from the back of an ass, and solo and ensemble singing and dancing. After the first season or two the emphasis was put more and more on the effects obtainable from spectacle and music rather than on the satire, broad as it was, that was the chief staple of the Orations.[18]

At least three contemporary viewers of these entertainments recorded their impressions. Horace Walpole saw a performance in the first season and wrote to George Montagu in a letter of May 12, 1752,

> it appeared the lowest buffoonery in the world even to me who am used to my uncle Horace. There is a bad oration to ridicule, what it is too like, Orator Henley: all the rest is perverted music. There is a man who plays so nimbly on the kettle drums, that he has reduced that noisy instrument to be an object of sight, for if you don't see the tricks with his hands, it is no better than ordinary. Another plays on a violin and trumpet together; another mimics a bagpipe with a German flute, and makes it full as disagreeable. There is an admired dulcimer, a favourite saltbox, and a really curious Jew's harp. Two or three men intend to persuade you that they play on a broomstick, which is drolly brought in, carefully shrouded in a case, so as to be mistaken for nothing but the action. The last fellow imitates farting and curtseying to a French horn. There are twenty medley overtures, and a man who speaks a prologue and epilogue, in which he counterfeits all the actors and singers upon earth.

The author of the *Adventurer*, No. 19, January 9, 1753, saw the "Animal Comedians," after being induced to attend by the "repeated ecomiums" on their performance. "I was astonished," he writes, "at the sagacity of the monkeys; and was no less amazed at the activity of the other quadrupeds;—I should have rather said, from a view of their extraordinary elevation, bipeds."[19] Mrs. Piozzi took the most sensible stand: "So it was low buffoonery, but it pretended to nothing better, and was wondrous droll, and what the wags call funney."[20] Low but droll buffoonery, it brought money to Smart's pockets and, in a few instances, to the pockets of the more needy. Shortly after Walpole expressed his disgust, Smart gave a benefit performance for "Francis Callaway Citizen of London, under Misfortunes, being unavoidably involved in a most litigious Chancery Suit." Other benefit performances were given in 1753 and 1754 for

"Decay'd and Antient Masons" and for "a Free Mason," facts which bring into relief both Smart's generosity and the strength of his Masonic affiliations.

The *Gentleman's Magazine*, its editorial fingers on the pulse of every one of its possible rivals, announced somewhat smugly in a footnote to its 1752 preface that "since our list of dead Magazines in our last preface, the *Old Woman*, is defunct, and her ghost appears at her *Oratory*," Smart had found it difficult to keep *The Midwife* going once he got involved in entertaining the public from the stage, and, while the periodical continued until about April, 1753, it did not make its monthly appearance with the regularity that it previously had. The first number of volume three had appeared on October 1, 1751, as scheduled, but it was not until late January of 1752 that the second number came out. It contained mostly pieces used in the Oratory. A third number was eked out with more Oratory pieces and other help; number four was the last to be issued. Inability to make the deadline for the last few numbers of *The Midwife* can be put down to two additional facts; Smart was getting his collection of poems ready for publication and he was in love again.

"*Poems on Several Occasions*, by Christopher Smart, A.M. Fellow of Pembroke-Hall, Cambridge," published in June, 1752, after having been announced as ready at least two years earlier, was printed for the author by William Strahan, one of the most eminent printers in London, and sold by J. Newbery, and by no other bookseller. The title page bore Horace's advice, "nonumque prematur in annum," which Smart had followed to the letter, his work on the collection going back at least to 1743 when he was showing the first part of *The Hop-Garden*, one of the poems in the collection, to his friend Theophilus Wheeler in Cambridge. The handsome volume, with plates by Smart's friends, Francis Hayman and Thomas Worlidge, sold for ten shillings, a fairly high price for the time, and boasted a list of subscribers that ran to several pages and seven hundred and fifty-one names.* Among them they accounted for eight hundred and fifty-four copies of the one thousand that were printed, with

---

*Strahan had printed 250 sets of Proposals and 400 receipts for subscriptions as far back as June of 1750 and Smart had had at least two years in which to collect subscribers. At one point he had sent the list of subscribers to Strahan in what he thought was final form only to recall it for additions and changes, thereby incurring further charges. Strahan Papers, BM Add. MS. 48800, opening 55.

Newbery himself taking twenty copies and a Major Taylor subscribing for ten. Since Smart had had several years in which to think about possible subscribers the names in the list represent virtually all his associations over the last twenty years of his life. Identifiable subscribers from Maidstone were the Honourable Miss Marsham, of one of the old families of that city, and John Mason, Esq.; doubtless there were others. Durham families are represented to a greater extent or are, at least, more easily recognized; among them the Bowes family accounted for seven books. Richard Dongworth, Smart's headmaster at Durham Grammar School, took two books; Ralph Carr, husband to Mary, Anne Vane's sister, subscribed; and both The Hon. Charles Hope-Vere, Esq., and his wife, the former Anne Vane, put themselves down for a book. Other Durham names were those of Fox, Eden, Dr. Wharton, Cooper, and, of course, the Vanes, with Harry Vane taking twelve books and six other members of the family subscribing for one copy each. Even the names of some of Smart's schoolfellows at Durham Grammar School are there: Richard Alderson, William Forster, William Harrison, and John Sharp were, with the exception of the first, men who had gone on to Cambridge or, in the case of Harrison, to Oxford. Newcastle, too, is represented by at least three subscribers. Both Smart's sisters and their husbands subscribed; so did his mother and a Miss Smart, who may have been of Durham county. His uncle, Major Webb, put himself down for one book. "Mr. Smart, Gray's Inn" and "Mr. Smart, Lambeth," one of them possibly the father of Miss Smart, make up the rest of the family represented in the list. "Miss Carnan," soon to be Smart's wife, appears, and there are a number of other misses who might have been the inspiration of one or another of Smart's poems. Members, both students and Fellows as well as ex-Fellows, of all the colleges of Cambridge subscribed; almost everybody Smart knew as student and Fellow at Pembroke bought a copy. The conspicuously absent name was that of Dr. Roger Long, Master of Pembroke. Members from most of the colleges of Oxford also subscribed; Smart's connection with *The Student* came into play here. Vauxhall names were rife: Arne, Boyce, Burney, Mrs. Cibber, Garrick, Havard, Lowe, Joseph Mawley, Dr. Pepusch, Rich, Rolt, Rosoman, Roubiliac, Tyers, Worgan, and John Lockman, now Secretary to the British Herring Industry. More purely literary men included William Collins, William Kenrick, Moses Mendez, Samuel Foote, Samuel Richardson, William

Whitehead, and Ben Sedgley among others. Strangely, the names of Henry Fielding, Samuel Johnson, and Arthur Murphy were absent. There was a generous number of noble subscribers, chief among them the Duke of Cleveland, and such church dignitaries as the Bishops of Chester, Gloucester, and London, as well as the Dean of York. Reverend gentlemen abounded, two of them listed as "The Rev. Mr. Anonymous." Medical men, among them Dr. James of Fever Powder fame, military men, lawyers, and schoolmasters swelled the list. "Mr. Morgan, Westminster," was doubtless one of Smart's neighbors; Sir Digby Legard was later to be mentioned in *Jubilate Agno*, as indeed were a large number of other subscribers, among them Mrs. "Fysh"; Paul Panton, Esq., was to befriend Smart after his release from confinement in 1763; William Murray had recommended Smart to Pope; the Delavals, both the wild Delavals and the serious one, a Fellow of Pembroke, were in the list; Harriot Pratt did not subscribe but her brothers did; even Voltaire was down for one book, though it is not known through whose agency his subscription was obtained. No area or activity of Smart's life was without its associations in this long list of subscribers. Surely it must have made Smart feel that he had arrived.

Smart chose to dedicate his work to the Right Honorable Earl of Middlesex and took occasion to point out that he was "Born within a few miles of your Lordship"—the Earl subscribed for only one copy of the poems. But Smart did not expect to find a wealthy patron, rather he hoped to consolidate his position in the hierarchy of London poets and by virtue of the fame that would be his to make it easier for himself to write for a living. One of the purposes of the collection was to exhibit the range and diversity of his poetic talent; a second was to demonstrate his scholarly abilities and erudition. With the first purpose in mind Smart included thirteen odes, a number of "Ballads, Fables, and other Miscellaneous Poems," some epigrams, the prologue and epilogue for *Othello*, a masque, two Latin translations, a georgic, and his Tripos poems with their English translation by Francis Fawkes. The second purpose was served by the Latin translations, one of Pope's *Essay on Criticism* and the other of Milton's *L'Allegro*—the promised Latin version of *Il Penseroso* never materialized—and by the epigraphs from Lucretius, Horace, Homer, Pliny, Virgil, Phaedrus, and Juvenal that he prefixed to some of the poems. To his Latin version of Pope's *Essay on Criticism* he added footnotes citing and quoting

Virgil, Cicero, Persius, and especially Quintilian. Many of the shorter poems had already appeared in print in one periodical or another, and while the *General Review, or Impartial Register* in its July, 1752, list of books devoted two full pages to Smart's collection, quoting from two of the poems, it also suggested that "in Justice to his Subscribers, and in Honour to himself" he should not have reprinted the earlier poems but should have put in their place the *Eternity* and *Immensity* poems and his "elegant" translation of Pope's St. Cecilia's Ode. Smart's most ambitious original poem was the georgic, *The Hop-Garden*, in a genre which, deriving from Virgil's poems on farming, set out to instruct readers how to do something; with Smart it was to show how one should grow and harvest hops. In his opening lines he stated unequivocally that all these things he would "teach in verse Miltonian," a decision that was largely predetermined for him, as previous writers in the genre had long established Miltonic blank verse as the medium for these poems. *The Hop-Garden* is remarkable for the poorness of the blank verse and the stilted Latinate quality of its language, for a few autobiographical glimpses of Smart and his sister Mary Anne, for little pictures of the Kent countryside where Smart grew up, for some attempt at depicting the workers in the hop fields as real men and women rather than idealized figures, and for a patriotic feeling for England and Kent. Smart's patriotism was to manifest itself more and more often in his poetry. Some of the lines, almost lost in the preponderance of bad verse, are good in and for themselves and give promise, both in terms of what they say and how they say it, of better poetry to come. Smart's observation of the sounds and movements of the fauna of his native Kent are caught in such lines as

> The swallows too their airy circuits weave,
> And screaming skim the brook; and fen bred frogs
> Forth from their hoarse throats their old grutch recite

and

> —the curs'd raven, with her harmful voice,
> Invokes the rain, and croaking to herself,
> Struts on some spacious solitary shore.

This is Smart at his best in this poem; at his worst he can write of one species of hops that

Nature to him
Has giv'n a stouter stalk, patient of cold,
Or Phoebus ev'n in youth, his verdant blood
In brisk saltation circulates and flows
Indesinently vigorous.

He paused sometimes to draw a moral; he sang the elegiac praises of a dead friend, for this too is Miltonic and sanctioned by tradition; he threw in a few compliments to dead authors and living noblemen; and, for good measure, spun out at some length the story of Hengist and Horsa. But then the georgic was the genre in which all this was allowed, and Smart, like Pope before him, was experimenting with genres and the language and themes appropriate to them.

One of the miscellaneous poems in the volume which had not appeared in print before this time was *The Lass with the Golden Locks*; in it Smart revealed that he was in love again.

I.

No more of my Harriot, of Polly no more,
Nor all the bright beauties that charm'd me before;
My heart for a slave to gay Venus I've sold,
And barter'd my freedom for ringlets of gold:
I'll throw down my pipe, and neglect all my flocks,
And will sing to my lass with the golden locks.

II.

Tho' o'er her white forehead the gilt tresses flow,
Like the rays of the sun on a hillock of snow;
Such painters of old drew the Queen of the Fair,
'Tis the taste of the antients, 'tis classical hair;
And tho' witlings may scoff, and tho' raillery mocks,
Yet I'll sing to my lass with the golden locks.

III.

To live and to love, to converse and be free,
Is loving, my charmer, and living with thee:
Away go the hours in kisses and rhime,
Spite of all the grave lectures of old father Time;
A fig for his dials, his watches and clocks,
He's best spent with the lass of the golden locks.

IV.

Than the swan in the brook she's more dear to my sight,
Her mien is more stately, her breast is more white,

Her sweet lips are rubies, all rubies above,
Which are fit for the language or labour of love;
At the park in the mall, at the play in the box,
My lass bears the bell with her golden locks.

V.

Her beautiful eyes, as they roll or they flow,
Shall be glad for my joy, or shall weep for my woe;
She shall ease my fond heart, and shall sooth my soft pain,
While thousands of rivals are sighing in vain;
Let them rail at the fruit they can't reach, like the fox,
While I have the lass with the golden locks.

Smart was through with Harriot Pratt and with the more accessible, if real, Polly; Anna Maria Carnan had taken their place.*

Anna Maria Carnan was John Newbery's stepdaughter. She was born on January 26, 1732, in Reading and at the time of her marriage to Smart in 1752 was twenty years old, ten years his junior. No record of the marriage has been found, giving rise to all manner of conjecture. Elizabeth LeNoir tells how her father was admitted to John Newbery's table and how "he became enamoured of Anna Maria Carnan, daughter of Mrs. Newbery by her first husband. Mr. Newbery had apartments at Canonbury House, then a sweet rural spot. In the absence of the elders of the family Mr. Smart prevailed upon Miss Carnan to go with him from thence to St. Bride's Church, where they were married, this being before the marriage act. Notwithstanding this rash step Mr. Newbery did not withdraw his assistance, but placed them at Canonbury House where I and my sister were born."† The ceremony, as Mrs. LeNoir points out, took place before the Marriage Act of 1753 which stipulated that the permission of father or guardian be necessary for those under twenty-one years of age and that the couple be resident at least four weeks in the parish from which they were married, as well as setting

---

*Polly is the heroine of Smart's *The Pretty Chambermaid*, another poem in the collection. John Newbery, thinly disguised as Mr. Folio in George Colman's *Terrae-Filius*, No. 3, July 7, 1763, refers to his daughter, actually named Mary, as "Polly." And a Polly appears elsewhere in Smart's poetry, a line in *Jubilate Agno* (C73), "God be gracious to Polly and Bess and all Canbury," attesting to her identity as a real person.

†Letter of July 13, 1831, p. 217. The statement that the marriage was performed at St. Bride's, located in Fleet Street is partly confirmed in that the Reverend G. W. Barnes performed almost all the marriages in that church during the period in question and a "Rev. Mr. Barnes, St. Brides" was one of the subscribers to Smart's version of the Psalms of David in 1765. See St. Brides Registers of banns of marriage in the Guildhall Library, London.

a number of other conditions. Since the young wife gave birth to their first daughter, Marianne, on May 3, 1753, and since she does not seem, from all accounts, to have been the kind of girl who would have allowed Smart any liberties before marriage, the most probable date for their marriage is some time in the summer of 1752.[21] Although Newbery had known nothing of the impending marriage he invited the couple to live at Canonbury or Canbury House, Islington, where he had rooms.

In Canonbury House Smart enjoyed a very short interval of happiness. His second daughter, Elizabeth Anne, was born there, and christened in St. Mary's Church on November 21, 1754; many years later she gave an account of that period. Referring to the time after her father's marriage, she writes that "he resided for some time with his wife in apartments at Canbury House belonging to Mr. Newbery. It was here that the writer of this article his youngest daughter was born and that she and her sister spent their earliest years under the care of Mrs. Fleming of whom the apartments were held. I well remember the high trees that screened the back of the dwelling." Behind Canonbury, she goes on to relate, lived a Justice of the Peace named Booth who owned "a large, lean mastiff, in very ill condition, whose howling was a great annoyance to the neighbors. One morning Mr. Smart going as usual to read the newspapers at the Public House, meeting there with Justice Booth, was accosted by him with: 'So, Mr. Smart, the dog's dead.' 'I am glad of it,' he replied. 'Why so, Mr. Smart?' 'Why because he was half starved and always howling: I had thoughts of being at the expense of a brace of pistols myself to put him out of his misery.' 'Pooh, pooh,' exclaimed the Justice—'not my dog—I mean the dog of Venice.' "[22] In another letter she wrote that Canonbury House was then "rented by a respectable old couple of the name of Fleming who were usually called Daddy and Mammy by their lodgers. I believe my father was not extremely particular in regard to his person for I remember the story of Mammy Fleming once calling him thus, 'Come here you little dirty dog, and let me wash your hands.' 'Aye, do so, Mammy,' said he and walked with her to the sink for the ablutions."[23] Smart remembered Canonbury in a touching line, "For I bless God for my retreat at CANONBURY, as it was the place of the nativity of my children," prompted by the "Let" line, "Let Ibhar rejoice with the Pochard a child born in prosperity is the chiefest blessing of peace" (*Jubilate Agno*, B1, 75). But whatever peace and happiness he found in the early months of his marriage and later, when his children were born, were tempered by the pressing necessity to earn more and more money. As a result of his marriage he lost his Fellowship at Pembroke and the yearly sum that brought him. Soon after his marriage Smart engaged, willingly or unwillingly, in another of those literary controversies that marked this period and which usually produced more heat than light.

When the amateur *Othello* for which Smart wrote the prologue and epilogue in March, 1751, was reviewed in the sixth number of the *Inspector*, a series of essays appearing in the *Daily Advertiser*, the essayist spoke of the prologue as "excellent" and the epilogue as "hardly inferior to it." As self-appointed arbiter of taste, John Hill, the author of these essays, could not afford to overlook an occasion that caused as much sensation as the performance of *Othello*; his praise of prologue and epilogue was welcome despite its source. For John Hill, later Sir John by virtue of being awarded the order of Vasa by the King of Sweden in 1774, had proved himself a source of considerable annoyance to all connected with him as he turned from one undertaking to another in an effort to make a success at something. He had, by 1751, already failed as an apothecary, botanist, actor, opera librettist, editor, and controversialist. Despite some abilities and a long list of publications over a very wide range of subjects Hill was and is remembered as the unlucky antagonist of a number of his betters, among them Lewis Theobald, David Garrick, Henry Fielding, and Christopher Smart. The fact that Smart praised Fielding, Hill's chief target of satire, and that he may even have contributed to Fielding's *Covent Garden Journal*[24] probably prompted Hill to turn some of his attention to him. When Smart took to the newspapers to reply to *The Impertinent*, an anonymous essay known to be by Hill, he referred to Fielding as "a particular friend of mine [who] was scurrilously treated" in Hill's essay.[25] Although Hill throve on literary guerilla warfare, he exercised considerable powers of forbearance when Smart reprinted in *The Midwife* an *Inspector* essay on the subject of "perspicuity" or clarity in literary style, prefixed by a satiric paragraph in which he congratulated himself for having rescued "this learned and useful Piece from the Oblivion into which it was likely to fall" and stated that the essay itself illustrated the faults of which it treated. The reprint of the *Inspector* essay, part of the second number of volume three of *The Midwife*, appeared by January 20, 1752. In April, Hill had an opportunity to retaliate, for he elected, in another *Inspector*, to remark upon a passage in the Seatonian poem *On the Immensity of the Supreme Being*. Writing as a self-constituted expert on these matters, he took Smart gently to task: "We find Mr. *Smart,* a Person of real and of great Genius, in a late Poem . . . in the Midst of Passages that would have done Honour to many an Antient, talking of *Shrubs of Amber,* as if that mineral Substance had been a Plant growing at the Bottom of the Sea." This, considering the nature of Smart's satiric remarks in *The Midwife,* was generous of Hill. His next notice of Smart, however, was an open invitation to warfare, for he castigated him as an author who wrote because he was hungry, a creature "all earth" and no spirit, an ass distinguished as laborious, "and as dull, and as indefatigable as he is empty," and more in the same vein. Hill tried to ward off suspicion of his authorship of this paper, entitled *The Impertinent* and dated August 13, by writing of himself as though he too were partially guilty of writing because of hunger. And in a further attempt to divert suspicion from himself, in the *Inspector* for August 25, he congratulated the public in not encouraging a second number of a paper, meaning the *Impertinent,* which among other things "cruelly and unjustly attacked Mr. Smart." But his attempts at anonymity were futile, for the August *Gentleman's Magazine* stated quite bluntly that Hill was known to be the author and exposed him to shame.

Hill was one of the reviewers for Ralph Griffiths' *Monthly Review* and to him fell the doubtless pleasant assignment of assessing the merits and defects of Smart's *Poems on Several Occasions.* He proceeded to do precisely that, praising much but condemning even more. His censures were almost wholly just, concentrating on *The Hop-Garden* and on the *Epithalamium* and glancing rather disparagingly at the Latin poems. He praised some of the odes and, strangely enough, the masque, *The Judgement of Midas.* And he concluded in a fashion certainly intended to mollify rather than further to exasperate Smart: "Enough will be seen in these and the other specimens selected from the more finished of these pieces to justify us in giving mr. Smart a place among the first of the present race of *English* poets. If the censures, which it is the character of this work to bestow as freely as it praises, shall warn him to be more attentive to the finishing his works for the future, there is no doubt of his becoming equal to most who have done honour to the last or the preceding age." But Smart seemed determined to take umbrage, probably feeling that even praise, and qualified praise at that, from somebody of Hill's ilk was worse than unqualified censure. Three or four months after publication of his review Hill got wind of the fact that Smart was preparing an elaborate attack on him and took to still another *Inspector* essay, December 6, 1752, to protest that Smart was biting the hand that had befriended him. "It was I," Hill exclaimed, "that introduced him to the World: His Bookseller took him into Salary, on my Approbation of the Specimens which he offered . . . I am afraid I have since been guilty of saying that he had Genius. Has he not reason to make me the hero of a Dunciad?" The next day the *Inspector* devoted most of its space to attacking Smart's productions, including his Oratory, "the meanest, the most absurd; and most contemptible of all Performances that have disgraced a Theatre," and to condemning his ingratitude. Again he claimed to have introduced him to Newbery. Newbery wrote in the pages of the *Daily Gazetteer* a public denial of this last statement, and in less than a week Smart followed with a denial of his own which appeared in at least two newspapers. Smart's statement ended with his expressed determination "to follow the Advice of my Friends, and bring the *egregious Coxcomb* to poetical Justice, in the *Hilliad*, the first Book of which will be published with all possible Despatch." Hill thereupon attacked Newbery in the *Inspector* for December 12; Newbery's friends to the number of four volunteered as character witnesses for him in the public press on December 15 and 18; next month, January, 1752, the *Hilliad* appeared. Two lines from Virgil's *Aeneid* (XII, 948–9) that served as epigraph boded ill for Smart's victim; " 'Tis Pallas, Pallas who with stroke sacrificed thee, and takes attonement of thy guilty blood," recalling the death of Turnus at the hands of Aeneas.

Smart had been frustrated by Kenrick in his attempt to bring out an *Old Woman's Dunciad*; the *Hilliad* was probably inspired as much by his desire to emulate Pope's *Dunciad* as by Hill's attacks. The Grub-Street industry was often kept going by these real or concocted literary enmities, and Smart had not had the opportunity to show what he could do in the tradition of the satiric poem which took its point of departure from the epic. Here was a chance to write a mock epic and he made the most of it. The title page announced the presence of "Copious Prolegomena and Notes Variorum. Particularly those of Quinbus Flestrin ESQ; and Martinus Macularius, M.D. Acad. Reg. Scient. Burdig. & etc. etc. etc."

and fulfilled its promise by "A Letter to a Friend at the University of Cambridge," signed by Smart, and an answer by somebody, probably Arthur Murphy, ostensibly at Cambridge.* Only after approximately twenty-five pages of further prolegomenous matter does the poem get under way, and even then four lines of verse are virtually lost on a page given over largely to footnotes, a pattern that was followed for the rest of the poem. Smart naturally adopts and distorts the conventions of the epic and the traditional forms in which the emendations and animadversions of classical editors were couched. Hill is addressed in mock-Miltonic terms, "O thou, whatever name delight thine ear,/ Pimp! Poet! Puffer! Pothecary! Play'r!," near the beginning of the poem, characterized as "A wretch devoid of use, of sense, and grace,/Th' insolvent tenant of incumber'd space" (the only lines in all Smart's poetry quoted in Johnson's *Dictionary*), and finally dismissed, "So long in gross stupidity's extreme,/ Shall H---ll th' ARCH-DUNCE *remain* o'er every dunce supreme." Smart praised Arne, William Boyce, Fielding, Hogarth, and Garrick in the poem, and "Orator" Henley and Dr. Rock, a notorious quack doctor, were satirized in the notes by Arthur Murphy, one of Smart's closest friends up to the time of his confinement.

Smart's introductory letter contained one short passage which shows that he knew that his besetting fault was the speed with which he composed his poetry. He wrote to his friend that the "Design and colouring of a poem, such as you have planned, are not to be executed in a hurry, but with slow and careful touches, which will give that finishing to your piece, remarkable in every thing that comes from your hand, and which I could wish the precipitancy of my temper would permit me to aim at upon all occasion." Joined with this "precipitancy of temper" was the necessity to write new pieces hurriedly in order to earn more and more money. Smart could not afford the time needed to lavish "slow and careful touches" upon his poetry, and his name was connected by his contemporaries with certain ephemeral publications representative of the hack work that kept many Grub-Street writers alive. When *Fun: A Parodi-tragi-Comical-Satire* was published in 1752, despite its satire of "Mother Midnight's Magazine" and "The Student" and

---

*"Quinbus Flestrin" appears at least nine times in Murphy's *Gray's Inn Journal*, and there is other external evidence for his participation in *The Hilliad*.

its reference to "an old Woman of a very bad character, one Mother Midnight," it was attributed to Smart. He, always touchy about his reputation as a poet, took to the *General Advertiser* of February 12, 1752, to protest his innocence of any connection with it. Similarly, the *Drury Lane Journal*, by Roxana Termagant, was thought by many to be by Smart, possibly because its twelve issues make a number of friendly references to Mrs. Midnight. In fact, the *Covent Garden Journal Extraordinary*, No. 2, January 20, 1752, speaks of Roxana Termagant whom the author has special reasons to believe is "no other than a SMART old Woman," adding, lest the identification be not complete, that she is accomplished at "Caudle-making," a reference to the Oratory. He and Bonnell Thornton were supposed to be members of an imaginary society called the Female Disputants which met at the Silent Woman in Broad Street, St. Giles, and was a rival to the male Robin Hood Society. Accounts of this society figured in Thornton's *Drury Lane Journal*. While the degree, if any, of Smart's participation in any of these can only be surmised, he was certainly one of the Grub-Street confraternity, whether he wished to be or not. One pamphlet of the same year, 1752, sums up the way somebody felt about these literary rows. Catchily entitled *The geese stript of their quills; or, proposals for depluming and rusticating the rival literati*, the digest of its contents in the *Monthly Review* reads in part,

> Our author's design in this small piece, which is written in a very genteel and sensible manner, is to reprove the *Inspector* and mr. S-----t for those strokes of obloquy, those dull sarcasms, those indecent revilings, with which they have lately loaded each other; and for which, our author thinks, they deserve to be expelled the *republic of letters*. . . . As to mr. *Smart*, his business, he tells us, should be to collect his random thoughts on various subjects, and to range them in proper *declamatory* order; by which means, we are told, he will have an opportunity of exerting his genius every *Monday* in the week, in a solemn *harangue* at the *Robin Hood society*.[26]

Smart was getting his share of attention; not to have been noticed would have been less welcome to him than bouquets such as these.

Another of the reasons Smart could not polish his poetry to his own satisfaction in 1752 was the continued success of his Oratory; the *Gentleman's Magazine* for January, 1753, says that it went on

"30 nights in all." Actually, in the 1752—3 theatrical season there were at least sixty-eight performances, stretching into May. However great or little a part he was now taking in these productions, he was of necessity having to give up valuable time to them. What is more, the writing of poetry for pleasure or for increased fame without any regard for money was one thing; entirely different was the realization that with a wife already pregnant and with his *Poems on Several Occasions* behind him he needed more than just the income he could get from isolated poems. His income from *The Midwife* was being choked off as the periodical languished in his hands and finally expired about April or May, Newbery doubtless realizing that Smart could no longer keep up the pace he had set and knowing that a longer run of the periodical would result in losses. To make up for this lost income and to meet the expenses of married life Smart almost surely was given additional hack work by his father-in-law, anxious to keep the newly wed couple at least solvent. Smart may have picked up small sums by writing an occasional piece or two for his friends; he wrote for or had at least one piece reprinted in his friend Murphy's *Gray's Inn Journal* No. 14 for January 20, 1753 (1756 ed.), where under the items of "True Intelligences" Murphy writes,

> The following satyrical Ballad on the reigning Taste of the Town has been handed about here this Week. It is said to be a *Jeu d'Esprit* of Mr. *Smart's*, whose Genius sometimes deigns to descend from Flights worthy of its Eagle-Wing, to the inferior Regions of Pleasantry, where it gaily amuses itself in Pursuit of elegant Trifles.

There follows "A New Ballad" of seven stanzas deploring the degeneracy of the stage which now substitutes pantomimes, animals, birds, etc., for the plays of Shakespeare and Jonson. Murphy had made occasional complimentary references to his friend's Oratory and he made room again in 1753 for another poem by Smart. In a May issue of the *Gray's Inn Journal* (No. 32) appeared a somewhat different version of a poem earlier printed in *The Midwife*. The poem, a clever verse epistle to a Welsh clergyman who had promised "the Author an hare" and then had not kept the promise, contains one of Smart's best known burlesque rhymes in "Tell me, thou son of great Cadwallader,/ Had'st thou an Hare, or hast thou swallow'd her?" Much more important is the little headnote to the poem which says that the "Author of an excellent Poem upon a very bad Subject, viz. the *Hilliad*, has been indisposed for some time past, but we had the Pleasure of seeing him here a few Days since, and the following pleasant Piece of Poetry shows that he has again held alliance with his Muse." Smart had been sick for a while, but there is no way of knowing the nature of his ailment.

Murphy's notices of Smart did not go totally unrequited; the latter praised Murphy's *Gray's Inn Journal* essay on the Naturalization Act in a letter written in Latin and dating from July, 1753, the same month the essay appeared. Briefly, he chides Murphy for not writing, accuses him facetiously of much sexual activity, and tells him how much he admires his writings. As for himself, he had been at the seaside with not unhandsome male companions and beautiful women, and could well believe the ancient writers who held that Venus was born of the sea.[27] Smart had probably gone to the Kentish coast where his sister Margaret, Mrs. Hunter, was either now living or was visiting with her husband William, a native of Margate who was finally to settle in Ramsgate, if he had not already done so by this time. The visit to the ocean would have come not too long after Anna Maria Smart had given birth to their first child in May.

Whatever Smart may have contributed to the work of others he could not have been realizing much money, if any, from these slight efforts. He must have been doing other work for he had little outside income upon which to depend. The one exception was the prize money for the Seatonian competition which he was again awarded, to nobody's surprise, including his own. The very great probability is that he was and had been for at least a while engaged in certain editorial chores for Newbery that finally saw publication as *The Muses Banquet*, a collection of songs, and *Be Merry and Be Wise*, a collection of jests and maxims, both advertised in the *Cambridge Journal and Weekly Flying-Post* for March 17, 1753, as published on that day.[28] Both collections contain much of his own work that Smart had already published elsewhere, largely in *The Midwife*. But, except for these, none of Smart's poems seem to have been reprinted in the periodicals in this year, a rather striking fact in the light of their popularity. One other work in this year has been claimed for Smart with some confidence; *Mother Midnight's Comical Pocket-Book*, a sixty-four-page pamphlet "by Humphrey Humdrum, Esq.," was printed for J. Dowse and published in December. There are some charming light verses and much of the nonsense that Smart had shown he could handle so cleverly in *The Midwife* as well as in others of his publications.[29] And in this same year Smart wrote a Latin Ode on St. David's Day; the poem which exists only in manuscript bears the words, "Humbly presented to his Royal Highness the Prince of Wales, by a Cambo-Briton." Smart had dedicated his *Solemn Dirge* on the death of Frederic, Prince of Wales, to Prince George, and the St. David's Day ode, with its reference to the Prince's father, dead less than two years, was an attempt to find royal favor and patronage. The English translation, which more than does justice to the original, shows the kind of thing Smart was reduced to.

> O Phoebus, who on Helicon's smooth-flowing streams
>   Pourst forth the sweetness of divine Thalia's art,
>   Come from thy temple. As I sing a higher theme
>   Inspire me, and with brighter beams bedeck the day.
>   To aid me in my task, the rivers gently sound
>   Among our vales, the prophet god among our hills
>   Is King, and Cambria too boasts of her native Muse.
>
> Hail, holy day! on which we all our annual joys
>   Express, and fittingly our Patron glorify.
>   Hail too, whose virtue and whose life recall thy sire,
>   Who bringst a glory to thy titles, and to fame
>   Bestowst an extra grace: All Hail, illustrious Prince!
>   Grant us thy favour and thy people bless. Receive
>   Thy Britons' prayers and deign to let us call you ours,
>   Great Child, whom Fame calls forth, adopted son of Splendour;
>   Whom the great ocean's king extols with all his waves.
>
> The day shall come when thou (no blot upon thy race,
>   But equal copy of thy sires in heart and life)
>   Shall enter in Fame's temple through the gate of Virtue
>   And see the kings and sages who are set within.
>   The day shall come when Gaul (what race more vain than that?)
>   Entire, with mingled awe and love, shall honour thee.
>   In thy hands shall it be to rule o'er worlds to come,
>   And peoples not yet found shall bow beneath thy laws,
>   While flourishes, with thy good auspices, most famed
>   Cambria, race most ancient of a former world.
>   As if among our Homeland's peaks, thy lofty head
>   Shall reach the sky, and straight the laurel crown be thine.[30]

95

Soon after Edward Cave, publisher of the *Gentleman's Magazine*, died on January 10, 1754, somebody, probably either Samuel Johnson or John Hawkesworth, suggested printing a number of Smart's poems in the pages of that periodical. Four of his poems were reprinted; some of those that appeared there for the first time were dug out of a seemingly bottomless reserve of earlier verse that Smart must have built up largely while at Cambridge. How much, if anything, he got for these contributions, some of them unsigned, is not known. After a two-year period in which none of his verse was published in the magazines Smart must have been gratified to see his poems to the number of about twenty appearing in almost every one of the monthly installments of the widely circulated *Gentleman's Magazine*. He was surely also gratified when he read in the September number of that same periodical an *Ode to February*, "Occasion'd by the birth-day of a beautiful lady born in that month.—Attempted in the manner of Mr. S----T," a close imitation of his poem on Harriot Pratt, *On the Fifth of December*, "Being the birth-day of a very beautiful young lady." Notable among the poems first printed in the *Gentleman's Magazine* this year was the *Ode to Lord Barnard*, celebrating the kindness of Harry Vane who had been granted the title of Viscount Barnard in April; the poem was introduced by a letter in which the correspondent hoped Mr. Smart would not be offended by its being made public. Notable too was the presence of a number of fables. Smart had already published some samples of what he could do as a fabulist in *The Midwife* and in his *Poems on Several Occasions*, published two years earlier. One of the projects that he never completed was a collection of "tales and fables in verse." The collection, if it ever had seen the light of day, would have been a gathering together of much of what Smart had already written in these two genres with possibly a few original pieces thrown in.

Charles Burney survived Smart by many years and reviewed in the *Monthly Review* the 1791 edition of his poems edited by Christopher Hunter. He wrote of Smart's fables, "We are inclined to believe that, after Gay, Smart is the most agreeable metrical Fabulist in our language; his versification is less polished, and his apologues in general are perhaps less correct, than those of Gay and Moore; but in originality, in wit, and in humour, the preference seems due to Smart." Certainly, if the number of times some of these pieces were reprinted in the eighteenth century is a just criterion of their popularity, they were highly thought of indeed. Where other writers of fables stuck pretty closely to animals as their protagonists Smart often used people or objects. Thus he has fables whose speaking characters are a bag-wig and a tobacco-pipe, a tea-pot and a scrubbing brush, or a brocaded gown and a linen rag. Or he will have a Miss and a butterfly, a blockhead and a beehive, or "Miss Abigail and the Dumb Waiter." Those of his fables which employed allegorical characters, *Care and Generosity* or *Reason and Imagination*, for example, seem from the number of times they were reprinted to have pleased his contemporaries most. And here in the fables his flair for reproducing conversation, already manifest in *The Midwife*, showed to striking advantage. The bag-wig, its nostrils assailed by the "vapours" of the tobacco-pipe, speaks.

> Bak'd dirt! that with intrusion rude
> Breaks in upon my solitude,
> And with thy fetid breath defiles
> The air for forty thousand miles—
> Avaunt—pollution's in thy touch—
> O barb'rous English! horrid Dutch!
> I cannot bear it—Here Sue, Nan,
> Go call the maid to call the man,
> And bid him come without delay,
> To take this odious pipe away.
> Hideous! sure some one smoak'd thee, Friend,
> Reversely, at his t'other end.
> Oh! what mix'd odours! what a throng
> Of salt and sour, of stale and strong!
> A most unnatural combination,
> Enough to mar all perspiration—
> Monstrous! again—'twou'd vex a saint!
> Susan, the drops—or else I faint!

The English pipe turns upon his Gallic attacker,

> Why, what's the matter, Goodman Swagger,
> Thou flaunting French, fantastic bragger?
> Whose whole fine speech is (with a pox)
> Ridiculous and heterodox.

continuing to the end of the fable to berate his opponent and to proclaim his Englishness.

Others of Smart's fables, most noticeably *The English Bull Dog, Dutch Mastiff, and Quail* and to a slighter extent *The Brocaded*

97

Gown and Linen Rag, proclaim the speakers' and Smart's pride in being an Englishman, although at the end of the *English Bull Dog* the arbitrating quail concludes that good can be found in every place. Along with this, and frequent enough to be of significance, is the situation in certain fables which finds persons or objects representative of higher and lower classes or ranks at odds with one another—with the representative of the lower ranks always having the better of the argument. This is true of *The Teapot and Scrubbing Brush, The Bag-wig and the Tobacco-pipe, The Brocaded Gown and the Linen Rag, Mrs. Abigail and the Dumb-Waiter,* and *The Country Squire and the Mandrake.* Smart may have unconsciously released feelings about his position in society through the medium of these fables. He did use the fables, it is clear, for a number of conscious purposes; to praise his friends, to recall something from his past life, to compliment a noble person, to introduce a humane or religious note, and even to puff one of Newbery's publications or Roubiliac's work as a sculptor. And in *Reason and Imagination,* published in 1763 after he was released from confinement, he could even refer to the treatment of the insane in jocular terms, "The Doctors will soon find a flaw,/ And lock you up in chains and straw." But one of the most memorable aspects of these fables is one they share with his verse epistles and a few other poems; that is, the burlesque rhymes he was so ingenious in devising: Witch in, kitchin; big-bellied, Farinellied; trust 'em, custom; fist on, Whiston; gaze on, blazon. On rare occasion some flash of poetry really not integral to the fable, catches the eye—"Cowslips, like topazes that shine,/ Close by the silver serpentine." Given the lightness of Smart's touch and the century's fondness for moralizing, it is easy to see why his fables were so admired.

Smart was going on with Mrs. Midnight's Oratory at this time and the writers of the *Connoisseur* in their seventeenth essay, May 23, 1754, could refer to "the melody of the *Wooden Spoon,* the *Jews-Harp,* and *Salt-Boy* at *Mrs. Midnight's*" in the confident expectation that their readers would know what they were talking about. The Oratory had had ten performances from March 4 through April 1 and would still be fresh in the mind of those who had seen it. As part of Mrs. Midnight's Concert the old instruments for producing music were closer in time to the *Connoisseur* essay, for under that name the Oratory had been put on in the Haymarket Theatre on April 22, 25, May 2 and 6. In July and August and for a few days in September the name was changed to the "British Roratory," then to "Sack Posset" for a couple of performances, then back to the "Old Woman's Oratory," then to the "New Carnival Concert" for one night, and finally, in October, amplified to "Mrs. Midnight's New Carnival Concert." On November 8 the *Daily Advertiser* noted that Mrs. Midnight had surrendered the Haymarket Theatre to Cleopatra, the first of whose Aetheopian Concerts took place in that same evening.[31] Up to October, then, Smart must have been devoting some time to the performances and deriving some income from them. Possibly the letter he wrote for the "The True Intelligence" section of the twelfth and final number of the *Entertainer*, published on November 19, was both a bit of byplay between himself and Arthur Murphy, the author of the periodical, and another bid for public attention for his entertainments. He writes

> SIR,
>
> I am what the world call an *accomplished LADY*, I rise at ten o'clock, breakfast at twelve, from twelve till four, I dress myself, at four I dine, go out at five, and retire at three o'clock the next morning; I am married, and have several children, but I leave the *poor little things* to the care of my husband; my peculiar qualifications consist in the art of painting my face, and dropping my fan; I have acquired the most engaging motion of the eyes and lips; I can cheat at cards tolerably well, and in one word, I am possessed of all the qualities that make up an accomplish'd woman; I beat my husband one hundred times every day and spend twice the rent of his estate every year; I love pleasure, and give a ball at my own house every week; and as I know you to be a man of *taste*, I hope we shall have your company next Thursday, till then farewell,
>
> MARY MIDNIGHT.

And Murphy answers

> *Madam,*
>
> I return you thanks for your kind invitation, and shall have the honour to wait upon you: I am persuaded nothing is ever wanting to the entertainment of a lady, who possesses all the qualifications peculiar to her sex; I have the honour to subscribe myself,
>
> *Madam,*
> *Your most oblig'd and very*
> *humble servant*
> CHARLES MERCURY.[32]

Newbery brought out *"Mrs. Midnight's* works compleat" in three volumes, that is, *The Midwife* in March, and in the same month Murphy wrote in the *Gray's Inn Journal* of the arrival of "the Earl of Pentweazle from his travels thro' *Europe*." Since Smart had used "Pentweazle" as a family name for a number of his pseudonyms and since the "Earl" was described as only four feet and ten inches tall—Smart was always conscious of his low stature—this may be a reference to him and may explain the line in *Jubilate Agno*, "God be gracious to Miss Leroche my fellow traveler from Calais" (D, 42) ; nothing is definitely known of a trip to the Continent. Again in March, at least in the March issues of the *Gentleman's Magazine*, there is a possible hint of Smart's state of health around this time, for a poem printed there for the first time is entitled *Ode to a Virginia Nightingale* and bears the explanatory addition, "Which was cured of a fit in the bosom of a young lady, who afterwards nursed the author in a dangerous illness." But Smart was always dipping into his reserve of poems and there is no compelling reason to believe that the illness was of this year, nor indeed is it absolutely necessary to accept the illness as a real one.

Whether ill or well, Smart accomplished little this year, even failing to compete for the Seatonian prize. This lack of activity is difficult to understand because the Smarts already had one daughter only a little over a year old and Anna Maria Smart was pregnant again. Their second daughter, Elizabeth Anne, was born on October 27. Records exist of loans made by Newbery to Smart and also to Anna Maria, and while no dates for these loans have survived they must have been given in this or the following year, for the Smarts had married in mid-1752 and by 1756 Smart had given Newbery reason to look less kindly upon him. The same records show a tailor bill for thirteen pounds for a coat for Smart at the rather expensive cost of seventeen shillings, six pence, per yard.[33] "During the far greater part of his life," writes Hunter, "he was wholly inattentive to economy; and by this negligence lost first his fortune and then his credit" (p. xxix) . Smart loved fine clothes, good food and drink, and the other pleasures of life; if he could not earn the money to indulge himself, he felt no compunction about borrowing. Whenever the loans were made or the fine coat ordered, the young couple were in debt and in need of a source of income. Smart was no doubt working on his prose translation of Horace, dated 1756 but announced in the *Gentleman's Magazine* for December, 1755, and possibly on the collection of "tales and fables in

verse" which never came into being. And he was probably doing
additional hack work of one kind or another for Newbery. About
this time Smart introduced Tom Tyers, son of the proprietor of
Vauxhall Gardens, to Samuel Johnson, a meeting which Tyers recalled years later. Tyers wrote that "Christopher Smart was at first
well received by Johnson." "This writer," he is referring to himself,
"owed his first acquaintance with our author [Johnson], which
lasted thirty years to that bard. . . . Johnson had been much indisposed all that day, and repeated a Psalm he had just translated,
during his affliction, into verse, and did not commit to paper. . . .
Smart, in return, recited some of his own Latin compositions. . . .
Poet Smart used to relate, 'that the first conversation with him was
of such variety and length, that it began with poetry, and ended
with fluxions.' "[34] Tyers' reference to his thirty-year friendship with
Johnson puts the first meeting somewhere in 1755; at this time at
least Smart was still "well received by Johnson." Smart's description
of his own first meeting with Johnson shows that the two men took
to each other, Johnson perceiving from the range of Smart's knowledge and his conversational abilities that the Fellow of Pembroke
was a man of parts. The eventual rupture between the two was of
Johnson's making; their friendship lasted six years at most.

Another relatively unproductive year was 1755, although Smart
did and projected more work than he had in the preceding year.
Only one performance of "Mrs. Midnight's Rout" at the Haymarket
for February 10, 1755, is recorded in the whole year; another source
of money was cut off. The Gentleman's Magazine, with Newbery
now the owner of one-twelfth share in it,[35] continued to publish
Smart's poems: two fables, the poem Lady Harriot and a musical
setting for the same poem, an epitaph on Richard Rolt's wife, and
an epilogue to a performance of Steele's The Conscious Lovers.
Probably only the epitaph on Mrs. Rolt, who died at Islington on
February 22, 1755, and the epilogue to Steele's play, for the performance of December 5, were new pieces. The poem to Harriot
Pratt was an old one, and the fables were probably part of the
collection Smart and Newbery had projected. In this year, in April
or May at the latest, he wrote the fable The English Bull Dog,
Dutch Mastiff, and Quail in the hope of receiving some tangible
token of recognition from Lord Hartington whose appointment as
Lord Lieutenant of Ireland it celebrates, although the fashion in
which the reference to him is brought into the concluding lines

suggests that Smart tacked it on to an already finished poem.[36] He was now, of course, getting his prose *Horace* ready for publication and this kept him busy. He remembered belatedly that the Seatonian prize money that he had neglected or been unable to compete for in 1754 would be very welcome and accordingly dashed off the *Goodness* poem just in time to receive the prize. Despite his need for money and because his pride would not allow him to refuse such a solicitation, he was one of the subscribers to Miss Mary Masters' *Familiar Letters and Poems on Several Occasions*, along with Johnson, Hawkesworth, Fawkes, and Samuel Richardson. Possibly he had subscribed because Harriot Pratt had, as had both her brothers and "Miss Astley (now Mrs. Pratt)," the wife of her brother Edward.* Some time this year also he was probably engaged in editing two more collections for Newbery. Both came out in 1756; the first, *A Collection of Pretty Poems for the Amusement of Children Three Feet High*, was published on February 2, while the second, *A Collection of Pretty Poems for the Amusement of Children Six Foot High*, appeared on March 17. Their contents, including a number of Smart's known pieces already printed elsewhere, and possibly some others not now identifiable as his, were not such as to make the editorial work especially onerous. Unless, of course, the necessity to be associated with such enterprises, coming at a time when Smart was so pressed, contributed to his eventual breakdown. Too often, since he had left Cambridge, he was left with no alternative but to take on subliterary chores that must have been deeply distasteful to him. He may, on the other hand, have found some relief from serious matters by pretending to get down on a level with the children for whom such collections were intended. And perhaps it is not merely chance that his last publication was a collection of *Hymns for the Amusement of Children*, a book whose title and part of whose format resemble those of the 1756 collections.[37]

The Works of Horace, "Translated Literally into English Prose; For the Use of those who are desirous of acquiring or recovering a competent Knowledge of the Latin Language" appeared in December, 1755, in two duodecimo volumes, convenient for carrying in

---

*If he was the Mr. Smart who dined at the Chaplain's Table at St. James's Palace on December 13 with Thomas Birch and a few others, his circle of acquaintances must be extended to include the indefatigable Tom Birch. Smart's acquaintance with William Dodd, then a Chaplain to the King, makes his presence there very possible. BM Add MSS 4478c fol. 279v.

one's pockets. A brief preface provides some interesting information on Smart's motives in translating Horace into prose and tells something about his feelings toward the whole enterprise:

> The following version being the work of a man who has made poetry, perhaps, too much the business of his life, some account of his motives for undertaking it may seem necessary. In the first place, then, there was reason to believe that a thing of this kind, properly executed, would be very useful to those who are desirous of acquiring or recovering a competent knowledge of the Latin tongue. Secondly, the extraordinary success which attempts of this kind have met with, though by men who manifestly did not understand the author, any otherwise than through a French medium, and tho' printed in large volumes, and sold at a proportionate price; gave sufficient reason for the translator to hope, that his labour would not be in vain; I say *labour*, for genius, if he had pretentions to it, could not have been exerted in the work before us.

After stressing again the "cheapness and convenience" of the edition and guaranteeing the accuracy of his version he turns to the "learned reader," who "need not be informed that this version was not intended for him; though some of the most eminent of that character have condescended to examine the manuscript, and given it the sanction of their approbation." The best editions were "diligently consulted; and it is presumed the judicious will find in the following sheets some emendations and improvements, which have escaped former editors." Smart takes his leave of the reader by quoting "the words of an old poet, which are applicable enough to this Undertaking."[38] The gist of the lines Smart quotes is to the effect that while the business in hand may seem to be mere child's play it is actually fraught with great difficulties. After the preface comes a Latin notice to his learned readers in which Smart informs them in essence that he has restored some rather immodest passages to decency. The Latin text and the English translation are *en face*; at the foot of the Latin text are textual notes recording emendations of previous editors while the English translation has explanatory notes, either original with Smart or gleaned from previous annotators.[39]

Almost nine years after the prose *Horace* was published John Hawkesworth visited Smart and wrote an account of that visit to Smart's sister Margaret. He found Smart "busy in translating Horace into verse" and, he goes on, "he told me his principal motive for translating Horace into verse was to supersede the prose translation which he did for Newbery, which he said would hurt his memory. He intends however to review that translation, and print it at the foot of the page in his poetical version."[40] Both the preliminary matter in the prose *Horace* and what Smart revealed to Hawkesworth tell quite eloquently of the mood in which he worked upon and saw his translation published. To this must be added the fact that Smart felt he had been cheated by Newbery in his payment for the translation. Brooding on the disagreeableness of the task that had been forced upon him and yet with more than his share of pride in his reputation and abilities as a scholar, Smart spent at least one miserable year preparing this translation. Concurrent with his work on Horace, he was doing some work, whether original or not, toward compiling the collection of "Tales and Fables in Verse" which, "adorned with Cuts, designed and engraved by the best Masters," was advertised as "In the Press, and speedily will be published" on the last page of the preliminary matter. Smart had not been idle despite the absence of much original published work in 1754 and 1755.

On November 11 Smart, described as "of the parish of St. Mary, Islington" (where Canonbury House was situated), and Richard Rolt signed a contract with Thomas Gardner, stationer, and Edmund Allen, printer, to provide material, or to have such material provided if they could not, for a periodical to be called the *Universal Visiter or Monthly Memorialist*. Edmund Allen was Samuel Johnson's friend and neighbor of Bolt Court, Fleet Street. And although Thomas Gardner had not published many books, Johnson maintained, in contradiction to Tom Davies' remark that Gardner was not "properly a bookseller," that "he had served his time regularly, was a member of the Stationers' company, kept a shop in the face of mankind, purchased copyright, and was a *bibliopole*, Sir, in every sense." On the same occasion he said, smiling, "What an excellent instance it [the contract] would have been of the oppression of booksellers towards poor authors," causing Boswell soberly to comment in a footnote that "Mr. Gardner, I am assured, was a worthy and liberal man."[41] The first number of the periodical was to appear on February 1, 1756, a fact which was announced in Smart's *On the Goodness of the Supreme Being* and which moved the poetaster John Lockman to another of his occasional poems with their extended titles.[42] Extraordinarily, all parties bound themselves for the optimistic period of ninety-nine years during which time they would not engage in any venture that would affect the success of the enterprise. Copy for each issue was to be delivered on the first day of each month prior to the actual month of publication, and for this Smart and Rolt were each to get one-fourth share after expenses were defrayed. The four bound themselves to one another in the sum of two hundred pounds, and any one of them could be free from the contract by giving due notice. Witnesses to the contract were Thomas Rosoman, proprietor of Sadler's Wells in Islington from 1743 on, and a William Harborne.[43] Rosoman is remembered in *Jubilate Agno* with the wish that "God be gracious to Thomas Rosoman & family" (D, 156). Rolt at one time or another wrote songs, cantatas, and other pieces for Sadler's Wells. That Smart should desert Newbery for Gardner is not surprising, for he complained bitterly to John Hawkesworth in 1764 that his father-in-law had given him only thirteen pounds for his translation of Horace and had turned over the other eighty-seven pounds of the promised one hundred pounds to Smart's family.[44]

From the very beginning it became evident that Smart would have trouble keeping to the terms of the agreement with Gardner. Before long, his friends had to help him supply material by writing pieces for his share of each monthly issue; Garrick, Burney, Percy, and probably Arthur Murphy offered their services or were asked to do so. The most famous contributor to the *Universal Visiter*, however, was Samuel Johnson, whose recently published *Dictionary* was praised by Smart in an essay entitled *Some Thoughts on the English Language*, which appeared in the opening number of the periodical.[45] Johnson said that he wrote "for some months" while Smart "was mad" but gave up writing for the *Universal Visiter* when it became evident that Smart's wits would not return to him; hence, the assumption is that Smart was mad for much, if not all, of the time he was engaged with Rolt in editing the periodical. Smart's heaviest contributions were in the earliest numbers, those for January, February, March, and April, and prose predominated over poetry. Besides pieces on Chaucer, Spenser, and Shakespeare he wrote the essay on the English language already mentioned and some "Literary Observations," the latter being less than a page in length. These last two pieces appeared in January; in February he devoted two pages to "Further Remarks on Dr. Lowth's celebrated Prelections," continuing his praise of the work he had characterized as "one of the best performances that has been published for a century" in the "Literary Observations." Two of his poems were printed in January; one of these, the *Secular Ode*, had been written over ten years ago, while the other, *To the Right Honourable Earl of Darlington*, congratulated Harry Vane on being appointed "Paymaster of His Majesty's Forces" on December 16, 1755. A third poem, *Stanzas, occasioned by the Generosity of the English, to the Distressed Portugese*, written some time shortly after the Lisbon earthquake on November 1, 1755, praises English charity.

> Where arts and arms astonish all the globe;
>> Where *Science* sweeps along with *Roman* mien;
> Where more than empress in her royal robe,
>> The majesty of *Liberty* is seen;
> Where countless graces croud the circling shore,
> Is there yet room for one perfection more?
>
> Yes, CHARITY! *Religion's* darling child;
>> See, the seraphic language of her look!
> Without her, anchor'd *Hope* in vain had smil'd,
>> And heav'n-ey'd *Faith* had almost clos'd her book:
> Without her, *Virtue* barren wou'd remain,
> And ENGLISHMEN, be ENGLISHMEN in vain.

Smart had already sounded the note of patriotism in his essay on the English language when he wrote that the Spanish language "is too grave, solemn, and formal; the *French* too light, precipitate, and coxcomical. The *Italian* is over-softened and emasculated with a redundancy of vowels; as the *German* is burthened and rendered barbarous by an harsh, unutterable, disagreeable concurrence of consonants. But the *English* tongue is majestic without softness, lively without lightness, and nervous without roughness."

Two epigrams signed "C" represent all the poetry Smart contributed in February. In March his sole poem, signed "S," was one entitled *To Health*, and in April three slight poems, two of which had already appeared in print, made up his part of the poetry section. Also presumably his in the April number was an essay, *Some thoughts on a national militia*. Thereafter his presence in the periodical is marked by an infrequent poem, sometimes one already printed, in the months up to October.[46] But the *Universal Visiter* was doomed almost from the beginning; the wonder is that it managed to run for an entire year. Besides being of some biographical value, the magazine shows Smart's increasing pride in his English-ness, a theme that emerges more strongly in his later poetry, and his preoccupation with metrics, a preoccupation that manifested itself early in his career and found its ultimate expression when he came to translate Horace into verse.[47]

A footnote to Smart's *Brief Enquiry into the Learning of Shake-spear* in the *Universal Visiter* speaks of "a society lately constituted to do honour to the memory of *Shakespear*. It is formed by a num-ber of very ingenious gentlemen, adepts in the polite arts, and patrons of merit, who intend annually to exhibit some patterns of their own excellence, at the same time that they assemble to com-memorate that of the divine poet. Mr. *Roubilliac* and Mr. *Havard*, at the last meeting, gave universal satisfaction; the former by a fine model of a bust for *Shakespear*, and the latter by an animated ode intended for music" (p. 127). Both Havard and Roubiliac were friends of Garrick; Roubiliac's model for a bust of Shakespeare was probably one of his first studies for the full-length statue completed for Garrick in 1758. And Roubiliac's first wife, Smart claims in a footnote to a later poem, "was a Smart, descended from the same Ancestors as Mr. Christopher Smart" (*An Epistle to John Sherratt, Esq.*). According to one writer, it was in the Bedford Coffee-House that there gathered "a little society of critics, calling themselves the Shakespeare Club, who affected to give laws on all things concern-ing the stage."[48] The Bedford was a famous place of resort, with Bonnell Thornton, Charles Macklin, Henry Fielding, Sir Francis Blake Delaval, Samuel Foote, William Hogarth, Thomas Arne, and Garrick as its habitués; and it was here too that John Hill, Smart, and Arthur Murphy frequently came. Smart even went so far as to date his *Hilliad* from the "Bedford Coffee-House, Jan. 16, 1753" in the preliminary matter of that work. From the roll of prominent men who frequented the Bedford, most of them known to Smart in varying degrees of intimacy, and from the reference to "the last meeting" of the Shakespeare Club in the footnote to his essay in the *Universal Visiter*, it is quite clear that Smart must himself have been a member of the society. Association with these men at this time in a club such as the Shakespeare did much toward keeping his spirits up.

While Smart was struggling to keep to the terms of his agreement with Gardner and Allen he still found time to assist friends. He wrote an epilogue for Murphy's farce *The Apprentice*, produced on

January 2, and he wrote a poem entitled *To the Author of Some Defamatory Verses against a Worthy Gentleman* for the June *Gentleman's Magazine*. A four-line version of this epigram, under the title *On a Malignant Dull Poet*, was not printed until 1824. The defamatory verses of the title probably lurk in some periodical of the day; Smart's reply reads,

> When the viper has vented its venom, 'tis said,
> That the fat heals the wound which the poison has made.
> Thus fares it with blockheads whenever they write,
> Their dullness an antidote proves to their spight.
> But had sense and keen satire attended the strain,
> That sense and keen satire had still been in vain;
> For ill-manag'd wit, like a suicide's sword,
> Turns its virulent point on the heart of its lord.
>   And since *Charles* leads a life undeserving of blame,
>   Detraction is only a foil to his fame.

Smart had a very good friend named Charles, Charles Burney, and while Burney had left London a few years ago he still made annual trips to the city. But the incident referred to might have taken place any time in the past ten years, since Smart had no hesitation about resurrecting old pieces even if their content had lost all point with the passage of time.[49] One other poem belongs to this year. Shortly after August, when it was reviewed in the *Monthly Review*, Smart wrote the *Hymn to the Supreme Being, on Recovery from a dangerous Fit of Illness*. As the poem was published by Newbery and dedicated to Dr. Robert James, whose Fever Powders Newbery was one of four persons having the sole right to vend, it is apparent that the publisher was ready to forgive his son-in-law's defection to Gardner. And since both Gardner's and Newbery's names appeared on the imprint of the first and second editions of the *Goodness* poem, on the second edition of the *Omniscience* poem, and on the third edition of the *Eternity* poem, all published in this year, it would seem that any differences that may have arisen were forgotten, either in the desire for profit or in the hope of helping Smart. What is more, both Newbery and Gardner used the second edition of the *Omniscience* poem to advertise works by Smart, the former printing a list of Smart's publications and promising speedy publication of the ill-fated collection of tales and fables, and the latter announcing publication of the second number of the *Universal*

Visiter. To Newbery's possible further credit must be added the fact that he brought out a third edition of the *Immensity* poem this same year.

The Hymn to the Supreme Being has been taken to be a hymn of praise to God for having restored the poet to his sanity after a fit of madness. Warrant for this belief has been found in such lines as "When reason left me in the time of need,/ And sense was lost in terror or in trance," "And exil'd reason takes her seat again," and "My mind lay open to the powers of night." Smart makes reference, in a footnote keyed to the first line of the *Hymn*, to the thirty-eighth chapter of Isaiah which tells how Hezekiah, "sick unto death," was told by the Lord to prepare for death and how, upon praying to the Lord, he was granted another fifteen years of life. What Smart could not know when he wrote the *Hymn* was that he, too, was to be granted only another fifteen years of life. But Hezekiah's illness was not mental, and much of what Smart says in his poem points to his own illness as a severe fever. "My sick'ning soul was with my blood inflam'd," he wrote, and

> My feeble feet refus'd my body's weight,
> Nor wou'd my eyes admit the glorious light,
> My nerves convuls'd shook fearful of their fate,
> My mind lay open to the powers of night.

In his dedication to Dr. James he is even more revealing,

> Having made a humble offering to Him, without whose blessing your skill, admirable as it is, would have been to no purpose, I think myself bound by all the ties of gratitude, to render my next acknowledgments to you, who under God, restored me to health from as violent and dangerous a disorder, as perhaps ever man survived. And my thanks become more particularly your just tribute, since this was the third time, that your judgment and medicines rescued me from the grave, permit me to say, in a manner almost miraculous.

Twice before, Smart says, Dr. James had rescued him from "the grave," hardly the way to say or imply that he had been saved from madness. Smart was soon to be confined, but the *Hymn* has nothing to reveal about the history of his madness, unless recurrent illnesses so wore him down that he finally succumbed the more easily to whatever forces drove him into the asylum. The review of the

Hymn in the August *Monthly Review* was little calculated to raise his spirits; again the tone was patronizing: "As this poem seems to have been the genuine effusion of gratitude, it would be cruel and invidious, to make it the subject of criticism; tho', otherwise, not the least exceptionable of this gentleman's performances. It is an instance, however, of the goodness of his heart, if not the fidelity of his muse."

Smart's own words in the dedication to Dr. James are the best point of departure for an investigation of his illnesses. His illness in 1756 was the third serious one he had suffered, if not in his adult life, at least by the time he settled in London and made the acquaintance of Dr. James. Some time in 1752 a London newspaper announced that "the ingenious Mr. Smart who has been very seriously ill of a Fever is now in a fair way to Recovery."[50] Here his illness is definitely said to have been a fever. Next comes the notice in his friend Murphy's *Gray's Inn Journal*, Number 32 for May 26, 1753, to the effect that Smart had been "indisposed for some time past, but we had the pleasure of seeing him here a few Days since"; this illness may not have been a serious one. And finally, there is the poem in the March, 1754, *Gentleman's Magazine*, *Ode to a Virginia Nightingale*, which speaks of a "dangerous illness" in which the author was restored to "mirth and health" by the same young lady who cured the bird. This last, if it refers to a real incident, may possibly look back to the illness of the preceding year, although Murphy's word "indisposed" would seem to bely that. Practically all the available evidence either states or strongly suggests that Smart suffered from recurrent fever of some kind; the lines in the *Hymn* that tell of loss of reason are easily interpreted as referring to the delirium that often accompanies fever. Important in this connection is a sentence in Smollett's statement of editorial policy in the April, 1756, issue of the *Critical Review* which reads, "They [the authors of the *Critical Review*] have nothing to say to the [Universal] Visiter, but that *they wage no war with Bedlam and the Mint*" (p. 287). The allusion, taken almost verbatim from a line in Pope's *Epistle to Dr. Arbuthnot*, l. 156, is to Smart and Rolt, editors of the *Universal Visiter*: the reference to Bedlam can only be to Smart. "Bedlam" need not mean that Smart was confined in Bethlem Hospital or anywhere else; it may only mean that Smollett thought he had lost his senses. Since Smart had included Smollett in a list of authors whom he admired in the fifth of his Castle-Building essays in *The Student,* the abuse he received from him in return seems excessive. John Armstrong, one of the "four gentlemen" who assisted Smollett, was praised in the same essay, and Thomas Francklin, another of the "four gentlemen," was at Cambridge while Smart was there and later was one of the judges who awarded him the Seatonian prize in 1752. Smollett's remark was much more cutting than Samuel Derrick's unfavorable review of the first number of the *Universal Visiter* for the *Critical.* Sarcastic almost throughout, he conceded only that Smart's *Secular Ode* "seems to be a work of genius, but executed in a loose rambling manner. The following stanza [the second] is a pretty imitation of *Spencer*" (pp. 85–8). Smart must have replied in some fashion to the review, bridling no doubt at the jeering patronizing tone, and Smollett retaliated with the Bedlam-Mint insult, at the same time attacking Smart's friend Murphy.[51] This glancing insult, possibly nothing more than a literary allusion, is one of the first contemporary references to Smart's madness. One other such reference is Dr. Johnson's well-known and unfeeling comment about the aid he gave Smart in the *Universal Visiter.* "I wrote for some months in 'The Universal Visiter', for poor Smart, while he was mad," Boswell reports him as saying in 1775, "not then knowing the terms on which he was engaged to write, and thinking I was doing him good. I hoped his wits would soon return to him. Mine returned to me, and I wrote in 'The Universal Visiter' no longer."[52] Hunter's comment on the *Universal Visiter* affair is so vague as to render it of little value; he writes of "Johnson, who, on the first approaches of Mr. Smart's malady, wrote several papers for a periodical publication in which that gentleman was concerned, to secure his claim to a share in the profits of it" (p. xxi).

Elizabeth Anne Le Noir's first letter to Sharp reveals much that has not hitherto been known about her father's illness.

> Previous to my father's showing any symptoms of insanity, my sister a child of three years old awoke one night screaming and saying that her *papa had lost his head.* This singular presentiment or whatever it may be called was soon after verified, and it was found necessary to confine him. He was committed by Mr Newbery to the care of a *Mr Potter* who kept a private house at Bethnal Green. There I remember to have been taken to see him by my mother and I retain a faint recollection of a small neat parlour in which we were received. He grew better, and some misjudging

friends who misconstrued Mr Newbery's great kindness in placing him under necessary & salutary restriction which might possibly have eventually wrought a cure, invited him to dinner and he returned to his confinement no more. He never recovered the clearness of his intellect though he continued to write and publish.*

Smart's first daughter, Marianne, was born on May 3, 1753; hence her nightmare occurred in mid-1756 at the earliest, at which time her father's madness had not manifested itself or been suspected. Elizabeth Anne was christened on November 21, 1754; her recollection of visiting her father in the private madhouse and her statement that "he returned to his confinement no more" after being invited out to dinner by friends puts the period of his residence with Mr. Potter some time after his year in St. Luke's Hospital, that is, at some time after May, 1758. Hence, Mrs. Thrale's report of a conversation between Dr. Burney and Samuel Johnson, "says Burney I vex to hear of poor Kits going to Chelsey:—'but a madman must be confined Sir—at Chelsey or elsewhere',"[53] would seem to be a generic reference to private madhouses, a number of which were in Chelsea. Since Mr. Potter's madhouse was a private one there are no records of the inmates.

Records were kept, however, at St. Luke's Hospital, very full and unambiguous records. An entry in its "Curable Patients Book" for July 30, 1751, to May 20, 1771, shows that on March 15, 1757, a petition was delivered for Smart's admission into the curable ward of the hospital. His parish was given as St. Gregory's, Middlesex, close to St. Paul's Cathedral, and he was recommended by Francis Gosling. He was admitted on May 6, 1757, and discharged, uncured, on May 11, 1758. The "Minute Books" of the same hospital tell the story in greater detail; the minutes are those of the weekly meetings of the Committee of the Hospital;

> March 18th 1757
> Read and approved the Petitions & Certificates on behalf of Christopher Smart, Eliz.th Morgan and Mary Montague. Ordered. That they be brought for Examination in their Turns.

*July 13, 1831, pp. 217–18 in Sharp MS 28. The Bethnal Green rate-books reveal that a George Pottar (spelled Potter in 1764) of Bethnal Green East Side paid the highest rates for his street and among the highest for the whole of Bethnal Green. He paid rates on three pieces of property as well as personal charges for several years, clear evidence of his means.

April 22d 1757
Ordered. That Christopher Smart and Eliz.th Morgan be brought for examination next Fryday.

April 29th 1757
The Friends on behalf of Christopher Smart having sent a Message to this Committee that the Person who was to bring him is out of Town and praying he may be continued on the List till next Fryday. Ordered. That he be continued accordingly.

May 6th 1757
Christopher Smart was examined. Ordered. That he be now admitted upon the usual Security being given.

May 12th 1758
Dr. Battie having acquainted this Committee that Christopher Smart (who was admitted 6th day of May 1757) continues disordered in his Senses notwithstanding he has been admitted into this Hospital above 12 Calendar Months and from the present Circumstances of his Case there is not Suff.^t reason to expect his speedy Recovery And he being brought up and examined. Ordered. That he be discharged and that Notice be sent to his Securities to take him away.

May 19th 1758
The Friends on behalf of Christopher Smart who was discharged uncured last Friday attending & praying the patient may be put upon the List to be readmitted at 5s. a week in his Turn. Ordered. That he be put upon the List accordingly.

March 28th 1760
Ordered. That Christopher Smart be brought next ffryday for Readmission at 5s. a week.

April 4th 1760
This Committee received a letter from the Petitioners on behalf of Christopher Smart that he wiii not be brought for readmission. Ordered. That his Name be taken off the List.

Everything in Smart's case went according to established procedure: the petition, the admission, the report by Dr. Battie, the two-year wait after being put on the list for the incurable ward, all are duplicated in the other entries in the minute books. Smart's name does not appear anywhere in the "Incurable Patients Book," disposing of the possibility that he may later have been readmitted to St. Luke's. What is more, while he could have gone to Bethlem Hospital from St. Luke's, he could not, such were the regulations at the latter place, have been admitted to St. Luke's if he had been discharged as uncured from Bethlem. No evidence exists that Smart was ever confined in Bethlem Hospital. His "friends" who acted on his behalf in getting him admitted to St. Luke's were Newbery, from whose parish he was admitted, and Francis Gosling, once himself a bookseller.

Smart was fortunate that he was admitted to St. Luke's Hospital rather than to Bethlem, or to one or another of the more undesirable private madhouses. St. Luke's is described by John Noorthouck in his *New History of London*, published in 1773:

> At the north-west corner of Upper Moorfields stands St. Luke's hospital for lunatics; a neat but very plain edifice: nothing is here expended in ornament, and we only see a building of considerable length plaistered over and whitened, with ranges of small square windows, on which no decorations have been bestowed. This hospital, which takes its name from its being situated in St. Luke's parish, is supported by private subscriptions, and is designed as an improvement upon Bethlehem, which was incapable of receiving and providing for the relief of all the unhappy objects for whom application was made. But no person is to be admitted who has been a lunatic above twelve calendar months; or who has been discharged as incurable from any other hospital for the reception of lunatics; or who has the venereal disease; is troubled with epileptic or convulsive fits, or is deemed an idiot; nor any woman with child. The hospital was opened in 1751, and is very amply supported since (pp. 755–56).

The foundation of the hospital on June 13, 1750, a year before its actual opening, was partly prompted by the abuses at Bethlem Hospital, as was made abundantly clear in an appeal for funds in the year of its foundation. One of the men very early associated with the new hospital was Dr. William Battie, one of the famous medical men of the eighteenth century. He was St. Luke's first physician, a post he held until he resigned it voluntarily in 1764. As a governor of Bethlem since 1742 Battie knew everything that could be known about the treatment of the insane there and he had no intention of allowing St. Luke's to become another Bedlam. He insisted that the insane be provided with "Servants peculiarly qualified" as attendants, that they have separate rooms and the diet of healthy people, and that they not be exposed to public view. In his

Treatise on Madness (1758) Battie explained that "the visits therefore of affecting friends, as well as enemies, and the impertinent curiosity of those who think it pastime to converse with madmen, and to play upon their passions, ought strictly to be forbidden." All in all, Dr. Battie was considerably in advance of his time in his views on madness and its treatment.

The nature of Smart's madness is impossible to diagnose at this distance in time. For Battie, "that man alone, is properly mad, who is fully and unalterably persuaded of the existence, or of the appearance, of anything which does not naturally exist, or does not actually appear to him, and who behaves according to such erroneous persuasion." Since Smart was in St. Luke's during Battie's administration, and since Battie himself pronounced him uncured, he must have been subject to hallucinations. Strong drink, taken often enough and in sufficient quantity, will have that effect, of course, but Battie, distinguishing between "original" and "consequential" madness, and stating that "madness frequently succeeds or accompanies fever," would allow only that excessive drinking could "become a very common, tho' remoter cause of Madness." Others differed: John Ball in his *Modern Practice of Physic*, 1760, lists "anxiety of mind" and too much "strong vinous or spiritous liquors" as "antecedent causes" of madness. Smart's mania, however it manifested itself, and it usually manifested itself in loud public prayer, did not stem from drunkenness; it was aggravated, however, by frequent recourse to the bottle. Ironically enough, as Mrs. Piozzi recognized, if Smart had prayed in the privacy of his home all might have been well for him. Her comment comes in a rather lengthy passage which represents the soundest contemporary judgment on Smart's case.

> The famous Christopher Smart, who was both a wit and a scholar, and visited as such while under confinement for MADNESS, would never have had a commission of LUNACY taken out against him, had he managed with equal ingenuity [that is, kept his eccentricities private]—for Smart's melancholy showed itself only in a preternatural excitement to prayer, which he held it as a duty not to controul or repress—taking *au pied de la lettre* our blessed Saviour's injunction *to pray without ceasing*.—So that beginning by regular addresses at stated times to the Almighty, he went on to call his friends from their dinners, or beds, or places of recreation, whenever that impulse towards prayer pressed upon his mind. In every other transaction of life no man's wits could be more regular

than those of Smart; for this prevalence of one idea pertinaciously keeping the first place in his head, had in no sense except what immediately related to itself, perverted his judgment at all: his opinions were unchanged as before, nor did he seem more likely to fall into a state of DISTRACTION than any other man; less perhaps, as he calmed every start of violent passion by prayer. Now, had this eminently unhappy patient been equally seized by the precept of *praying in secret*; as no one would then have been disturbed by his irregularities, it would have been no one's interest to watch over or cure them; and the absurdity would possibly have consumed itself in private, . . . I well remember how after the commission was put in force, poor fellow! he got money from the keeper of the mad-house for teaching his little boys Latin—a proof, as vulgar people would imagine, that his intellects were sound; for mean observers suppose all *MADNESS* to be *PHRENZY*, and think a person *INSANE* in proportion as he is wild, and disposed to throw things about—where as experience shows that such temporary suspensions of the mental faculties are oftener connected with delirium than with *mania*, and, if not encouraged and stimulated by drunkenness, are seldom of long duration.[54]

This account derives from an earlier one in which she writes that while Smart prayed in secret he was not thought mad "but soon as the Idea struck him that every Time he thought of praying, Resistance against y^t divine Impulse (as he conceived it) was a Crime; he knelt down in the Streets, Assembly rooms, and wherever he was when the Thought cross^d his Mind—and this indecorous Conduct obliged his Friends to place him in a Confinement whence many mad as he remain excluded, only because their *Delusion* is not known."[55] Smart's misfortune was that he could not leave others in peace; he needed only to have kept to himself and all would have been well.

Dr. Johnson's remarks on Smart's madness are among the kindlier of those recorded by Boswell on his "poor friend Smart." "My poor friend Smart," Johnson is supposed to have said, "shewed the disturbance of his mind, by falling upon his knees, and saying his prayers in the street, or in any other unusual place. Now although, rationally speaking, it is greater madness not to pray at all, than to pray as Smart did, I am afraid there are so many who do not pray, that their understanding is not called in question." At another time Johnson said, "I did not think he ought to be shut up. His infirmities were not noxious to society. He insisted on people praying with him; and I'd as lief pray with Kit Smart as any one else. Another charge was, that he did not love clean linen; and I have no passion for it."[56] The Reverend Mr. Whitefield tells how he was able to secure the release of a young man confined to Bethlem Hospital because he had fasted for nearly a fortnight, because he "prayed so as to be heard four Story High," and because he had sold his clothes and given the money to the poor.[57] Smart had no friend to free him from confinement even though he did not go to the lengths that Whitefield's young friend had.

The form Smart's mania took is known; why he should have succumbed at all is not known. Hunter implies that a number of circumstances formed a chain of events that led to his confinement. Smart, he says, was born prematurely and was weakly; as a consequence he was given cordials as a child and youth, a practice that led to his fondness for drink. This same love of drink coupled with worry about money, "acting upon an imagination uncommonly fervid, produced temporary alienations of mind; which at last were attended with paroxysms so violent and continued as to render confinement necessary" (p. xx). Another, much later, hypothesis has it that Smart clearly

> suffered from manic depressive insanity or cyclothymia, a disorder characterized by recurrent attacks of depression and excitement or predominantly by one or the other. Smart himself said, 'I have a greater compass both of mirth and melancholy than another.' This is a deep-rooted constitutional infirmity, which often influences the temperament of the sufferer even during his periods of normality. The cardinal symptoms of mania are excitement, elation, and what is called 'the flight of ideas,' in which the stream of thought is continuous but fragmentary, the connections being determined by chance associations between the fragments. In Smart's case the mental illness was not the result of his drunkenness, but he drank because he was mentally unstable.[58]

There is no question but that Smart drank too much, but this was a forgivable failing. His bouts of loud public prayer were another matter. Mrs. Piozzi tells us, possibly taking Johnson's "any other unusual place" as a point of departure, that Smart "went on to call his friends from their dinners, or beds, or places of recreation, whenever that impulse towards prayer pressed upon his mind." Smart himself acknowledges this propensity: "For I blessed God in St James's Park till I routed all the company," he writes in *Jubilate Agno*, adding, "For the officers of the peace are at variance with me,

and the watchman smites me with his staff" (B1, 89, 90) . The reference to the watchman indicates that he was no nice observer of the
time of day or night when he felt compelled to drop to his knees
and pray. He was not "noxious" to society, but he was an unexpected source of annoyance to his friends and to his family—and to
utter strangers. No respecter of persons, he would force whoever was
nearest him to kneel and pray, to the amusement of passersby and
to the extreme annoyance of his victim. And so it was—a familiar
figure to the officers of the peace who soon tired of his eccentricity, a
cause of considerable embarrassment to his wife and to his father-in-
law, and a figure to be pitied even by those who did not possess one
iota of his poetic genius—that Smart was sent to St. Luke's Hospital
in the hopes that he might there be cured. For Dr. Battie believed
that "Madness, like several other animal distempers, often ceases
spontaneously, that is without our being able to assign a sufficient
reason; and many a lunatic, who by the repetition of vomits and
other convulsive stimuli would have been strained into downright
Idiotism, has when given over as incurable recovered his understanding." Whatever harsh treatment he may have suffered later, no
violence or other cruelty was allowed at St. Luke's.

When Smart emerged from St. Luke's Hospital on May 11, 1758,
he was still uncured and his friends put his name on the waiting list
for a place in the incurable ward. Some eight months later, on
January 17, 1759, the *Public Advertiser* announced a benefit performance of Aaron Hill's *Merope* and a new farce entitled *The
Guardian* at Drury Lane for a "Gentleman, well known in the
Literary World, who is at present under very unhappy Circumstances." The performance, originally set for January 26, did not
actually take place until February 3 at which time Garrick, the
prime mover behind the benefit, appeared in his new farce with
Yates, O'Brien, Miss Pritchard, and Mrs. Clive. William Havard,
another friend of Smart's, took the role of Poliphontes in *Merope*.
The occasion was much publicized, with Smart's friends, among
them Murphy, Rolt, and William Woty, all writing poems deploring his condition and eulogizing his poetry. A broadside announced
quite bluntly that the performance was for "Mr. Christopher
Smart." *Lloyd's Evening Post* for February 2 printed Murphy's
poem with the words "On reading a Paragraph, hinting at the kind
Concern which a Manager of Drury Lane Theatre show'd, for the
unhappy Mr. Christopher Smart." And the same occasion prompted

John Lockman, a member of the group at Vauxhall, to some verses which he titled "A Thought on reading a Play Bill for Merope, to be performed at Drury Lane Theatre, on Saturday, 3 Feb. 1759, for the Benefit of his ingenious Friend Mr. Christopher Smart." It remained, however, for an announcement of the benefit performance to state that it was for "Christopher Smart in the Mad House."[59] Thomas Gray was in London and must have read the announcement of the benefit, for he promptly wrote to William Mason on January 18 to tell him about the upcoming performance and to announce that "poor Smart is not dead, as was said." Mason's reply confirms that some of Smart's friends believed that he had died; possibly they had heard nothing about his confinement in St. Luke's and had lost sight of him for a while. The stay at St. Luke's would certainly have been kept as quiet as possible by Smart's friends and family. Mason wrote back to Gray, "This resuscitation of Poor Smart pains me, I was in hopes he was safe in that state where the best of us will be better than we are & the worst I hope as little worse as infinite Justice can permit. But is he return'd to his senses? if so I fear that will be more terrible still, pray, if you can dispose of a Guinea so as it will in any sort benefit him (for tis too late for a ticket) give it for me." Benefit performances for people in distress were common at this time; Smart, as Mrs. Midnight, had given such benefit performances when he was acting in his Orations. But Smart, who was "under the pressure of severe distress," Hunter writes, was not permitted by his "friends" to "refuse" the profits of the benefit (p. xx), evidence that he was still proud enough and aware enough to wish to be spared the shame of receiving public charity. Smart's "severe distress," as Hunter puts it, does not mean that he was then in confinement: if anything, it suggests only that he needed money desperately.* Even the caustic *Critical Review*, no friend to Smart, when it took notice of *The Guardian*, published, significantly enough, by Newbery, was gracious enough to write that the "generous and charitable occasion upon which this translation was first exhibited on an English theatre renders it sacred from criticism." Eight years earlier Smart had praised Garrick in *The Midwife* for giving benefit performances for "Persons in Distress"; his gratitude to the actor must have been warm indeed in 1759.

Newbery's publication of Garrick's *Guardian* may be put down

---

*The only other reference to his being confined at the time occurs in the *Gentleman's Magazine* in 1779, twenty years after the event.

simply to an instinct for profit; the fact that it was the afterpiece at his unfortunate son-in-law's benefit performance may point, however, to his prior participation in the whole affair. He was probably one of the friends who prevailed upon Smart to allow the benefit to take place at all, and it was he, even more probably, who took it upon himself to get him admitted to St. Luke's. Smart was admitted from Newbery's parish and he was recommended to the governors of the hospital by a former bookseller, a man sure to be known to Newbery. Every indication tends to put Newbery in a good light with respect to his dealings with his son-in-law. He loaned him money, he found plenty of hack work for him, he may have set him up in his venture on the stage, he took him to live at Canonbury with him, and he set aside profits from certain publishing ventures for him. Smart's daughter Elizabeth Ann LeNoir wrote of Newbery that "no individual was ever more extensively useful his means considered, his door was always open to needy authors, and his purse and patronage were at their service. My father was of this number, and admitted to his table."[60] Newbery praised Smart's poetry in print even at a time when Smart almost surely wanted nothing more to do with him, seeing him as one of the agents of his downfall. And Arthur Murphy, Smart's closest friend in these years, wrote in a *Gray's Inn Journal* essay that, "While a *Smart* subsists among us, I cannot help thinking it an indelible Reproach to the Age, that he has not any where found a Mecaenas;" in 1786 Murphy added here, "A bookseller is his only friend, but for that bookseller, however liberal, he must toil and drudge." The implication is unmistakable: no matter how liberal and friendly Newbery was, it was shameful that Smart should not be free to write what he wanted when he wanted. Reproaches may be leveled at the age, but not at Newbery. In an essay by *"The Female Student,"* that is by Smart, in *The Student*, a bookseller is described in uncomplimentary terms, and there is every reason to believe that Newbery sat for the portrait. How much is bitterness, how much raillery, there is no way of knowing, but the periodical was Newbery's and the supposition is that he took it all in good part. At much the same time, what is more, Smart more than once refers to "my friend Mr. Newbery" in *The Midwife*. Newbery loaned money to Johnson and to Goldsmith and to others; his desire to be repaid in money or in literary drudgery bespeaks him a businessman but not a tyrant. There is no truth in the view that sees him driving poor Smart to the utmost of his abilities and then clapping him in an asylum when he could no more profit from him. During Smart's confinement at St. Luke's, Newbery and his stepson Thomas Carnan brought out two editions of *The Nonpareil*, a collection of pieces from *The Midwife*, and in 1758 the former printed a second edition of the Seatonian poem *On the Power of the Supreme Being*, both possibly with the intention of helping Smart. Certainly these publications did nothing to hurt Smart's reputation at a time when he was virtually forgotten. Smart was not an easy man to get along with; he and Newbery, only nine years his senior, came from different backgrounds and had little in common. One was a poet and scholar, the other a shrewd business-man. Had it not been for Anna Maria Smart, his stepdaughter, Newbery might have abandoned the poet much earlier. Writers were easy to come by.

The *Gentleman's Magazine* for December, 1758, carried Smart's fable of *The English Bull Dog, Dutch Mastiff, and Quail* with an introductory note reading, "The following Fable, which has been handed about in private, was written by the ingenious Mr. Christopher Smart, Late of Pembroke Hall, Cambridge, when his Grace the Duke of Devonshire (then Lord Hartington) was appointed Lord Lieutenant of Ireland." As an occasional poem it was written shortly after the event it celebrates in its concluding lines: Lord Hartington was appointed to his post in Ireland in April, 1755, and arrived in Dublin early the following month. Hence its belated publi-cation in somewhat revised form, at the end of 1758 may be some slight evidence that Smart was at liberty between his release from St. Luke's and his next confinement. At least he may have been living for a short time at home or in the home of friends, possibly even with his father-in-law, for there also exists the extremely re-mote possibility that he had a hand initially in Newbery's collection of travels, *The World Displayed*, published one volume a month from December 1, 1759, to July 1, 1761.[61] This kind of editorial chore, plus the exhumation and publication of the *English Bull Dog* fable, may have been all he was thought capable of in the latter half of 1758. However, the poems written by his friends at the time of the benefit performance prematurely and mistakenly mourn his permanent incapacity for further poetic effort, for, in about a month or so, Smart was engaged in a long and unique poem to which he was to give a little time each day for the next four years. The poem, *Jubilate Agno*, would have confirmed the worst suspicions of Smart's enemies and caused much distress among his friends if they had seen it, for it is seemingly an incoherent outpouring of whatever came into the writer's diseased mind. Actually, it is not that at all; it is the central document in Smart's life, both as a poet and as a man.

IV.

JUBILATE AGNO, 1759-1763

Smart's whereabouts between May 11, 1758, and February 3, 1759, are unknown; he left St. Luke's Hospital as an "uncured" lunatic on the earlier date and was given a benefit performance by Garrick on the later. Since he was uncured, and since there is no positive evidence of any original work during these nine months, the assumption is that he was kept by friends or was confined in a private madhouse. Mrs. Elizabeth LeNoir remembered being taken by her mother to see her father, "committed by Mr Newbery to the care of a *Mr Potter* who kept a private house at Bethnal Green" and being received in a "small neat parlour."[1] As Smart's wife had left London for Dublin and had already set up shop there by January 3, 1759, as announced in the *Gazetteer and London Daily Advertiser* for that date, and as she was back in Reading managing the *Reading Mercury* by January 25, 1762,[2] she must have taken little Elizabeth to see Smart at Potter's either shortly before she went to Dublin or after she returned. Many years later Elizabeth wrote that "on my poor father's derangement Mr. Newbery sent my mother to Ireland to settle an agency for the sale of James's Powders; she was there two years; and soon after her return she was established with her eldest brother John in the business at Reading."[3] Of the two possibilities the former seems more plausible; Elizabeth was only four years old in November, 1758, and would, as she did, remember little about the visit. What is more, she says that an encounter with Dr. Johnson in which she asked him why he made such "strange gestures" happened at "Canonbury (called Canbury) House where I was born and spent the first seven years of my life."[4] She and her sister were left behind with the Newberys when their mother went to Dublin, for Elizabeth was christened on November 21, 1754; hence, when her daughter was seven years old, in November, 1761,

Anna Maria Smart was back in England, and probably in Reading, preparing to take charge of her stepfather's newspaper. At some time between Smart's release from St. Luke's Hospital and his wife's departure for Dublin, he had entered the madhouse with the small neat parlor in Bethnal Green, for Elizabeth LeNoir says that when he left there "he returned to his confinement no more. He never recovered the clearness of his intellect though he continued to write and publish." Potter's, then, was the last place in which Smart was confined for insanity.

Mrs. Piozzi says that Smart "would never have had a commission of lunacy taken out against him" if he had not made a public display of his eccentricity.[5] She refers to the procedure by which a number of people could swear to a person's unsoundness of mind before commissioners under a writ of *de Lunatico Inquirendo* and thus have him committed, although the enforcement of the commission did not preclude that the lunatic had had and might continue to have lucid intervals. Under the conditions of such a commission the suspected person was deprived of all control over land, buildings, finances, etc., and a relative was appointed to take charge of these for him. Smart's statement in *Jubilate Agno* that he "made over" his inheritance to his mother may mean that it was she who was given control over whatever small estate he had when he was confined in Potter's madhouse. And although Potter's establishment, being a private madhouse, had no legal authority for existence, keepers of such places were excused as long as their management was exercised properly. Confinement in a private madhouse in the eighteenth century, before corrective legislation was enacted in 1774, was usually accompanied by shockingly cruel physical and mental abuse. Beatings, purgings, forced feedings, sexual assault, and primitive and filthy living conditions were the rule. The exceptions were the madhouses run by such men as Dr. Battie or Dr. Nathaniel Cotton, the poet, but their fees were very high. William Cowper spent a year and a half with Dr. Cotton at his private asylum at St. Albans; William Collins was less fortunate, for it is thought that he was put into the hands of a man named Mac-Donald who kept a madhouse in Chelsea and who took little care of those in his charge. There were madhouses other than Potter's at Bethnal Green, a group in Chelsea, a well-known one in Hoxton, and a number of others, all doing a profitable business. Confinement in these places was often the unfortunate lot of a woman who stood in the way of her husband's pleasures or of a man or woman whose estate and property could in this fashion be taken over by an unscrupulous relative. A writer in the *Gentleman's Magazine* for January, 1763, points up the difference between "*public* hospitals" and "*private* Mad-houses" in these words: "In *these* charitable institutions for the relief of Maniacks," referring to the hospitals, "no impatient heir can be gratified; no austere relation can be indulged; and no ties of consanguinity broke or suppressed" (p. 25). Understandably, the keepers of these madhouses were not eager to have the identity of their inmates known nor their own doings too closely enquired into. Another writer in the *Gentleman's Magazine*, in the March, 1763, number, writing of one of the Chelsea madhouses, said that "it appears also, that the persons confined in this house, were denied the use of pen, ink and paper, and secluded from all commerce with the world, being constantly denied, if any enquiry was made after them at the house" (p. 126). In its "Historical Chronicle," under the date November 28, 1763, the *Gentleman's Magazine* reported the indictment of "the master and servants of a certain mad-house" for the unlawful detention of a young gentleman, who was "confined in a strait waistcoat, tied down 17 nights and days, denied the use of pen, ink and paper" (p. 612). The "Historical Chronicle" for May, 1766, carried the story of "a lady of fashion" who was caused to be confined in a madhouse and who was "deemed by the court to be sane in mind" (p. 245), while a correspondent in the same magazine, in December of the same year, offered suggestions for reforms, pointing out that "the unhappy persons who are privately betrayed into these prisons . . . are confined in dungeons, scarcely bigger than a grave, without pen, ink, paper, books, or society; without possibility of complaint to any but those, whose interest it is to continue the oppression" (p. 577). A revolting description of the ill-usage afforded prisoners in private madhouses and the ease with which a husband, for his own purposes, could cause his wife to be confined for a few days or for years forms part of the "Historical Chronicle" for April, 1772. One woman, upon a personal examination by a Justice Wilmot, was "found . . . apparently sane, and in a truly pitious situation, having a hole quite through her hand, which it is more than probable, was occasioned by some violence from her inhuman keepers" (pp. 195–196). The aftermath of this same affair provided matter for three closely printed columns in the "Historical Chronicle" for July.[6]

Smart was fortunate to be in Potter's hands; his wife and daughter were allowed to visit him as were some of his friends. Toward the end of his confinement he was visited by the Sherratts, probably by Richard Rolt and his wife, and by Miss Sheels of Queen's Square, since he says of them in the *Epistle to John Sherratt*,

> 'Tis blessing as by God we're told,
> To come and visit friends in hold.

It is thought that Dr. Johnson visited him in his confinement, for he told Burney that Smart "has partly as much exercise as he used to have, for he digs in the garden. Indeed, before his confinement, he used for exercise to walk to the alehouse; but he was *carried* back again."[7] This, coupled with Boswell's remark, upon the occasion when he and Johnson visited Bedlam in 1775, "I had been informed that he had once been there before with Mr. Wedderburne (now Lord Loughborough), Mr. Murphy, and Mr. Foote," has been taken as evidence that Johnson went to see Smart.[8] And Smart's prayer in *Jubilate Agno* that "God be gracious to Samuel Johnson" (D, 74), written on April 24, 1762, has been used to suggest that the visit took place about this time. But the visit to Bedlam could not have been to see Smart, both because Smart was never in Bethlem Hospital nor, in all probability, in an asylum to which the public was allowed access. On the visit with Murphy and Foote and Wedderburne, Johnson's attention was drawn to a man beating his straw, supposing him to be William, Duke of Cumberland, further evidence that the reference to Bedlam was to Bethlem Hospital and not, generically, to any asylum. Nor could he have visited Smart when, on August 24, the latter prayed for him, for from August 16 to September 26, 1762, Johnson was not in London.[9] Johnson's visit to Bedlam probably took place in July of 1762 when he, Murphy, and Wedderburne had come together in the matter of his pension.[10] Whatever kindnesses Johnson may have shown Smart, and they were not many, they did not include visiting him in the asylum; the remark about Smart's digging in the garden need be no more than hearsay. Johnson would seem, on the basis of a letter to Anna Maria Smart, written in late 1758, to have sympathized with the poet's wife rather than with him. "Madam," he addresses her,

To enumerate the causes that have hindered me from answering your letter would be of no use; be assured that disrespect had no part in the delay. I have been always glad to hear of you, and have not neglected to enquire after you. I am not surprised to hear that you are not much delighted with Ireland. To one that has passed so many years in the pleasures and opulence of London, there are few places that can give much delight; but we can never unite all conveniences in any sphere; and must only consider which has the most good in the whole, or more properly which has the least evil. You have gone at the worst time; the splendor of Dublin is only to be seen in a parliament winter; and even then matters will be but little mended. I think, Madam, you may look upon your expedition as a proper preparation to the voyage which we have often talked of. Dublin, though a place much worse than London, is not so bad as Iceland. You will now be hardened to all from the sight of poverty, and will be qualified to lead us forward, when we shrink at rueful spectacles of smoky cottages and ragged inhabitants. One advantage is also to be gained from the sight of poor countries; we learn to know the comforts of our own. I wish, however, it was in my power to make Ireland please you better; and whatever is in my power you may always command. I shall be glad to hear from you the history of your management; whether you have a house or a shop, and what companions you have found; let me know every good and every evil that befalls you. I must insist that you don't use me as I have used you, for we must not copy the faults of our friends; for my part I intend to amend mine, and for the future to tell you more frequently that I am, &c.

Sam. Johnson[11]

Not a word about Smart, not even an allusion to him. Mrs. LeNoir wrote that "Dr. Johnson was kind to my mother under her misfortunes. I have often heard her tell of her dining with him, with two gentlemen whom she believed to be Italians" and also that Johnson sent Anna Maria a present of game.[12] For Johnson, then, the misfortune was not Smart's but his wife's.

Anna Maria Smart had gone to Dublin, leaving her children with her mother and stepfather. There she opened a shop and sold, among other things, Dr. James's powders at "Mr. McMahon's in Cape Street Dublin," a fact that was announced in the newspapers as early as January 3, 1759, and as late as June 27 of the same year. Resident in Dublin was her sister-in-law Mary Anne who had married Richard Falkiner, son of a gentleman of County Tipperary, at some time between 1744 and 1752, at which later date she and her husband subscribed to Smart's *Poems on Several Occasions*. One account has it that while Falkiner was "eating his dinners in London, previous to being called to the Irish Bar (called 1741), he made the acquaintance of Christopher Smart, and subsequently married his sister, Mary Anne Smart."[13] Falkiner was actually admitted to the Irish Bar in 1745,[14] and Smart was going into London as early as 1744, when he ran up a tailor's bill there, so that the two may have become acquainted that early. In Dublin Anna Maria Smart would have the advantage of her sister-in-law's presence and immediate access to the society of her friends. That Smart's wife should have sought some way to earn her own livelihood attests to her considerable strength of character and to her undoubted capacity for the management of a business, a capacity she later showed by her long years as publisher of Newbery's newspaper in Reading. For she stayed only two years in Dublin, the first issue of the *Reading Mercury* published under her name appearing on January 25, 1762. If she was concerned about the fate of her husband, she did nothing except on one occasion to visit him in the madhouse. From her father and stepfather she inherited and learned a shrewd sense of business, but she had no great liking for literature. "My Mother," writes Mrs. LeNoir rather caustically, "altho' married to an author (or perhaps from that very circumstance) had a great dislike to anything relating to literature, and though she was like her father in law always willing to assist distressed authors, she discouraged all propensity to authorship in her own family."[15] In another letter Mrs. LeNoir, who is probably a prejudiced witness, said of her mother that "Queen Bess herself was not more absolute."[16] Anna Maria had, as a young woman of twenty, been persuaded by Smart to elope. Within a year of the marriage she had given birth to a child; the following year, in November, 1754, she gave birth to another. Her husband began to show signs of his madness in less than two years after the birth of the second child and even before this he was improvident, inconsiderate, and too fond of the bottle. She later told Christopher Hunter, who recorded it in his biography of Smart, that her husband was so thoughtless that he often "invited company to dinner, when no means appeared of providing a meal for themselves" (pp. xxviii–xix). In another anecdote Hunter tells how Smart having undertaken "to introduce his wife to my Lord Darlington, with whom he was well acquainted; he had no sooner mentioned her name to his Lordship, than he retreated suddenly, as if stricken with a panic, from the room, and from the house, leaving her to follow overwhelmed with confusion" (p. xxix). The worth of this anecdote is somewhat tempered by the fact that at the time it could have taken place Smart was diverting the public as Mother Midnight on the stage and had been for some time. Such activity is little compatible with the degree of shyness he is supposed to have possessed. How much love there was between Anna Maria and her husband can only be guessed at, but it was not great enough to survive his years of confinement as a madman. The fault was almost entirely Smart's, for he alienated many friends while she seems to have been widely respected. Johnson's letter is one indication of how one of her husband's former friends felt about her, and when she died in 1809 her obituary notice in the *Gentleman's Magazine* described her as "a woman, the virtues of whose heart, in all relations of life, whether to her kindred or her friends, were a pattern worthy of imitation." And Margaret Hunter, Smart's other sister, in a letter to Anna Maria written in the late 1760's, speaks of "the tender respect which I shall always bear you, for your many actions towards me of affectionate and friendly regard."[17] She must have been sorely tried by her husband not to have offered to help him in the last eight years of his life, the years after he came out of Potter's madhouse, years when she was very well off. Except for his daughter Elizabeth's one visit to the madhouse, Smart did not see either of his children again for the rest of his life.

During the period beginning on or about January 4, 1759,[18] then, to January 30, 1763, when he broke off part way down a page of that document, Smart was engaged in writing his *Jubilate Agno*, only about one third of which survives.[19] From what remains of the poem it appears that Smart had intended throughout to write matching pairs of verses, the first all beginning with the word "Let" (except for the very first two lines) and the companion verses all with the word "For," thus achieving an antiphonal effect. Originally he may even have envisaged public performance of his song of praise, and in some parts of the *Jubilate* the links between Let and the corresponding For verses are either unmistakable or can be worked out.* Many pairs of lines, or even sometimes the relation

---

*Thus, the first Let line of section B1 reads, "Let Elizur rejoice with the Partridge, who is a prisoner of state and is proud of his keepers," and the corresponding For line reads, "For I am not without authority in my jeopardy, which I derive inevitably from the glory of the name of the Lord," where the link is the idea of imprisonment or confinement, called "jeopardy" by Smart.

between two parts of the same line, depend upon rather recondite areas of knowledge, for not only was Smart a determined punster in four languages, English, Latin, Greek, and Hebrew, but he had also remembered strange and out-of-the-way bits of information from his very wide reading. And he had books and periodicals to which he could refer, in the former for names of plants, animals, and Biblical figures, and in the latter for the events going on around him in London, England, and Europe. Smart was not cut off from the world while he was in confinement, and there were few events of any national importance that he did not in one fashion or another record in *Jubilate Agno*.

Smart did not willingly enter Potter's madhouse and he conceived and continued to nourish a deep-rooted bitterness toward all those who had a part in having him confined, as well as against those who acquiesced in the action. His stepfather had had him confined, and the other members of the Newbery and Smart families had made no move to stop him; his betrayal, Smart felt, was by members of his family, and he felt no compunction about registering his complaints against them in *Jubilate Agno*. A number of lines, written between July 28 and August 31, 1759, during the earliest part of his confinement, reflect the depth of his initial hurt and anger. One of his first concerns was about his reputation, and on the first of the above dates he wrote, "For my existimation is good even amongst the slanderers and my memory shall arise for a sweet savour unto the Lord" (B1, 3). He was troubled, too, lest he be cuckolded while separated from his wife, and on August 31 wrote, "For they throw my horns in my face and reptiles make themselves wings against me" (B1, 115). And between these dates he wrote various lines whose meanings are immediately seen or soon discovered. "For I am come home again, but there is nobody to kill the calf or to pay the musick," (B1, 15) he complained in a line anticipatory of some he was to write in the *Epistle* to Sherratt upon his release from confinement,

> 'Tis you that have in my behalf,
> Produc'd the robe and kill'd the calf;
> Have hail'd the *restoration day*,
> And bid the loudest music play.

He knew he was a prodigal son; all he wanted was forgiveness. On the following day he wrote, "For there are still serpents that can speak—God bless my head, my heart, & my heel" (B1, 18). And within the space of the next three weeks he accused his enemies of having turned his wife against him, "For they have seperated me and my bosom, whereas the right comes by setting us together" (B1, 59) ; he accused his family of deceit in words taken almost literally from the Book of Job, "For my brethren have dealt deceitfully as a brook, and as the stream of brooks that pass away" (B1, 74); and he went so far as to cry out that his death was desired, "For they lay wagers touching my life.—God be gracious to the winners" (B1, 92). While much of his bitterness was given vent thus early in *Jubilate Agno*, he returned later at various times to record his feelings, particularly his acute sense of having been deserted by everybody, in other lines. On October 24, 1759, in the midst of some lines on the coffin, the cradle, and the purse, he expressed this as "For the purse is for me because I have neither money nor human friends" (B1, 283), qualifying the last word in deference to his cat Jeoffrey whom he first mentions as early as August 19, "For I am possessed of a cat, surpassing in beauty, from whom I take occasion to bless Almighty God" (B1, 68). Having been deserted, a word he found occasion to pun upon in this same poem, he sought solace in the company of a cat and in the cultivation of a few flowers.

Provided with pen and ink and paper, allowed visitors, digging in the garden, playing with and talking to his cat, reading books and periodicals, possibly even allowed a few hours' accompanied freedom from confinement, Smart spent almost exactly four years in the private madhouse at Bethnal Green. Part of each day of that confinement was ritually devoted to the composition of one, two, or three pairs of lines that were then written down neatly in the document he entitled *Jubilate Agno*. This poem, for so Smart considered it and so it is, is many things: it is a prolonged, antiphonally conceived hymn of praise to the Lord, in which Smart calls upon all creatures to join him in adoration of their Maker. As such it is not without a tradition and antecedents. It is a spiritual and historical journal of four years in the life of its composer, mirroring his moods, telling of his daily activities, revealing his suffering and gradual reconciliation to his lot, chronicling his illnesses, and giving his reaction to trivial and domestic events as well as to the more momentous and public ones that were taking place outside his restricted world. It is also the storehouse of a tremendous fund of knowledge that ranges over many fields, showing Smart's intimate acquaintance with many books and suggesting his probable acquaintance with many others, old and new, familiar and esoteric. It is a trying ground for the poetry that Smart was to publish in the years after he left the madhouse, a trying ground where methods and devices could be experimented with and tested, where ordinary words could be placed in unusual juxtaposition to others and uncommon words could be essayed to see what effect their sight and sound and associative background might have, and where the themes of that later poetry would be given greater prominence than they had in the poetry before 1759—in lines of a strange beauty which had been glimpsed but never plainly revealed before this time in his poetry. And it is, above all else, the unique expression and implicit description of a crisis in the life of a man, for the improvident, intemperate, hail-fellow-well-met Grub-Street hack and sometime public entertainer who suffered himself to be put away as a madman in 1759, walked out of his confinement four years later a different person. He was a different man and a different poet; the predominant features of his new existence as man and poet had always been there in him, but it took years of confinement, deprived of the bottle, sex, and the other ways in which one could indulge himself, to bring them out. Smart hints at this himself in the line, "For stuff'd guts make no musick; strain them strong and you shall have sweet melody" (B2, 307) , by which he means that a state of repletion ("stuff'd guts") will not produce great music—or poetry—but once the guts are strained, that is, made usable for stringed instruments, or, as part of the sustained pun, when the artist is made to undergo extreme pressures of one sort or another, then the melodies that are created will be sweet.

Arriving in London, a bachelor with expensive tastes and love for gay company, Smart had managed to get along for two or three years on what he got from Pembroke and what he earned by his writing. This income he supplemented when need arose by applying to one or another of his friends for a loan. But when he married he lost his income from his fellowship at the same time that he took on the responsibility of a wife, and, in the next two years or so, of two children. Not only did he have to provide for their needs; he also had to depend more and more on his writing and editing to allow him to live the kind of life to which he had become accustomed. As a result he was under considerable pressure from 1753 on, and it is probable that as he saw the debts accumulating he took refuge more and more in drinking. With the increased drinking his own personal expenditures mounted and his capacity for creative work declined. The Newberys, solidly middle class and eminently respectable, tried to straighten out this son-in-law for whom they had not bargained, lending him and his wife money and seeing to it that he had plenty of literary chores. But their efforts and those of Smart's friends made no impression upon him. He continued to drink and spend money foolishly and the pressure on him mounted and mounted. And yet all the strain of these years was as nothing to that which awaited him in the asylum. No matter how much he drank in the years before and after his marriage and before he entered the madhouse, and no matter how importunate his creditors were during those same years, he still had his wife and the two little girls and his friends—and his freedom. All this changed when he was put into Potter's care. However kindly his keeper may have been disposed to look upon him, Smart was suddenly deprived of strong drink, the companionship of his family and friends, whatever love his wife bore for him, and his precious freedom. He had known confinement in St. Luke's Hospital and that experience had left its mark upon him, even though Dr. Battie was the most enlightened man of his time in the treatment of the insane. With the year at St. Luke's to look back upon and a future of uncertain duration in the private madhouse before him, Smart's frame of mind in the first months of his confinement was desperate. With the passage of the months and as he marked in *Jubilate Agno* the various anniversaries of his stay in the madhouse, he became more and more used to his new existence and made the most of what opportunities were allowed him. And as he cast off the extreme bitterness of his feelings and came gradually to feel less self-pity he began to find his real nature as a man and a poet. Just as his body had been hardened and renewed by the forced abstention from alcohol and from the exercise in the garden so his spirit was refreshed and his creative power reinvigorated and finally fully defined. Now, while under confinement, he was able to release the poetry that had welled up in him before but had been refused complete expression because other, more lucrative forms of expression necessarily took precedence. He had never had the leisure to write the kind of poetry of which he was capable; the poetry which he wrote before his confinement, as he confessed to Murphy in the prolegomenous matter of the *Hilliad*, did not have the benefit of any loving care and polish. Now he had more time than he knew what to do with, and the poetry he wrote during these years profited immensely from his enforced leisure.

Except for a possible occasional short trip outside the madhouse, and the welcome advent of a visitor now and then, Smart spent four lonely years at Bethnal Green.[20] Like other lonely men and like others who could not afford to turn their thoughts inward too often and too long he had to find ways to keep his mind active. The eighteenth century bred many such men; of Smart's acquaintance Gray and Johnson were so afflicted. Any task, however seemingly insensate, so long as it fixed the attention to it, was welcome. Johnson counted the number of lines in Latin poems and revised his *Dictionary*; Gray always had something going forward. Smart began *Jubilate Agno* and wrote one, two, or three pairs of lines in it every day, partly because he had to find some means of recording what was boiling in his mind, and partly for the assurance it gave him to know that each day, and possibly at fixed times for different days, he would be at his appointed place for writing. He almost never revised on paper what he once put down on the folio pages of *Jubilate Agno*; the care and polish that he was unable to give his other compositions he lavished on this one, writing down in final form only what he had cast and recast in his mind. Some of the lines, even the majority of them possibly, demanded reference to one or more books or to contemporary newspapers and periodicals before they could be given their final and accurate form. Long lists of animals and plants and equally long lists of Biblical names, appearing in *Jubilate Agno* in the same order that they did in one or another book of natural history and in the Bible, need not be attributed to a phenomenal memory. Smart had some books and could doubtless ask Newbery and others to procure more for him. A scholar collects books, some more than others, and Smart, sometime Fellow of Pembroke, would have at least a small library of his own. But much more than names and information derived from books found its way into *Jubilate Agno*.

Early in the confinement Smart wrote such lines as "For I have seen the White Raven & Thomas Hall of Willingham and am myself a greater curiosity than both" (B1, 25); Thomas Hall was a young child with the physical development of a man whom Smart had described in *The Student* as "the young giant." Smart therefore claimed to be a greater freak or spectacle than either he or the white raven. About two weeks later, he complained, seeming to refer to taunts hurled at him, that "Silly fellow! Silly fellow! is against me and belongeth neither to me nor my family" (B1, 60); the very next day he wrote "For they pass by me in their tour, and the good Samaritan is not yet come" (B1, 63). All this seems to point to the presence of unwelcome sightseers. Within another two weeks he wrote "For I pray the Lord JESUS that cured the LUNATICK to be merciful to all my brethren and sisters in these houses" and "For they work me with their harping-irons, which is a barbarous instrument, because I am more unguarded than others" (B1, 123, 124). Here he states plainly that he is or has been subjected to physical abuse and seems to associate himself with the lunatics of both sexes confined in asylums or madhouses. But about a week later he exclaimed gratefully, "For I bless God that I am not in a dungeon, but am allowed the light of the Sun" (B1, 147). Earlier he wrote, in the present tense, "For the officers of the peace are at variance with me, and the watchman smites me with his staff" immediately after having written, in the past tense, "For I blessed God in St James's Park till I routed all the company" (B1, 89). While much in *Jubilate Agno* is clear or resolvable, Smart's comments on his own state and treatment, especially in the first months of his confinement, cannot be accepted without question. Whenever the subjective element enters into, or can be read into, statements made in *Jubilate Agno*, comparatively little reliance can be put in their factual truth or accuracy. Only when Smart is not writing about himself, or at least when he is not writing about matters touching on his confinement and his family, for example, are his statements completely acceptable. Thus, there is no reason to question his motives when he reports on his physical ailments, mentions events and persons of his early life, or even when he expresses opinions about events taking place in the world outside his restricted sphere of activity. Smart wrote an autobiographical document in *Jubilate Agno* and revealed much about himself in it, but he did write it in a madhouse not long after having been released as an uncured lunatic from St. Luke's Hospital and, like similar documents by persons whose sanity was never in question, it is not always to be trusted.

Smart does not say plainly that he found life in the madhouse unbearable, at least until he learned to subdue his desires. He had always been, or adopted the pose of being, of a strongly amorous nature. One of his first poems, written when he was thirteen, shows how observant he was of the female bosom, and the poetry written before his first confinement returns often and lovingly to that portion of the feminine anatomy. Some of his poems are more outspoken than others in their sexuality, although the context is usually facetious or semi-facetious. One of his poems in *The Student* in 1751, *The Author Apologises to a Lady for his being a Little Man*, seeks to persuade the fair one that "carnage" does not make the man, tells her that her breasts were "made to be press'd, not to be crush'd," and finally challenges her to put him to the test,

> Then, scornful nymph, come forth to yonder grove,
> Where I defy, and challenge, all thy utmost love.

His crambo ballad, *Lovely Harriote*, concludes suggestively enough, with the advice that she "to marry ought," and he steps forward himself as prospective groom,

> Then may I hug her silken Yoke,
> And give the last, the final Stroke,
> T' accomplish lovely *Harriote*.

And again and again in the early poetry he states or insinuates his readiness and capacity for amorous encounter. When, therefore, in *Jubilate Agno*, he writes "For I bless God in the strength of my loins and for the voice which he hath made sonorous" (B1, 80) he is giving himself his due. He and Anna Maria had wasted no time in getting a family. Separation from his wife, whatever intellectual distance had always existed between them, was something he felt sorely. He protested against this early in his confinement, "For they have seperated me and my bosom, whereas the right comes by setting us together" (B1, 59). But Anna Maria had already been in Dublin for almost a year when Smart wrote this line and they may never have seen one another again. Forced to do without sex, Smart vacillated between praise of chastity and sexual desire, covertly revealed. In the earliest part of *Jubilate Agno* he wrote "Let Susanna bless with the Butterfly—beauty hath wings, but chastity is the Cherub" (A, 92), praising Susanna for her adamant refusal to succumb to the lust of the two elders. Again, he could write "For beauty is better to look upon than to meddle with and tis good for a man not to know a woman" (B1, 103) and "For CHASTITY is the key of knowledge as in Esdras, Sr Isaac Newton & now, God be praised, in me" (B1, 194) . But suddenly he would drop the pose and remember what it was to be with a woman, to be with his wife; "For the angel GRATITUDE is my wife—God bring me to her or her to me" (B2, 324) , he wrote and then, in the very next line, with his mind still on what he had written the previous day, for he was writing only one line or pair of lines a day in this part, he added "For the propagation of light is quick as the divine Conception." Only a week earlier he had written three lines on three consecutive days which led, after an interruption of four days, to the two just quoted. In these he wrote

> For the SUN is an intelligence and an angel of the human form.
> For the MOON is an intelligence and an angel in shape like a woman.
> For they are together in the spirit every night like man and wife.

He used one of the oldest of all sexual images, the sun, as the male reproductive force. The same thought is echoed about three months later in the line "For when she [the moon] rises she has been strengthned by the Sun, who cherishes her by night" (B2, 430). And in a few other lines he may be using sexual imagery consciously or unconsciously. His fear that his confinement might give his wife the liberty to make a cuckold of him is expressed directly at least once and may lurk behind the numerous references to horns in the poem. One other deprivation seems not to have tortured him as much as might be expected; he wrote, perhaps ruefully, "For I have abstained from the blood of the grape and that even at the Lord's table" (B1, 5) .

Smart missed his children too. They were only babies when he had to spend a whole year in St. Luke's, and he could not have had too much time to become reacquainted with them before being committed to Mr. Potter's care. Two of the most touching lines in *Jubilate Agno* reveal his emotion at the thought of his little daughters,

> For I bless God for my retreat at CANBURY, as it was the place of the nativity of my children.
> For I pray God to give them the food which I cannot earn for them any otherwise than by prayer. (B1, 75, 76)

Both lines are introduced by corresponding lines in the Let section which show how close the two parts of the poem could be:

> Let Ibhar rejoice with the Pochard a child born in
> prosperity is the chiefest blessing of peace.
> Let Elishua rejoice with Cantharis God send bread
> and milk to the children.

More than two years after he began *Jubilate Agno* he suddenly remembered to ask God to be "gracious to Polly and Bess and all Canbury" (C, 73), and still later he included a Mrs. Hind, another resident of Canbury, one about whom nothing is known, in his prayers for God's graciousness (D, 8). He remembered his wife late in the poem on two occasions; both times he thinks of her kindly, asking God's graciousness and mercy for her (C, 108 and 128). His sister Margaret's son Christopher is mentioned in a spirit of good will; the boy was about eleven years old when Smart wrote "For I have a nephew CHRISTOPHER to whom I implore the grace of God" (B1, 65). And late in 1762 he prayed again for Christopher and his parents and brothers, "Lord have mercy on William Hunter his family," using the old possessive form as he was to in the Psalms (D, 133).* Smart had tasted happiness briefly at Canbury House, there he had lived with his wife, there his children had been born, and there, inevitably, his thoughts returned as day followed day in the madhouse with no prospect of release to bolster his spirits.

Other figures and events recalled themselves to his mind; after all, he had plenty of time for recollection. He thought of Shipbourne and Fairlawn and Maidstone where he had spent his childhood. He rejoiced to attribute to God his deliverance from the venom of the vipers that he had caught as a youth. He remembered some of the local lore of Kent, especially some of the common names of the flowers and plants that grew there and their real or fancied virtues. And he recalled, as he did so often in his poetry, the river Medway. Recollections of Durham, of school under Dongworth, of Raby Castle and the Vane children, especially of Anne, and of a number of the prominent people of that Cathedral city are more

---

*The line "God be gracious to Christopher Peacock and to all my God-Children" (B2, 346) may be a reference to an actual godchild; the Peacocks were an old Durham family, two of whose members had borne the name Christopher in the seventeenth and early eighteenth centuries.

frequent than memories of places and people in Kent. Many of the canons of Durham Cathedral are named; possibly Smart felt some kinship with them because old Peter Smart his ancestor had once been a canon himself. He dutifully remembered to ask God to be gracious to the Duke of Cleveland who had continued for some years after the Duchess's death to send him the forty pounds annual gift she had instituted. Of the area around Durham, other than Raby Castle, he mentioned only Newcastle, and then in a line whose meaning is elusive: "For I bless God for my Newcastle friends the voice of the raven and heart of the oak" (B1, 121). Names from the ten Cambridge years flood the pages of *Jubilate Agno*, a very few of them even now remembered, most of them obscure. A few of the terse mentions of Cambridge contemporaries revived in Smart's mind incidents that occurred while he was there. One such reference, "God be gracious to Cutting (C, 134), probably recalled to him the rustication in September, 1744, of Leonard Cutting, a Pembroke undergraduate student, for "great enormities," for so the Master, Dr. Roger Long, described his crime or misdemeanor. On January 12, 1762, soon before his release, Smart celebrated the anniversary of the founding of Pembroke with a line in *Jubilate Agno*, having written a poem on the four-hundredth anniversary of that occasion nineteen years earlier, while then at Pembroke. And not only does he remember Harriot Pratt and her brother Jermyn in calling upon God to be gracious to them, but he also does not forget their home in Ruston and their father. More remarkable is his inclusion of the name of one of the Pratts' friends or neighbors, a Mr. Pigg, whose name or character had left its impress upon his mind. "For I bless God for the immortal soul of Mr Pigg of DOWNHAM in NORFOLK," he wrote in August, 1759 (B1, 116), following lines in which he speaks of and lists "men who bear the names of animals" with whom he had "a providential acquaintance." Mr. Pigg's family is remembered a few months later in a line "For Kittim is the father of the Pygmies, God be gracious to Pigg his family" (B2, 387), which may contain a pun on Smart's nickname as well as reference to the diminutive stature of which he was quite conscious. And it was the first part of "Pygmies" of course that led him to include the name of a family he had met while visiting the Pratts.

Smart's references to Cambridge University, taken together, contain a curious yet understandable ambiguity.[21] But his loyalty to

Pembroke was unswerving and he blessed all its benefactors. Most significantly, at one point, in a line which he himself dates as "Novr 5.th 1762. N.S.," he expresses the very revealing desire that "The Lord magnify the idea of Smart singing hymns on this day in the eyes of the whole University of Cambridge" (D, 148). Twice in his academic career he had had many, if not all, of the eyes of the University upon him; once when he had preached a sermon before the Mayor of Cambridge and a second time when he had given a speech on the anniversary of the martyrdom of King Charles I.[22] The desire to sing hymns, probably his own, before the assembled University stemmed as much from the contemplated satisfaction of occupying the center of attention as from the laudable intention of contributing to the moral uplift of his hearers. Smart had taken the principal part in his Cambridge play and he had been the focus of public attention as Mother Midnight in night after night of the Oratory, yet it was not to the larger audiences of London or to the more intimate one of his own college that his thoughts went back but to an audience composed of the men who made up Cambridge University. Among these he would have envisaged, if they were still there, the men whose names he recorded in *Jubilate Agno*. Those who had left the University would be there to see and listen to their old friend, making the trip back from the various parts of England to which their fortunes had taken them. Francis Gulston and Richard Halford, both of Pembroke, linked together in grateful recollection, probably as students of his, "God give me to bless for Gulstone & Halford" (D, 115), would be there. Also there, proud of their fellow Pembrochian, would be Nathaniel Acton, Thomas Baker, Leonard Cutting—long since back from his rustication, Edward Musgrave, Charles Wilkinson, John Smith, gentle Mr. Peele, William Mason—down from the North for the occasion, Thomas Gray —still his friend though he may have had sufficient provocation not to be, and Richard Forester, who had taken the role of "the gentle Fair" in Smart's Cambridge play. The other members of the cast of *A Trip to Cambridge* would be there in a body, headed by Richard Stonhewer of Trinity and Peterhouse, their prompter. And from Christ's there would be George Heartley, Richard Marsh—who had gone to Durham school with Smart, Charles Hingeston, and John Bill; from King's, Richard Lyne, Christopher Anstey, and William Draper; from Caius, Jermyn Pratt, brother of the lovely Harriot, and Thomas Anguish; from Trinity, John Higgs, John Rust, and

Stephen Whisson, who had been one of the moderators the year Smart took his Bachelor of Arts degree; and from Clare, St. John's, Emanuel, Sidney Sussex, and Magdalene would come, respectively, William Whitehead—now Poet-Laureate, John Abdy, William Affleck, Brook Bridges, and John Delap, who had joined with Smart and others in mourning in verse the death of the Prince of Wales in 1751. Some of those whom Smart would have wished there were dead, and he prayed God to have mercy on their immortal souls.

Nearest in mind to Smart in the madhouse, however, were the years he had spent in London. Curiously enough, with the exception of the reference to Canonbury House in Islington, he mentions no building in the city. He seems not to have observed too closely the works of man; rather his eye was on the alert to note the wonders of God's creation. And so it was that he rarely remembered and re-corded in *Jubilate Agno* the purely man-made phenomena of the places in which he had lived. But the men who had been his friends or acquaintances or with whom he had been associated in the busi-ness or pleasures of life in London were of course still fresh in his memory and he put their names down, recording most of them in the last half-year of his stay in Potter's establishment. A number of the names in section D of his poem were those of people, probably relatively unknown to him in any other connection, who had sub-scribed to his *Poems on Several Occasions* in 1752. His gratitude to them and to those who were already subscribing to *Mother Mid-night's Orations*, and possibly even to the version of the Psalms he was deep into, made itself known in the line "Let Quarme, house of Quarme rejoice with Thyosiris Yellow Succory—I pray God bless all my Subscribers" (D, 221), written on January 14, 1763, a little more than two weeks before his release. A Robert Quarme, Esq., had subscribed to the 1752 *Poems* and his name led Smart to think of all his subscribers. While every line in section D starts with a surname and many of them then suggested to him somebody of the same name whom he knew, he did not always make any reference to this latter fact, and conjecture, sometimes bordering on certainty, must supply the deficiency. When he wrote, "Let Hind, house of Hind rejoice with Paederos Opal—God be gracious to Mrs Hind, that lived at Canbury" (D, 8) no question arises. Similarly, in the line "Let Ascham, house of Ascham rejoice with Thyitis a precious stone remarkably hard. Let God be gracious to Bennet" (D, 53), there can be no doubt that he was thinking of his friend James Bennet, the nominal editor of Ascham's English works—Samuel Johnson did the actual editing—father of little Kitty to whom Smart had written a poem in 1752, and headmaster of the school attended by Christopher Hunter, Smart's nephew. Chief among those Smart singled out, with Mrs. Hind and James Bennet, from his London years were the men who entertained at Sadler's Wells, Vauxhall Gardens, and the theaters. He felt especially kindly to Jonathan Tyers, proprietor of Vauxhall Gardens and to his son Tom, as well as to his performers, for twice he invoked God's favor for them (B2, 455, and D, 144). When he thought about Dr. Arne and Charles Burney and of Hogarth and Sir James Thornhill he was again thinking of Vauxhall Gardens for all, with the exception of Thornhill, Hogarth's father-in-law, were employed there at one time or another, in one capacity or another. From Sadler's Wells he remembered Thomas Rosoman, who had witnessed the *Universal Visiter* contract; Mr. Granier, one of Rosoman's actor-dancers;[23] and Peter Hough, an epitaph for whom had appeared in *Mother Midnight's Comical Pocket-Book*, 1753 (D, 56, 160, and 110) . In one line he linked four men whom he knew: "Let Flexney, house of Flexney rejoice with Triopthalmos— God be gracious to Churchill, Loyd and especially to Sheels" (D, 62) . William Flexney, London bookseller, was to sell Smart's 1763 *Poems on Several Occasions* and the *Psalms* in 1765; Smart's verse *Horace* was "Printed for W. Flexney" in 1767. And Flexney had also published poetry for Charles Churchill, Robert Lloyd, and the Reverend James Sheels. Sheels died soon after this line was written and Smart was asked to write his epitaph. He even remembered to ask God to be gracious to Warburton (C, 40), whom he had attacked in the satiric dedication to his *Horatian Canons of Friendship* in 1750 and with whom he had had no further dealings. At least two names, Hopwood and Ruston (76 and 105), were invested with melancholy remembrance of his year in St. Luke's Hospital, for a Mary Hopwood was discharged from there uncured on March 3, 1758, and Ann Ruston was discharged on June 30, 1758; both were there while Smart was.[24] With time it is possible that more of these names in section D will prove to have had some associative significance for Smart.

Section D of the *Jubilate*, its Let lines lost, may represent a falling off of interest on Smart's part, and yet it may have been, in the missing part, one of the richest components of the whole. The preceding extant part, section C, is barest and least rewarding in the Let lines, with a rather monotonous and terse listing of Biblical names coupled with an equally arid catalogue of plants occasionally interspersed with the name of a bird or another creature. Occasionally too, a bit of information, a recorded date, or the wish that God be gracious to a person or an institution ("God be gracious to Durham School") lends some warmth of interest to the Let lines, but most of them are on the order of

> Let Ramah rejoice with Cochineal.
> Let Gaba rejoice with the Prickly Pear, which the Cochineal
> feeds on.
> Let Nebo rejoice with the Myrtle-Leaved-Sumach as with the
> Skirrel Jub. 2^d.
> Let Magbish rejoice with the Sage-Tree Phomis as with the
> Goatsbeard Jub: 2^d.
> Let Hashum rejoice with Moon-Trefoil. (1–5)

The corresponding For lines,

> For H is a spirit and therefore he is God.
> For I is a person and therefore he is God.
> For K is king and therefore he is God.
> For L is love and therefore he is God.
> For M is musick and therefore he is God.

are not remarkable as poetry but they, part of one of three such alphabetical improvisations, show Smart's preoccupation with language and his fondness for puns, if nothing else. But elsewhere in the For lines of section C are whole passages of greater power and significance, and with a bare exception or two they have no discoverable link with the corresponding passages starting with Let. So, too, it may be with the missing For lines of section D; in fact, the greater richness of reference in the Let lines of D over those of C make it probable that the missing For lines in D were also richer than those in C. In addition, the Let lines of D are full of statements and allusions to contemporary events as well as to Smart's own affairs. Some of these last contain hints that Smart knew that he was soon to be released,

> Let Forward, house of Forward rejoice with Immussulus a kind of
> bird the Lord forward my translation of the psalms this year.
> Let Quarme, house of Quarme rejoice with Thyosiris yellow Suc-
> cory—I pray God bless all my Subscribers.

JUBILATE AGNO, 1759-1763

Let Larkin, house of Larkin rejoice with Long-wort or Torch-herb—
God give me good riddance of my present grievances.
Let Halford, house of Halford rejoice with Siren a musical bird.
God consider thou me for the baseness of those I have served
very highly. (220—223)

In the last two lines, written on January 15 and 16, 1763, about two weeks before his release, he appears to look forward to his freedom and even to be meditating some kind of vengeance against those who put him in Potter's madhouse. On January 28, he asked God to "be gracious to John Sherrat," the man who procured or engineered his release; two days later he wrote the last line of *Jubilate Agno.*

Section D contains more implicit information about Smart's activities and probable frame of mind than it does explicit statements to these effects. First, the very fact that he had progressed in his scheme of things through most of the classes of creatures and had coupled them with figures from the Bible up to this time but now turned to common, and some uncommon, surnames lends unusual significance to this final section. Since he had not exhausted all possible Biblical names there was some reason for the shift. That reason was a renewed and sharpened interest in the affairs of the outside world. As early as Christmas day, 1759, he had written, "For I bless God that I dwell within the sound of Success, and that it is well with ENGLAND this blessed day. NATIVITY of our LORD N.S. 1759." (B2, 353), evidence, in the reference to the celebrations for English military and naval successes during the year, of his awareness of the great events taking place. On March 14, 1760, he noted that there was a general fast on that day (B2, 433), and a year later, on March 10, 1761, he asked God to "give grace to the Young King" (C, 35). George III had succeeded his father on October 25, 1760; on March 3, 1761, he had made a speech before Parliament about the salaries of judges, and this may have led Smart to make his entry in the *Jubilate*. On September 30, 1762, the same day the news was reported in the *London Gazette*, Smart wrote "I give the glory to God, thro Christ, for taking the Havannah," and himself added the date (D, 112). But these are virtually all the references to the doings of the great. An occasional line also shows that he was not entirely oblivious to the momentous occasions in the lives of the obscure; on September 16, 1759, he asked God's graciousness for "the CAM & to DAVID CAM and his seed for ever" (B1, 162), an unmistakable reference to the birth of three sons to the wife of David Cam on the twentieth of August, an event which found its way into the register of births, marriages, and deaths in the *Gentleman's Magazine* and other periodicals.

Evidently Smart read the notices of births, marriages, and deaths with very keen interest, for the names in many other lines in D can be traced to them. Sometimes the interval between an actual event and Smart's record of it is so brief that he must have gotten it from a newspaper or by word of mouth rather than from the monthly register in magazines such as the *Gentleman's*. Thus, when he writes "Let Clare, house of Clare rejoice with Galeotes a kind of Lizard at enmity with serpents. Lord receive the soul of Dr Wilcox Master of Clare Hall" (102) on September 20, 1762, he is mourning the death on September 16 of Dr. Wilcox who, four times in his capacity as Master of Clare Hall and once as Vice-Chancellor, had been one of the judges to award him the Seatonian prize for the best poem on the attributes of God. A number of the names in this section, appearing in the newspapers and periodicals, recalled to Smart's memory people of the same name—only some of whom he knew personally. "Let Digby, house of Digby rejoice with Glycyrhiza & Sweetroot. God be gracious to Sr Digby Legard and his Son and family" (165), written on November 22, 1762, was prompted by the birth of Sir Digby's son on the fourth of November. While any connection between Smart and the Legard family is still to be established, he was certainly acquainted with the fact that the Reverend James Merrick was preparing a version of the Psalms, and therefore when he read of the death on Christmas day, 1762, of a Mr. Merrick he wrote on December 30, "Let Merrick, house of Merrick rejoice with Lageus a kind of Grape. God all-sufficient bless & forward the Psalmist in the Lord Jesus" (203). He seems especially to have been interested in men who attained great age and recorded the names of many who far exceeded the Biblical three score and ten, having revealed his concern about man's longevity in section C; "For I prophecy that men will live to a much greater age, this ripens apace God be praised" (88). One final example out of the many that remain must suffice. Since monthly magazines such as the *Gentleman's* came out about the first week of the month following that for which the issue was published, that is, the October number would be available in the first week of November, some of Smart's entries would be much later than the event they record. Therefore, the reference to "Miss

Leroche my fellow traveler from Calais" (D, 42), while it was written on July 23, 1762, probably stemmed from the marriage of a Miss Laroche on June 2, 1762.[25] There is no other evidence that Smart ever visited the Continent, if in truth he did, but a Miss Laroche does figure in the large circle of his London acquaintants. She was one of two sisters who took part in the amateur *Othello* in 1751 for which Smart wrote the prologue and epilogue.[26]

Failure to recognize some of the complexities of the extant lines of D has resulted in a virtual dismissal of that section as the least interesting and revealing part of the poem. While the possible associations from Let to For lines cannot, in the absence of the latter, be guessed at, certain vertical associations, that is, from one Let line to the succeeding one, emerge to indicate that Smart was not merely filling his paper at random, having given up all thought of design and coherence. Relationships between parts of a single line also reveal unexpected depths of complexity. Thus, when he wrote, early in D, "Let Fisher, house of Fisher rejoice with Sandastros kind of burning stone with gold drops in the body of it. God be gracious to Fisher of Cambridge & to all of his name & kindred" (12), it should be clear that he knew or knew of somebody named Fisher in Cambridge. At least two Cambridge men of that name may have been known to him; one was a John Fisher, banker. The other is the likelier candidate, for the *Cambridge Journal* for October 21, 1752, announces a concert by Mr. Burney "at Wisbeach at the Free School," "The first violin with a Solo, etc., by Mr. Fisher from Cambridge, who will likewise perform a Solo on the Violincello." Charles Burney was Smart's friend and Smart loved music, hence he probably knew the musical Mr. Fisher from Cambridge. But he had included all of the Fisher name and kindred in a general blessing, and it is, therefore, quite probable that he also had in mind the Reverend Peter Fisher who died at Staindrop, county Durham, in 1793 at the age of eighty-five, having been rector there for fifty-six years. For Smart was in Durham and visiting Raby Castle near Staindrop in 1737 and 1738, the first two years of the Reverend Mr. Fisher's tenure there. And surely, if Smart remembered the rector of Staindrop, he did not couple the name of Fisher with "Sandastrus kind of burning stone with gold drops in the body of it" without being aware of the Staindrop equals stone-with-gold-drops association.

Vertical association can be seen in the following lines.

Let Snow, house of Snow rejoice with Hysginum a plant
dying Scarlet.
Let Wardell, house of Wardell rejoice with Leiostreum a
smooth oyster. God give grace to the black trumpeter
& have mercy on the soul of Scipio. (179–80)

Valentine Snow was a famous trumpeter for whom Handel wrote
the obbligato parts in many of his oratorios; in January, 1753, he
was appointed Sergeant Trumpeter to the King and continued in
that post until his death in 1770. His name and his accomplishments as a trumpeter led Smart to think of a black, as opposed to a
white (Snow), trumpeter, either real or fancied, and if the latter he
may have dubbed him Scipio with Scipio Africanus in mind. Snow
came to mind in the first place because of line 177, "Let Abington,
house of Abington rejoice with Lea a kind of Colewort praise him
upon the sound of the trumpet," but if the intervening line "Let
Adcock, house of Adcock rejoice with Lada a shrub, which has
gummy leaves" (178) is in any way connected with the stream of
association the link is still to be discovered. Somewhat more
straightforward are these two lines:

Let Dongworth, house of Dongworth rejoice with Rhymay the
Bread-fruit. God be gracious to the immortal soul of
Richard Dongworth.
Let Randall, house of Randall rejoice with Guavoes. God
give Randall success. (28–9)

Richard Dongworth was headmaster of Durham school while Smart
was there; Thomas Randall succeeded to the post on Dongworth's
death in February, 1761, having served under him for many years.
"Rhymay the Bread-fruit" and "Guavoes" are both to be found on
the same page of Anson's *Voyage Round the World in the Years
MDCCXL.I.II.III.IV*, 1748, compiled by Richard Walter, M.A., a
book whose printed subscription list includes "Pembroke-Hall Library" and a "Reverend Mr. Smart." Smart names the work in line
11.* However full Smart's mind may have been of possible release
from the madhouse and of plans for his future life he did not
abandon *Jubilate Agno* to incoherence. In the *Song to David* particularly and in the Psalms and *Hymns and Spiritual Songs* to a

*In lines 10, 20, 21, 22, and 23, fish and plants that are mentioned or described
in the *Voyage* are listed. Earlier, in B, 154, Smart is evidently paraphrasing
Anson's account of the fish called the Torpedo.

lesser extent he was to show that he could build a highly intricate poetical structure; in *Jubilate Agno* he was learning how this was to be done.

Of the many books from which Smart drew for *Jubilate Agno*, one work overshadows all the rest.[27] Smart's familiarity with the Bible was intimate, and, while there is no need to believe that he was capable of holding in his memory long lists of names from that work, it is also clear that he quoted from it and alluded to it from memory. For the Bible and the Book of Common Prayer are, after all, the two books that provide the pervasive background to the *Jubilate*. He knew the Aprocrypha, and when he wrote in line A 80 "Let Savaran bless with the Elephant, who gave his life for his country that he might put on immortality," his reference can be tracked down to I Maccabees vi, 43–6, where "Eleazar also (surnamed) Savaran . . . put himself in jeopardy, to the end he might deliver his people and get him a perpetual name . . . he crept under the elephant, and thrust him under and slew him: whereupon the Elephant fell down upon him, and there he died."[28] Other works united to contribute to the uniqueness of Smart's poem, sometimes directly and at other times as a result of a way of thinking which he found congenial and shared with their authors. While it is sometimes possible to trace a line to one of the physico-theological writers of the late seventeenth or early eighteenth century it is more important to realize that he had assimilated their doctrine and made much of it his own. He knew, with John Ray, that the wisdom of God was manifested in the works of the creation, and although he might have remembered or recently read in William Derham's *Physico-Theology, or a Demonstration of the Being and Attributes of God from the Works of Creation* that wasps "frequent" wood that is "dry and sound but never any that is rotten,"[29] when he wrote "Let Zorobabel bless with the Wasp, who is the Lord's architect, and buildeth his edifice in armour" (A, 101), he might just as easily have observed the wasps' building techniques for himself. Zorobabel, or Zerubabel, helped to rebuild the Temple and as such was important in Freemasonic history; Smart seldom does only one thing at a time in most lines of *Jubilate Agno*. And although he may have read much about birds and fish and plants and precious stones and even stored away much of that information, he had access to a copy of Pliny's *Natural History* in Philemon Holland's translation, Eleazar Albin's *Natural History of Birds*, and either

Philip Miller's *Gardener's Dictionary* or one or more works similar to it—and he impressed them into service repeatedly. For the names of fish, some of them listed in crude alphabetical order, he went to Conrad Gesner's *Historiae Animalium* in one of its many editions.[30]

Even in the relatively barren Let lines of section C Smart can be seen to take advantage of an impressive range of erudite learning or a well-stocked collection of books. For such a seemingly uninteresting line as "Let Jarib rejoice with Balsam of Capivi. The Lord strengthen my reins" (50), while it may be one of several lines in which Smart voices his concern about his health, is based on the medical lore of his day. Balsam Capivi, according to Ralph Thicknesse's *Treatise of Foreign Vegetables*, 1749, "wonderfully deterges . . . the reins" (p. 224). A few lines after the reference to Balsam of Capivi and one of its medicinal virtues Smart writes "Let Elasah rejoice with Olibanum White or Male Frankinsense from an Arabian tree, good against Catarrhs and Spitting blood from which Christ Jesus deliver me" (68), and Thicknesse again provides an explanation of the line and is candidate for Smart's source. Devoting four pages to the subject, he explains that the names Male and Female "Frankinsense" derive from the phenomenon of resinous droppings from a tree often coming together two and two to resemble "the Testicles of Men, or the Breasts of Women." He records the views of some who claim that the substance comes only from Arabia, and states that it is held to be good, taken internally, for "coughs" and "spitting of Blood" and externally efficacious in "Fumigations for the head in Catarrhs" (pp. 256–59). Later in *Jubilate Agno* Smart introduces the name Thicknesse in the line "Let Thickness, house of Thickness rejoice with The Papah a fruit found at Chequetan" (D, 23), right in the midst of a number of lines including creatures and plants found in Anson's *Voyage*. This juxtaposition makes it still easier to believe that Thicknesse's was one of the books Smart knew or had. Elsewhere in this section he writes that hemlock is "good in the outward application" (146) and confirmation exists in *The Compleat Herbal, or the Botanical Institutions of Monsr. Tournefort*, 1730, which says that the juice of the hemlock "boil'd in a splenetick plaister, is applied outwardly" (77). "Let Sanballat rejoice with Ground Moss found sometimes on human skulls" (92) leads, among other possible sources, to John Parkinson's *Theatrum Botanicum*, 1640, where, on p. 1313, the reader is regaled with a picture of a skull with moss growing out of it and the following text: *"Muscus ex cranio humano.* The Mosse upon dead mens sculles. . . . It is a whitish short Kinde of Mosse somewhat like unto the Mosse of Trees, and groweth upon the bare scalpes of men and women that have lyen long, and are kept in Charnell houses in divers Countries." While no certainty exists that Smart's knowledge of this grisly subject came directly or indirectly from the *Theatrum Botanicum*, that knowledge was accurate. He may also have gone to Parkinson's work for his remark on Tormentil, which he described as "good for hemmorhages in the mouth even so Lord Jesus" (74), for there it is said to be "most excellent to stay all kindes of fluxes of blood or humour, in man or woman, whether at the nose, mouth, belly, or any wound in the veines, or anywhere else" (p. 395).

Other books which Smart knew or owned and used in some fashion for *Jubilate Agno* have left slight traces by which their presence can be discerned. When he writes of "Parcas who is a serpent more innocent than others" (B, 96), the same creature, its name there spelled "Parea," can be found in Edward Topsell's *Historie of the Foure-Footid Beastes*, 1607, under the general heading "Of Innocent Serpents." Further strengthening the possibility that Smart used Topsell is the fact that he speaks of the hare and his adversary and the urchin and his adversary (A, 22 and 32), and Topsell uses "adversary" of the enemies of both the hare and the urchin. In four consecutive lines on echoes, especially in one of these, "for ECHO is greatest in Churches and where she can assist in prayer" (B1, 237), presumably meaning that prayers are thus doubled, he may be remembering either Robert Plot's *Natural History of Oxfordshire* or his *Natural History of Staffordshire*, or both, since both treat of echoes, the former having something to say about that phenomenon in churches.[31] His dependence on Pliny's *Natural History* in Philemon Holland's translation was great, so great that in at least one place it led him into error. He says of a bird with the Latin name Percnopteros that it "haunteth the sugar-fens" (B1, 178), echoing Holland's words, "haunting lakes, fens," used to describe a bird discussed in the same paragraph with Percnopteros in such a way as to cause confusion between the two. To the roll of books and areas of learning he knew may be added others which he might have known, among them emblematical literature, cabalistic lore, and the writings of various mystical authors. Some part of the symbolism in a number of lines may, and even doubtless does, derive from Freemasonic literature and ritual.[32]

Excluding natural history from the discussion of Smart's interest in science and his knowledge of its various ramifications, the heaviest concentration on scientific matters is in the *For* lines in section B1, starting with line 157 and continuing to the end. In section B2 the lines dealing with science are interspersed among a variety of others, although it is in this latter section that he deals with eclipses, the propagation of light, snow and frost, the precession of the equinoxes, the problem of ascertaining the longitude, equivocal generation, the phenomenon of the horizontal moon, and Newton's "notion of colours." To this impressive list may be added the subjects he touched upon in B1: gravity, centripetal and centrifugal forces, elasticity, magnetism, "the mechanical powers"—that is, shears, wedge, inclined plane, etc.,—friction, "the movement of bodies," hydrostatics, the ascent of vapors, the barometer, the air-pump, sound, echoes, and a few others. However superficial and sometimes mistaken some of his ideas about science may be, or seem to be, he knew something about a great many scientific subjects. Upon his first meeting with Samuel Johnson their conversation began with poetry and ended with fluxions, a branch of mathematics, sometimes called the infinitesimal calculus, which has to do with the rate and proportion at which a flowing or varying quantity increases its magnitude. Such an acquaintance with science is not entirely surprising; Smart was educated at Cambridge where the sciences reigned supreme.[33] When in mid-century voices were raised decrying the quality of education students received at Cambridge, the Bishop of Lincoln, Dr. John Green, reported the arguments of the vindicators of the University on this, and on other aspects, in *The Academic*, published in 1750. There he could write that "Mathematicks and Natural Philosophy are so generally and so exactly understood, that more than twenty in every year of the Candidates for a Batchelor of Arts Degree, are able to demonstrate the principal Propositions of the *Principia*; and most other Books of the first Character on those subjects. Nay, several of this Number, they tell you, are no Strangers to the *higher Geometry* and the more difficult Parts of the Mathematicks: and others, who are not of this Number, are yet well acquainted with the Experiments and *Appearances* in natural Science" (p. 23). Small wonder that Smart and

Gray bewailed the obscurity into which classical studies had been cast.

Smart cannot, of course, have known all or even a considerable fraction of the scientific books in use at Cambridge around mid-century and earlier, but some lines in *Jubilate Agno* echo the words of one or another scientific work closely enough to warrant the assumption that he had it in mind or close at hand. His knowledge of other works may be assumed from the range of topics common to the lines dealing with science in *Jubilate Agno* and to those works themselves. In the former category is Robert Hooke's *Posthumous Works*; 1705 Hooke's "I proceeded next to shew that this Propagation of Light was to all imaginable Distance in a Moment or Instance of Time" (p. 99) served as direct source for Smart's "For LIGHT is propagated at all distances in an instant because it is actuated by the divine conception" (B1, 284). Less close verbally, but still close enough to warrant the theory that Smart also took his cue from it, is Hooke's statement, "Coherence nothing but Similitude of Parts and Motions" (p. 191), which becomes in *Jubilate Agno*, "For Attraction is the earning [that is, yearning] of parts, which have a similitude in the life" (B1, 165). In the latter category is the Abbé Noel Antoine Pluche's work, titled *Spectacle de la Nature: or Nature Display'd*.[34] Some of Smart's lines may have come right out of Pluche, always allowing for the special slant that he gives to his textbook sources. In five lines, all written from September 17 to 22, 1759, Smart makes statements about elasticity, fire, the shears, and mechanical principles (B1, 164–181), all of which bear some kinship with Pluche's treatment of the same topics. In Pluche's words, speaking of the inclined plane, "the Resistance diminishes with regard to the Power, as the Length in the inclined Plane increases with regard to the vertical Height," and the "same Advantage is found, with the same Proportion, in the Use of the Wedge."[35] "For the power of the WEDGE," writes Smart in B1, 180, "is direct as it's altitude by communication of Almighty God," following this with the line, "For the Skrew, Axle & Wheel, Pulleys, the Lever & inclined Plane are known in the Schools."*

Smart could almost equally well have gone to other books for

---

*Other subjects treated by both Smart and Pluche are the origins of fountains, of snow, of rain, of thunder and lightning, and of other atmospheric phenomena, shells, circulation of sap, "double Flowers," and the nature of colors. A few verbal parallels in some of these last bolster up the belief that Smart had recourse to *Nature Display'd*.

some or most of his information; among these would have been such works as J. T. Desaguliers' *Mathematical Elements of Natural Philosophy*, translated from the Latin of William Gravesande, 1731; Robert Green's *Principles of Natural Philosophy*, 1712; and Bernard Nieuwentyt's *Religious Philosopher*, translated from the Dutch by J. Chamberlayne, 1730.

Chamberlayne's translation of Nieuwentyt's work bears the long, elaborate, and inclusive subtitle, "The Right Use of Contemplating the WORKS of the CREATOR.

I. In the wonderful Structure of Animal Bodies, and in particular Man,
II. In the no less wonderful and wise Formation of the ELEMENTS. and their various Effects upon Animal and Vegetable Bodies. And,
III. In the most amazing Structure of the HEAVENS, with all its Furniture. *Designed for the Conviction of Atheists and Infidels.*"

As a possible further inducement to the prospective buyer a letter to the translator from Mr. Desaguliers, himself a well-known writer and translator, was procured and printed; among other commendatory remarks he writes, "He that reads *Nieuwentyt*, will easily see that a *Philosopher* cannot be an *Atheist*; and if it were true, that a Smattering in *Physics* will give a proud Man a Tincture of *Atheism,* a deep Search into Nature will certainly bring him back to a Religious Sense of GOD'S Wisdom and Providence." The arguments employed to convince the unbelieving of the existence of God are the familiar ones; since the human body, the systems of plants, and the celestial phenomena are so intricate on the one hand and so regulated by demonstrable laws on the other, there must be a creating and controlling hand. And that hand is God's. Books like Nieuwentyt's and scores of others inspired the spiritual philosophizing Smart indulged in in so many of the lines devoted to scientific matters. But Smart was a poet as well as a philosopher and he added still another dimension to the physico-theological explanations of Nieuwentyt and others. For him the tides "are the life of God in the ocean, and he sends his angel to trouble the great DEEP" (B1, 157). The loadstone also contains "the Life of God, and there is a magnet, which pointeth due EAST" (B1, 167), he wrote, following this with a line of strange and vivid beauty, "For the Glory of God is always in the East, but cannot be seen for the cloud of the crucifixion." For him, too, "WATER is not of solid constituents, but is dissolved from precious stones above" (B1, 196) and the "ASCENT of VAPOURS is the return of thanksgiving from all humid bodies" (B1, 208). Where a scientist would write that "the Time of the *Equinoxes* each Year will *precede* the Time in which it happened the Year before," Smart wrote, "For the PRECESSION of the Equinoxes is improving nature—something being gained every where for the glory of God perpetually."[36] And to him thunder and lightning are nothing more than "the voices of God direct in verse and musick" and "a glance of the glory of God" (B1, 271–2). There is no madness here; there is deep religious feeling and poetry. A few years before entering Potter's madhouse he had written in the Seatonian Prize poem *On the Power of the Supreme Being*:

> Survey the magnet's sympathetic love,
> That wooes the yielding needle; contemplate
> Th' attractive amber's power, invisible
> Ev'n to the mental eye; or when the blow
> Sent from th' electric sphere assaults thy frame,
> Shew me the hand that dealt it!—baffled here
> By his omnipotence, Philosophy
> Slowly her thoughts inadequate revolves,
> And stands, with all his circling wonders round her,
> Like heavy Saturn in th' etherial space
> Begirt with an inexplicable ring.

At the time these lines were written there was no question whatsoever about Smart's sanity.

Although Smart persisted in giving his own religious and poetic twist to the formulae and laws and explanations found in scientific works, he had thought seriously about certain problems and put down his conclusions in the *Jubilate*. Newton's philosophy, despite sporadic opposition, held the day, and it was in the *Jubilate* that some of his principles were first examined in a purely non-scientific work. Earlier, in the Seatonian poem *On the Omniscience of the Supreme Being*, published in 1752, Smart had held the emigrating nightingale up as an example of the instinctive knowledge of direction with which God had endowed his creatures, for she "instant knows/ What Newton, or not sought, or sought in vain." And although man cannot hope to gain knowledge reserved for Divinity, Newton attained to the highest degree of that knowledge accessible to man.

> Illustrious name, irrefragable proof
> Of man's vast genius, and soaring Soul!

In much of what he wrote about science in his *Jubilate* Smart was in accord with Newton and his popularizing disciples; in important ways he clashed with them. What Smart felt about the man Newton is fairly plain from the two lines in which he names him. In the first of these, "Let Conduit, house of Conduit rejoice with Graecula a kind of Rose. God be gracious to the immortal Soul of Sr Isaac Newton" (D, 170), he is led to Newton by the name of John Conduit, husband to the philosopher's niece. In the second, he identifies himself with Newton in a context that is plainly approbratory, "For CHASTITY is the key of knowledge in Esdras, Sr Isaac Newton and now, God be praised, in me," following immediately with a qualifying line which casts doubt on Newton's philosophy but in no way derogates from his worth as a man, "For Newton nevertheless is more of error than of the truth, but I am of the WORD of GOD" (B1, 194—95). And "Newton is ignorant for if a man consult not the WORD how should he understand the WORK?" (B1, 220) continues the charge that Newton's fundamental error was not one of inaccurate observation of phenomena but of the interpretation consequent upon that observation. At one point Smart declares that "Newton's notion of colours is ᾽αλογος unphilosophical," contrary to reason, unaccountable, groundless, and after declaring that the "colours are spiritual" develops a spectrum of his own that begins with white and progresses to pale, which "works about to White again" (B2, 651—63). Smart had in mind the passage in the *Optics* which reads, "And if at any time I speak of light and rays as coloured or endued with colours, I would be understood to speak not philosophically and properly but grosly, and according to such conceptions as vulgar people in seeing all these experiments would be apt to frame. For the rays to speak properly are not coloured. In them there is nothing else than a certain power and disposition to stir up a sensation of this or that colour."[37] Bishop Berkeley had attacked Newton's "notion of colours," and, while it is possible that Smart, who also shared with Berkeley the same belief about the phenomenon of the horizontal moon, "she appears bigger in the horizon because she actually is so" (B2, 426), may have known the latter's work directly, he also could have derived his knowledge from more than one secondary source.[38] Thus, the arguments Berkeley advanced in his explanation of the phenomenon of the horizontal moon are part of an appendix to Robert Smith's *Opticks*[39] and the Bishop's *Essay on Vision* is cited in a footnote in Smith's chapter "Concerning our

Ideas Acquired by Sight." Some of Smart's other anti-Newtonianism was probably learned from the pages of Robert Green's *Principles of Natural Philosophy* where, as in Smart after him, the possibility of squaring the circle is discussed and where, on the subject of colors, one could read that "no one ever imagin'd them to reside anywhere but in ourselves."[40] Both Smith and Green had been Cambridge professors; their books were among those in use at the University around 1730. Smart's spiritual philosophizing was not, therefore, spun entirely from the web of his unaided imagination, and even though his final statement of one or another scientific principle may seem bizarre he knew whereof he wrote.

With all its wealth of biographical material on Smart's life, the spiritual as well as the everyday, *Jubilate Agno* is even more valuable as a continually unfolding picture of a poet finally approaching the realization of his full powers. Virtually everything that was to mark his greatest poetry, the *Song to David*, the Psalms, and the *Hymns and Spiritual Songs*—the verse translation of Horace to a much lesser extent—is present in the *Jubilate*. The great religious themes are prominent; the whole poem is, of course, one long hymn of praise, based in part on the Benedicite of the liturgy and in part on portions of the Bible. Charity, invested with human attributes, is named in two lines, "For I pray to give his grace to the poor of England, that Charity be not offended & that benevolence may increase" (B1, 29) and, more graphically, "For Charity is cold in the multitude of possessions, & the rich are covetous of their crumbs" (B1, 154), a possible echo, in its latter half, of the story of Lazarus the beggar.[41] But it is gratitude, the major note in Smart's song of praise, that sounds through most strongly. The hold it had on his mind is seen in two lines, the first of which is the strongest expression of this theme in all his poetry. "For the sin against the HOLY GHOST is INGRATITUDE" (B2, 306); whatever William Cowper and others conceived the unforgivable sin to be, Smart was in no doubt; it was ingratitude. "For the angel GRATITUDE is my wife—God bring me to her or her to me" (B2, 324), he writes a little later, possibly with Anna Maria in mind, but even more probably in the hope that some grateful person would bring about his release. In yet another line, the meaning of which is far from clear, he has Timon rejoice with the Crusion and then adds, "The Shew-Bread in the first place is gratitude to God to shew who is bread, whence it is, and that there is enough and to spare" (B2, 207). And finally, he also writes "For there is no invention but the gift of God, and no grace like the grace of gratitude" (B1, 82). Gratitude, praise, and charity: these were the themes he wove into the *Jubilate*, sometimes boldly and plainly and at other times more faintly but never really abandoning them for long.

Smart was not praising his God in verse solely in *Jubilate Agno* in the years in the madhouse. For a man who had turned out literary and subliterary work for about five or six years with the speed he had, despite all the welcome and unwelcome interruptions to literary activity, the three pairs of lines he ritually wrote daily in that poem were far from enough to keep him busy. He had a garden to dig in and a cat to keep him company, but he needed intellectual activity, and he turned to books and the writing of other poetry to keep his mind from turning in upon itself. A number of verbal and phrasal similarities between *Jubilate Agno*, concentrated in sections A, B1, and B2, written from about the beginning of his confinement to August 26, 1760, and the *Song to David*, the Psalms, and the *Hymns and Spiritual Songs* makes it highly probable that Smart was engaged upon those latter poems at the same time that he was writing the former. Further, similarities in the *Song to David*, the Psalms, and the *Hymns and Spiritual Songs* suggest that they were being written either concurrently or very near in time to one another, and in the light of the number of separate poems in the Psalms and *Hymns and Spiritual Songs* the former assumption is more likely. While it is always possible that the similarities are merely coincidental, their numbers and the closeness of the parallels are so great that the theory of concurrent composition is more attractive than that of a kind of haphazard echoing of former work. Absence of such similarities between the poetry up to *Jubilate Agno* and the great religious poems after *Jubilate Agno* also reinforces an already extremely plausible theory. Smart's earliest modern biographer long ago pointed out what he termed coincidences of expression between the *Song* and the Psalms, finding the following common to them: clust'ring spheres, his talent and his term, the man of God's own choice, trumpet and alarm, multitudes in mail, good in grain, the briny broad, the cherub and his mate, the lion and the bear, and bastion's mole.[42] Even more numerous are the parallels between *Jubilate Agno* and the *Song* and between *Jubilate Agno* and the Psalms. Parallels between *Jubilate Agno* and the *Hymns and Spiritual Songs*, some of which extend to the *Song*, when added to the number shared by the *Song* and the Psalms and *Hymns and Spiritual Songs* taken together, or by the *Song* and one of the latter two taken by itself, swell the total impressively. And some slight further evidence is had in the parallels between the Psalms and the *Hymns and Spiritual Songs* which were printed together in 1765.[43]

A Song to David appeared on April 8, 1763, approximately nine weeks after Smart left the madhouse. No one believes he wrote that long and highly intricate masterpiece in those nine weeks. At the same time, on the last page of the *Song*, he solicited subscribers for the Psalms and the *Hymns and Spiritual Songs*, stating that copy was already in the hands of the printer. The Psalms were not published until 1765 but specimens appeared more than once in the interval. In *Jubilate Agno* itself a cluster of references allude to his hymns twice, to his version of the Psalms four times, and to his subscribers once.[44] Smart is not here building castles in the sky, referring to yet unwritten works which he plans to turn to when he gets out; he is speaking of work either completed or very near completion. With the exception of a very few lyrics and a number of translations in his poetic version of Horace's works Smart later wrote nothing that so much as approached the beauty of the *Song*, the Psalms, and the *Hymns and Spiritual Songs*. Only toward the very end of the seven and a half years that he lived after his release did he manage to catch again something of the simplicity and sincerity and feeling of those poems in the *Hymns For the Amusement of Children*, they, too, written under great pressures. Besides the parallels that exist between *Jubilate Agno* and the great religious poetry published between 1763 and 1765 there are other points of similarity. Smart's use of old words—amerce, earn (yearn), bean (bene=bless), to brisk, lowth, existimation—in *Jubilate Agno*, while not without occasional parallel in the earlier poetry, becomes quite pronounced in 1763 and after. A coinage, "innatation"; a nonce-verb, "to camel," used of his cat Jeoffrey; and a few other striking usages—"distribute" as adjective, "prank" as an object, and "redoubted"—also anticipate a distinctive feature of the later poetry. Alliterative doublets, sporadic in appearance in his poetry up to 1756, become more frequent and look ahead to the heavy use that distinguishes the poetry of the last period.* Some alliterative

*Magnifical and mighty, pleasantry and purity, malignity or mischief, magnitude and melody, prudence or providence, pleasant and pure, neither a swordsman nor smith, beef and breeches, a stick or a straw, witches and wizards, duly and daily, and mirth and musick.

157

patterns, although not pronounced enough to be called a device, tend to resemble variations on the alliterative doublet.† And in some of these alliterative combinations Smart seems to go out of his way for one or the other of the parts, suggesting that the practice was a deliberate one. Occasionally, too, he will link one part of a line with another by using different alliterative groups. Thus, he writes "Let Meshullam bless with the Dragon, who maketh his den in desolation and rejoiceth among the ruins" (A, 86), taking the first group from Jeremiah ix.11. Or, in another place, he will speak of the Fieldfare as "a good gift from God in the season of scarcity" (B1, 57), in this fashion making poetry out of the fact that this particular thrush remains in England in the winter and is also good to eat.

Jubilate Agno, its lines very often deriving now from the Bible, now from an ornithological work, or still another time from a scientific textbook is a highly articulated and methodical poem. Besides its "sources" and the clearly visible use of certain poetic devices, its structure, part of which comes from the liturgy and part from the practice of the poets of the Old Testament, is not something left to chance. Some part of the structure consists of horizontal and, less frequently, vertical associations and also, of course, of associations between two parts of the same line. Some part of it also comes from the conscious effort to link lines vertically by using parallel constructions and approximately the same number of syllables:

> For the tides are the life of God in the ocean, and he
> sends his angel to trouble the great DEEP.
> For he hath fixed the earth upon arches & pillars, and
> the flames of hell flow under it.
> For the grosser the particles, the nearer to the sink, &
> the nearer to purity, the quicker the gravitation. (B1, 157–9)

And this group is preceeded by two lines that also form a small division:

> For I pray to be accepted as a dog without offence, which
> is best of all.
> For I wish to God and desire towards the most High, which
> is my policy.

---

†The result is phrases like temporal thrift, cloud of the crucifixion, parry by prayer, chastity is the Cherub, magnanimity of meekness, mead of the musician, and had not malice been multitudinous.

These last two lines have nineteen syllables each; their corresponding Let lines contain, respectively, twenty-three and twenty-six syllables, with the break coming about at the middle of each. Much of this deliberate balancing of the lengths of lines and of parts of lines is attributable to the influence of Robert Lowth's published lectures on the sacred poetry of the Hebrews, and from that work Smart would also have derived something of his practice of parallel constructions.[45]

With such antecedents as guides, with a sizable collection of books at his disposal, and employing various poetic devices Smart wrote his *Jubilate Agno*. Before confinement in Potter's madhouse he had in various poems given promise of an ability to paint a picture in a few lines—the description of the ring-dove's nest in the poem *On the Immensity of the Supreme Being* was much admired as were some of the passages in the *Morning Piece* and *Noon-Piece* —but even in the earliest part of the *Jubilate* he was already developing this ability to an extent and in a way that he could not have done in the hectic years before 1759. Now he no longer needed a few lines; a few words were enough for the sketch, and the creature whose likeness he was striving for was captured in his quintessential being. The porcupine is "the creature of defence and stands upon his arms continually"; the weasel "sneaks for his prey in craft, and dwelleth at ambush"; and the elk is "the strenuous asserter of his liberty, and the maintainer of his ground."[46] Sometimes only a word or two was needed to evoke a quick impressionistic picture. In successive lines he wrote of three fish, the grampus, "who is a pompous spouter"; the shark, "who is supported by multitudes of small value"; and the goldfish, "who is an eye-trap."[47] His ability in extended portraiture can be seen in the seventy-four lines which he lavishes upon Jeoffrey his cat, catching him in every conceivable act and movement of the feline repertory (B2, 697–770). On infrequent occasion he combines a physical and spiritual picture, trying to suggest at one and the same time outward appearance and what appears to him as inward reality: "For the warp & woof of flowers are worked by perpetual moving spirits" (B2, 501) or "For LIGHTNING is a glance of the glory of God" (B1, 272), where part of the effect is auditory, owing to the alliteration, and part visual. Sometimes the effect achieved by an isolated line, "For the nets come down from the eyes of the Lord to fish up men to their salvation" (B1, 131), defies description.

Poetical fragments, lines, and passages of great beauty abound in *Jubilate Agno*. Smart writes, "For there is no rain in Paradise because of the delicate construction of the spiritual herbs and flowers" (B2, 376), giving a glimpse of the heavenly terrain he had more than once envisaged. His eye for terrestrial flora and fauna, everywhere pervasive, may be exemplified by his description of the dragonfly, "who sails over the pond by the wood-side and feedeth on the cressies" (A, 100). Coming to David's name early in his catalogue of Biblical figures he is moved to dwell longer upon him than upon any other figure before or after, remembering him in his capacity as musician, "Hallelujah from the heart of God, and from the hand of the artist inimitable, and from the echo of the heavenly harp in sweetness magnifical and mighty" (A, 41). And in a number of lines concerned with musical instruments, after having spoken of harpsichords, harps and viols, the German flute, the common flute, and the trumpet, he suddenly returns to a consideration of the harp and writes four lines that have few counterparts in English poetry.

> For GOD the father Almighty plays upon the HARP of
> stupendous magnitude and melody.
> For innumerable Angels fly out at every touch and his
> tune is a work of creation.
> For at that time malignity ceases and the devils themselves
> are at peace.
> For this time is perceptible to man by a remarkable
> stillness and serenity of soul. (B1, 246—9)

Written in the early days of October, 1759, these lines bear comparison with anything in *A Song to David*, published four years later but almost surely being written at this time. The *Song* is no freak; rather it is a natural and predictable outgrowth of *Jubilate Agno*. At least once the description of a creature in the latter is better poetry than in the former, for when Smart wrote of the "Sword-Fish, whose aim is perpetual & strength insuperable" (B1, 129) he was unable to improve upon that sketch in the more finished lines of the *Song*, "Strong through the turbulent profound/Shoots xiphias to his aim." Sometimes a line has an evocative power that is independent of the meaning, which may be uncertain or entirely elusive. Possibly some still uninvestigated area of proverbial literature will yield the meaning of "For in my nature I quested for beauty, but God, God hath sent me to sea for pearls" (B1, 30); in the meantime none of the magic of the line is lost.

JUBILATE AGNO, 1759-1763

Fascinated as he was with the mystery of language and the real or fancied relationships that he saw between various languages, Smart used *Jubilate Agno* as a document in which he could both experiment with and explain his theories. At its most obvious this preoccupation with the possibilities of language gave rise to three exercises on the alphabet in which arbitrary meanings or identities were given to each letter. The first such exercise begins

> For A is the beginning of learning and the door of heaven.
> For B is a creature busy and bustling.
> For C is a sense quick and penetrating.
> For D is depth.
> For E is eternity—such is the power of the English letters
> taken singly.
> For F is faith. (B2, 513–18)

The alphabet, minus J and V, is run through; a line, "For in the education of children it is necessary to watch the words, which they pronounce with difficulty, for such are against them in their consequences," is added; and then a second exercise is embarked upon,

> For A is awe, if pronounced full. Stand in awe and sin not.
> For B pronounced in the animal is bey importing authority.
> For C pronounced hard is ke importing to shut. (B2, 538–40)

and again, with the same exceptions, through Z. Once more, at the beginning of section C, Smart does the same thing; this time each letter is given an identity and is proclaimed, therefore, to be God.[48] Sounds meant much to him and he associated certain words with particular musical instruments, ending a series of ten lines devoted to such associations with "for beat heat, weep peep &c are of the pipe" (B2, 596) and then continuing,

> For every word has its marrow in the English tongue for
> order and for delight.
> For the dissyllables such as able table &c are the fiddle
> rhimes.
> For all dissyllables and some trissbyllables are fiddle
> rhimes.
> For the relations of words are in pairs first.
> For the relations of words are sometimes in oppositions.
> For the relations of words are according to their distances
> from the pair.

Meanings of words, the actual meanings and those meanings which could be wrenched from the composition of certain words, afforded him opportunity for a number of atrocious puns. "For the Mouse (Mus) prevails in the Latin" (B2, 638), he writes in exemplification of his theory that "the power of some animal is predominant in every language" (B2, 627), and then explains, "For Edi-mus, bibi-mus, vivi-mus—ore-mus" (B2, 639). Equally outrageous is, "for two creatures the Bull & the Dog prevail in the English. For all the words ending in ble are in the creature. Invisi-ble, Incomprehensi-ble, ineffa-ble, A-ble" (B2, 645—6). He took advantage of this last, however, to list some of the attributes of God. And he could make a word mean its very contrary, for when he writes that "Adversity above all other is to be deserted of the grace of God" (B2, 328) he catches himself up a few days later and writes that "being desert-ed is to have desert in the sight of God and intitles one to the Lord's merit" (B2, 333). Smart's fondness for alliteration, for coining new words and reviving old ones, and for using words in unusual senses are all part of his fascination with the latent potentialities of language.

Everywhere in *Jubilate Agno* there are rich rewards for the student of Smart's life and poetry. His state of health while in confinement is seen in a number of ejaculations from "God bless my throat" (B1, 179), written on September 22, 1759, through a series, "Catarrhs and Spitting blood from which Christ Jesus deliver me," "good for old coughs and asthmas," "Lord have mercy on my breast," and "The Lord Jesus strengthen my whole body" (C, 68—71), written in March, 1761. He was always conscious of his small stature and he wrote "For I am a little fellow, which is entitled to the great mess by the benevolence of God my father" (B1, 45), in other lines giving his sympathy to the pygmies in their warfare against their enemies (B1, 148, and B2, 378). His awareness of his condition is most plainly stated in a line which derives partly from the Gospel according to St. Mark iii:21, "For I am under the same accusation with my Saviour—for they said, he is besides himself" (B1, 151). His fondness for animals, unforgettably expressed in the lines on his cat Jeoffrey, extends even to the wolf, "which is a dog without a master, but the Lord hears his cries and feeds him in the desert" (A, 76). And he prays to God to "be merciful to all dumb creatures in respect to pain" (B1, 183). At another time he is prompted by something he has just written, "Let Horton, house of Horton rejoice with Birdlime," to add "Blessed be the name of the Lord Jesus against the destruction of Small Birds" (D, 195). In the *Song to David* this feeling for his fellow creatures comes out strongly in the forty-second stanza,

> Open, and naked of offence,
> Man's made of mercy, soul, and sense;
>   God arm'd the snail and wilk;
> Be good to him that pulls thy plough;
> Due food and care, due rest, allow
>   For her that yields thee milk.

and in his last work there is a hymn on "Good-Nature to Animals." *Jubilate Agno* looks back on work done as well as forward to work yet to be published. Closest verbally to something written before confinement is the line "Let Hillel rejoice with Ammodytes [a sand-burrowing snake], whose colour is deceitful and he plots against the pilgrim's feet" (B1, 24) which echoes lines in the poem Smart wrote on the return of the King to England in 1748, "Nor Stratagem, the subtlest snake of war, / Plots to entangle ev'ry Pilgrim's feet."

Jubilate Agno is a product of some four years spent in a mad-house. While it was being written Smart was at work on those poems which transcend in beauty and order anything he had published earlier; only his contemporaries found madness and aberration of genius in the *Song to David* and the other religious poetry; their sanity is now unquestioned. The *Jubilate* has much in common with the poetry published in 1763 and after, and where it seems to deviate into nonsense or madness it seems to do so only because some fact known to Smart himself or to most of his contemporaries is now obscured by the passage of two hundred years and the occurrence of several revolutions in taste and education. Smart and his contemporaries were nourished on and read books which are either virtually unknown or entirely forgotten today. A small detail of history, such as the knowledge that Titus Oates was once a chaplain in one of Cromwell's regiments, may help to explain why a reference to Oliver Cromwell in the latter half of one line (B1, 274) leads Smart to the name Titus in the first part of the following line, even though in doing so he skips a name in the book of the Bible which might be expected to appear where Titus intrudes. And the line "Let Agur bless with the Cockatrice—The consolation of the world is deceitful, and temporal honour the crown of him that creepeth" (A, 73) yields a rich harvest when one knows that the cockatrice (Topsell is one authority) is called Bazilicos in Greek and Regulus in Latin, the king of serpents, and has a crown on its head. Almost surely there is no line or a pair of lines that does not have its logical explanation which was known to Smart but is temporarily baffling to us.

And thus it was, day by day, line by line, that Smart marked the passing of another fraction of the time he was condemned to spend in the madhouse. Other men would have found different outlets or would have entirely succumbed to despair; he had his God and his poetry.

V.

LONDON, 1763-1765

London was undergoing a severe cold spell in December, 1762, and January, 1763; the Thames was frozen and the wherrymen were unable to work. John Wilkes' name was on everyone's lips. The Cock Lane ghost was still very much a topic of conversation, and one James Rice, a broker, intruded himself on public attention by forging a letter of attorney for thirty thousand pounds in stock. On the first of January William Whitehead, Poet Laureate, produced his usual New Year's Ode; on the thirteenth Sir George Pocock arrived at Plymouth aboard the Namur after a hazardous trip from Havannah from where the fleet had sailed on the third of November; on the seventeenth eight criminals received sentence of death at the end of the sessions at the Old Bailey; and on the eighteenth the Queen's birthday was celebrated with its usual splendor. On the twenty-first, sixty-four gentlemen became Bachelors of Art at Cambridge, and on the same day the *Daily Advertiser* reported that "a young fellow was detected in a criminal Action in a Cell in Bethlem Hospital, with one of the poor Lunaticks." On the thirty-first, sermons were preached on the anniversary of the martyrdom of King Charles the First before both the House of Lords and the House of Commons. And also on the thirty-first Christopher Smart was released from a 'four-year confinement—although he may have enjoyed temporary intervals of freedom—in Potter's madhouse. In one of the last lines of *Jubilate Agno* he had asked "God be gracious to

John Sherrat"; the line was written on the twenty-eighth of January. *An Epistle to John Sherratt, Esq.* is one of four poems in a little volume published by the end of July, 1763. Smart appended a two-line epigraph from Ovid's *Tristia*, part of a poem to a faithful friend, to the effect that "These things shall ever remain fixed in my inmost heart and I will be an everlasting debtor for this life and mine." The second stanza of the poem contains the autobiographical references:

> Well nigh sev'n years had fill'd their tale,
> From Winter's urn to Autumn's scale,
> And found no friend to grief and *Smart*,
> Like Thee and Her, thy sweeter part;
> Assisted by a friendly pair
> That chose the side of CHRIST and PRAY'R,
> To build the great foundation laid,
> By one sublime, transcendent maid.
> 'Tis well to signalize a deed,
> And have no precedent to plead;
> 'Tis blessing as by God we're told,
> To come and visit friends in hold;
> Which skill is greater in degree,
> If goodness set the pris'ner free.
> 'Tis you that have in my behalf,
> Produc'd the robe and kill'd the calf;
> Have hail'd the *restoration day*,
> And bid the loudest music play.
> If therefore there is yet a note
> Upon the lyre, that I devote,
> To gratitude's divinest strains,
> One gift of love for thee remains;
> One gift above the common cast,
> Of making fair memorials last.

Smart puts the period of his "grief," not necessarily synonymous with confinement, at almost seven years; he thanks Sherratt and his wife and the Rolts, the "friendly pair," so identified in Smart's footnote; and he identifies as "Miss A.F.S.—. Of Queen's—Square," in another footnote, the "one sublime, transcendent maid" who had started the move to have him released. John Sherratt was a small businessman, not particularly wealthy, who was given to charity.*

* As one of the proprietors of an Antigallican privateer he petitioned on June 24, 1763, for a bounty or pension for the losses he suffered, and when his will was proved on October 4, 1766, he was found to have left two messuages or

How he joined the Rolts and Miss Sheels of Queen's Square in their eventually successful efforts to get Smart out of the madhouse is not known. Miss Sheels was a good friend of the Burneys who had been living in Poland Street since their return to London in 1760.[1] James Sheels, brother of Smart's benefactress, died on October 29, 1762, aged 24; he was the subject of Smart's poem, *Epitaph on the late Mr. Sheels, Written at the Request of his Father,* first printed in Dr. William Dodd's *Christian Magazine* in January, 1763, and then again in Smart's *Poems on Several Occasions* in 1764. Sheels had served as clergyman for no longer than fifteen months when he died, and Smart, in the last two lines of his poem, offered consolation to his parents and sister: "Let God's good-will, at our expence be done./As *Christ* demands a brother and a son." Since the poem is signed with Smart's full name, some people, it is obvious, did not think him mad in late 1762 and early 1763. Dr. William Dodd, a friend of Johnson's, was editing the *Christian's Magazine* for Newbery; he printed Smart's *The 100th Psalm, for a Scotch Tune* in the January to June, 1761 supplement of his periodical, an *Epitaph on a Young Clergyman* in August, 1761, and reprinted the *Epitaph on the Death of Master Newbery* in March, 1762, as "From the 'Art of Poetry, on a new plan,' just published," another of Newbery's publications. Dodd had been admitted to Clare College, Cambridge, as a sizar on October 2, 1745, and was at Cambridge during the next four years while Smart was still there. He, too, was a Freemason, and he and Smart could have become acquainted either at Cambridge or in London where Dodd was ordained a priest on June 17, 1753. Other of Smart's friends were writing for Dodd's magazine; the mainstays of the poetry columns for the first volume were Francis Fawkes and William Woty, and there was a Latin poem by Robert Lowth in the very first number. They too may have had something to do with the publication of Smart's poetry in the *Christian's Magazine*. Other friends, principally Bonnell Thornton, were instrumental in getting Smart's *Epitaph on Henry Fielding* printed in the *St. James's Magazine*, edited by Robert Lloyd and to which both Thornton and Charles Churchill were contributing. Smart had already invoked God's blessings upon Churchill and Lloyd in *Jubilate Agno* (D, 62). The Fielding epitaph appeared in the

---

tenements in Shoreditch to his wife, ten pounds to his daughter, and two guineas to a charity school. T29/35/p. 110 in Public Records Office and 9/Tyndal/923/fol. 355 in Somerset House.

second volume of the magazine (March through August, 1763); the third volume (September, 1763, through February, 1764) reprinted five of Smart's pieces from the *Universal Visiter*. Again, if Smart did not get paid for any of these pieces, he welcomed their appearance or reappearance.

Shortly before his release Smart had had the satisfaction of seeing published *Mrs. Midnight's Orations; and other Select Pieces: as they were spoken at the Oratory in the Hay-Market, London.* Though they were "Printed for the EDITOR" and he is nowhere named, the work is Smart's and represents another less than arduous plan to make money. All he did was to collect orations and poems that had been used in the Old Woman's Oratory and add a dedication to the right Honourable Lady Caroline Seymour.[2] To the end he appended *The Gifts: A Dramatic Interlude.* "As it was intended to be presented at the Theatre in the Hay-Market, London. Set to Music by Mr. Joseph Gaudry." Mr. Gaudry had appeared with Mrs. Midnight in a benefit performance of Mrs. Midnight's Concert and Oratory on March 6, 1760, and for that occasion had sung a new cantata of his own composition.[3] *Mrs. Midnight's Orations* is an interesting volume because it gives the only text of some pieces performed at the Oratory; even more important is the light it throws on Smart's whereabouts and activities.[4] In addition, in his dedication, conceived as a New Year's gift to Lady Caroline, he speaks of "the MUSES, (to whom, & their Hawkers, I have been a faithful Drudge for these five and twenty Years)"; since this was written, or at least published, in January, 1763, Smart was putting the beginnings of his poetry at about 1738, when he had already been for four or five years at Durham Grammar School. Of further interest is the announcement on the verso of the title page, "At the Desire of many of the Encouragers of this Work the Subscribers Names are omitted," a statement which points to a subscription list that was being made up while Smart was still in the madhouse and, except for the fact of possible embarrassment in promoting the work of a madman, affords no other clue to the reasons which prompted the encouragers of the work to print it without the names of the subscribers.

Smart had returned to the region about St. James's Park, Westminster, where he had lived as a bachelor; this time he took rooms with a Mrs. Barwell whose house was located in Park Street. Hawkesworth visited him in 1764 and wrote that he was "with very decent people, in a house most delightfully situated with a terras that overlooks St. James's Park, and a door into it."[5] Here, in pleasant surroundings in a fine residential section of the city, Smart put the last touches to *A Song to David*. It was published on April 6, and was printed "for the Author; and sold by Mr. Fletcher, at the Oxford Theatre, in St. Paul's Church-yard; and by all Booksellers in Town and Country." For reasons best known to himself Smart had asked James Fletcher, presumably the younger, not previously connected with any of his work, to act as principal bookseller for the five hundred copies of the poem he had had printed. Crowded at the foot of the last page of the poem was the announcement that on the same day proposals for a new translation of the Psalms of David were published. The work, to be printed by subscription, was to be accompanied by a "Set of Hymns for the Fasts and Festivals of the Church of England"; specimens of the work could be had from a number of booksellers, in two coffee-houses, and from the printer, C. Say, "who has Copy in his Possession." Smart had not been idle in the years from 1759 through 1762; although the *Psalms* were delayed, they were in an advanced state of readiness.

A Song to David bears as epigraph on its title page the first two verses from II Samuel 23, "DAVID the Son of JESSE said, and the MAN who was RAISED UPON HIGH, the ANOINTED OF THE GOD OF JACOB, and the SWEET PSALMIST OF ISRAEL, said, The SPIRIT OF THE LORD spake by ME, and HIS WORD was in my Tongue." Smart chose the twenty-third chapter of the second book of Samuel principally because of his belief that the spirit of the Lord spoke by and through him, Smart himself, as well as through David, but he was conscious too of the catalogue of David's mighty men to which most of the chapter is given over, for in *Jubilate Agno* and in poems published shortly after the *Song* he was to emphasize the heroic qualities of famous warriors.[6] As his first major poem in many years *A Song to David* was Smart's bid for renewed recognition; except for the reprinting of some of his poems and the composition and publication of a very few new ones, he had done nothing that would be remembered since his *Hymn* in 1756. His anticipation of the kind of critical notice his poem would receive was exceptionally keen.

First to review the *Song* was John Langhorne in the *Monthly Review* for April. Langhorne's tone throughout was one of genuine pity devoid of smug condescension. "From the sufferings of this ingenious Gentleman," he writes, "we could not but expect the performance before us to be greatly irregular; but we shall certainly characterise it more justly, if we call it irregularly great. There is a grandeur, a majesty of thought, not without a happiness of expression in the following stanzas." Thereupon he quotes stanzas ten, seventeen, eighteen, twenty-one, and forty and comments, "There is something remarkably great, and altogether original, in the last quoted stanza." But he then goes on to say that some passages are "almost, if not altogether, unintelligible," citing the seven pillars passages (stanzas 30–37) and providing an ingenious conjecture as to their interpretation. Some of Smart's allusions, he finds, "relate frequently to subjects too little known, and far fetched"; again, however, he does not dismiss them with this, but gives his own explanation of two such allusions. And in his last sentence he makes his one overt reference to Smart's confinement and begins the legend about the composition of the poem: "It would be cruel, however, to insist on the slight defects and singularities of this piece, for many reasons; and more especially, if it be true, as we are informed, that it was written when the Author was denied the use of pen, ink, and paper, and was obliged to indent his lines, with the end of a key, upon the wainscot." All in all, this was a temperate, generous, and intelligent review. Not so, however, was that in the *Critical Review*, where there was no real attempt to understand the poem. Two sentences sufficed there: "Without venturing to criticize on the propriety of a Protestant's offering up either hymns or prayers to the dead, we must be of the opinion, that great rapture and devotion is discernable in this ecstatic song. It is a fine piece of ruins, and must at once please and affect a sensible mind." The implications are clear; the poet was to be pitied and his effort was to be put down to a fit of ecstasy, no term of praise at that time. All this Smart, of course, read: what he could not know were the comments that were being written in letters and made in conversations. William Mason saw the *Song* and concluded that Smart was as mad as ever;[7] James Boswell sent the poem to Sir David Dalrymple, characterizing it as "a very curious composition, being a strange mixture of *dun obscure* and glowing genius at times." Boswell also sent Smart's *Poems* to Dalrymple, saying "His *Genius and Imagination* is very pretty. The other pieces have shivers of genius here and there, but are often ludicrously low. Poor man, he has been released from his confinement, but not from his unhappy disorder. However, he has it not in any great height. He is not a poet of the first rank."[8] Boswell was mouthing the prevailing opinions; the *Song* was a product of insanity; some of Smart's recent poems were "pretty;" others were "low," by which he meant not on acceptable poetic subjects couched in appropriately conventional poetic language.

Eighteenth-century literary critics, both the professionals and the amateurs, could usually cope with recondite allusions in the poetry they sat in judgment upon; occasionally they confessed failure, but then they laid the blame on the poet and damned his obscurity. Langhorne recognized the difficulties in the *Song*; he recognized too that Smart's allusions could be traced and identified if one knew the books to which he had gone. But only a few of Smart's contemporaries shared the erudition that spilled over into *Jubilate Agno* and the *Song*, as well as into others of his works. Thomas Gray, in some respects, was like Smart in the wide-ranging knowledge which found its way into some of his poetry to the bafflement of most of his readers. But where Gray, especially in some of his Odes, demanded knowledge of English history, Italian poetry, Elizabethan and later drama, and a number of other subjects on the part of his readers, most of Smart's allusions can be traced to herbals, bestiaries, and volumes on natural history. He himself thought it necessary to identify "Ivis" of stanza fifty-three of the *Song* as the hummingbird in a footnote, and it is well that he did, for his source for the name is still unknown. But the major crux in the poem is the passage listed in his contents as "Shews that the pillars of knowledge are the monuments of God's work in the first week." Here, he designates each day in the week of creation by a letter of the Greek alphabet in order as follows: Alpha, Gamma, Eta, Theta, Iota, Sigma, and Omega. Attempts to discover why these particular letters were chosen have led to conjectures about Freemasonic symbolism, Cabalistic thought (and a combination of the two), and to Smart's imperfect recollection of Greek and hence the garbled spelling of a word formed by the letters as they stand. But Smart's reason for assigning these letters in this order to the days of creation almost surely awaits someone's stumbling upon the right book. And yet, aside from the seven pillars and the references to natural history, and, of course, the constant Biblical echoes and allusions, the subject matter of the *Song* should not have proved overwhelmingly difficult for his contemporaries. Certainly a poem on David, King of Israel, from Smart's hands could have come as no surprise.

Smart had identified himself with David at least as early as the Seatonian prize poem *On the Immensity of the Supreme Being*, published in 1751, where, in the very opening lines, he wrote, "Once more I dare to rouse the sounding string,/*The poet of my God*," calling attention immediately by the italics to his assumed role. *On the Power of the Supreme Being* begins with a quotation from "the anointed poet." And it is he whom Smart invokes, under the name of Orpheus, "for so the Gentiles call'd thy name,/Israel's sweet psalmist," in the first two verses of the poem *On the Goodness of the Supreme Being*. His statement about Orpheus comes from the reading he did at Pembroke, for one of the books he withdrew from the library, Patrick Delany's *Historical Account of the Life and Reign of David*, contains the question "What if *Orpheus* in *Thrace* was no other than *David* in *Paran?*," followed by a long argument designed to prove the truth of this theory. Smart returned to Orpheus in *Jubilate Agno* where he wrote,

> For the story of Orpheus is of the truth.
> For there was such a person a cunning player on the harp.
> For he was a believer in the true God and assisted in the
>   spirit. (C, 52–4)

Here, Orpheus' belief "in the true God" links him with David, who appears in *Jubilate Agno*, under his own name, as an ancestor of Smart's in two ways:

> For the ENGLISH are the seed of Abraham and work up
> to him by Joab, David, and Naphtali. . . . (B2, 431)

and

> For the WELCH are the children of Mephibosheth and
> Ziba with a mixture of David in the Jones's. (B2, 435)

As the son of an English father and a Welsh mother, albeit her name was not Jones, Smart could feel doubly close to David. And when Smart turned again to David in the *Jubilate* he did so with a kind of nostalgia for a golden age when men were "ten feet high in general" (C, 91) and each had "a glorious horn upon his forehead"

(C, 119). David was the hero of Smart's longings, a warrior, scholar-poet, and worshipper of God.

Not all men, however, looked upon David as an exemplar of all the virtues. Pierre Bayle in his *General Dictionary*, another book Smart had borrowed from Pembroke library, had had doubts about David; not about his greatness, but about his virtuousness. His account of him begins, "David, King of the Jews, was one of the greatest men in the World, though we should not consider him as a Royal Prophet, who was a man after God's own heart."[9] The title page of Patrick Delany's account of David even promised a consideration of "Mr. Bayle's Criticisms, upon the *Conduct* and *Character* of that Prince." Bayle had gone to I Samuel 13:14, for the words "a man after his [God's] own heart," and years later when Samuel Chandler preached a sermon on the death of George II on October 25, 1760, he had it published under the title *The character of a great and good King full of Days, Riches, and Honour* comparing the dead monarch to David, both in the title, from I Chronicles 29: 28, and throughout his text. Chandler's fulsome sermon provoked an anonymous reply with the title *The Life of David, or the History of the Man after God's own Heart*, published in February, 1761, and variously ascribed to Peter Annet, John Noorthouck, and Archibald Campbell. David fares very poorly indeed in this work, many of whose arguments are a sarcastic elaboration of those introduced decades earlier by Pierre Bayle. Toward the end of his work the anonymous writer takes a "retrospective view" of his narrative, summing up David's career in a "few words":

> A shepherd youth is chosen by a disgusted prophet to be the instrument of his revenge on an untractable king. To this end he is inspired with ambitious hopes, by private inauguration; is introduced to court, in the capacity of a harper; and by knocking down a man with a stone, whom, if he had missed once, he had four more chances of hitting; and from whom, at the last, he could have easily run away; he was advanced to the dignity of son-in-law to the King. So sudden and unlooked-for a promotion, within sight of the throne, stimulated expections already awakened; and Saul soon perceived reasons to repent his alliance with him. Being obliged to retire from court, he assembled a gang of ruffians, the acknowledged outcasts of their country, and became the ring-leader of a lawless company of banditti. In this capacity he seduces his brother-in-law Jonathan, from his allegiance and filial duty; and covenants with him, that if he obtained the kingdom, Jonathan should be the next person in authority under him. He obtains a settlement in the

dominions of a Philistine prince, where, instead of applying himself laudably to the arts of cultivation, he subsists by plundering and butchering the neighbouring nations. He offered his assistance to the Philistine armies, in the war against his own country, and father-in-law; and is much disgusted at their distrust of his sincerity. He however availed himself of the defeat and death of Saul, and made a push for the kingdom. Of this he gained only his own tribe of Judah: but strengthened by this usurpation, he contested the remainder with Saul's son, Ish-bosheth, whom he persecuted to the grave. Ish-bosheth being assassinated by two villains, with intention to pay their court to the usurper; he is now King of Israel. In which capacity he plundered and massacred all his neighbours round him at discretion. He defiled the wife of one of his officers, while her husband was absent in the army: and finding she was with child by him, he, to prevent a discovery, added murder to adultery; which being accomplished, he took the widow directly into his well-stocked seraglio. He then repaired to the army, where he treated the subjected enemies with the most wanton inhumanity. A rebellion is raised against him by his son Absalom; which he suppressed, and invited over the rebel-general, to whom he gave the supreme command of his army, to the prejudice of the victorious Joab. After this he cut off the remainder of Saul's family, in defiance to the solemn oath by which he engaged to spare that unhappy race: reserving only one cripple from whom he had no apprehensions: and who, being the son of Jonathan, gave him the opportunity of making a merit of his gratitude. When he lay on his death-bed, where all mankind resign their resentments and animosities, his latest breath was employed in dictating two posthumous murders to his son Solomon! and, as if one crime was more wanting to complete the black catalogue, he clothed all his actions with the most consummate hypocrisy; professing all along the greatest regard for every appearance of virtue and holiness.

Whereupon he exclaims, "This, Britons! is the king to whom your late excellent Monarch has been compared! What an impiety to the Majesty of Heaven! What an affront to the memory of an honest Prince!"

The Life of David did not go unanswered; Chandler, who never turned his back on a controversy, wrote a Review of the History of the Man after God's own Heart in 1762, exposing and correcting the falsehoods of his attacker. This, in turn, provoked a Letter to Dr. Samuel Chandler by the anonymous author; and Chandler's last word, to the extent of two volumes, A Critical History of the Life of David was published posthumously in 1766. Others took up the cudgels against David's denigrator. In April, 1761, "A Protestant Layman" wrote a rather dispassionate letter to the *Gentleman's Magazine* on the faults of the pamphlet and, among other considerations, claimed for David one virtue that appeared "very striking" to him, "his constant love to his country," which he went on to exemplify. Greater prominence was given to *The Life of David*, or, as it was commonly referred to, *The History of the Man after God's own Heart*, by a fifteen-page review in the *Monthly Review* for April in which much is quoted from it. One month earlier the *Critical Review* had given it a page and a half and dismissed it, after quoting a few passages, with the statement that "Such dangerous buffoonery needs no comment." On January 24, 1762, the Reverend William Cleaver preached a sermon at Oxford entitled *An Inquiry into the True Character of David King of Israel*, which was published at Oxford that same year, and John Newbery printed *Reflections on the Moral and Religious Character of David* by the Reverend John Francis in 1764. Both books defended David. Smart was in confinement, writing *Jubilate Agno*, when the controversy began; the portion of that document written between August, 1760, and March, 1761, has not survived, so that Smart's comment on the death of George II is unknown. That he would have commented is virtually certain; few events of major importance went unnoted in *Jubilate Agno*. Although the *Song to David* may have been finished in one form or another by the time of the King's death, when Smart left the madhouse in January, 1763, he doubtless knew of the attack on his hero and felt that his poem was another vindication of David's character. Perhaps it is no accident that the *Song* in its final form should launch immediately, after three stanzas of invocation, into "The excellence and lustre of David's character in twelve points of view, . . . proved from the history of his life," as the contents has it, and that the last line of stanza five should be read, "The man of God's own choice." Thus, there was a timeliness about the appearance of the *Song* that should have insured it a greater degree of success and attention than it gained.

Smart's identification with David is implicit in part of the breakdown of the "Contents" that he prefixed to the *Song*. There he describes the contents of verses, or stanzas, seventeen through twenty-six as "He consecrates his genius for consolation and edification.—The subjects he made choice of—the Supreme Being—angels;

men of renown; the works of nature in all dirctions, either particularly or collectively considered." He might have been listing some of the subjects of his own poetry, beginning with the Seatonian poems on the attributes of the Supreme Being and working his way through the other subjects upon which he had written poems himself. And in the very progress of cataloguing these subjects, as he goes on to do in the *Song*, he was once again reverting to a feature of his poetry that is remarkable both early and late in his development, the enumeration, usually in similar order, of God's creatures by families and according to rank. In fact, as he devotes one stanza to each of David's subjects, God, angels, man, the world, plants, fowl, "fishes," beasts, and gems, various sections of *Jubilate Agno* come to mind, for there more than anywhere else he allowed himself to expatiate on God's creatures, animate and inanimate. And *Jubilate Agno* anticipates in various of its lines the very words of these same stanzas of the *Song*.* In addition, when Smart describes stanzas fifty and fifty-one as containing the "transcendant virtue of praise and adoration" he might just as logically have been speaking of one of the major themes of his own poetry. While there was no fanfare announcing the publication of the *Song* Smart had put a very great deal of himself into that poem.

That Smart should have thought it necessary to list and describe the subjects of the *Song* stanza by stanza in his "Contents" attests to the care with which the poem is constructed, a fact which is borne out by the advertisement for the *Song* added to the 1763 *Poems on Several Occasions*. There Smart writes, "This Song is allowed by Mr. *Smart's* judicious Friends and Enemies to be the best Piece ever made public by him, its chief fault being the *exact* REGULARITY and METHOD with which it is conducted." Part of the exact regularity and method is seen in Smart's division of the poem into groups of three and seven stanzas or multiples thereof. He had already revealed the fascination that numbers held for him in *Jubilate Agno* where, after stating that "there is a mystery in numbers," he says that "every thing infinitely perfect is Three" and that "Seven is very good consisting of two compleat numbers" (C, 19, 22,

---

*The former's "CHERUBS & their MATES" leads to the *Song's* "the cherub and her mate"; "the Coney, who scoopeth the rock" to "Her cave the mining coney scoops"; "a Nosegay in the medow" to "the nosegay in the vale"; gums & balsams" to "Choice gums and precious balm"; "there be millions of them in the air" to "Michael with his millions"; and "the Mackerel, who cometh in a shoal" to "The shoals upon the surface leap."

and 31). Even within his groups of stanzas there are links or associations that further demonstrate the pains he took to make this long
poem a unified whole.[10] Most striking of these devices, and of
course the simplest and most effective at the same time, was repetition, especially of an adjective as the first word in two successive
stanzas followed by the use of the same word in its comparative
degree as the first word of the third stanza. Smart had experimented
with this many years before in the prologue to his play *A Trip to
Cambridge*, performed at Pembroke in 1747, in which one series of
lines reads,

> Swift to the soul the piercing image flies,
> Swifter than *Harriot's* wit or *Harriot's* eyes;
> Swifter than some romantic traveller's thought;
> Swifter than British fire when *William* fought.

One whole division of the *Song* is held together by the words "For
Adoration," first used in an introductory and transitional stanza,
the fifty-first, and then repeated in the next twenty-one stanzas;
each time the words descend one stanza, so that in stanza fifty-three
they appear in the second line and in stanza fifty-four in the third,
and so on. The effect is not one of a gratuitous display of ingenu-
ity but rather a striking exhibition of what Smart could achieve by
such a device.

Smart's knowledge of the Bible and particularly of those parts
that retell the story of David, I and II Samuel, extended even to
minute details. Stanza seventy-six of the *Song* and the first two lines
of stanza seventy-seven illustrate the way in which a few words
recalled from II Samuel became the inspiration for some magnificent poetry. In II Samuel, 1:23, Saul and his son Jonathan are
described as "lovely and pleasant in their lives, and in their death
they were not divided: they were swifter than eagles, they were
stronger than lions"; in II Samuel, 3:1, the house of David is compared to the house of Saul: "Now there was long war between the
house of Saul, and the house of David: but David waxed stronger
and stronger, and the house of Saul waxed weaker and weaker." Of
this Smart made

> Strong is the lion—like a coal
> His eyeball—like a bastion's mole
> His chest against the foes:

Strong, the gier-eagle on his sail,
Strong, against tide, th' enormous whale
Emerges as he goes.

But stronger still, in earth and air,
And in the sea, the man of pray'r.

Whatever else went into the making of these lines, recollection of the Saul and Jonathan and eagle and lion association with the consequent description of David as stronger than the house of Saul contributed a major part. Almost no stanza is wholly independent of some Biblical influence; sometimes this takes the form of clear echoes, more often the stanzas of the *Song* bear within them only shadowy resemblances of their source.[11]

Much of what causes the *Song* to stand out from the other poems of the period, both the religious and the non-religious, arises from a few mannerisms which had made their appearance in the Seatonian prize poems and were to reappear in the *Psalms* and *Hymns and Spiritual Songs* in 1765. Smart used the alliterative doublet too often for it to be anything but a deliberate part of his poetic style.* Further adding to the over-all effect of the poem is a number of triplets; "All period, pow'r, and enterprize/Commences, reigns, and ends" is an example of two triplets, one following the other, which parallel and balance one another, each member of the first triplet corresponding respectively to its fellow in the second. Smart had used this pattern in his *Hymn* in 1756 where "deeds, thoughts, and words" are followed by "work, conceive, and speak."† At one point Smart combines an elaborate alliterative doublet with a triplet: "Whence bold attempt, and brave advance,/ Have motion, life, and ordinance." Such excessive use of triplets leads to the suspicion that Smart, planning divisions of his poem in blocks of three stanzas or multiples thereof, quite artfully introduced the device and had the "perfect" nature of the number three in view both for the groups of stanzas themselves and for elements within stanzas. Alliteration

---

*The *Song* contains, and in some of the following examples shares with other poems by Smart, the pairs, hail and hear, bless and bear, pray'r and praise, ministry and mead, sense and soul, foul and fond, great and glad, last and least, meat and med'cine, the peril and the prize, the fasting and the fear, and his talent and his term.

†Simple triplets include travel, spade, and loom; number, sign, and scheme; foot, and chapitre, and niche—in successive stanzas—above, beneath, around; meekness, peace, and pray'r; mercy, soul, and sense—also in successive stanzas—man, beast, mute; man, soul, and angel; great, beautiful, and new; hell, and horror, and despair; and finally in the very last line, DETERMINED, DARED, and DONE.

also plays a major role in the effects Smart strove for. Hunter remarks of an earlier poem, the ode on Harriot Pratt's birthday, that
"its chief blemish is the too frequent and affected use of alliteration"
(p. xxxiii).* Awareness of Smart's widespread use of this device
reveals the dependence he put upon it. A few epithets, "never-
wasting" bloom and "heart-directed" vows; some uncommon words,
meed, grutch, respire, laud (as noun); and a few uses of another
device of poetic diction, "briny broad" for the ocean and "fleece"
for sheep, also contribute to the character of the poem, if not always
necessarily to its excellence. Occasionally the syntax is so inverted
and the telescoping of phrase and thought so extreme that the
meaning still continues to be elusive.[12]

Despite the amount of praise that has been lavished upon the
Song, and most of it is merited, the poem is palpably uneven. Some
of the less meritorious passages may suffer from an excess of the
devices Smart employed, but the best passages transcend the use of
those same devices—or they are used so skillfully that they do not
intrude upon the reader. While the Song contains the best of his
poetry it must yield precedence, so far as sustained excellence is
concerned, to one or two of the Hymns and Spiritual Songs where,
because of their limited scope, Smart was able to write a better,
unified poem. But nothing in any of the rest of his poetry comes up
to the best passages in the Song, and here one forgets alliteration,
doublets and triplets, and everything else except the pictorial quality of the verses. Smart had displayed this quality to good advantage
in the 1752 Poems on Several Occasions and in the Jubilate Agno: in
the Song he carried it to a height that he never reached again. Some
of this quality is seen in the earlier stanzas of the poem, as in the
picture of animals in stanza twenty-four, or of the hummingbird and
the bell-flowers in stanza fifty-three, or of the laurels and crocuses
seen against the "snow-clad earth" in stanza sixty-one, but it is
really in the climax of the poem, beginning with stanza seventy-two
and continuing, almost without interruption, through the penulti-
mate stanza, that this aspect of Smart's art and genius is most perfectly realized. The pictures succeed each other with breath-taking

---

*Some of the more remarkable instances, for the figure is pervasive in the Song,
are "Serene—to sow the seeds of peace" and "plant perpetual paradise," both from
stanza 12. Sometimes, as in stanza 23, he places an alliterative doublet, "peace or
prey," in immediate juxtaposition with an alliterative line, "They that make
music, or that mock." At least once the alliteration extends for two lines: "And
sense and soul detained;/ Now striking strong, now soothing soft" (stanza 28).

speed; the mind's eye cannot adjust quickly enough to one before another is thrust upon it. "Beauteous the fleet before the gale," Smart writes, and the eye and mind join forces to visualize an armada with sails straining in the wind as waves dash high above the advancing prows. But before the picture has had time to reveal any of its details the mind and eye must shift quickly, and the ships and wind and waves must give way to a vast army of men in armor with plumed helmets and weapons aligned, "Beauteous the multi-tudes in mail,/ Rank'd arms and crested heads." And then succeeds a quiet, shaded garden, "Beauteous the garden's umbrage mild," and there is a wrench as the mighty symbols of armed conflict are displaced by the garden with its "Walk, water, meditated wild,/ And all the bloomy beds." The lion, "the gier-eagle on his sail," and "th' enormous whale," all primates in the great chain of being, are drawn with a few quick strokes.[13] But, fittingly enough, the greatest effects are reserved for the end of the poem when, gathering speed, for the lines demand an almost frenzied haste, picture follows picture so fast that one is dazzled,

> Glorious the sun in mid career;
> Glorious th' assembled fires appear;
>   Glorious the comet's train:
> Glorious the trumpet and alarm;
> Glorious th' almighty stretch'd-out arm;
>   Glorious th' enraptur'd main.
> Glorious the northern lights astream;
> Glorious the song, when God's the theme;
>   Glorious the thunder's roar:
> Glorious hosanna from the den;
> Glorious the catholic amen;
>   Glorious the martyr's gore:

And as these auditory and visual effects are brought together and the speed diminishes, the poem comes to a calm and majestic close.

> Glorious more glorious is the crown
> Of Him that brought salvation down
>   By meekness, call'd thy Son;
> Thou at stupendous truth believ'd,
> And now the matchless deed's atchiev'd,
>   DETERMINED, DARED, and DONE.

Small wonder that critics and readers put this all down to madness, complete or vestigial; nothing like this had come their way before.

July, 1763, saw the publication of another slender volume by Smart. Simply titled *Poems*, it contained an allegorical fable, *Reason and Imagination*, addressed to Kenrick, Smart's one-time literary antagonist and now his friend; an *Ode to Admiral Sir George Pocock* who had recently returned from the capture of Havannah and who had been Smart's neighbor in St. James's Street over ten years earlier; an *Ode to General Draper*, Smart's contemporary at Cambridge; and the *Epistle to John Sherratt, Esq.* For epigraph to the collection Smart belligerently quoted the first three lines of the fifth fable of Phaedrus' fifth book which he translated in 1765 as

> In ev'ry age, in each profession
> Men err the most by prepossession;
> But when the thing is clearly shown,
> Is fairly urg'd, and fully known,
> We soon applaud what we deride,
> And penitence succeeds to pride.

Critics who recognized the lines as coming from the fable of the countryman who concealed a pig and thus confounded those who derided him for what they thought was his attempt at imitating a pig's squeal were warned that they were in the presence of natural talent and should comport themselves accordingly.

The main poem, *Reason and Imagination*, tells of the refusal of Reason to wed Imagination, insisting that they should be allies but nothing closer. While the fable found favor with his contemporaries, the most interesting poems in the little volume are the two odes. That to Pocock begins with a striking image,

> When CHRIST, the seaman, was aboard
> Swift as an arrow to the *White*,
> While Ocean his rude rapture roar'd,
> The vessel gain'd the Haven with delight.

One stanza of the same poem was as applicable to the poet as to his subject; Smart had his own circumstances in mind when he wrote

> And yet how silent his return
> With scarce a welcome to his place—
> Stupidity and unconcern,
> Were settled in each voice and on each face.

LONDON, 1763-1765

As private as myself he walk'd along,
Unfavor'd by a friend, unfollow'd by the throng.

A number of Smart's friends forgot him during the years from 1759
to 1763; their names do not appear in the list of subscribers for the
Psalms and never come up in connection with him after his release.
Inevitably he allowed some of his feeling to vent itself in his poetry.
From the ode to a naval man Smart turned to the ode to a military
man, seeming in his poetry to identify himself with, or to be fasci-
nated by, heroic figures. In August, 1759, Smart had written in
Jubilate Agno "For I bless God that I am of the same seed as Ehud,
Mutius Scaevola, and Colonel Draper" (B1, 19), associating himself
with three military heroes of three different cultures. William
Draper, a Colonel in 1759, was promoted to Brigadier-General in
June, 1762. Smart's theme in his ode on Draper is that the English
or Christian hero, exemplified by Draper, who was a Master of Arts
of King's College, is one who combines talents and learning with
his military skill and prowess:

> A heroe, that prefers a higher claim
>   To God's applause, his country's, and his own;
> Than those, who, tho' the mirrour of their days,
> Nor knew the Prince of Worth, nor principle of praise.

Here, as in the ode to Pocock, Smart invokes "God's applause" as
the highest praise man can aspire to or win. What if, Smart devotes
most of his poem to saying, your deeds are not commemorated by
statues, coins, paintings, etc. Your worth is recognized by your
monarch and in my verse, and

> Thyself and seed for which there is no doom,
>   Race rising upon race in goodly pride;
> Shall ever flourish root, and branch, and bloom,
>   Shall flourish tow'ring high and spreading wide;
> To carry God's applauses in their heart,
> To shew an ENGLISH face, and act an ENGLISH part.

Again Smart is concerned with neglected merit; again he has himself also in mind. One other passage reveals something about Smart.
As he rouses himself as a poet to do justice to his subject he cries
out,

181

My Muse is somewhat stronger than she was,
    In spite of long calamity and time,
Arouse, Arouse ye! is there not a cause?
    Arouse ye lively spirits of my prime.

Concentrated in these two odes is much that is revelatory of the poet who had emerged from confinement a changed man. Most of his poetry, whether religious or not, would have some expression of religiosity in it; much of it would have somewhere embedded in it a personal note of bitterness, usually subdued or hidden as the poet took on one guise or another. Somehow Smart's pride in his Englishness was strengthened in his confinement and he tended more and more to lay great stress on the virtues and advantages of being a native of England. He had struck this same note again and again in *Jubilate Agno*, rising to the climax in the line "For I am descended from the steward of the island blessed be the name of the Lord Jesus King of England" (B1,137).[14] But absent from this volume and rarely to appear in these last years was the light bantering voice of the young man about town who was ready to compose a set of verses on even the most trifling occasions.

Smart's *Poems* was enthusiastically reviewed in the *Cambridge Chronicle* for July 23.

> The Public will receive the same pleasure on the perusal of this poem [*Reason and Imagination*], as we find from the accidental meeting of an old friend after a long absence. The world has been so often entertained with the ingenious productions of Mr. Smart, that anything from his hand must awaken our attention; and this little Fable will at the same time gratify and reward their curiosity. Poets are indeed often termed Enthusiasts, and that rather from the extravagance and rant of folly, than from any impulsory feelings of real Genius. It may perhaps in this immoral and irreligious age do Mr. Smart small credit that he appears as an advocate for Christianity; the Coxcomb and the Fool, who laugh at what they do not understand, may deride such unfashionable attempts; while the Man of Wit, who often too fatally misemploys it, and the Man of Parts, who scandalously betrays them, ought to blush.

After deducing the moral and praising the tale again the reviewer contents himself with "laying the plan" of the poem before his readers and extracting a few passages from it. But Smart's pleasure at this notice of his work was short-lived; the *Monthly Review*, a more widely read and powerful medium, was cruelly blunt,

Instead of entering on the merit of these poems, we shall transcribe
a few lines of Milton's SAMPSON, and leave our Readers to make
the application:

> This, this is he, softly awhile
> Let us not break in upon him;
> O change beyond report, thought, or belief! . . . .
> . . . .
> By how much from the top of wondrous glory
> To lowest pitch of abject fortune are thou fall'n![15]

The *Critical Review*, referring to an angry statement Smart had
appended to the back of the *Reason and Imagination* volume to
the effect that the writers for the *Critical Review* possessed neither
religion nor learning as manifested by their remarks on *A Song to
David*, went on to say,

> A writer must be possessed of an equal portion of madness and
> malignity to deny Mr. Smart his praise as a poet, which we allow in
> its full extent. A kind of Postscript, however, annexed to these
> poems, calls for our notice, or rather our thanks, as Mr. Smart's
> own words to any rational reader, must more than justify the char-
> acter we gave of his song to David (See the Critical Review for
> April, 1763, p. 324.) He is pleased to term our observation to be
> 'stupendous impudence against the truth of Christ Jesus, who has
> most confidently affirmed this same David to be alive in his argu-
> ment for the resurrection.'
>
> Did our criticism of Mr. Smart's last production require any
> further elucidation; we might produce the fact of his inscribing a
> poem to John Sherrat, ESQ. and his encomiums upon one Rolt,
> whom the world has unanimously damned both as a poet and
> historian.[16]

Rolt had been damned as a historian by Smollett in the *Critical
Review* in March, 1756, in his review of the former's *History of
South America*; John Sherratt, an obscure merchant, was not
thought worthy to be the subject of a serious poem. Smart had
always been too sensitive to criticism; at this time it must have been
especially galling to him, and the *Critical Review* could not have
been crueller than to asperse the abilities and character of the two
men who had done so much to procure his release from confinement. He never forgot the treatment accorded him in that periodical.

Proposals for a version of the *Psalms* had been printed at the back
of *A Song to David* and Smart's friends were already getting sub-

scribers for him. Mason wrote to Gray from York on June 28, 1763, saying,

> I have got about 10 Subscribers to Smart & dont know how to transmit him the money. Stonehewer advises me to keep it, as he hears he is in somebodys hands who may cheat him. I have seen his Song to David & from thence conclude him as mad as ever. But this I mention only that one should endeavor to assist him as effectually as possible wch one cannot do without the mediation of a third person. If you know any body now in London (for Stonehewer has left it) whom I can write to on this subject pray tell me. Tis said in the papers he is prosecuting the people who confined him. if so, assisting him at present is only throwing ones money to the Lawyers.

Gray replied soon thereafter from London,

> I think it may be time enough to send poor Smart the money you have been so kind to collect for him, when he has drop'd his lawsuit, wch I don't doubt must go against him, if he pursues it. Gordon (who lives here) knows, & interests himself about him: from him I shall probably know, if he can be persuaded to drop his design. there is a Mr Anguish in Town (with whom, I fancy, you were once acquainted) he probably can best inform you of his condition & motions, for I hear, he continues to be very friendly to him.[17]

Richard Stonhewer, prompter for Smart's Cambridge play in 1747, was a Durham man who had received a Bachelor of Arts from Trinity College and then a Master of Arts from Peterhouse. Through his pupil, the Earl of Euston, later third Duke of Grafton, he had received a number of governmental posts. John Gordon had acted in Smart's play; he too was a Durham man, attending Durham Grammar School while Smart was still there. Both he and Stonehewer were Fellows at Peterhouse. Thomas Anguish, so identified by Mason, of Boswell Court, Lincoln's Inn, was a scholar at Caius College from 1742–6; by 1763 he had become Accountant General. Since Smart had asked "God be gracious to Lyne & Anguish" in 1759 in *Jubilate Agno* (B1, 288) it is clear that they had become acquainted well before 1763, possibly while they were at Cambridge, for Lyne is doubtless Richard Lyne, elected a Master of Arts of King's in 1741. Lyne was also Chaplain to the King from 1744–1767. Smart had friends in positions from which they could do him much good.

Mason's report that Smart was prosecuting the people who confined him reveals that the latter may have had recourse to his ancient right to traverse in the hopes of proving that he had been untruly found a lunatic. Since nothing more is heard of the prosecution, of which no records exist, Smart either did not get the necessary consent of the Chancellor or, if he had been found a lunatic under two inquisitions or commissions, found he had no right to traverse.[18] His reasons for wanting to prosecute were less motivated by a desire for revenge than by the desire to be cleared of the stigma of madness. Although he may have been permitted an occasional outing in the years from 1759 to 1763 he spent almost all of that time in Potter's madhouse, and no matter how much activity, poetical, physical or otherwise, he carried on, there must have been entirely too much time for brooding on all the wrongs, real and fancied, that had been done him. Smart was a gentle and charitable man, even in the very depths of despair and himself in need of all the charity that could be given, but he had suffered too much not to want in some fashion to retaliate for what he felt was his unjust confinement. There could be no thought of reconciliation with his family; all that was left for him was to clear his name and to write his poetry. He had already seen how much his poetry suffered in the eyes of the public through the critics' unkind references to his past confinement and their unsubtle hints that he was still mad. His translation of the Psalms, the most ambitious literary project he ever undertook, with the possible exception of the verse translation of Horace, would demonstrate to all that he had lost neither his sanity nor his poetic powers.

Accordingly, on September 8, 1763, he issued separately published "Proposals for Printing, by Subscription, A New Translation of the Psalms of David. To which will be added, a Set of Hymns, for the Fasts and Festivals of the Church of England." The conditions bespeak the care with which the work was planned and the imminence of its publication:

I. The Work will be printed in One Volume Quarto, on a fine new Letter, and handsome Paper.

II. The Measure is kept up for all the old favourite Tunes; and for the new Measures, there will be new Musick composed by Dr. *Boyce*, Mr. *Howard*, and other eminent Masters, which will be published in an Appendix to the Work for such as chuse it.

III. The Price to Subscribers will be Ten Shillings and Six-pence; half to be paid at the Time of Subscribing, and the other half on the Delivery of the Book, which is ready for the Press, and will be published with all convenient Speed.

IV. A List of Subscribers Names will be printed.

Smart also apologized for the delay in publication, referring to the proposals appended to *A Song to David* which assured the public that copy for the Psalms and Hymns was already in the hands of the printer: "N.B. In order to make the PURCHASER full amends for postponing the Work, the Paper and Print will be much better, and every Thing conducted in a more elegant Manner, than was promised in the former Proposals." No fewer than ten London booksellers as well as others at Cambridge, Oxford, York, Durham, and Dublin would receive subscriptions for the author, and subscribers could also leave their money with Mr. Willock at the Rainbow Coffee-House and Mr. Blyth at John's Coffee-House. Smart had added two London booksellers, Laurence and Flexney, and the five from outside London to the number appearing in his first announcement of the proposals at the end of *A Song to David*. Again, as with *A Song to David*, he must have done a considerable amount of work on the Psalms and the Hymns in order to be able, so soon after his release, to promise their speedy publication. As specimens of his translation he included Psalms XLV and CXLVIII, both of which appear unchanged in the published version. But whether he had not completed the whole work or whether publication awaited a larger subscription, the promise was not to be kept for almost two more years. He seized the occasion, however, to advertise the *Song to David* and the *Reason and Imagination* volume at the end of the proposals, describing the former as "a Poem composed in a Spirit of Affection and thankfulness to the great Author of the Book of Gratitude, which is the *Psalms* of DAVID the King." Once again he saw fit to elevate gratitude to one of the highest ranks in the hierarchy of virtues.

In the meantime, another small volume of poems came out in time to be reviewed in the November number of the *Monthly Review*. This was Smart's *Poems on Several Occasions*, containing the poems *Munificence and Modesty*; *Female Dignity, to Lady Hussey Delaval*; and *Verses from Catullus, after Dining with Mr. Murray*.

Three epitaphs, those on the Duchess of Cleveland, Henry Fielding, and the Reverend James Sheels, plus the *Epitaph from Demosthenes*, made up the rest of the volume. Again, as with the *Reason and Imagination* volume, much of the poetry had been resurrected. Since the Duchess of Cleveland had died many years ago in 1742, Smart must have written the epitaph while at Cambridge and sent a copy to the bereaved family; he could have done no less, being the recipient of an annual sum of forty pounds from her. The epitaphs on Fielding and on Sheels had appeared already in the periodicals for this year. Nor could "The Famous General Epitaph" from Demosthenes, ten lines in length, and the poem to Mr. Murray, six lines in length, add much to the bulk or quality of a volume whose chief claims upon public attention were the poem *Munificence and Modesty* and the slighter poem *Female Dignity*. Since William Murray had been created Baron Mansfield in 1756 there exists the possibility that Smart, referring to him as Mr. Murray, may have written the little poem to him much earlier. *Female Dignity, Inscribed and Applied to Lady Hussey Delaval* was written for the wife of John Hussey Blake Delaval, whose undergraduate career at Pembroke in Smart's time there was brought to such a rapid end. Other than the fact that Smart places female dignity above all other feminine graces and excellences nothing need be said about a poem whose chief purpose was to flatter the wife of a wealthy acquaintance. *Munificence and Modesty* is said, in its subtitle, to owe its existence to a hint from a painting of Guido. It is a religous and allegorical fable with some verbal echoes or anticipations, depending on when it was written, of Smart's major religious poetry. On the whole, the volume was hardly such as to improve his reputation. Psalm XLV was given on the last page as a specimen of his proposed translation; this was the work he had fastened his hopes upon, while in the collections leading up to it he was simply marking time.

The *Critical Review,* never a periodical to avoid a literary quarrel, continued its attack, beginning with a barely disguised sneer at the meagerness of Smart's collection: "This is a very small collection of poems, containing only seven short copies of verses. We wish, from a regard to the reputation of Mr. Smart, who formerly made a considerable figure in the world of literature, that they had been suppressed, as they can do him no honour." Upon this, the first three lines of *Munificence and Modesty* are quoted and the reviewer remarks, "Which whoever can either understand or admire, has more penetration than we can pretend to." Finally,

> But we will say no more of Mr. Smart: Peace be to the manes of his departed muse. Our sentiments with regards to this unfortunate gentleman are such as every man must feel on the same melancholy occasion. If our readers are desirous to know what they are, we must refer them to the fine lines at the end of Mr. Churchill's epistle to Hogarth.[19]

Churchill's conclusion, on Hogarth's supposed madness, includes such lines as "And sunk, deep sunk, in second childhood's night," and "To drivel out whole years of idiot breath," words whose sting would still be great despite the last couplet, "The greatest genius to this fate may bow;/ Reynolds, in time, may be like Hogarth now." Since the epistle to Hogarth had been published only four months before this review, it was still fresh in the minds of the public.

Smart, who had infinitely more to lose than his attackers, had unwisely added an unusual advertisement to the back of the *Munificence and Modesty* volume. In it he claimed proudly that his *Reason and Imagination* volume had "been honoured with the approbation of the first names in the Literary World" and went on to summon the *Monthly Review*, which had damned it "after an invidious silence of a considerable Time," to "the Bar of the Publick, to answer the following Queries."

> Whether there is any Thing they hate as much as
> Truth and Merit?
> Whether they had not depended upon their *malignity*,
> for the Sale of their Book from the beginning?
> Whether the writings of Mr. *Smart* in particular
> (his Prize Poems excepted) have not been constantly
> misreported to the Publick, by their despicable Pamphlet?
> Whether the Reverend Mr. *Langhorne* has not the
> poetical Department of the Monthly Review?
> Whether a certain *scandalous fellow*, who has
> oppressed Mr. Smart for these many years, did not wait upon *Griffiths*,
> and complain that he had been treated too mildly in a former Review?
> Whether the said *scandalous fellow* did not give Griffiths and
> others Money to defame Mr. *Smart*, as far as they dared?
> Whether, if this was not the Case, they do not act their Mischief
> without Motive, and serve the Devil from affection?

Smart's query about Langhorne was only partly true. Langhorne had reviewed only the *Song to David* of Smart's poems up to this time; the reviewer of the two subsequent volumes, those containing *Reason and Imagination* and *Munificence and Modesty*, is not known.[20] Possibly Smart was thinking of John Hill in his references to "a certain scandalous fellow," but whatever he may have thought he would gain from this action the only result was to alienate the *Monthly* further. While the periodical felt obliged to notice Smart's angry accusations it did so obliquely and not without dignity.

> We are glad to find that, notwithstanding all that this ingenious bard has so long suffered, neither the glow of his imagination, nor the harmony of his numbers, are in the least impaired.—We say no more, as we have the mortification to learn, from some angry queries, and groundless insinuations, printed at the end of these poems, that, in spite of the sincere regard we have so often expressed, and always felt, for a writer of so much merit, he, from whatever fatality, has most unhappily misconstrued what we lately intended as a proof of our high veneration for the abilities which God so bounteously bestowed upon him.—As it appears to him so unpardonably criminal to affix any limitation whatever, to the praises which he thinks due to all his Writings, he may rest assured, that he will, for the future, have very little cause to be offended with us, on that account.[21]

Had Smart occasionally been willing to turn the other cheek, had he not been so painfully sensitive about his poetry, he would have had a much easier time of it. He had many friends, some of them even writing for the *Monthly* and the *Critical*, and they would in time have seen to it that he was spared some of the harsher criticism that he was so adept at provoking.

Smart could not have earned much money from his poetry in 1763, or if he did, he squandered it, for efforts were being made at this time to help him financially. John Newbery continued his kindness toward his son-in-law, setting apart for his benefit the profits from the *Martial Review, or General History of the Late War*, a publication in which Goldsmith had a hand and which was announced as published in the *Gentleman's Magazine* for September. At about this time or a little later Goldsmith was also doing something on his own for Smart, for among his "papers at his death was found a copy of an appeal to the public for poor Kit Smart, who had married Newbery's step-daughter ten years before, and had since, with his eccentricities and imprudences, wearied out all his friends but Goldsmith and Johnson."[22] This appeal was to have been printed and circulated, for Bishop Percy describes it as a "Paper, which [Goldsmith] wrote to set about a subscription for poor Smart the mad poet: (I believe this last was never printed.)"[23] But Smart himself was not idle; he could not depend upon others. Smollett's *British Magazine, or Monthly Repository* for September, 1763, printed "A New Song, Supposed to be written by Mr. Smart," which begins "Where shall Celia fly for shelter" and is one of the poems to form part of his next collection.

The end of the year and the beginning of the next was marked for Smart by the resurrection of some of his *Universal Visiter* pieces in the *Universal Museum, or Gentleman's and Lady's Polite Magazine* for December and January and in the *St. James's Magazine* for January and February. Next Month the *Universal Museum* reprinted *Reason and Imagination* which was described as "By the celebrated Mr. Christopher Smart." Whether Smart knew Arthur Young the editor or not, such notice was welcome; Smart could use all the favorable mentions he could get. His work and his name were being kept alive as he continued to solicit subscriptions for his version of the Psalms and to plan and work on other literary projects. The quest for subscribers led Smart to enlist the help of Paul Panton, a contemporary of his at Cambridge who was residing in Anglesea, North Wales. Panton was a collector of Welsh manuscripts with a wide circle of acquaintances and did much for Smart in the years between 1764 and 1769; he had also subscribed to Smart's *Poems* in 1752. Smart's first surviving letter to Panton is dated January 10, 1764: "Being about to put my book to the press forthwith I desire the favour you would immediately send me the names of such subscribers as you have been so kind as to procure & make their payments to you by your Agent in Town, who probably will subscribe himself, if you will be so good as to desire him. I am now at Mrs. Barwell's in Park Street Westminster."[24] Smart signed himself "Your most obliged and affectionate friend"; he must have become more closely acquainted with Panton in London, as the latter was admitted to Lincoln's Inn in 1744, the same year he was admitted to Trinity Hall as a pensioner. Smart's pride, while certainly still alive, was not so great now; he could baldly ask Panton to urge his agent to subscribe for a copy of the Psalms.

Smart's statement that he was about to put his book to press and his request for the names of the subscribers Panton had got for him implies that all was in readiness and that the list of subscribers would be printed along with the rest of the book. But he was still on the lookout for more subscribers, and on June 8, 1764, he signed a receipt acknowledging the "Revd Mr. Percy's" payment of "Five Shillings and Three-pence, being the first Payment for one Copy of A new translation of the Psalms of David, and a Set of Hymns for the Fasts and Festivals of the Church of England; which I promise to deliver, when published, to the Bearer hereof, on Payment of the other Moiety." Percy's receipt was number 1438; Smart probably had 1500 of them printed up as opposed to the modest 400 he had ordered for his *Poems* of 1752.[25] While he was building up his subscriber's list Smart was also turning his talents in a new direction. On the second of April his first oratorio, *Hannah*, was performed at the King's Theatre in the Haymarket. The music was by John Worgan, organist and composer for Vauxhall Gardens, who had also composed the music for Smart's *Solemn Dirge* on the death of the Prince of Wales in 1751. *Hannah* was a failure; there was only the one performance. Blame for the failure probably rests more squarely on the shoulders of the composer than those of the librettist, but reading the libretto as poetry divorced from its musical score still hardly does Smart justice, for there is very little that is memorable in his verses. Contemporary comment was limited to the friendly *St. James's Magazine*'s commendatory remark in its May issue that the oratorio had "some poetical merit." The *Critical Review* was silent; the *Monthly Review* devoted three noncommital sentences to it, although it did admit that there were "some airs superior to most we meet with in performances of this kind."

Smart's versification of the story of Hannah in I Samuel is a wooden thing, and his choice of this particular episode in the Bible is difficult to explain. Hannah is childless and is taunted by Peninnah, Elkanah's other wife. Finally Hannah's prayers for a son are answered and she dedicates him, Samuel, to the service of the Lord. No analogy exists between this story and Smart's own life; only once does he strike a note that may be interpreted as personal. In an air that describes the terror of the benighted pilgrim he writes,

> But oh how sweet
> At Home to meet,
> With her that loves him best!

Anna Maria Smart had made no effort to help or solace her husband; he, for his part, bitter at his confinement, would have little or nothing to do with the rest of his family. Possibly he may have thought of his children when he came to Hannah's song of thanks to the Lord for answering her prayers, but, if he did, his rendition of his original does not show it. Where the Bible has "My heart rejoyceth in the Lord, mine horne is exalted in the LORD: my mouth is inlarged over mine enemies: because I rejoyce in thy salvation," Smart has

> My Heart with Transport springs,
> To thee the King of Kings;
>   My Tongue has learnt a nobler Tone:
> Mine Enemies despair,
> While Record thus I bear,
>   Salvation is of God alone.

Much of the rest is of a piece with this; *Hannah* was hack work, done for the money it would bring, money that would keep Smart going until the Psalms were published. An advertisement of the Proposals for the Psalms occupied the last page of the oratorio; there Smart grasped the chance to add, "This Translation has met with the Encouragement of many Bishops and other dignified Clergymen, together with all the eminent Writers of Poetry and Musick," a reference to the names in his growing list of subscribers. Even yet, however, he was not prepared to publish.

Toward the end of his confinement, during which he wrote *Jubilate Agno* and was working on his own version of the Psalms, Smart knew and could speak generously of a rival version. On December 30, 1762, a month before his release, he wrote "Let Merrick, house of Merrick, rejoice with Lageus a kind of Grape. God all-sufficient bless & forward the Psalmist in the Lord Jesus" (D, 203). He was referring to the Reverend Mr. James Merrick's translation, sponsored by Newbery. Literary London was very much aware that both Smart and Merrick were nearing the completion of their translations of the Psalms, and the *Public Advertiser* of June 12, 1764, reprinted Psalm 126 in the version of each, prefacing this with the statement that "In order to oblige our Readers with the Pleasure of comparing the respective Merits of two rival Translations of the Psalms, we have inserted the following Specimens." The newspaper further informed its readers of the names of some of the booksellers from whom subscriptions for Smart's version could be had. Again it is clear that Smart was still hoping for more subscribers. Again, too, as he had already done a number of times in the last year and a half, he brought out another small collection of poems. The volume took its title from the main poem, *Ode to the Right Honourable the Earl of Northumberland, on his being appointed Lord Lieutenant of Ireland*, "Presented on the Birth-day of Lord Warkworth. With some other pieces." Smart described himself on the title page as "A.M. Some time Fellow of Pembroke Hall in Cambridge, and Scholar of the University," the first time the latter had appeared in print since it made up part of the title page of the Latin version of Pope's St. Cecilia's Ode in 1743. The reference is, of course, to the Craven Scholarship that he had won in open competition in 1742, an honor which he was to recall in subsequent publication. Its resurrection in these years, but only on the title page of some of his works, is indicative of his continuing pride in his academic achievements of the Cambridge years. He had lost much; this could not be taken from him.

Besides the title poem the volume contained *To the Hon. Mrs. Draper, On being asked by Colonel Hall to make verses upon Kingsley at Minden, On a Bed of Geurnsey Lilies, The Sweets of Evening*, a *Song* beginning "Where shall Caelia fly for shelter," two epitaphs, and an epigram. The *Song*, printed in September, 1763, in the *British Magazine*, the poem on the Guernsey lilies, and the *Sweets of Evening* are among Smart's most charming short lyrics.[26] The first of these is a return to the light jocular vein of the early London years; the other two lyrics are in a more muted tone, but they too breathe optimism. Mrs. Draper, wife to General Draper upon whom Smart had written an ode in his 1763 *Poems*, may have been the subject of a complimentary poem because her husband had subscribed for forty copies of the Psalms, yet to be printed. Colonel Hall also subscribed to the Psalms as did General Kingsley; the latter was of Maidstone.[27] Since the Battle of Minden was fought on August 1, 1759, Smart's poem was probably written years earlier than its appearance in 1764. So, too, with the *Ode to the Earl of Northumberland*, as Smart himself confesses in his advertisement to the collection:

Though the following Piece was in a degree received at a certain place, and something handsome done (according to custom) yet

193

such was the modesty of the excellent person to whom it was addressed, that the Printing of it was so far from being approved of, that very positive injunctions were given to the contrary.

The author therefore was content to have the Manuscript handed about amongst his friends for their private entertainment, determining at all events to abide by his obedience.—But at length having the honour to communicate it to a great and worthy friend, who has been for some years in the country, he persuaded him to make it public, urging that the suppression would in a degree be a loss to letters; and as for any blame about the matter, he was ready to take that upon himself. This is an honourable Gentleman who has a most profound respect to my Lord Lieutenant, and whose commands were not likely to be resisted, as they were given with equal authority and benevolence, and in the true spirit of an Englishman, born to encounter opposition and triumph over difficulty.

Quite clearly Smart was not above carrying his flattering occasional poems around in person in the expectation that something handsome would be done. On this occasion, however, he had double expectation of reward; not only was he celebrating the Earl's appointment as Lord Lieutenant of Ireland on April 20, 1763, but he presented the poem on August 14, the twenty-first birthday of the Earl's son. The poem itself is not remarkably better or worse than such poems generally are. And while Smart went back a year for his poem on the Earl of Northumberland and some ten years for the epigram, he reached even farther back for the epitaph on the late Duke of Argyle, who died October 4, 1743.[28] The inevitable proposals for the Psalms made up the last page of the volume.

Alert for another opportunity to disparage Smart's poetry, the July *Critical Review* pounced on the advertisement he had foolishly printed with the poems. "Mr. Smart informs us," the unknown reviewer wrote, "in the advertisement prefixed to this poem, that the excellent person to whom it is addressed was so far from approving of the printing it, that he gave very positive injunctions to the contrary. We shall add, that this was a proof not only of the noble lord's modesty, but of his taste and good sense." The *Song*, the reviewer admitted was "pretty, and well turned." Langhorne reviewed the collection in the September *Monthly Review* and complained that "there is in the later productions of Mr. Smart, a *tour* of expression, which we many times are at a loss to understand; and it often seems to us, that his words as well as his sentiments, are rather too much under the influence of imagination," probably having *The Sweets of Evening* in mind. He found the last stanza of the title ode, curiously enough, "really very pretty" and concluded with the dubious compliment that "the little pieces added to this Ode, are not destitute of merit." The friendly *Public Advertiser* remarked on July 24 that in "the Ode now before us Mr. Smart appears plainly to have written from his own feelings and to have avoided the beaten track of undistinguished adulation." But whatever the reviewers found to criticize and to praise, Smart was again writing some poems of a high order of excellence.

A few months after publication of the *Ode* Smart received a call from his old friend John Hawkesworth, recently returned from visiting Smart's mother and sister Margaret at Margate. In a letter dated October, 1764, Hawkesworth reported on his visit.

Dear Madam,

I am afraid that you have before now secretly accused me, and I confess that appearances are against me; I did not however delay to call upon Mr. Smart, but I was unfortunate enough twice to miss him. I was the third day of my being in town seized with a fever that was then epidemic, from which I am but just recovered. I have since my being in town this second time called upon my old friend, and seen him. He received me with an ardour of kindness natural to the sensibility of his temper, and we were soon seated together by his fire side: I perceived upon his table a quarto book, in which he had been writing, a prayer book and a Horace: after the first compliments, I said I had been at Margate, had seen his mother and his sister, who expressed great kindness for him, and made me promise to come and see him; to this he made no reply; nor did he make any enquiry after those I mentioned; he did not even mention the place, nor ask me any questions about it, or what carried me thither. After some pause, and some indifferent chat, I returned to the subject, and said that Mr. Hunter and you would be very glad to see him in Kent: to this he replied very quick, 'I cannot afford to be idle;' I said he might employ his mind as well in the country as in town, at which he only shook his head; and I intirely changed the subject. Upon my asking him when we should see the Psalms, he said they were going to press immediately: as to his other undertakings, I found he had compleated a translation of Phaedrus in verse for Dodsley at a certain price, and that he is now busy in translating all Horace into verse, which he sometimes thinks of publishing on his own account, and sometimes of contracting for it with a bookseller; I advised him to the latter, and he then told me he was in treaty about it, and believed it would be a bargain: he told me his principal motive for translating Horace into verse, was to supersede the prose translation which he did for Newbery, which he said would hurt his memory. He intends however to review that translation, and print it at the foot of the page in his poetical version, which he proposes to print in quarto with the Latin, both in verse and prose, on the opposite page; he told me he once had thoughts of printing it by subscription, but as he had troubled his friends already, he was unwilling to do it again, and had been persuaded to publish it in numbers, which, though I rather dissuaded him, seemed at last to be the prevailing bent of his mind: he read me some of it: it is very close, and his own poetical fire sparkles in it very frequently; yet, upon the whole, it will scarcely take place of Francis's, and therefore, if it is not adopted as a school book, which perhaps may be the case, it will turn to little account. Upon mentioning his prose translation, I saw his countenance kindle, and snatching up the book, 'what,' says he, do 'you think I had for this?' I said I could not tell, 'why,' says he, with great indignation, 'thirteen pounds.' I expressed very great astonishment, which he seemed to think he should increase by adding, 'but, Sir, I gave a receipt for a hundred'; my astonishment however was now over, and I found that he received only thirteen pounds because the rest had been advanced for his family; this was a tender point, and I found means immediately to divert him from it.

He is with very decent people, in a house most delightfully situated with a terras that overlooks St. Jame's Park, and a door into it. He was going to dine with an old friend of my own, Mr. Richard Dalton, who has an appointment in the King's library, and if I had not been particularly engaged, I would have dined with him. He had lately received a very genteel letter from Dr. Lowth, and is by no means considered in any light that makes his company as a gentleman, a scholar, and a genius less desirable. I have been very particular, dear Madam, in relating all the particulars of this conference, that you may draw any inference, that I could draw from it, yourself.

I should incur my own censure, which is less tolerable than all others; if I did not express my sense of the civilities I received from you and Mr. Hunter, while I was at Margate: I have Mrs. Hawkesworth's express request in a letter now before me to do the same on her part: if you, or any of the family come into our part of the country, we shall be very glad to accomodate you with a table and a bed; you will find a cheerful fire-side and a hearty welcome. If in the mean time I can do you any service or pleasure here, you will the more oblige as you the more freely command me.

Our best compliments attend you, Mr. Hunter, your young gentleman, and Mrs. Smart, not forgetting the ladies we met at your house, particularly one who I think is daughter to Mrs. Holmes.

Hawkesworth's picture of Smart is one of a man who thinks he has suffered unjustly at the hands of his family and is determined he will have no more to do with them. So drastic a decision must have come hard, for he loved his sisters; he wrote fondly of "gentle Mariane" in *The Hop-Garden* and at some unknown date, presumably before 1759, he sent one of his sisters a New Year's gift of a pocket book accompanied by a poem that shows how he felt about her before the rift occurred.

> Of all returns in man's device
> 'Tis gratitude that makes the price,
> And what sincerity designs
> Is richer than Peruvian mines.
> Thus estimate the heart's intent,
> In what the faithful hands present.
> This volume soon shall worth derive
> From what your industry shall hive,
> And then in every line produce
> The tale of industry and use.
> Here, too, let your appointments be,
> And set down many a day for me;
> Oh! may the year we now renew
> Be stor'd with happiness for you;
> With all the wealth your friends would choose,
> And all the praise which you refuse;
> With love, sweet inmate of the breast,
> And meekness, while in blessing, blest.

His sole purpose now was to re-establish himself as poet and scholar, and at the same time make his living by writing. His prayer book was always at hand and some literary project either going forward or being planned. While Hawkesworth may have concealed the extent of Smart's excitability from his family, there is no hint that Smart was still afflicted. Indeed, Hawkesworth reassures Mrs. Hunter that her brother was seeing and corresponding with men of scholarly interests; he had an engagement to dine with Richard Dalton, keeper of the pictures and antiquarian to His Majesty, and he had received a "genteel letter" from Dr. Lowth. Smart had praised the latter's lectures on Hebrew poetry in the *Universal Visiter* and had profited from them in writing *Jubilate Agno*. Smart, Hawkesworth further assures the family, "is by no means considered in any light that makes his company as a gentleman, a scholar, and a genius less desirable." Among those that Smart could still count as friends were a number of composers, some of whom set his Psalms to music. One of these was Dr. James Nares, father of the philologist

Robert, to whom Smart addressed a delightful verse epistle in this
year or the next.

> Smart sends his compliments and pray'rs
> Health and long life to Dr. Nares—
> But the chief business of the Card,
> Is 'Come to dinner with the bard',
> Who makes a mod'rate share of wit
> Put on the pot, and turn the spit.
> 'Tis said the Indians teach their sons
> The use of bows instead of guns;
> And ere the striplings dare to dine,
> They shoot their victuals off a pine,
> The Public is as kind to me,
> As to his child a Cherokee;
> And if I chance to hit my aim,
> I chuse to feast upon the game;
> For panegyric or abuse
> Shall make the quill produce the goose,
> With apple-sauce and Durham mustard,
> And cooling pye o'er laid with custard.
> Pray please to signify with this
> My love to Madam, Bob, and Miss,
> Likewise to Nurse and little Poll—
> Whose praise so justly you extol.
>
> P.S. I have (don't think it a chimaera)
> Some good sound Port and right Madeira.

Smart's conviviality was not dead; he still enjoyed acting the hos-
pitable host to friends. He enjoyed his wine, good wine to be drunk
appreciatively and not guzzled in great quantities. And he had not
lost his ability to toss off the little facetious sets of verses with their
burlesque rhymes which he had so often written before 1756.

But Hawkesworth's letter may also have been intended to show
Mrs. Hunter and Mrs. Smart that Christopher was not idle. The
Psalms were going to press immediately, and Smart had completed a
verse translation of Phaedrus' fables for J. Dodsley, successor to
Robert Dodsley, the bookseller who published some of Smart's
poems in the *Museum* almost twenty years earlier. *A Poetical
Translation of the Fables of Phaedrus*, another work whose title
page bore the information that the translator had been Scholar of
the University, was published in December, 1764, although it is
dated 1765. It was announced as published on the seventeenth by

the *Public Advertiser* and some extracts were printed in that same newspaper three days later with a favorable comment. Smart dedicated the volume to Master John Hussey Delaval because of "the great and frequent favours" which the author had received from his "amiable and excellent parents." The youngster is praised for his abilities and character; there is a little disquisition on the similarity between Gay's fables and those of Phaedrus; and there is a final injunction to the boy to mention Edward Moore's *Fables For the Female Sex* to his "fair sisters." An advertisement confirms that Smart, proud that he had been Scholar of the University, took some scholarly pains with this edition. He writes,

> We trust that the Public is herein presented with the completest Phaedrus that has hitherto appeared for the use and entertainment of young gentlemen. In the first place, it is the only one we know of that is totally free from offence; a very serious and important point in respect to tender minds. Secondly, we have taken great care to give an accurate edition of the original on the opposite page, availing ourselves, as far as was expedient, of the great Dr. Bentley, *Gudius,* and others. Lastly, there are several evident restorations made, which are not to be met with elsewhere, upon no less weighty reasons than the adjusting of the measure, or something equally valid. Upon the whole, the young reader by this explanatory version and parsing index, will get the drift of the author's meaning, learn his syntax, and make a better progress in the tongue, than he would do by a mere prose translation, which is rather too great a help.

Possibly because Phaedrus, as a fabulist, was not worth as much of his time as the prose Horace had been and the verse Horace was to be, Smart added only about twenty notes to the text, applauding some of Richard Bentley's emendations, making an emendation of his own, explaining a number of references, and disagreeing with Bentley in three places. "It is amazing that this should escape Bentley," he exclaims in one note, proud to have caught the great scholar in an error of omission.

Smart, as an original writer of fables himself, was eminently qualified for the work he had undertaken. His decision to omit what the *Critical Review* termed "several fables of indelicate turn" was praised by a reviewer for that periodical in the September issue, but after comparing one fable in the Latin original with Smart's English version the reviewer concluded, "Phaedrus is remarkably concise; this version is more diffuse. In some places the translator has embellished the author's narration, and given an ingenious turn to a simple expression: but he has not refined his language with a proper degree of nicety and care; many of his verses are encumbered with feeble expletives and unnecessary words." Langhorne reviewed the translation for the *Monthly Review*, in January, 1765, contenting himself with the opinion that Phaedrus' Latin was not for beginning students but that the version might still be useful. Certainly the considered judgment and moderate language of the *Monthly*'s notice of his work should have quieted Smart's suspicion that Griffiths' publication, and Langhorne in particular, were determined to do him all the harm they could. This is all the more remarkable in that Langhorne could really bear a grudge. Griffiths wrote in a letter, "I would not trust him," he is referring to another of his reviewers, "when he reviews the works of a *friend*, nor indeed of an enemy, for in either case no impartiality is to be expected from him. Poor Langhorne was the same, and many a scuffle have we had about *favour* and *resentment*."[29] Since the Rev. Mr. Langhorne was one of the subscribers to Smart's version of the Psalms, he was evidently willing to forget Smart's accusations against him.

Despite Smart's assurance to Hawkesworth in October, 1764, that his Psalms "were going to press immediately," the long-awaited work did not come out for almost another year. In his original proposals appended to *A Song to David* he had told prospective subscribers that C. Say, the printer, already had copy. When he advertised the proposals at the back of his *Ode to the Earl of Northumberland*, more than a year later, he informed his readers that subscriptions were received by various booksellers and "also by Messrs. Richardson and Clark, Printers, in Fleet-Street." But when the Psalms were finally published they were printed by Dryden Leach, a wealthy printer with large shares in several newspapers. Part of the delay in the printing of the work was due to Smart's desire for more subscribers; part of it was because he had trouble deciding on a printer. And while he solicited more subscriptions and met with his printer, or corrected proof, James Merrick's rival version of the Psalms went steadily forward, being advertised in Newbery's *Public Ledger* on July 4, 1765, as ready to be delivered by that bookseller, anticipating publication of Smart's translation by more than a month. On July 7 the *Public Advertiser* mentioned the musical settings of the Psalms promised by Smart in 1763; four days later Smart himself announced in the *General Advertiser* that the Psalms and Hymns

would be published on August 12. Another notice in the *Public
Advertiser* on August 14 announced the publication of the musical
settings, but they did not appear until October 31. In the meantime the Psalms and Hymns, with the *Song to David* thrown in,
came out as promised on August 12. A number of Smart's friends in
the musical world were represented in the composers of the forty-
five separately published melodies for the Psalms. William Boyce
and James Nares each wrote six; the others who contributed were
Samuel Howard, John Stanley, Joseph Baildon, Samuel Long, Benjamin Cooke, John Randall, Edmund Aston, Thomas Wood, and
George Berg, a tribute to Smart's ability to keep old friends. Separately published and printed for J. Walsh, a bookseller specializing
in the publication of music, these musical settings for the Psalms
made no lasting impression upon the public and were never reprinted. Charles Burney, Smart's staunchest friend, continued his
kindnesses by helping to build up the roster of musicians who composed these melodies for the Psalms.

Other friends solicited subscriptions for him, Paul Panton in
Wales, William Mason in the north, and Miss Sheels in London.
For when the Psalms were published a printed list of subscribers,
736 in number and accounting for 858 copies, accompanied it;
again, as in 1752, people from all the places and areas of activity
familiar to Smart were represented. Not only did Miss Sheels, the
young lady who helped bring about Smart's release from confinement, subscribe, as did both her parents, but she added other subscribers. One of these appears in the list as "Lady unknown, by Miss
Sheeles." Close by the name of Miss Sheels was that of "John Shar-
ratt, Esq."; only Rolt of Smart's deliverers could not afford to subscribe. Both Paul Panton and his wife subscribed, and a number of
the Welsh names in the list attest to his efforts on Smart's behalf.
The people of Maidstone were represented by at least three names;
there were more subscribers from Durham, including six members
of the Vane family. Smart's sister Margaret and her husband, William Hunter, each subscribed and were instrumental in getting a
few subscriptions from among their friends in Ramsgate and Margate in Kent. Smart's other sister had married Richard Falkiner, a
wealthy barrister; between them they accounted for ten books.
Francis Smart, the poet's cousin, took one book; the only other
Smart of the list was "Mrs. Smart, senior." Anna Maria Smart did
not subscribe. Smart's aunt Sarah and her husband, now Colonel

Webb, both subscribed, as did a Mr. William Webb. Many of Smart's companions and colleagues of the years in Cambridge, now distinguished in the list as "Reverend" gentlemen, appeared; Addison, his tutor; Dr. Long, D.D.F.R.S., Master of Pembroke Hall; Rev. Mr. Brown, the redoubtable James Brown, who led the fight against Long in the battle of the Fellowships; the Reverend Dr. John Gordon, who had attended Durham school and had acted in Smart's Cambridge play; Richard Stonhewer, prompter for that same play and a staunch friend of Smart's during his last years; the Reverend Thomas Anguish, Clerk, who looked after Smart's interests when he left confinement; and many others. Most of these men had made their mark in the world or had settled into a comfortable life in the university or were respected members of the clergy. Smart too could have had such a life; he chose not to and now he had to enlist their aid. Others who were solicited and responded were the Delavals, the Pratts (but not Harriot), Smart's neighbors in Park Street and its immediate environs, the booksellers, a surprising number of military and naval men, several physicians, and a generous number of Bishops, Lords, Right Honourable gentlemen, and Reverend gentlemen. Henry Venn, contemporary with Smart at Cambridge, had subscribed to the 1752 *Poems*; now, a distinguished evangelical clergyman, he bought two copies of the Psalms and probably got friends in the evangelical movement also to subscribe.[30] Both the Duke of Cleveland and the Earl of Darlington were listed. From the world of music and entertainment there were virtually all the names of the men with whom Smart had had any connection: Arne, Beard, Boyce, Garrick, Hogarth, Lowe, Hayman, Havard, Howard, Rosoman, the Tyers, Worlidge, and, of course, Charles Burney. Writers in the list included Armstrong, Colman, Cowper, Churchill, Cumberland, Dodd, Fawkes, Grainger, Gray, Hawkesworth, Lloyd, Mason, Murphy, Smollett, the Wartons, Whitehead, Woty, and Edward Young. Enmities were forgotten for the moment: Smollett who had dealt Smart at least one cruel blow in the *Critical Review*, Grainger who had reviewed the *Goodness* poem harshly in the *Monthly Review*, Kenrick who had crossed imaginary swords with Smart more than a decade ago, Langhorne whom Smart accused of persecuting him in the pages of the same *Monthly Review*, Gray who probably had good reason to look less than kindly upon him, all were touched by Smart's plight. At least, if all were not moved by pity, they did subscribe. So too did others, men whose names make up part of the history of Smart's last years; among these are the Reverend R. Lowth, Bonnell Thornton, and Richard Dalton. Certain names recall Smart's own recollection of them in *Jubilate Agno*: Mr. Bird, Sir Digby Legard, Mrs. Stede, and Gulston. And there were other names that may have concealed biographical significance. Was the Reverend Mr. Maxwell, Chaplain to the Asylum, by any remote chance Francis Kelly Maxwell, admitted as a sizar at Pembroke in 1747 and ordained priest in London in 1753, who presumably resided in London from 1753 or 1755 to 1780? What asylum was referred to? Did Smart know the musician Charles Avison or, more probably, did one of his Newcastle friends get him to subscribe? Who were Samuel Blackwell, Esq., of Gloucester, ten books; Ralph Lodge, Esq., and Richard Parrott, Esq., each of whom took six books; and William Shurrock, five books? Who procured the subscriptions of "His Excellency Gov. Pownal" for four books and that of the "Hon. William Clifton, Esq. Chief Justice of Florida?" Smart may have known the ex-governor of New Jersey, Massachusetts, and South Carolina at Cambridge, as he received his Bachelor of Arts from Trinity College in 1743, but there is no evident connection with Clifton. However the full list of subscribers came into being, Smart clearly still had many friends and well-wishers. Conspicuously absent again was the name of one of Smart's early friends in London, Samuel Johnson.

Johnson did subscribe to a translation of the Psalms but it was to James Merrick's. Also among the subscribers to Merrick's version were Johnson's newly made friends, Henry Thrale and his wife, as well as another good friend, Bennet Langton. If Johnson bestirred himself in anybody's behalf at this time, it was obviously in Merrick's. Inevitably both Merrick and Smart were able to obtain subscriptions from the same people; oddly enough, Dr. William Battie, under whose care Smart had been at St. Luke's Hospital, subscribed for two copies of Merrick's Psalms but not to Smart's. Merrick's subscription list was heavy with Reverend gentlemen and members of the nobility; Smart's was much more heterogeneous. Where Smart could sign himself "Some time Fellow of Pembroke Hall, Cambridge and Scholar of the University," Merrick could write himself "Late Fellow of Trinity College, Oxford"; and where Smart had, in his proposals, written of the encouragement his translation received from "many of the Bishops and other dignified Clergymen," Merrick could write in his preface that his Psalms had been "favoured with a revisal" by the Reverend Dr. Lowth, Prebendary of Durham, who was also "pleased to encourage and advise [its] publication." But where Smart's version was "adapted to the Divine Service," as the title page proclaimed, and "the measure is kept up for all the old favourite tunes; and for the new measures there will be new musick, composed by Dr. Boyce, Mr. Howard, and other eminent masters, which will be published in an Appendix to the work for such as chuse it," as had been announced as far back as the proposals of September 8, 1763, Merrick was forced to state in his preface that his version had not been "calculated for the uses of public Worship." Still with his eye on Smart's claims for his Psalms, he wrote that "the translator knew not how, without neglecting the Poetry, to write in such language as the common sort of people could be likely to understand: For the same reason he could not confine himself in general to stanzas, nor, consequently, adopt the measures to which the tunes used in our Churches correspond." The truth of the matter is that he contented himself with only five "meters," specimens of which he gives in his seven versions of the *Gloria Patri* at the end of the Psalms. While he makes some use of three simple stanzaic forms and occasionally of trochaic tetrameter couplets, the bulk of the work is in iambic octosyllabic couplets; Smart, on the contrary, uses an almost bewildering variety of stanzas, with a marked preference for the *Song to David* stanza. His exercise on the *Gloria Patri* at the end of the Psalms runs to twenty-five different measures.

Smart's volume included the *Hymns and Spiritual Songs for the Fasts and Festivals of the Church of England* and a reprinting of the *Song to David*. Contemporary readers, influenced by the adverse notices of Smart's previous poetic efforts, overlooked or were incapable of appreciating the merits of his Psalms and Hymns, and his collection never went into another edition; Merrick's Psalms were printed in a second edition in the following year. Reviews in the *Critical Review* and in the *Monthly Review* were hostile to Smart and expressed strong preference for Merrick's version as a whole, giving quoted comparisons of specific psalms. The latter was true of the *Critical Review* which said of the translation of one passage that Smart's had a "ludicrous appearance" while Merrick's translation of the same passage was in "a more poetic style." In other comparisons Merrick had "more dignity," or his lines were "much more tender and pathetick," or he translated with

"delicacy and spirit" and with "elegance and variety" passages for
which Smart received no praise. Praise of Merrick's version brought
the review to an end; Smart's version was not mentioned by name
in the summing up but there was no mistaking the oblique reference to it: "The reader will undoubtedly be glad to find that the
Psalmist is at last delivered from a crowd of wretched poets, who
had overwhelmed his native grace and dignity under the rubbish of
their despicable schemes: the admirers of these beautiful compositions may read them with pleasure in Mr. Merrick's translations."[31]
A review of Merrick's work in the *Monthly Review*, extending to
some six pages, devoted a single paragraph of comment to Smart's
volume: "As Mr. Smart so highly resented the manner in which we
mentioned some of his late productions, and as we found he was so
sensibly hurt by what we said of them, however justly or however
tenderly we expressed ourselves, this consideration drew from us a
promise, that he should, for the future, have little cause to be
offended with us on that account: indeed some unhappy circumstances in this gentleman's life, seem to have given his latter writings a peculiar claim to a total exemption from criticism. Accordingly, we chuse to be silent, with regard to the merit of the present
publication."[32] Prospective buyers of the Psalms had had a chance
to compare the respective versions of Psalm CXXVI in June of 1764
when they were printed in the *Public Advertiser*. Something of the
quality of the rival versions can be further had from comparison of
the familiar twenty-third Psalm in the two editions. Merrick chose
the meter of *L'Allegro* and *Il Penseroso*.

> Lo, my Shepherd's hand divine!
> Want shall never more be mine.
> In a pasture fair and large
> He shall feed his happy Charge.
> And my couch with tend'rest care
> 'Midst the springing grass prepare.
> When I faint with summer's heat,
> He shall lead my weary feet
> To the streams that still and slow
> Through the verdant meadow flow.
> He my soul anew shall frame,
> And, his mercy to proclaim,
> When through devious paths I stray,
> Teach my steps the better way.
> Though the dreary vale I tread

By the shades of death o'er spread,
There I walk from terror free,
While my ev'ry wish I see
By thy rod and staff supplied,
This my guard, and that my guide.
While my foes are gazing on,
Thou thy fav'ring care hast shown;
Thou my plenteous board hast spread,
Thou with oil refresh'd my head;
Fill'd by Thee my cup o'er flows;
For thy Love no limit knows:
Constant, to my latest end
This my footsteps shall attend,
And shall bid thy hallow'd Dome
Yield me an eternal home.

Smart chose a more conventional hymn stanza,

THE shepherd Christ from heav'n arriv'd,
My flesh and spirit feeds;
I shall not therefore be depriv'd
Of all my nature needs.

As slop'd against the glist'ning beam
The velvet verdure swells,
He keeps, and leads me by the stream
Where consolation dwells.

My soul he shall from sin restore,
And her free pow'rs awake,
In paths of heav'nly truth to soar,
For love and mercy's sake.

Yea, tho' I walk death's gloomy vale,
The dread I shall disdain;
For thou art with me, lest I fail,
To check me and sustain.

Thou shalt my plenteous board appoint
Before the braving foe;
Thine oil and wine my head anoint,
And make my goblet flow.

But greater still thy love and grace
Shall all my life attend;
And in thine hallow'd dwelling place
My knees shall ever bend.

But either because he was not entirely satisfied with this or because he felt that this Psalm, like some others, deserved more than one translation, he offered an alternate version, falling back upon the *Song to David* stanza.

CHRIST Jesus has my name enroll'd,
And to his own peculiar fold
   Above all want consign'd;
Thou hast to ghostly welfare brought
The sheep, thy precious blood has bought,
   O shepherd of mankind.

Me plac'd beneath the blue serene,
In pastures ever fresh and green,
   Where all is peace and still,
He feeds—and sets me on the brink
Of living waters, there to drink
   Of comfort and my fill.

He shall convert my carnal heart,
And every Christian grace impart,
   To fix me in his way;
For by his hallow'd name he swore,
And for the sake of that no more
   Shall David ever stray.

Yea tho' from hence my journey lies
Down thro' the vale of tears and sighs,
   And up the steep of pain,
No terror shall my course withstand;
Thy rod and staff are still at hand
   To check me and sustain.

Thou shalt add plenty to thy grace,
And heap my board before their face,
   My troublers to confound;
The head that thou hast lifted up,
Thou hast anointed, and the cup
   Of my salvation crown'd.

The goodness and the grace divine,
Shall constant all along the line
   Of utmost life extend;
And I shall in thy temple dwell,
In thankful psalmody to tell
   Of transport without end.

What repelled contemporary reviewers of Smart's version was the lengthy elaboration of each verse of his original. A poet who expanded "The Lord is my shepherd, I shall not want" to four or six lines must of necessity, they felt, add extraneous matter or merely repeat himself in a fashion with which they could not sympathize. The "native grace and dignity" of the original, the *Critical Review* had written censoriously, had been buried "under the rubbish" of the "despicable schemes" of a "crowd of wretched poets." Merrick's more straightforward and unimaginative renditions were thought to preserve the simplicity and dignity of the original, and they did so in a way which made no demands upon the critics' understandings or powers of appreciation. His was a safe translation; Smart's, laboring under the disabilities that these same critics had discovered and proclaimed in their reviews of his work after 1762, was obviously poetically heterodox.

No reviewer of the Psalms, neither Smart's nor Merrick's, noticed or thought fit to call attention to the fact that Smart based his version largely or wholly on the Book of Common Prayer while Merrick went back to the Bible. Thus, for the second verse of the first Psalm the Bible has "But his delight is in the law of the Lord, and in his law doth he meditate day and night" where the Book of Common Prayer renders it as "but his delight is in the law of the Lord: and in his law will he exercise himself day and night." Merrick's version reads "But, possess'd with sacred awe,/ Meditates, great God, thy law"; Smart's "This ['God's holy law'] as his exercise he takes" is as obviously linked with the word "exercise" in the liturgy as Merrick's version is linked with the word "meditate" in the Bible. Similar dependence on the Bible and the Book of Common Prayer, respectively, occurs elsewhere in the two versions. Smart's decision to follow the Book of Common Prayer accords, of course, with the announced intention in the Psalms, for a prefatory note on the verso of the half-title reads, "In this translation, all expressions, that seem contrary to Christ, are omitted, and evangelical matter put in their room;–and as it was written with an especial view to the divine service, the reader will find sundry allusions to the rites and ceremonies of the Church of England, which are intended to render the work in general more useful and acceptable to congregations."[33] Here, too, Smart's critics, particularly the reviewers for the *Critical Review* who had questioned the orthodoxy of some of his beliefs as expressed in the *Song to David*, might have found matter for adverse comment, but their tactic with the Psalms was for the most part to ignore Smart and praise Merrick. Some slight balm to the wound was the *Christian's Magazine's* reprinting of Psalms 117, 123, and 142 in December; Dodd or Newbery, or both, thus charitably provided Smart with a bit of free advertising.

Smart's translation of the Psalms was an inevitable sequel to *A Song to David*; first, a song of praise to the poet-scholar of God and then a reworking of his songs in praise of God. Both were in his mind during the years of his confinement, and he almost surely worked at the *Song* and the Psalms in this same period, occasionally borrowing, consciously or unconsciously, an image or a peculiar collocation of words from one for use in the other. The first suggestion that he attempt a version of the Psalms came at least as early as 1752, for that year marked the end of the activity of James Crockatt the bookseller, whom Smart a decade later in *Jubilate Agno* prayed for and described as "the first to put me upon a version of the Psalms" (D, 210). Smart had thought much about the problems of versifying the Psalms and he had increasingly become convinced that a new version with new melodies was needed for use in the Church of England. His first venture in this direction was a version of the forty-second Psalm in the *Universal Visiter* for October, 1756; and since his original contributions to this periodical had virtually ceased by May it is probable that the Psalm was of earlier composition. This was not, however, the version that he used in the Psalms of 1765. One other Psalm, the one hundredth, "for a Scotch Tune," appeared in the *Christian's Magazine* for August, 1761, and was almost surely his; it too gave way to a new version in 1765, as it contained such Scotticisms as "mickle;" and "gang," and "menceful." But the fact that the one hundredth Psalm should be for a particular tune and that Smart had prayed for musicians to set his Psalms while he was still in confinement shows clearly that the new version of the Psalms was inseparable in his mind from new musical settings for them. However unrealistic all this may have been, it served to sustain him in hope for a number of years.

Smart's identification of himself with David went back to the Seatonian prize poems, expressed itself obliquely in the *Song to David*, and emerged most strongly in the Psalms, for in these last poems he could not but help think of himself as he rendered the prose of the Book of Common Prayer version of the Psalms into

verse. How close David's circumstances seemed to his own in Psalm
XXXI:

> My name was nam'd as a reproof,
> That neither friend nor foes,
> Nor neighbours came beneath my roof,
> And my companions kept aloof,
> As other company they chose.
>
> The world have all my deeds forgot,
> And I am in the place
> Of one, whose memory is not,
> Whose body damps sepulchral rot,
> And like an useless broken vase.
>
> For I have heard the godless crowd
> In blasphemy and strife,
> And fear on every side's avow'd,
> While fraud and faction are allow'd
> To meet, and scheme against my life.

Both Gray and Mason, in 1759, were surprised to learn that Smart
was still alive; he had been in the place of one whose memory was
not. In Psalm XXXV Smart found another occasion to recall certain
events in his own life:

> But in my distress they jested,
> Yea the very abjects met,
> Making mouths, my peace infested
> Without ceasing or regret.
>
> Fawning gluttons, in conjunction
> With the mimicking buffoon,
> Gnash their teeth without compunction,
> And my miseries importune.

In *Jubilate Agno* he had stated that he was looked upon as a freak
and had even repeated some remarks made upon his condition,
"For Silly fellow! Silly fellow! is against me and belongeth neither
to me nor my family" (B1, 60). The alienation from his family that
was the most grievous result of his confinement was paralleled in
Psalm LXIX where he could write

> I am become to all my kin
> As foreign to their care;

My mothers children from within
Refuse me entrance there.

And he sympathized keenly with the psalmist in Psalm CII, lamenting the loss of his wife and virtually hugging his miseries to himself
in a paroxysm of self-pity.

I have labour'd my researches,
Pond'ring on my lonely state,
Watching as the sparrow perches
On the house without his mate.

For their malice advantageous
This my case my foes deride;
All day long they are outrageous,
That against me are ally'd.

For with tears these ashes steeping,
I have eaten them for bread;
And my cup with bitter weeping
I have mingled on my bed.

In these and in other passages Smart saw himself in one aspect of his
life, the darker.

Smart of necessity leaned heavily on his original. He could not
stray too far from the words and thoughts of the Psalms he was
translating, but he could and did introduce imagery and words of
his own. And he could and did give greater prominence to some
elements in his originals. His fondness for naval imagery, for example, induced him to resort to it where there was not the slightest
warrant for it in his original. Psalm XVIII, verse 44, reads, in the
Book of Common Prayer, "A people whom I have not known: shall
serve me." Smart, in his version, takes ship to arrive at the lands of
this people,

My swelling sails shall be unfurl'd,
And to reform a distant world,
Thou shalt my fleets convoy;
And nations from thy word remote,
I to thine honour will devote,
And in thy ways employ.

Where Psalm XXXI, verse 9, in the liturgy has "Thou hast not shut
me up into the hand of the enemy: but set my feet in a large room,"

SMART: SCHOLAR OF THE UNIVERSITY

Smart writes

> Thou hast not given me up, nor bound
>   Within the stranger's hand,
> Nor in the streights hast run aground
> My vessel, but secure and sound
>   Hast brought her to a spacious land.

In Psalm XXXIII, verse 12, he has Christ holding the helm of a ship, figuratively, of course; in the last verse of Psalm LXVIII, the Lord "stands all-pow'rful on the prow." Where the psalmist has an empty raging sea Smart places a navy in its midst (Psalm LXXXIX, verse 10). And in the first verse of Psalm CXIX, NUN, Smart speaks of his vessel gliding "safe to the destin'd port," directed by the light of the word of God, in place of the simple words, "Thy word is a lantern unto my feet: and a light unto my paths." This recourse to naval imagery is striking, and while Smart, who identified himself with fighting men, found in his source and employed images taken from land battles, he introduced the naval imagery without the sanction of his original. In a poem written almost immediately after his release from confinement in January, 1763, Smart thanks John Sherratt for bringing about his freedom, despite the difficulties in his way, in the following image,

> To run thy keel across the boom,
> And save my vessel from her doom,
> And cut her from the pirate's port,
> Beneath the cannon of the fort,
> With colours fresh, and sails unfurl'd,
> Was nobly dar'd to beat the world.

Possibly the ocean, one of God's most stupendous creations, in its vastness—he more than once called it "the vast profound" in his religious poetry—symbolized freedom to him who had been forced to spend too much time in cramped quarters.

Smart introduced more than just a small cluster of naval images into his version of the Psalms; taking his cue from Horace, the Latin author he studied more closely than any other, he felt free to experiment with language. While the number of words coined originally by him in the Psalms is small, he resurrected a number of words which had been used before but were rare indeed in 1765. Sometimes he produced an epithet which was only a variation of one he had found in the Bible, his "mercy-beams" and "mercy-gate" being readily manufactured on the analogy of the Bible's "mercy-seat," but nonetheless helping to create the sense of a vocabulary somewhat removed in time from 1765. Also aiding in this was Smart's return to the old possessive form, almost without exception in "Christ his," used time and again and again. Other epithets also contributed to the seeming remoteness of his language. Thus he has "heart-directed," "heav'n arrested," and "heav'n-directed" in the Psalms and others formed in the same way in the *Hymns and Spiritual Songs*.[34] Adding something also to the strangeness of his version were the coinages "godchildhood," "imblossom'd," and "unreef," the last used of a flag. More often, however, Smart used a perfectly familiar word in a way in which few other writers had thought to employ it. One such word, a favorite with him, was "sublimes," used as a verb and meaning to transmute into something higher and better. While "to sublime" was not out of place in scientific writing, it made a strange appearance in the Psalms. But there are many many more words which, while not used in the Bible, seem properly to belong there; and Smart almost invariably uses these words more than once.* Some words make but a single appearance, but they too lend something to the general impression of the far-away and unusual.† Much of the unique effect that the language of Smart's Psalms has, insofar as vocabulary is concerned, does not derive from the Bible. But the familiar, and equally important, part of that vocabulary and the imagery dependent upon it is of course Biblical; contemporary readers and reviewers expected the latter; they were unprepared for the former.

Many of Smart's most memorable effects in the Psalms are based only in part on the Bible, if indeed some of them owe anything at all to that source. Those "multitudes in mail" of stanza seventy-eight of *A Song to David* and of the second verse of Psalm LXVIII owe nothing to the Bible; the word "mail" occurs there only twice and never in conjunction with multitudes. "Stupendous," the key word in the Psalms and one which Smart used effectively before and after 1765, is never used in the Bible; its numerous appearances in

---

*A partial list would include respire, convex, affiance, laud (used as a noun twelve times), mows, ghostly (meaning spiritual), sempiternal, promulge, redoubted, to plume, restiff, lave, penitential, and educe.

† Among these are words such as imbrue, rives, gratulation, amerce, abjects, lowth, rancle, obnubilated, to straw, implead, cield, decachord (non-Biblical), bruit, to canton, dehort, and adjure; some of these are Biblical, most are not.

the Psalms, some twenty-five times and almost always associated with God, do much toward creating the uniqueness of that collection. Smart's use of this word suggests something of the awe and humility he feels before the spectacle of God's immensity and parts of his creation. The "bastion's mole" of stanza seventy-six of the *Song to David* and of the third verse of Psalm XXXI also owes absolutely nothing to the Bible. Examples abound, Smart employing unusual images or achieving fresh effects with "clust'ring spheres" and "pillar'd arches," with "choice gums" and "cocoa's purest milk," and with "shoals" that "upon the surface leap" and "the mutes that sea contains," none of which derive from the Bible. His dexterity in various stanzaic forms and his facility in the repetition, parallelism, and syntactical inversion that Robert Lowth had found in Hebrew poetry must always be linked with his deeply conscious effort to create striking effects with unusual words in unusual juxtapositions.

One more aspect of the Psalms makes for further uniqueness. As he had in the *Song*, Smart carried the device of repetition to exceptional extremes, his Psalms being remarkable for the constant use of doublets and triplets, often linked alliteratively, so that with the repetition of a particular pair or trio of words the major motifs of the poems are made to stand out clearly and boldly. The very last words of his last Psalm are "praise and pray'r," the companion themes of the whole collection, an alliterative pair that is found ten times in the psalms and seven times in the accompanying *Hymns and Spiritual Songs*. At one point in the Psalms it is stretched to a triplet, "By praise, by patience, and by pray'r"; at another time it is qualified as "publick pray'r and praise."* Occasionally there will be an alliterative triplet: "weakness, want and woe" or "plenty, pow'r and peace," or "malice, multitudes and might."

Some of these usages, the doublets and triplets, the alliteration—"good in grain" occurs in *A Song to David*, four times in the Psalms, and in the preface to Smart's verse *Horace* in 1767, as a further example—the few coinages, the old words resurrected, may seem by themselves to be too weak or infrequent to make much impression in the thousands of words in the Psalms. However, not all the examples have been listed and, more importantly, the collective presence of these devices gives the Psalms the peculiar quality

---

*Other such combinations are grace and goodness, fraud and faction, fraud and force, work and word, bear and bless, watch and ward, and his talent and his term.

that causes them to stand out from Merrick's version and from most of the religious poetry of the period. Unfortunately for Smart, not even his staunchest friends, many of them poets themselves, understood what he was trying to do and they thought it best for his sake to say nothing about his Psalms. William Mason, who with Stonhewer did most of all Smart's friends to help him after he came out of confinement, wrote an essay "On Parochial Psalmody" in 1782 in which he examined metrical versions of the Psalms; he mentioned Merrick once or twice but never Smart.

The Psalms are not without their faults. Occasionally the syntax is so tortured as to make Smart's meaning obscure; equally often there are rather ill-defined allusions to Biblical matters which compound the difficulties already set up by the terseness and economy of expression in many passages. And then too the besetting sin of poetic diction makes itself felt in the usual ways. Some of Smart's verbal revivals are not felicitous, even though they lend an air of remoteness to his verses. The "pensile house" of the storks; "reduce" and "educe" used in their root Latin meanings; "obnubilated souls" and "supplicate the knee;" all these, with some others, must have alienated even contemporary readers. Smart's fondness for an unusual and Latinate poetical vocabulary had been parodied in his Grub-Street days; he was still open to criticism on the same score. He coined new epithets and used many old ones. He relied on or lapsed into certain of the somewhat worn-out circumlocutions of the poets who wrote about nature and found themselves wanting to vary the names of God's creatures, influenced of course by a long tradition. Hence there are "feather'd millions," and "finny shoals," and the sea becomes, variously, the "briny" depth, broad, and bath. Fish are described as "mute." Taking his cue from the Biblical "firstlings" and "fatlings," Smart has his "younglings" and "kidlings"; and the river Kidron "purls." Yet the uses of poetic diction in the thousands of verses of the Psalms are relatively few and would hardly have provoked comment in his own time.

Accompanying the Psalms were the *Hymns and Spiritual Songs for the Fasts and Festivals of the Church of England,* thirty-five poems, each of which was appropriate for a holy day of the Church of England. Robert Nelson had long ago written a prose *Companion for the Fasts and Festivals for the Church of England,* and there had been at least two earlier sets of hymns designed for the calendar of the Church,[35] but Smart owes nothing to any of them; indeed he writes two hymns where Nelson has only one fast and festival and has some hymns, "King Charles the Martyr" and "The King's Restoration," for example, that are naturally not in Nelson, since they celebrate events that happened after Nelson's death. But Smart's hymns are, for the most part, poetry of a very high order of excellence while Nelson's work is intended as nothing more than a vademecum for the worshipper. Smart, constantly experimenting with stanzaic forms and poetic techniques, adopted a system of linking one hymn to the next by repeating a word or idea—or by association—from the last line or stanza of the one to the first line or stanza of the other. Sometimes the links defy immediate recognition, but they are there. Sometimes the association that joins two hymns exists only on a verbal level, as in the end of number XI, where a reference to bell ringers prepares the way for the opening line of number XII, "Pull up the bell-flow'rs of the spring" and for a reference in the next two lines to the "ring" of a "chearful song." All the hymns are brought into a unified whole by the appearance of "WORD" as the last word of the last hymn harking back identically to the first "WORD" of the first hymn. Although the device may seem mechanical and contrived Smart so employed it that it comes as a delightful surprise at first and, later, as something to look forward to. Again, as in the Psalms, the stanzaic forms are varied; unlike his practice in the Psalms, however, the *Song to David* stanza is used sparingly. His source for the *Hymns*, as it had been for the Psalms, was the Book of Common Prayer. That other more secular areas of Smart's large store of reading and knowledge should have made their presence felt was inevitable.

Inevitably, too, the themes that predominated in the volumes of poetry that appeared one after the other from 1763 to 1765 were present in the *Hymns and Spiritual Songs*. Here, in Hymn VI, "The Presentation of Christ in the Temple," Smart not only raised his own voice in praise and gratitude but also took it upon himself to speak for all creation,

> I speak for all—for them that fly,
>   And for the race that swim;
> For all that dwell in moist and dry,
> Beasts, reptiles, flow'rs and gems to vie
>   When gratitude begins her hymn

going on, in subsequent stanzas, to call upon each of the families of creatures listed in the quoted stanza to praise God. This method of gathering a number of objects, ideas, or qualities together in one stanza and then allowing scope for fuller treatment in successive stanzas was one of the formal features used with such extraordinary effect in *A Song to David*. As in the Psalms and elsewhere in his work Smart gloried in the achievements of the English, even to the point of suggesting that the English language might suffice "To make nations good and wise" (Hymn XV), echoing *Jubilate Agno*, "for the ENGLISH TONGUE shall be the language of the WEST" (B1, 127). And, as he had before, he turned to contemplate England's might on the ocean, nowhere more extensively or proudly than in Hymn XVII, "The King's Restoration," a hymn that gave him the welcome opportunity to rehearse the history of British naval exploits. Of five successive stanzas beginning "we thank thee" he devotes the third entirely to this theme,

> We thank thee for the naval sway
> Which o'er the subject seas we claim;
> And for the homage nations pay,
> Submissive to the great Britannic fame;
> Who soon as they thy precious cross discern,
> Bow lowering to the staff on our imperial stern.

Like John Donne before him Smart saw the mast on a ship as a symbol, a "precious cross" or, as in Hymn XXI, "Christ's triumphant cross," or, again, as in the fable, *A Story of a Cock and a Bull*, "the British cross" (here possibly the Union Jack). But it is in Hymn XVII that he calls the roll of England's great admirals and sea-fighters: "Howard, Frobisher, and glorious Drake"; and "Forest, Suckling, Langdon"; and Queen Ann "cherish [ing] with her wing/A Russell, Shovel, Rook, a Benbow, and a Byng." Only in one other poem, the *Ode on Admiral Sir George Pocock*, published two years earlier, did he sound the praises of England's naval heroes so fully, there claiming for Pocock that

> Not HOWARD, FROBISHER, or DRAKE,
> Or VERNON'S fam'd *Herculean* deed;
> Not all the miracles of BLAKE,
> Can the great Chart of thine exploits exceed.

A faint anticipation is to be seen in *The Hop-Garden* where Vernon and Warren are described as "British demi-god[s]." And it is in Hymn XXVI, "The accession of King George III," an event which occurred on October 25, 1760, arousing the suspicion that the poem was written for that occasion, that Smart attributes the success of our "gallant fleets" to the fact that Christ Jesus was "at the helm."

Some of Smart's loveliest lines occur in the Hymns; the birth of Christ moves him to describe the effect of this momentous event,

> Spinks and ouzles sing sublimely,
>   'We too have a Saviour born,'
> Whiter blossoms burst untimely
>   On the blest Mosaic thorn.
>
> God all bounteous, all-creative,
>   Whom no ills from good dissuade,
> Is incarnate, and a native
>   Of the very world he made. (No. XXXII)

Characteristically, he gives his birds their less common names, preferring them to the more familiar "finches and blackbirds." But in yet another hymn, Number XIII, "St. Philip and St. James," written for May 1, he writes of the "black-bird" and the "goldfinch." The whole of this latter hymn epitomizes, in so much as any one hymn can do that, what Smart accomplished in this collection.

> Now the winds are all composure,
>   But the breath upon the bloom,
> Blowing sweet o'er each inclosure,
>   Grateful off'rings of perfume.
>
> Tansy, calaminth and daisies,
>   On the river's margin thrive;
> And accompany the mazes
>   Of the stream that leaps alive.
>
> Muse, accordant to the season,
>   Give the numbers life and air;
> When the sounds and objects reason
>   In behalf of praise and pray'r.
>
> All the scenes of nature quicken,
>   By the genial spirit fann'd;
> And the painted beauties thicken
>   Colour'd by the master's hand.

LONDON, 1763-1765

Earth her vigour repossessing
    As the blasts are held in ward;
Blessing heap'd and press'd on blessing,
    Yield the measure of the Lord.

Beeches, without order seemly,
    Shade the flow'rs of annual birth,
And the lily smiles supremely
    Mention'd by the Lord on earth.

Couslips seize upon the fallow,
    And the cardamine in white,
Where the corn-flow'rs join the mallow,
    Joy and health, and thrift unite.

Study sits beneath her arbour,
    By the bason's glossy side;
While the boat from out its harbour
    Exercise and pleasure guide.

Pray'r and praise be mine employment,
    Without grudging or regret,
Lasting life, and long enjoyment,
    Are not here, and are not yet.

Hark! aloud, the black-bird whistles,
    With surrounding fragrance blest,
And the goldfinch in the thistles
    Make provisions for her nest.

Ev'n the hornet hives his honey
    Bluecap builds his stately dome,
And the rocks supply the coney
    With a fortress and an home.

But the servants of their Saviour,
    Which with gospel-peace are shod,
Have no bed but what the paviour
    Makes them in the porch of God.

O thou house that hold'st the charter
    Of salvation from on high,
Fraught with prophet, saint, and martyr,
    Born to weep, to starve and die!

Great to-day thy song and rapture
    In the choir of Christ and WREN

219

When two prizes were the capture
Of the hand that fish'd for men.

To the man of quick compliance
Jesus call'd, and Philip came;
And began to make alliance
For his master's cause and name.

James, of title most illustrious,
Brother of the Lord, allow'd;
In the vineyards how industrious,
Nor by years nor hardship bow'd!

Each accepted in his trial,
One the CHEERFUL one the JUST;
Both of love and self-denial,
Both of everlasting trust.

Living they dispens'd salvation,
Heav'n-endow'd with grace and pow'r;
And they dy'd in imitation
Of their Saviour's final hour.

Who, for cruel traitors pleading,
Triumph'd in his parting breath;
O'er all miracles preceding
His inestimable death.

Here is Smart's observant eye for the details of nature; here is his insistence on "praise and pray'r"; here, too, is the simple device of triplets, "prophet, saint, and martyr" and "to weep, to starve and die," which marks all of his religious poetry and derives ultimately from the Old Testament. Indeed, in the rather short compass of these *Hymns* he uses proportionately many more doublets, particularly of the alliterative variety, than he does in the Psalms. Various other usages, including exact verbal echoes, link the Hymns with the Psalms and form a kind of pattern which becomes increasingly visible in these works of his late years. Despite the beauty of so much of the poetry in the Hymns and despite the unmistakable religious fervor in them, the reviewers said nothing about them; the Hymns could only have made them ill at ease. Indeed, the very attempt to provide hymns for the church year was suspect, smacking of evangelicalism. While there is no doubt, from Smart's designating some of his Psalms to be sung to one or another "old" tune and from the existence of the *Collection of Melodies* for them, that he hopefully foresaw his Psalms taking the place of the established psalms of the liturgy, he gave no clear sign that he expected the same for the *Hymns and Spiritual Songs*. Had he done so, he would again have been disappointed. Having failed to achieve his end, he was compelled to go on to other work.

Smart's name is linked with a curious work of this same year entitled *A Defence of Freemasonry*, a refutation of another Freemasonic work, *Ahiman Rezon*, published earlier in 1765. The actual "defence" covers about forty pages and has appended to it "A Collection of Masons Odes and Songs. Most of them entirely new;" the pamphlet was printed for the author and sold by W. Flexney and by E. Hood. While the "defence" has been claimed for Smart, there is no solid evidence for the attribution.[36] Last in the collection of songs is "A Song by Brother C. Smart, A.M., Tune, 'Ye frolicksome Sparks of the Game'," which confirms Smart's participation in Masonic affairs but does nothing for his reputation as a poet.[37] Along with Smart's there are songs by brother Masons from various parts of England; some bear the notation that music was composed for them, one of these settings being by Smart's friend Dr. Boyce. A Brother H. Jackson who wrote some songs for the collection appears in the announcement of Mother Midnight's New Carnival Concert for September 26, 1754, at which time a "Mason's Ode, set by Gilder, Words by Jackson, sung by Masons" formed part of a benefit performance for "Pittard le Charpentier and a Free Mason." In 1765 Smart could have been attending Masonic lodge meetings in scores of places in London, although he probably went to a lodge near his rooms; the Bell Tavern, King St., Westminster, was not too far from Park Street. Since he used Storey's Gate Coffee-House, St. James's Park, as a place from which to write a number of letters in the next four years, he may also have attended meetings near that establishment.[38] If he was paid for his song, or if, as seems improbable, he edited the *Defence*, his gain could only have been slight. He needed more than sporadic small sums of money; he needed a steady and impressive income.

VI.

LONDON, 1766-1771

For sheer length and sustained excellence nothing Smart had written hitherto could compare with the combined Psalms and *Hymns and Spiritual Songs.* Some six years at least had gone into their composition, with interruptions of one nature or another either slowing his progress or bringing it to a temporary standstill. With the *Song to David* and the *Jubilate Agno* also behind him Smart felt that he had come to a turning point in his life as a poet when the Psalms and their accompanying *Hymns and Spiritual Songs* were published, reviewed, and so soon forgotten. His need to keep busy and his circumstances—as well as his pride—had earlier set him to translating Horace into verse, and with the failure of the Psalms he applied himself to that task more vigorously. But the translation was far from complete and the arrangements for its printing and publication were, if anything, still abortive. Soon after the New Year, in serious trouble, he wrote to Paul Panton again; the letter, dated January 10, 1766, was written from Storey's Gate Coffee-House.

> D^r^ S^ir^
> I shou'd have dispatched your books according to your commands, but lost your letter & the directions therein contained.—It will be a very kind thing to collect the 2^d^. payments for me & send them & you shall have the books as soon as I am repossessed of the directions.—For you must know I was lately arrested by my printer for Eighty Six pounds & must have gone to jail for that very book, from which I was in hopes of [?] ingenuous bread, if it had not been for a kind friend, who cou'd not bear to see my tears—I am going to impose another tax upon my friends for a new Volume of Missellaneous Poems, which nothing but absolute want shou'd have compelled me to—Pray let me hear from you soon—
>
> Your most obliged
> & affectionate
> Christopher Smart[1]

Panton had collected subscribers for the Psalms and the first moiety of their payments; Smart was now asking for the second moiety which he had to have before he could send off the books. Other subscribers had not come forward to pay the second moiety, and Smart had written on January 3 to Granville Sharp of Durham, residing at this time in London, inquiring how to dispose of the unclaimed ten copies of the Psalms for which John Sharp, Archdeacon of Northumberland, had subscribed. Granville Sharp in turn wrote to the Archdeacon.

A few days ago I received a letter from Mr. Smart desiring

directions where to send the 10 Books of his Psalms for which you subscribed, and signifying that he had been arrested by his Printer for £86, and that he "must have finished an unfortunate life in jail had it not been for the good nature of a Friend, who could not bear to see his tears."—In return, I desired him to send the Books to me (which I have since received) and said I would take your directions for the disposal of them; so please to inform me in your next, how you will have them sent.

I wish some kind of place, or employment, could be found for poor Smart; surely he must be very capable of earning a comfortable subsistence, if he was but put in the way of it.[2]

When Smart wrote to Panton he echoed the words of this letter. At the time these letters were written he was hard at work at the verse translation of Horace upon which Hawkesworth saw him engaged in late 1764, but he was also contemplating "a new Volume of Missellaneous Poems," to be sold by subscription. He had told Hawkesworth in 1764 that "he once had thoughts of printing" his verse Horace "by subscription, but as he had troubled his friends already, he was unwilling to do it again." Since he had published three works by this method, the 1752 *Poems, Mother Midnight's Orations* in 1763, and the Psalms, his pride quite naturally forbade a subscription for the Horace. But by the time he wrote the letter to Panton he had faced possible imprisonment for debt and he was desperate. His solution, as always, was to publish something as quickly as possible, this time in the hopes that the translation of Horace would be adopted as a school text and run into successive editions. He clung to this last hope and, in order to realize it, he fell back upon the subscription scheme again for the miscellaneous poems.

A letter to George Colman in the following month, February 27, from "St James's Park next door to the Cockpit," echoes the one to Panton:

Sir:
I find myself reduced by the necessity of the case again to tax such of my friends as are disposed to do me the honour of their names

I am with much respect
Your obliged Servant
Christopher Smart.

I observe from the conversation in general on your late performance, that either your benevolence has won you more affection, or your wit commanded more applause (both I suppose) than that of any person in my memory.[3]

Colman and Garrick's *The Clandestine Marriage* had had its premiere exactly a week before Smart's letter gave flattering recognition of the play's success. Colman, a close friend of Robert Lloyd and of Bonnell Thornton, had subscribed to the Psalms and could be counted on to do the same for the new poems. Smart cherished the project for some two more years at least, for at the end of the second and fourth volumes of the verse *Horace*, published in the autumn of 1767, he had elaborate proposals printed. As with the Psalms there were to be a number of copies on Royal paper; unlike the previous proposals, however, the subscriber could pay the whole amount immediately if he wished. And lest anyone suspect that this was to be nothing but a reprint of old poems Smart promised that none of his 1752 *Poems* would be included. Some of the booksellers who had taken in subscriptions for the Psalms were to serve in the same capacity again.

Granville Sharp's kindly wish that "some kind of place, or employment" could be found for Smart had occurred to Richard Stonhewer, and on April 22 of this year Smart was put first in the list to fill the next vacancy in the number of Poor Chevaliers of the Chapel of St. George at Windsor Castle.[4] Had he been fortunate enough to secure this place, which he never did, he would have been given lodgings at Windsor and about thirty pounds a year; for this he would have been required to assist at prayers in the Chapel every day, hardly an onerous existence for one who was happiest on his knees rendering homage to God. But fate was unkind again, and Smart was not to end his days in the peace of a hostel. Stonhewer's part in this charitable action is revealed in a letter Smart wrote to Panton on January 22, 1767, again from one of his favorite haunts, Storey's Gate Coffee-House.

> Dear S^r
>
> Mr Mason the King's Chaplain coming lately to Town waited on Mr Stonhewer to enquire after me & seemed affectionately anxious concerning the state of my affairs. Mr Stonhewer informed him, that he had procurd me to be put upon the lists of Expectants for a Poor Knight of Windsor, but that there was no likelihood of a vacancy for some years. Mr Mason then proposed an annual Subscription of a guinea or two yearly amongst my friends. Sundry

gentlemen have come in to this goodnaturd Scheme, which was
none of my own devising: but being urged by Mason I made
application to such of my Benefactors, whose wishd goodness in a
manner gives me warrant.

I am D^r S^r,
Y^r most obliged &
most obedient Ser^t
Christopher Smart

Smart had had to swallow whatever pride remained to him. Mason's
suggestion that he be supported by an annual subscription of one or
two guineas a year by his friends would have been anathema to him
a little more than a year ago, but the spectre of debtor's prison had
terrified him, and he had so far forgotten his manliness as to break
down into tears on the occasion of his arrest. Stonhewer did not
rest content with getting Smart on the list for a place at the Chapel
at Windsor, for some time after August 15, 1766, when he became
private secretary to the Duke of Grafton, his former pupil and now
First Lord of the Treasury, he must have been instrumental in
procuring an annual pension of fifty pounds from the government
for him.[5]

With fifty pounds a year Smart should have been able to live
quietly and comfortably but he was congenitally incapable of living
within his means. On February 12, 1767, he wrote once more to
Paul Panton; again he was in need.

Dear Sir
    I am sorry any mistake shou'd happen by my directing the letter
to the wrong place, however your most friendly & obliging answer
came in very good time. I communicated the contents to M^r
Mason, who is at present in a very pitiable state of anxiety concern-
ing his wife, which he lately married & is now dangerously ill. He
has not succeeded very well with regard to numbers, & his plan
rather interferes with the present application I am making for Subscribers to a 2^d Vol. of Missellaneous Poems. I beg the favour you
wou'd order your Bookseller to dispatch the [?] watchd Psalms
to Pater Noster Row as fast as possible, they being wanted in
London. Once more give me leave to repeat my best thanks for
your generous intentions in my favour & believe me to be with
much affection & respect

your most oblig'd old friend
& humble Ser^t
Christopher Smart

Balancing in his mind the conflicting advantages of a private subscription as opposed to a public one for his projected volume of
miscellaneous poems, a subscription actually under way, he made
the best of both worlds by accepting two guineas from Panton
shortly after he wrote to him in February. His acknowledgement
came in a brief letter of April 24.

> My Dear Friend,
>   I acknowledge the receipt of two guineas paid me with much
> Politeness by Dr Wynn, being the annual contribution you are
> pleased to lay upon yourself in my behalf agreeable to the plan
> proposed by Mr Mason.
>
>   I am with much respect
>   affection &
>   thankfulness
>   ever yours to command
>   Christopher Smart.

The tone of these last two letters to Panton is calmer, more dignified than those written shortly after Dryden Leach had taken legal
action to collect the eighty-six pounds owed him. Smart felt surer
of himself; he could depend on a small circle of devoted friends to
continue their yearly subscription and he was getting the verse
Horace ready for the press. With its publication and possible subsequent adoption as a school text he would be able to hold his head
up again and dispense with the charity that had kept him alive.
Cognizant of the favors done him by Francis Fawkes over the years
he reciprocated to some slight degree by subscribing to his translation of the *Idylliums of Theocritus*—despite his ever present
need.

   *The Works of Horace, Translated into Verse. With a Prose In-
terpretation, for the help of Students. And Occasional Notes.* "By
Christopher Smart, A.M. Sometime Fellow of Pembroke Hall, Cambridge, and Scholar of the University" was published in August in
four attractive octavo volumes. For the epigraph Smart chose some
lines from his poet's first book of epistles where Horace speaks of
himself, "I was the first to plant free footsteps on a virgin soil; I
walked not where others trod. Who trusts himself will lead and rule
the swarm,"[6] evidently feeling that he too in some way was a pioneer, although he was by far not the first to attempt a verse *Horace*.
His dedication was to Sir Francis Blake Delaval, the Othello of the
amateur production of Shakespeare's play in 1751; the first sentence

of the dedication explains his reason for undertaking the work at all. "Should you ask me," he addresses Sir Francis, "what could be my inducement to undertake the following work at my time of day, and after three or four applauded persons, I must fairly answer, that I made my version of Horace for the same reason, as he wrote the original,

> —Paupertas impulit audax
> Ut versus facerem—."

After this frank admission of his need for money Smart did the expected and praised Sir Francis and, in a footnote, his brother Edward, a Fellow of Pembroke. With these preliminaries out of the way, he gave his full attention to a long preface.

Smart's Preface to the verse *Horace* is in some respects an *apologia*; at "his time of day"—he was forty-five years old in 1767—he felt obliged to justify both the present work and to a lesser extent his past life as a poet. This was his most extended piece of literary criticism, far longer and more ambitious than the critical remarks which accompanied his *Ode on Musick for St. Cecilia's Day* in 1746. The personal note, present in 1746, is very strong in the *Horace* preface, with an almost immediate identification of poet and translator in the statement that the "Horatian boldness, cannot be attempted with any success, save by men of some rank with them and affinity in the spirit." Since Horace was distinguished by an "unrivalled peculiarity of expression, which has excited the admiration of all succeeding ages," Smart felt obliged to offer proof of his qualifications for reproducing that excellence in his translation. Accordingly, he recalled to his readers the earliest of his published translations, that of Pope's St. Cecilia's Day ode into Latin: "I beg leave therefore to assure the Reader, that I did not set about my work without the consciousness of a talent, admitted of, and attested to, by the best scholars of the times both at home and abroad. Mr. Pope in particular, with whom I had the honour to correspond, entertained a very high opinion of my abilities as a translator, which one of the brightest men amongst our Nobility will be ready (I trust) to certify, should my veracity in this matter be called to question" (p. viii). The nobleman he referred to was William Murray, Baron Mansfield, who had encouraged him to write to Pope. No event in his life meant more to him as a poet than Pope's few words in praise of his abilities as a translator. But even Pope, Smart went on, had left "no remarkable instance" of a translation or imitation of Horace which captured his *curiosa felicitas,* although, he admitted, "this is a beauty, that occurs rather in the Odes, than the other parts of Horace's works; where the aiming at familiarity of style excluded the curiosity of choice diction" (p. ix).

As he turned to a brief discussion of the Odes, Smart singled out the fourth book, "which *Horace* wrote with all his might by the united force of judgment and genius, under the patronage and applause of *Augustus* and the whole world," and hoped that if his version were considered worthy to be put alongside those of Cowley, Pope, and Atterbury, "it will be thought no mean literary atchievement for a single man, who was very far from having such superlative advantages" (p. x). Despite his solitary and troubled state he claimed to have made "certain new discoveries, and put disputed passages out of all question." And after naming the Latin edition he used as his text, explaining the paucity of his footnotes, and congratulating himself on being careful "concerning all passages of Offence" (p. xi), he came to one of the major ideas expounded in his Preface.

> Besides the *Curiosa Felicitas,* so much of *Horace* by himself, there is another poetical excellence, which tho' possessed in a degree by every great genius, is exceeding in our Lyric to surpass; I mean the beauty, force and vehemence of *Impression*: which leads me to a rare and entertaining subject, not (I think) any where much insisted on by others.
>
> *Impression* then, is a talent or gift of Almighty God, by which a Genius is impowered to throw an emphasis upon a word or sentence in such wise, that it cannot escape any reader of sheer good sense, and true critical sagacity. This power will sometimes keep it up thro' the *medium* of a prose translation; especially in scripture, for in justice to truth and everlasting preeminence, we must confess this virtue to be far more powerful and abundant in sacred writings (p. xii).

In illustration of scriptural examples of "impression" he quotes a few lines of Hebrew and translates them himself, following them with two examples from Virgil, again in his own translation.

Smart had been thinking of this talent or gift of impression at the very least as early as February, 1760, when he wrote in *Jubilate Agno,* "For my talent is to give an impression upon words by punching, that when the reader casts his eye upon 'em, he takes up the image of the mould wch I have made" (B2, 404). Thus, he felt himself especially endowed to undertake a translation of Horace into verse. And because the following are among the major themes of his poetry as well as of the writers of ancient Greece and Rome he further identified himself with them. For he writes that "we must take this along with us, however, that the force of *Impression* is always liveliest upon the eulogies of patriotism, gratitude, honour, and the like" (p. xiii) . Nor was he at a loss for passages to exemplify his stand, quoting Virgil, Homer, and Dionysius and taking opportunity to bring in references to and brief quotations from Sir John Denham and Scaliger. His pride in his own discernment and abilities as a translator even caused him to quote a passage from Pope's Homer and his own version, closer to "the sense and spirit of the original" according to him (p. xvi). Then after devoting five pages to illustrating Horace's skill in "impression," Smart turns to the second major idea in his Preface, possibly having had it partly in mind when he thought of his work as a pioneer attempt. He leads rather dramatically into his subject, "I come now to a piece of classical history, which seems to have been a secret to all commentators of *Horace* from the beginning," and after two more sentences he reveals his discovery: "To retard the reader no longer the first part of that essay [the *Ars Poetica*] is a manifest ridicule of the Metamorphoses of *Ovid*, who was in high esteem at the *Court of Augustus* for that work, which, however, beautiful for music and painting, had nothing to recommend it to the judgment and taste of *Horace*, who well know [*sic*] that the business of poetry is to express gratitude, reward, merit, and promote moral edification" (p. xxii). Unfortuately, Smart did not know that Horace had died well before Ovid had even begun the *Metamorphoses*. Seven pages are devoted to a proof of his theory and then he closes on a personal note, again one of self-pity:

> Good-nature is the grace of God in grain, and so much the characteristic of an *Englishman*, that I hope every one deserving such a name will think it somewhat hard, if a gentleman derived from ancestors, who have abode upon their own Lordship six hundred years in the County Palatine of *Durham*, should have been reduced in a manner by necessity to a work of this kind, which if done in a state, he had more reason to be satisfied with, had been more likely to have given satisfaction.

P.S. It is no more than justice to the merit of Mr. *Flexney*, to acknowledge, that ever since I have been engaged with him in this work, he has constantly treated me with much friendship and good-nature, which I hope will serve him amongst such gentlemen and scholars, as have occasion for a good Bookseller.

William Flexney's name was one in the list of booksellers who took in subscriptions for Smart's Psalms as early as the proposals of September 8, 1763; he sold the 1763 *Poems on Several Occasions* and was one of the three booksellers who sold the Psalms when they were finally published. Although he also published the verse *Horace*, Smart's *Parables*, published in the next year, were printed by W. Owen. No printer or publisher, save Newbery, had a long association with Smart.

Smart's Preface reveals much about him; it is the last and the longest of his public utterances. Not only did he insist, as he had done in his previous translations, principally the prose *Horace* and the Phaedrus, on his qualifications for the task before him, but he also included in his prolegomena scholarly statements about the editions used as texts, the number and kinds of his notes, and his own emendations and conjectures. While his major translations were done in the hope of striking a rich mine of revenue and were largely for use as school texts, he always had an eye on the learned reader who knew how such editions should be carried out and would be sure to carp at him for not adhering to scholarly protocol. In addition, in the Preface, he demonstrated that he had been engaged in more than a superficial fashion with the question of Horace's uniqueness as a poet and, as a direct consequence, with the ancillary question of the abilities and gifts demanded of a translator of that poet's work. His quotations in Hebrew and Greek, as well as in Latin poets other than Horace, were included for the sake of his arguments, of course, but they were also designed as further evidence of his scholarly credentials. In the second volume of the *Horace*. Smart also wrote that "in order to exercise the student in the Horatian measures, and at the same time (as I trust) to give him no mean entertainment, I have subjoined my translation of Mr. Pope's Ode on St. Cecilia's day, written when I was a youth, and for which I had the honour of a very handsome letter of thanks from that celebrated Author." Smart's theory that Horace was ridiculing Ovid's *Metamorphoses* in the first part of the *Ars Poetica* had excited him and he hoped that other scholars would be convinced of the strength of his case and be similarly excited. But accompanying this need to reiterate his fitness for the task he had set himself was a note of bitterness. All his projects had failed to bring him the relief he needed; the Psalms, far from rescuing him, at one time seemed about to bring him to a debtor's prison. He could not go on turning out volume after volume of poems and translations; his health, never robust, could not stand the physical and mental strain involved in another large literary project. The collection of miscellaneous poems which he had been advertising never materialized; it was one thing to project it, and another, at this stage, to bring it into being. And so, feeling sorry for himself, he informed the reader in his dedication that his version of Horace had been undertaken because of sheer poverty, returning to this complaint in the Preface where he stressed his solitary state and lack of advantages while working on his translation. Finally, in an excess of self-pity and bitterness, he laid claim to a six-hundred-year old name, lamenting that one so descended should have been reduced to this kind of work.

Either Ralph Griffiths did not see fit to have the *Horace* noticed in his *Monthly Review* or none of his writers would agree to review it, for it is not even listed in that periodical. The rival *Critical Review*, however, accorded it second place in its August issue, allotting it ten and a half pages and quoting generous portions of Smart's translations, if not always commenting generously upon them. Whoever wrote the review had his say about what a translator of Horace should be capable of and then proceeded to see how Smart came up to those standards. The reviewer's preoccupations were often with minutiae: "bedaub'd" in one passage, "Say what slim youth, with moist perfumes/Bedaub'd," gives us "an indelicate idea of the lover;" in the lines, "Who without breach shall hug the pleasing chain;/Nor ever any bick'ring strife," the "idea of *hugging a chain without a breach* is ridiculous; and the word *bick'ring* is coarse and superfluous;" and of another line "Yet, goddess, of rich Cyprus queen," he wrote that the "word *rich* can have no meaning in this place; we rather suppose that *beatam* signifies *happy,* alluding to the patronage of Venus." Comparing Smart's version in various places with the original, he meted out praise and censure with rather more of the latter than of the former. One stanza "is not inelegantly translated;" in "this version there is neither delicacy of sentiment, nor elegance of style;" "this translation is not unpleasing, but may be read without admiration;" the translator "makes the passage absurd as well as unpoetical." But, he admits, in one passage "Mr. Smart has caught the spirit of the Roman poet, except in the concluding line" and in general he "preserves the sense of his author, and sometimes breathes a true poetic spirit, of which take the following instance."

Quo me, Bacche rapis &c. Lib. 1. Ode 25.
Bacchus, with thy spirit fraught,
Whither, whither am I caught?
To what groves and dens am driv'n,
Quick with thought, all fresh from heav'n?
In what grot shall I be found,
While I endless praise resound,
Caesar to the milky way,
And Jove's synod to convey?
Great and new, as yet unsung
By another's lyre or tongue,
Will I speak—and so behave,
As thy sleepless dames, that rave
With enthusiastic face,
Seeing Hebrus, seeing Thrace,
And, where feet barbarian go,
Rhodope so white with snow.
How I love to lose my way,
And the vastness to survey
Of the rocks and desarts rude,
With astonishment review'd!
O of nymphs, that haunt the stream,
And thy priestesses supreme!
Who, when strengthen'd at thy call,
Can up-tear the ash-trees tall,
Nothing little, nothing low,
Nothing mortal will I show.
'Tis adventure—but 'tis sweet
Still to follow at thy feet,
Where so e'er you fix your shrine,
Crown'd with foliage of the vine.

Another poem is quoted in Smart's translation to show his use of a measure more "familiar" than heroic verse in his rendition of the satires and epistles, and the reviewer then quotes Smart's rather long exposition of his theory about the first part of the *Ars Poetica* and Ovid's *Metamorphoses*. The reviewer concludes by list-

ing the scholarly apparatus in the edition and by complimenting
Smart on his decision to omit or give "an inoffensive turn to all
those passages which have a tendency to suggest immodest ideas;
tho' he has not been so extremely scrupulous in this point, as some
supercilious and unmerciful editors of Horace, who have expunged
seventeen of the odes and epodes, besides many passages in others
which they thought exceptionable." Considering the acrimony of
previous reviews of Smart's efforts he should have been pleased,
or at least relieved, at the moderate and judicious tone taken in the
review of his *Horace*. The *Critical Review* was notoriously censori-
ous; to have come off so well was a triumph of sorts.

When John Hawkesworth visited Smart in 1764 and in a letter
described how he found him translating Horace into English verse,
"He read me some of it," he wrote to Smart's sister Margaret in
Margate, "it is very clever, and his own poetical fire sparkles in it
very frequently; yet, upon the whole, it will scarcely take place of
Francis's; and therefore, if it is not adopted as a school book, which,
perhaps, may be the case, it will turn to little account." Hawkesworth referred to Francis's *Horace* in the obvious expectation that
Margaret Hunter would know what he was talking about, such was
the popularity of this translation of the Latin poet. Philip Francis,
unsuccessful dramatist and able political pamphleteer, had translated the odes, epodes, and *Carmen Seculare* in two volumes in
1742,—in 1746 he added the satires, epistles, and *Art of Poetry*. The
four volumes were revised in 1747 and were reprinted again and
again, having gone into some eight or nine editions by 1767, a two-
volume edition appearing in 1765 while Smart was at work on his
own version. Samuel Johnson, presumably with some knowledge of
Smart's version, as well as that of other translators, told Boswell in a
conversation in 1778 that "the lyrical part of Horace never can be
perfectly translated; so much of the excellence is in the numbers
and the expression. Francis has done it the best; I'll take his, five
out of six, against them all."[7] Smart knew Francis's translation, of
course, and he also knew that his version would be compared to it
by prospective buyers. Fortunately for him, so strongly was Francis's
translation intrenched, the *Critical Review* did not once refer to
that earlier translation. The *Monthly Review*'s failure to notice
Smart's *Horace* was probably an unconscious act of kindness, for
when it reviewed William Duncombe's *Works of Horace in English
Verse, By Several Hands* in 1758 Francis's version came up immedi-

ately: "That gentleman's version," wrote the reviewer, "particularly of the Odes, is highly Horatian: it is moral without dulness, gay and spirited with propriety, and tender without whining," and the rest of the review was little more than comparison of various passages in Duncombe's edition with Francis's, with the latter's translation preferred in every instance.[8] Francis's translation was constantly in Smart's mind as he worked on his own.

Smart had given more of his time to Horace than to any other single author, classical or modern. He translated his works into prose and then, dissatisfied with that version, put in two or three years on a verse translation. And it was to Horace he turned, both while at Cambridge and in his first two years in London, as a congenial model to be followed and imitated. As early as 1743-4 when he was awarded the Bachelor of Arts degree he sought and found in Horace a poem which he could use as a point of departure for a lighthearted set of verses celebrating his delivery from lectures. The Roman poet's "Exegi monumentum aere perennius," Book III, Ode xxx, is one in the tradition which claims greater longevity for his poem than can be expected for any other of the works of man. Taking the first line for his epigraph, Smart then wrote,

> 'Tis done: I tow'r to that degree,
>   And catch such heav'nly fire,
> That HORACE ne'er could rant like me,
>   Nor is *King's* chapel higher.—

And where Horace asks Melpomene to crown his locks with Delphic bays, Smart ends his poem by asking Banks, a tailor, to invest him with the graduate's gown, square-cap, and hood. He was next attracted to Horace's ode on the decayed beauty Lyce who refuses to acknowledge that her day is past and still hopes to arouse desire in men.[9] In imitation of this poem Smart wrote his own version, entitling it *To Lyce* and bringing in references to contemporary people. And when he made his first bid for recognition in literary London it was with the *Horatian Canons of Friendship*, an imitation of the third satire in Horace's first book of satires, published in 1750. Soon after this Miss Nelly Pentweazle, that is, Smart, translated the very first of Horace's odes, the first to Maecenas, and published it in *The Midwife* in 1751. In the 1752 *Poems on Several Occasions* another Horatian imitation appeared; this was called *The Pretty Chambermaid* and went back to the fourth ode of the second book for its inspiration. Of all these, only the ode *To Maecenas* is an exercise in translation; in it Smart uses the *Song to David* stanza and expands the thirty-six lines of his original to twice their length. And while Horace's straightforward Ode xxx of Book III becomes a springboard for some undergraduate fun in verse, Smart finds his natural ambient in the poems *To Lyce* and *The Pretty Chambermaid* and only now and then in a sparkle of satiric brilliance in the *Horatian Canons of Friendship.*

Smart's best poetry before 1759 was the humorous love verse that he wrote to various young women with whom he was in love in his own precipitate fashion. With these poems should be put those whose purpose is less than serious and in which the poet adopts the tone of a man of the world conversing with his peers. This kind of poem, commoner before 1759, was infrequent with Smart after 1763, but he recaptured it in a few of his own verse epistles. It was only natural, therefore, that his best translations in the verse *Horace* should be those in which his talent for this semi-serious, semi-facetious light lyric should coincide with the same quality in his original. His best efforts were in the translations of the odes as a whole and especially of the kind of ode that gave him opportunity to loose his natural bent. Horace's *To Lydia,* Book I, Ode viii, is a lyric in which the poet "animadverts upon Sybaris, a youth distractedly in love with Lydia, and wholly dissolved in pleasures," a subject to which Smart could do ample justice.

> I charge thee, Lydia, tell me straight,
>   Why Sybaris destroy,
> Why make love do the deeds of hate,
> And to his end precipitate
>   The dear enamour'd boy?
> Why can he not the field abide,
>   From sun and dust recede,
> Nor with his friends, in gallant pride
> Dress'd in his regimentals, ride,
>   And curb the manag'd steed?
> Why does he now to bathe disdain,
>   And fear the sandy flood?
> Why from th' athletic oil refrain,
> As if its use would be his bane,
>   As sure as viper's blood?
> No more his shoulders black and blue
>   By wearing arms appear;
> He, who the quoit so dextrous threw,

>And from whose hand the jav'lin flew
>   Beyond a rival's spear;
>Why does he skulk, as authors say
>   Of Thetis' fav'rite heir,
>Lest a man's habit should betray,
>And force him to his troops away,
>   The work of death to share?

In "dear enamour'd boy," from Horace's "amando," and in "Nor with his friends, in gallant pride,/ Dress'd in his regimentals, ride," from Horace's "Cur neque militaris? Inter aequales equitet," something of the quality of Smart's characteristic idiom in this translation of Horace's works emerges. Sybaris is no remote figure from the pages of an old book; he is a contemporary young officer in love with a somewhat coquettish young lady who has so distracted him that he forbears to go riding in his regimentals—a gratuitous and happy touch—with his fellows. Philip Francis calls Sybaris a "too amorous Boy" and asks "Or why no more with martial Pride,/ Amidst the youthful Battel ride," closer to Horace in this last than Smart with his "regimentals."[10]

The differences between Smart's version and Francis's can be further seen by comparison of their translations of Book I, Ode xxiii, another poem in which Smart might be expected to appear to best advantage. Francis makes this of it:

>Chloe flies me like a Fawn,
>Which through some sequester'd Lawn
>Panting seeks the Mother-Deer,
>Not without a panic Fear
>Of the gently-breathing Breeze,
>And the Motion of the Trees.
>If the curling Leaves but shake,
>If a Lizard stir the Brake,
>Frighted it begins to freeze,
>Trembling both at Heart and Knees.
>But not like a Tyger dire,
>Nor a Lion, fraught with Ire,
>I pursue my lovely Game,
>To destroy thy tender Frame.
>Haste thee, leave thy Mother's Arms,
>Ripe for Love are all thy Charms.

Smart's translation reads,

Me, Chloe, like a fawn you fly,
That seeks in trackless mountains high
    Her tim'rous dam again;
Alarm'd at every thing she hears,
The woods, the winds excite her fears,
    Tho' all those fears are vain.
For if a tree the breeze receives,
That plays upon the quiv'ring leaves
    When spring begins to start;
Or if green lizards, where they hide,
Turn but the budding bush aside,
    She trembles knees and heart.
But I continue my pursuit,
Not like the fierce Getulian brute,
    Or tyger, to assail,
And of thee life and limbs bereave—
Think now at last 'tis time to leave
    Thy mother for a male.

At times, both in this poem and in others Smart is more literal, at other times Francis is. But where Francis rejects Horace's "montibus aviis" for the rather pretty and familiar—even traditional—"sequester'd Lawn," Smart is satisfied with a very literal "trackless mountain." His "She trembles knees and heart" adopts Horace's Latin construction, "Et corde & genibus tremit," doing away with any preposition, a daring of which Francis was incapable. Francis's "tender frame" becomes in Smart "life and limbs," both one of his alliterative doublets and at the same time a more concrete phrase than the again unsurprising one chosen by his predecessor. Finally, for the last line of a poem is so strategically important, especially in a poem such as this, Smart stays with Horace in his "Think now at last 'tis time to leave/ Thy mother for a male" when all that Francis can rise to is "Haste thee, leave thy Mother's Arms,/ Ripe for Love are all thy Charms." Francis is too polite here, "love" is too delicate a euphemism for Horace's "viro;" Smart's "male" begs no question.

Smart's early imitations of Horace affected his translation of many in the latter's poems. His manner was already fixed in some degree, and, where in the imitation he could allow himself great latitude, in the translation he limited himself somewhat but still took certain freedoms which derive ultimately from those same translations. *To Lyce*, written about 1750, introduces modern names for those of Horace's contemporaries and adds details rather liberally.

At length Mother Gunter the Gods hear my prayer,
They have heard me at length, Mother Gunter,
Yo're grown an old Woman yet romp drink & swear,
And attest the tricks of a young Pounter.

You invoke with a voice that tremblingly squeaks
Brisk Cupid tho sure of denial;
He shuns you and basks in the blossomly cheeks
Of Miss Gubbins who plays on the viol.

He flyes from the Trunk y^t is sapless and bare,
To the pliant young Branches he comes up;
Age has hail'd on thy face, & snow'd on thy hair,
And thy green Teeth have eat all thy Gums up.

Nor thy Sack, nor thy Necklace, thy Watch, nor thy Ring,
Have restored thee to youth, or retarded
Those years, which Old time and his friend Vincent Wing
In the Alamanack long have recorded.

O where is that beauty, that bloom, & grace,
Those Lips that would breath Inspiration,
That steal me away from myself, and gave place,
To no Creature save Joan in the nation.

But poor Joan is dead, and has left you her years
As a Legacy which gracious Heaven
Has join'd to your own, which a Century clears,
And is just Mad'm the age of a Raven.

Then remains a Memento to each jolly Soul,
Who of Venus's Club's a stanch Member,
That Love hot as Fire must be burnt to a coal,
As the Broomstick concludes in an Ember.[11]

The translation actually improves upon the colloquial, conversational tone of the imitation.

Lyce, the gods my vows have heard,
　　At length they've heard my vows;
You wou'd be beauteous with a beard,
　　You romp and you carouse:
And drunk, with trembling voice, you court
　　Slow Cupid, prone to seek
For better music, bloom, and sport,
　　In buxom Chia's cheek.
For he, a sauce-box, scorns dry chips,
　　And teeth decay'd and green;

Where wrinkled forehead, and chapt lips,
    And snowy hairs are seen.
Nor Coan elegance, nor gems,
    Your past years will restore;
Which time to his records condemns,
    With fleeting wings of yore.
Ah! where's that form, complexion, grace,
    That air—where is she, say,
That cou'd my sick'ning soul solace,
    And stole my heart away?
Blest! who cou'd Cynara succeed,
    As artful and as fair—
But fate, to Cynara, decreed
    Few summers for her share.
That crow-like Lyce might survive,
    'Till lads shou'd laugh and shout,
To see the torch, but just alive,
    So slowly stinking out.

For the most part the translation is less poetic in the sense that there are no "sapless and bare" tree trunks and no "pliant young Branches" but rather "dry chips." Nor does Mother Gunter sport a beard, whereas Lyce is given one, without any warrant in Horace's text for such an addition. And while the poem on Mother Gunter ends with the reminder that "Love hot as fire must be burnt to a coal, / As the Broomstick concludes in an Ember," the lads of the poem to Lyce laugh and shout "To see the torch, but just alive, / So slowly stinking out," a more fitting end for "an antiquated courtezan" (Smart's translation of Horace's "meretricem vetulam") whose "teeth decay'd and green" and "chapt lips" would insure a bad breath. Francis does not endow Lyce with a beard; and for him Cynara "died in beauty's bloom" where Smart has fate decree her "few summers for her share." Smart's "crow-like Lyce" is "the raven's rival" in Francis, and the latter's version ends more literally, but much less memorably, as the torch spreads a "sickly Gleam" and expires "in a Smoke." One way in which Smart consciously strove to emulate the urbane Roman was by using the current modes of speech of polite and impolite London society. He had shown, certainly as early as *The Midwife,* that his ear was attuned to the give and take of coffeehouse conversation; he improved in his ability to reproduce such conversation in the material he wrote for Mrs. Midnight's entertainments; and he had lost none of this ability when he translated Horace. One has only to turn to his translation of the epistles and satires to see this aspect of his art in operation.[12]

Smart's concern in translating Horace into verse, partially dictated by the desire to have the new version supersede his prose translation, which, he told Hawkesworth, "would hurt his memory," was even more dictated by the hope of making money. Since he could hope to obtain this end only by having his version adopted as a school text, he had to stress certain aspects of his work. Much of this was to be accomplished in his Preface; the rest was to be left to the scholarly apparatus he included. Among the four volumes were placed a Latin life of Horace, a chronological synopsis of Roman history, Dacier's Latin preface to the Satires, and an analysis of the various metrical schemes used by Horace—with examples. Footnotes, excluding those that had already accompanied the prose version, displayed the editor's erudition as he cited Rodellius, Plutarch, Aesop, Erasmus, Suidas, the Bible, Pythagoras, and Cicero and quoted Persius, Livy, and Homer. Most numerous, however, were the explanatory and historical notes which elucidated allusions, identified persons, and explained customs, sports, peculiarities of word and expression, and the like. Very few notes were devoted to disputed readings and very rarely was an emendation suggested. But by far the greatest preoccupation in the apparatus was the concern to explain and imitate Horace's meters. The breakdown of specimens of the Horatian meters numbered twenty-two varieties and listed each poem that fell into each category, the favorite scheme being one which emerged in Smart's translation as two iambic lines of eight syllables, one of ten, and one of twelve, rhyming aabb. Thus, the opening stanza of Smart's version of Book I, Ode xxvii, reads

> With glasses form'd for joy to fight,
> Is what the Thracians do in spite;
> Let Bacchus know no barb'rous customs here,
> But keep the modest God from bloody discord clear.

For his version of this ode Francis chose octosyllabic couplets.

Further, even more impressive, evidence of Smart's interest in rendering Horace's meters as closely as he could is in the thirty-eighth ode of the first Book where, under the title, there is the notation, "In the original metre exactly." In this poem he showed what he could accomplish with the rarely used and difficult Sapphics. Horace speaks to his servant,

> Persian pomps, boy, ever I renounce them:
> Scoff o' the plaited coronet's refulgence;
> Seek not in fruitless vigilance the rose-tree's
>   Tardier offspring.
>
> Mere honest myrtle that alone is order'd,
> Me the mere myrtle decorates, as also
> Thee the prompt waiter to a jolly toper
>   Hous'd in an arbour.

When Smart came to the eleventh ode of the first book he again saw fit to draw attention to his practice of sticking faithfully to the original meter, for there he wrote that in order to "imitate the metre of the original, the longest measure in the English tongue (much in use amongst our old poets) is here introduced: but, for convenience of printing, one line is severed into two." His first stanza reads,

> Seek not, what we're forbid to know
>   The date the Gods decree
> To you, my fair Leuconoe,
>   Or what they fix for me.*

Not only was he providing a new translation of Horace, but he was also writing a primer on Latin metrics as an extra inducement to prospective adopters. He had already established the fact of his dexterity in handling various stanzaic forms in the Psalms and *Hymns and Spiritual Songs*; with the publication of the verse *Horace* he drove the point home further.

Secondary to his desire to copy Horace's metrics exactly was his desire to follow his original in his theories of diction as put forth in the *Ars Poetica*. There was nothing novel in this, as he had made the substance of those remarks his practice very early in his career as a poet. But here, translating the very poet who had laid down the precepts that a poet should resurrect old words, coin new ones when need arose, and use unusual words or more common words in un-

---

* He used the same form in the eighteenth ode of this same Book and added a footnote referring to his original note. And in a note to the *Ars Poetica* he turns again to metrics and cites both Phaedrus and Terence in support of his argument.

usual senses, Smart felt that he should focus attention on his practice as it exemplified those precepts. Thus, in the lines "From Saturn sprung, do thou convey/ That Caesar hold the second place" (Book I, Ode xii), the word "convey" is a word "attempted," so reads his footnote, "in the peculiarity of Horace–grant by delegation, make over your right." His definition suggests some kinship with "conveyance" in the legal sense of that word, so that his attempt here was not too farfetched. As he had done before, he managed to give his language a certain patina of remoteness by the use of the old possessive form, especially with a proper name, backed up by the employment of old or unusual words.* His bolder attempts involved the use of a few words in an unusual sense, often by the unmysterious device of using a noun or adjective as a verb. The south wind "serenes the sky" and Venus "careers with all her might." Only one coinage has hitherto been noted, the adjective "assentatious," meaning "obsequious" or "servile," but it was an easy step from "assentation," an obsequious, servile act. Somewhat more imaginative was "alloquial," of or pertaining to the action of addressing others. "Vastation," the act of laying waste, while frequent in the period from 1610 to 1660, had not been used for more than a century.† "Begirl'd," of the twentieth ode of the third book, is more the sort of quasi-humorous nonce word Smart could be expected to invent. But in all these he was conscious that he was following in Horace's tracks. One other feature of his verse in these translations, quite perceptible in his first volume and then strangely disappearing almost entirely, was his old mannerism of linking two nearly allied words by alliterations.* Once, prominently in the last line of a poem, he manages a triplet; whimsy, wantoness, and wrath. Once, startlingly, there is a vivid reminder that the poet who was translating the pagan Horace was a Christian who had been put away in a madhouse because he insisted on praying too much too publicly. Coming upon a passage in the third satire in the first book of satires which he translated as "Till words at length, and sounds they found,/ To ascertain their thoughts by sound," he burst out in

---

*Hight (called or named), ken (as verb), to straw, younglings, grutch, laud (as noun), amerce, respire, and by my fay.

†*OED* gives the first use of "alloquial" to De Quincy in 1840 and 1663 as the last date for "vastation."

*Examples are ruffles or restrains, ruin and wrath, pow'r and pomp, restor'd and repossess'd, pomp and pride, madness or mettle, in prudence and in peace, and each glory and each grace.

a footnote, "The understanding of Horace was so benighted, that he supposed language to be gradual, and of human invention—nevertheless the Lord is the WORD, and all good words proceed from him [sic], as sure as nonsense and cant are derivable from the adversary." Some eight years earlier, while in Potter's madhouse, Smart had written in *Jubilate Agno*, "Let Mason rejoice with Vulvula a sort of fish—Good words are of God, the cant from the Devil" (B1, 237), the name of the fish suggesting the Latin word for the female genitalia to him and leading him to protest that the devil was responsible for cant.

Whatever the merits of Smart's version, Hawkesworth's opinion that it would not replace Francis's proved accurate; the verse *Horace* never went into a second edition, and Smart was again in need. Late in this year, just three days before Christmas, John Newbery died. Even Smart, however, could not have been so sanguine as to expect that Newbery would have made provision of any kind for him in his will. Although his efforts to prosecute those who had had him committed to the madhouse were abortive, Newbery must have been made aware of his intentions. However kindly Newbery may have been, he could not and did not feel obliged to help a son-in-law who was unable to curb his excesses at least to the point where he could take care of his wife and children. Anna Maria Smart had been given the management of the *Reading Mercury* in 1762; the first issue she published appeared on January 29 of that year. She needed no help from her husband; she offered him none. But Newbery was determined that Anna Maria, who had been persuaded by Smart to elope with him, should not again be swayed by him. Accordingly, when he died in 1767, his will was specific on this point. He gave one moiety or half part of his printing utensils, household goods, and the newspaper and his business in Reading to John Carnan; the other moiety, the will reads, "I give and bequeath to my said son ffrancis Newbery upon Trust and to and for the sole use and Benefit of my said Daughter in Law Anna Maria Smart and I do order and direct that the same or any part thereof shall not be subject or lyable to the Debts power or Controul of her present Husband or to the power or Controul of any person or persons whatsoever."[13] Newbery was shrewd to the last; helping his improvident son-in-law was one matter, but allowing him the slightest opportunity to get his hands on any part of his wife's patrimony was another.

On the fourth day of the New Year Smart wrote two letters, one from Storey's Gate Coffee-House to Paul Panton and the other from the Cockpit Royal to Charles Burney; the subject was the same. "Dear Sir," he addresses Panton,

> It is now the anniversary of Mason's kind plan in my favour, which I humbly take the liberty of reminding you of—You sub-cribed two guineas last year & promised to continue it—if every man, that had much more cause to use me kindly had been pos-sessed of your generous sentiments, I should have been well enough off with regard to circumstances—I pray God bless you & many happy years attend you!
>
> Your most affectionate &
most obliged friend &
Servant
Christopher Smart
>
> Are we to entertain the hopes of seeing you in Town?

And "Dear Sir" he also addresses Burney, one of his first London friends,

> Many thanks for your kind & generous Subscription of 2 guineas for 1768 likewise for the same sum sent in the name of Mr Sher-man [?] I bless God for your good nature which please to take for a Receipt.—I had made application to Mrs Skinner at the same time—She immediately remitted the money, which however was necessary as immediately to return—& was done accordingly—I wish you & your family many happy years & am most sincerely
>
> & affectionately
y^r obliged ser[14]

Smart's gratitude expressed itself in the closing lines of the two letters. Burney had solicited Mrs. Skinner's subscription of two guineas; Fanny, his daughter, writing in her diary on June 29, 1769, characterized the good lady as "an intimate acquaintance" of her father "and a very clever woman." She was doubtless the Mrs. Skinner who subscribed to the Psalms, along with the "Rev. Mr. Skinner, Chaplain to his Grace Archbishop of York."* With Burney, Panton, Mason, Stonhewer, the unknown Mr. Sherman,

---

*John Skinner had matriculated at St. John's College, Cambridge, a year later than Smart entered Pembroke; he was Public Orator of the University from 1752 to 1762, at which latter date he became sub-dean of York, a position he held until his death in 1805. He was appointed Chaplain to the Archbishop of York in 1761.

and Mrs. Skinner all contributing two guineas annually and with an indeterminate but not large number of others doing the same, Smart could look forward to a substantial New Year's gift every year. He continued, however, to manage to spend the money subscribed by this small group of friends, his annual fifty pounds governmental pension, and whatever he got from his publications, and he continued to be in need. His yearly income, aside from any money from his writings, was more than enough to provide for all his necessities; somehow he spent far more than he should. Possibly he had taken to the bottle again, although there is no contemporary comment to this effect; more probably he was simply trying, as he had while at Cambridge, to live up to the standards of dress and entertainment of his well-to-do friends. Whether he dissipated, or just lived beyond his means as he had ever done, he became more and more frantic in his efforts to augment his income.

Although he had projected a collection of miscellaneous poems, Smart turned, sometime after the publication of the verse *Horace*, to a form which he had already attempted with very little success. His oratorio *Hannah* had been performed for one night only; on March 8, 1768, his second oratorio, *Abimelech*, with music by Samuel Arnold, suffered the same fate. The libretto was sold at the theatre, the Theatre Royal in Covent Garden, and hence brought in some money, but hopes of a run with one or more benefit nights for the author and composer were immediately dashed. Arnold was not a particularly gifted composer, and Smart was not at home in this idiom; indeed, *Abimelech* shows a marked decline from the earlier oratorio. Smart went to the story of Abraham and Sarah and Abimelech in the twentieth chapter of Genesis for his libretto, recounting how Abimelech sent for Sarah, Abraham's half-sister and wife, and was deterred from knowing her by a dream in which God appeared to him and threatened him with death if he should carry out his purpose. At his worst Smart could write a chorus for Phicol and his guards,

> Obey, ye brave, the king's command,
> And on your needful duty stand;
> With might defend the gates you bar,
> —Here we are—here we are.

and at his best, writing on a theme dear to him, he could give Abraham the following air,

O great to conquer and to spare,
    Which could all obstacle subdue;
Do thou, my Saviour, form my pray'r;
    Be thou my word and music too.
Bless all thy host that on thee wait,
    Whate'er their title or degree,
Transcendant Good, sublimely great,
    Are less than nothing without thee.
Bless all mankind beneath the sun,
    Who know thee, and who know thee not,
Bless all that creep, that fly, that run,
    Or in vast ocean have their lot.
And, Oh, thy special blessing send,
    On all that Abraham calls his own,
But chief, my fair domestic friend,
    Still to be mine, and mine alone.

The last four lines, with their reference to Sarah as "my fair domestic friend," were necessary for the slight plot and should, if possible, be forgotten. Reviewers for the *Monthly* and *Critical* were kind to Smart and Arnold; they did not so much as notice their oratorio.

Very soon after the failure of *Abimelech* the *London Chronicle* for March 31 carried an announcement of "a very proper Present at the approaching Festival, for young Ladies and Gentlemen." The gift appropriate to Easter was Smart's *Parables of our Lord and Saviour Jesus Christ*, "Done into familiar verse, with occasional applications, for the use and improvement of younger minds." Here too he described himself as "Sometime Fellow of Pembroke-Hall, Cambridge, and Scholar of the University," evidently not at all ashamed at having descended from the verse translation of Horace to a mechanical versification in octosyllabic couplets of the parables of Jesus. Smart dedicated the volume, printed for W. Owen, a bookseller with whom he had not previously been associated, to the three-year old son of his friend Bonnell Thornton, of Orchard Street, Westminster. The dedication, dated February 24, 1768, closes, "I am with the greatest Sincerity and the most inevitable Affection to the eldest Son of BONNELL and SYLVIA THORNTON, Your most hearty Friend." Smart, himself still living in Westminster and not allowed to see his own children, probably visited the Thorntons and watched the growth of little George. He did not foresee, what a less naive person almost surely would have, that unfriendly critics would pounce upon a book dedicated to a three-year-old child. Ralph Griffiths' *Monthly Review* did precisely that: "This

version of the Parables is, with great propriety, dedicated to Master
Bonnell George Thornton, a child of three years old." The reviewer
then quoted one of the Parables, "A Piece of Silver," in preparation
for his final sneer, *"Familiar* verse, indeed, as the title page justly
intimates."[15] An example of one of the shorter parables (there are
eighty-three) will serve to illustrate what Smart considered familiar
verse and what he meant in his title page by "occasional applications."

PARABLE III

The Kingdom of Heaven compared to a Grain of Mustard-seed.

Then did he to the throng around
Another parable propound.
So fares it with the heavenly reign
As mustard-seed, of which a grain
Was taken in a farmer's hand
And cast into a piece of land.
This grain, the least of all that's sown,
When once to full perfection grown,
Outstrips all herbs to that degree
Till it at length becomes a tree
And all the songsters of the air
Take up an habitation there.

Christ laid (at first an infant boy)
The basis of eternal joy;
And from humility, his plan,
Arose the best and greatest man,
The greatest man that ever trod
On earth was Christ th' eternal God,
Which as the branch of Jesse's root
Ascends to bear immortal fruit.
From contradiction, sin and strife,
He spreads abroad the tree of life;
And there his servants shall partake
The mansions, that the branches make;
There saints innumerable throng,
Assert their seat, and sing their song.

The *Critical Review* for April devoted a few more sentences to its
notice of the Parables than the *Monthly Review* had; its verdict was
the same however.

> We do not remember to have met with any poet whose composi-
> tions are more unequal than those of Mr. Smart. Some of his pieces
> are distinguished by undoubted marks of genius, agreeable imagery,
> and a fine poetical enthusiasm. Others are hardly superior to the
> productions of Sternhold or Quarles. The work before us is of the
> lower class, containing about seventy parables, and some other
> passages of the New Testament, in plain, familiar verse, adapted to
> the capacities of children; to whom it may certainly be of use, as it
> will serve to give them an idea of our Saviour's discourses and
> furnish them with pious instructions; but it is not calculated to
> please their imaginations or improve their taste in poetry, as the
> reader will perceive by the following specimen.

Thereupon the parable of "The Lost Sheep" was quoted without
further comment. Had the periodicals been silent, as they had been
with *Abimelech*, they would have performed Smart a service, but he
had angered the reviewers and they had not yet forgotten or re-
lented.

Although hurt and further embittered by the reviews of the
Parables, Smart found some solace with friends, old and new. Sometime soon after the subscription list for the Psalms was closed, at the
very earliest, for none of their names is on it, he had moved into a
new circle of acquaintances. A Mr. John Kempe who died in 1823
was the subject of a "Memoir" in the *Gentleman's Magazine* for
that year; the author of the memoir writes that "Mr. John Kempe
for some years resided at the house of his father, who lived according to the true style of old English hospitality . . . many eminent
persons of the day were the frequent guests of his table. Among
these were Romney the portrait painter, and Stubbs the animal
painter, Dixon the celebrated mezzotinto engraver, Mr. N. Kempe's
sister the lovely Lady Hamer, Sir Thomas Robinson, the unhappy
poet Smart, and the Rev. Mr. Inkson." John Kempe himself is
quoted to the effect that "Smart loved to hear me play upon my
flute, and I have often soothed the wanderings of his melancholy by
some favorite air; he would shed tears when I played, and generally
wrote some lines afterward." Nicholas Kempe, John's father, lived
for many years at a house in Ranelagh-Walk, Chelsea; with Sir
Thomas Robinson he was one of the original proprietors of
Ranelagh Gardens which lay next to the grounds of his mansion.
Smart probably owed his introduction into this group to his acquaintance with so many of the figures in the world of entertainment of the period. His new friends were the kind of people he felt

most at ease with, people for the most part of some distinction in one art form or another.[16] None of them, with the exception of Romney, is ever mentioned by Smart in any connection. Romney, who had come to London in 1762 and was unknown until he competed in the Society of Arts painting competition in 1763, is mentioned in the *Epistle to John Sherratt, Esq.* John Dixon came to London about 1765, further confirmation that some of the members of this group came together after this date. Had Smart known the members of this group while he was gathering subscribers for the Psalms, there is no doubt that one or more would have been approached and would have subscribed. He probably joined the group as late as 1769, for some time between January 2, 1769, when he wrote a letter from Storey's Coffee-House in Westminster, and July 29, 1769, when he was described as "of Chealsea" in an indenture, he had given up his lodgings with Mrs. Barwell and moved to Chelsea. If he was welcomed into the Kempe home this late, his association with the young musician and the others was short-lived.

About this time, too, Fanny Burney, records her impressions of him as he came to see her father. On September 14, 1768, she writes,

> Mr. Smart the poet was here yesterday. He is author of the "Old Woman's Magazine". . . and of several poetical productions; some of which are sweetly elegant and pretty—for example: "Harriet's Birth Day," "Care and Generosity,"—and many more. This ingenious writer is one of the most unfortunate of men—he has been twice confined in a mad-house—and but last year sent a most affecting epistle to papa, to entreat him to lend him half-a-guinea! —How great a pity so clever, so ingenious a man should be reduced to such shocking circumstances. He is extremely grave, and has still great wildness in his manner, looks, and voice; but 'tis impossible to *see* him and to *think* of his works, without feeling the utmost pity and concern for him. . .

Next year, on October 4, 1769, Smart gave her a rose, "blooming and sweet as if we were in the month of June. 'It was given me,' said he, 'by a fair lady—though not so fair as *you*!' I always admired poetical licence!— . . . . This, however, is nothing to what he afterwards amused himself with saying."[17] Young Fanny saw Smart in various moods, grave and gay; the times when the latter prevailed must have been progressively fewer. When Fanny, much later, edited her father's memoirs she wrote of Smart in these years that "whatever belonged to that hapless poet seemed to go in constant deterioration; his affairs and his senses annually and palpably darkening together; and nothing, unhappily, flourishing in the attempts made for his relief save the friendship of Mr. Burney."[18]

One of the ways in which Burney sought to help his needy friend is related in the former's own words: "In 1769 I set for Smart and Newbery Thornton's burlesque Ode, on St. Cecilia's day. It was performed at Ranelagh in masks, to a very crowded audience, as I was told; for I then resided in Norfolk. . . . All the performers of the old woman's Oratory, employed by Foote, were, I believe, employed at Ranelagh on this occasion."[19] Bonnell Thornton's *Ode on St. Cecilia's Day, Adapted to the Ancient British Musick*, first set to music by Dr. Arne in 1763, was an enormously successful burlesque of the traditional ode for St. Cecilia's day, one of which Smart had written himself in 1746. Thornton's preface to the first publication of the Ode in April, 1749, claims its superiority over the odes of *"Johnny Dryden, Jemmy Addison, Sawney Pope, Nick Rowe*, little *Kit Smart*, &c, &c, &c."* The instruments used are reminiscent of those employed in Mother Midnight's entertainments, consisting of Jews-harp, salt-box, marrow-bones and cleavers, and a hurdy-gurdy. As John Newbery had died in 1767, the Newbery associated with Smart in Burney's account was probably Francis Newbery, John's son, inheritor of the publishing business, a scholar, a poet, and a lover of music with an interest in private theatricals. Doubtless Nicholas Kempe and Sir Thomas Robinson, Smart's acquaintances who held shares in Ranelagh Gardens, were also involved in the performance, part of whose purpose, if not all, was to help Smart. This sort of enterprise, whatever part Smart took in the preparation of the performance, was one that he loved, for it gave him a chance to give full play to his natural talent for making people laugh.

Another friend of Smart's, John Wilkes, was in prison when an ode in commemoration of his birthday "Written by Christ. Smart, A.M." was "performed" on October, 1769, at the Devil Tavern, Temple Bar, a popular place for concerts and lectures since 1752. Smart may have known Wilkes as early as 1750, about which time he wrote his witty extemporaneous couplet on the latter's squinting eyes.[20] They would inevitably have been brought together at some time by mutual friends, Wilkes being admitted into membership in the Sublime Society of Beef Steaks in 1754, a society which included Smart's friends Francis Hayman and John Beard, and Dr. William Barrowby, who subscribed to his *Poems* in 1752. Barrowby also frequented Bedford's Coffee-House where Smart and some of his new London friends, including Murphy, who may also have been a member of the Beef Steaks, used to gather.* Others of Smart's friends who belonged to the Beef Steaks Society were Garrick, William Havard, Hogarth, and Bonnell Thornton.[21] Wilkes did not subscribe to Smart's *Poems* in 1752, but he repaired that omission in 1765 with a subscription to the Psalms. And Smart, for his part, was sympathetic to Wilkes's ideas for, in *Jubilate Agno*, he wrote, "Let Adoniram the receiver general of the excise rejoice with Hypnale the sleeper adder./ For I stood up betimes in behalf of LIBERTY, PROPERTY and NO EXCISE" (B1, 107). The two almost coincided in the King's Bench Prison, Wilkes being discharged on April 17, 1770, while Smart was committed on April 26. Smart's performance at the Devil Tavern on October 31, 1769, was surely inspired as much by the realization that he could capitalize on Wilkes's notoriety and the widespread popular sympathy his case had aroused as by his adherence to Wilkes's principles. He was seizing upon every opportunity to add to an income which never proved adequate to his needs and desires.

About this time, and almost surely no earlier than August, 1765, when her name appeared in the subscription list printed with the Psalms, Smart's mother died. Smart's sister, Margaret Hunter, wrote to Anna Maria Smart from Margate on the eighth of May, neglecting to add the year date.

My Dear Sister

I am very sorry that after so Long an interval, I should renew our correspondence on a melancholy occasion, but I owe it to the tender respect which I shall always bear you, for your many actions toward me of affectionate and friendly regard, to inform you that it has pleased God to take our poor Mother to his Mercy out of this scene of sorrow and disappointment, for such it has been to her on many sad accounts; she departed Last night at about a quarter past 8. There is a paper in her own handwriting giving orders about her Funeral. Six of the poorest Widows of the place are to be pall bearers to have each a stuff Gown, to be saved out of the price of the Coffin, which is to be a very mean one, besides these we are ordered to make no invitations, but this days post carrys a Letter to

*George Lambert, one of the original twenty-four members of the society, subscribed to the Psalms, and Anthony Askew, M.D., who had been admitted in 1750 had put himself down for four copies of the 1752 *Poems*, with members of his family accounting for six more.

my Brother to tell him if he thinks of coming to the Buring he must be at Margate by next Tuesday night. God Bless you, and yours, my dear sister, with every Happiness that does indeed deserve the name. I hope you and I shall see each other again in this World, if not I humbly trust we shall meet in the Blissful Regions of Love, Harmony, and everlasting friendship,

Yours truly affectionate
M. Hunter.[22]

Smart may have gone to see his mother buried, but the bitterness he harbored against his family probably kept him in London; as he had told Hawkesworth four years earlier, he could not afford to be idle.

But matters got worse and worse; with the exception of the performance of Bonnell Thornton's burlesque ode on St. Cecilia's Day and his own ode in commemoration of John Wilkes's birthday, both in 1769, Smart entered into a period of even greater frustration and bitterness, attributing all his misfortunes to a malignant destiny. In this frame of mind and under the circumstances in which he found himself this year, sustained work of any worth was impossible for him. At the beginning of the year, as had become almost habitual with him, he wrote to Paul Panton to discover what had happened to the annual subscription of two guineas. Panton had, in fact, sent the money in the fall to a friend who had previously received the money for Smart, but a series of unlucky happenings kept the money from the poet. Accordingly, he wrote on the second day of the New Year from his usual haunt,

> Dear Sir
>
> I send this for the favour of your annual two guineas, which I am in want of God knows; tho' by the Death of Frank Smart I am direct heir to an Estate of six hundred pounds a year: but so obstinate is my adversity, that a thousand obstacles are thrown in the way of my just claim. I heartily wish you my compliments of the season many cheerful returns of the year & am with affectionate respect
>
> Your most obliged Ser^t
Christopher Smart.

Francis Smart, Smart's cousin, had died in August or September, 1768, leaving him nothing in his will. Smart was referring to the Snotterton estate which had descended to Francis Smart and which, without being specifically mentioned in his will, was bequeathed with all his other lands to three other members of the Smart family.[23] Smart had some legitimate reason to suppose that the Snotterton estate would descend to him, but the law was such that Francis could dispose of it as he wished, despite the fact that Christopher, as his first cousin, was his heir at law. But Snotterton was sold, the sale being recorded in an indenture of January 17, 1770, realizing six hundred and forty-seven pounds for the beneficiaries of Francis Smart's will after the huge mortgage was paid by the new owner, Lord Darlington. Smart profited only to the extent of the five shillings given him for the use of his name on the indenture, which he did not, however, sign.[24] The disappointment he experienced was so keen that he never recovered from it.

Smart was so pressed again that he needed Panton's two guineas desperately. What is more, two months after writing to his Welsh patron he waited upon Granville Sharp in London to ask what had happened to still another charity of which he was the beneficiary. James Sharp, one of Granville's eight brothers, wrote to another brother, John Sharp, Archdeacon of Northumberland, to tell him of Smart's visit; the letter is dated February 10, 1769. "Granville also desires I will tell you that poor Kit Smart has been with him, desiring that you will not forget the Charity he has had of £10 from the Trustees, he says it is of great consequence to him."[25] Through his Durham connections Smart had been able to get a grant from the Trustees of the estate of Nathaniel Crewe, third Baron Crewe of Stene and once Bishop of Durham, who had died in 1722 and left the money from his Northumberland estates to be used for charitable purposes.[26] James and John Sharp and four other members of the family had subscribed to the *Psalms*, with John taking ten copies; John and two others had subscribed to the 1752 *Poems*. John Sharp had been in Durham school with Smart, had entered Trinity College, Cambridge, the same year Smart was admitted to Pembroke, and had evidently not forgotten his friend in the time of his greatest need. In 1758 Sharp had become a trustee of Crewe's estate, a fact which Smart capitalized upon. But bad luck continued to dog Smart's footsteps, the ten-pound charity, like Panton's two guineas, was late in arriving and he had to write to or call upon somebody to plead that the money be forthcoming. Still another letter of this year, one from a minor poet named Cuthbert Shaw to George Allan, Esq., bears pathetic evidence of the depths Smart had reached. Shaw had once been an usher in the Darlington Free Grammar School; his first poem, *Liberty*, was inscribed in 1756 to the Earl of Darlington. At some time he was associated with John Newbery as a partner in the profits from the sale of a patent medicine called the *Beaume de Vie*, whose virtues he celebrated in verse. And in the summer of 1761 he acted at Drury Lane under Arthur Murphy and Samuel Foote. He could have become acquainted with Smart through any one of these circumstances. George Allan was a famous antiquarian and private printer of Darlington. Shaw writes, "I beg your pardon for having troubled you with a letter relative to Mr. Smart, whose pretensions, I am since informed, are merely visionary, and indeed from that and other circumstances, I am led to believe he still retains something of his former insanity. I have withdrawn myself from him for some weeks past. I hope, or at least am willing to flatter myself, your not answering my letter proceeds from the above frivolous application."[27] In 1768 Shaw had achieved great popularity with a highly successful poem on the death of his wife which went into a second edition in 1769; he was, therefore, in a position to help Smart in one way or another. Ironically, he was of low moral character and given to dissipation and improvidence, but even such as he could withdraw himself from Smart. What visionary pretensions Smart was entertaining is not known; he was probably trying to borrow money or procure help of some kind on the strength of his conviction that he would fall heir to the Snotterton estate. Since Allan had started to print works free shortly before this time, Smart may even have approached him to print something for him.

One ray of hope lightened the gloom of this year, if only for a brief moment. Smart's brother-in-law Thomas Carnan had taken over his stepfather's business, and word reached Smart that he was ready to effect a reconciliation with him. Accordingly, on April 16 Smart wrote a letter to Carnan which cost him much turmoil of mind, bitter as he was against Newbery and his family. But he needed kindness as much as he needed more solid help.

> Dear Sir/
> Being informed first by Mr. Leach & afterwards by Messrs Mason & Stonhewer that you have determined very benevolently in my favour, I think it incumbent upon me to be thankful. Indeed if mercy be not shewn me somewhere or other I do not see how I can possibly escape a prison. I congratulate you on your kind resolu-

tion, as you may depend upon it, that it will not only be finally a great thing for yourself, but people even now will applaud your generosity and good nature. I desire my duty to Mrs. Newbery and will wait on you or give you the meeting when and where you will please to name.

Yours most sincerely and affectionately,
Christopher Smart.[28]

Dryden Leach, Smart's debt to him having been paid by a friend, was disposed to help him to some extent. Since Smart assured Carnan that whatever it was he was going to do for him would "be finally a great thing for yourself," the latter had probably volunteered to publish something for him, something which Leach may himself have been reluctant to undertake. This was doubtless the *Hymns for the Amusement of Children* which Carnan published. Mason and Stonhewer, it is clear, still kept watch over Smart and did everything they could for him.

Somehow or other, with Carnan's help and that of older friends, Smart managed to stay out of debtors' prison for almost exactly a year beyond the date on which he wrote to his brother-in-law. During this time he was a welcome visitor at the Burneys, continually flattering young Fanny. Presumably he received his annual pension and the subscription money sent him by his friends and presumably he did some work on the *Hymns* for children. But he was contracting new debts or holding off demands for the payment of old ones, until finally on April 20, 1770, somebody's charity or patience ran out and his forebodings proved true; he was arrested at the suit of a James Bright who held his promissory note for nineteen pounds, nineteen shillings, six pence and who entered six separate claims for the standard sum of thirty pounds apiece for various unidentified goods and services. Smart was unable to raise bail and was sent to prison on April 26. There he remained awaiting trial before his old friend Mr. Murray, now Lord Mansfield, until February, 1770, at which time a jury brought in a verdict for the plaintiff for the sum of forty pounds, ten shillings. No friend came forward to pay his bail or to satisfy Bright's demands, probably aware that the cause was hopeless. For in March of 1770, while Smart was in the King's Bench Prison, a Peter Robinson brought in a second complaint of trespass against him for forty pounds.[29] The complaint was perforce forgotten, but if both Bright and Robinson had been paid, other tradesmen would surely have also appeared to claim their due. Reluctantly Smart's friends decided that he would at least for the present be better off in prison than at liberty. They did what they could to soften the blow, Carnan and Burney procuring the privilege of the Rules for him. With all allowances for the facetious note in the following letter, it is apparent that Smart was no stranger to arrest and imprisonment, for he wrote to somebody who inquired his whereabouts:

> Sir.
> After being *six* times arrested: *nine* times in a spunging house: and *three* times in the Fleet-Prison, I am at last happily arrived at the King's Bench.
>
> Kitt. Smart.[30]

At least he had not lost his sense of humor.

The King's Bench Prison was used for the confinement of debtors and those guilty of "libel and other misdemeanours." It was described in 1773 as "situated in a fine air; but all prospects of the fields, even from the uppermost windows, is excluded by the height of the walls with which it is surrounded. It consists of two rows of small houses, forming a street between them, where the prisoners open shops and follow their professions. At one end of this range is a larger house called the State-house, where those prisoners who can afford it are accomodated with more agreeable apartments than in the other parts of the prison. Opposite the State-house is a neat chapel; and beyond them is a large open spot of ground which is converted into a public garden."[31] At Smart's time the Rules was an area of about three miles south and west of the prison itself, containing all kinds of entertainment but public houses and theatres; those who purchased the privilege of the Rules could walk in St. George's Fields, which their less fortunate fellows could not even catch a glimpse of from within the prison. Tobias Smollett was imprisoned in the King's Bench for three months in 1759 for defamation of character; the following year he described the place in the novel *The Adventures of Sir Launcelot Greaves.*

> the prison of the King's Bench, . . . is situated in St. George's Fields, about a mile from the end of Westminster Bridge, and appears like a neat, little regular town, consisting of one street, surrounded by a very high wall, including an open piece of ground, which may be termed a garden, where the prisoners take the air, and amuse themselves with a variety of diversions. Except the en-

trance, where the turnkeys keep watch and ward, there is nothing in the place that looks like a gaol, or bears the least colour of restraint. The street is crowded with passengers. Tradesmen of all kinds here exercise their different profession. Hawkers of all sorts are admitted to call and vend their wares as in any open street of London. Here are butchers'-stands, chandlers'-shops, a surgery, a tap-house well frequented, and a public kitchen, in which provisions are dressed for all the prisoners gratis, at the expense of the publican. Here the voice of misery never complains, and indeed little else is to be heard but the sounds of mirth and jollity. At the farther end of the street, on the right hand, is a little paved court leading to a separate building, consisting of twelve large apartments, called state-rooms, well furnished and fitted up for the reception of the better sort of Crown prisoners; and on the other side of the street, facing a separate division of ground called the common side, is a range of rooms occupied by prisoners of the lowest order, who share the profits of a begging-box, and are maintained by this practice, and some established funds of charity. We ought also to observe, that the gaol is provided with a neat chapel, in which a clergyman, in consideration of a certain salary, performs divine service every Sunday. [Chapter XX.]

Smollett had an easy time of it during his three months imprisonment, but he had plenty of money, and the frequent visits of his friends made his confinement more than bearable.

While Smollett and others who could afford to purchase whatever they wanted in prison did not, as a consequence, suffer any hardships and could look back upon the period of confinement without horror, those without money lived in a most distressing state. One of Smart's fellow prisoners was a Mr. James Stephens, a very vocal and literate person who led a group of those imprisoned for debt in their demand to know by what law they were held in confinement. Stephens was allowed to appear before a court and plead their common case, evincing a surprising knowledge of English law, but he and his fellows received no satisfaction. This was in May and June, 1770; early in 1771 he wrote on behalf of three hundred and forty prisoners to the House of Lords, and he and another prisoner addressed a petition to Lord Mansfield—all to no avail.[32] Living with his father and mother in the prison was young James Stephens, between ten and twelve years old, who later wrote his memoirs and described the prison, its daily life, and some of his father's friends. He wrote of the prison that it was "far less cleanly and commodious then than it has now become, it since having been burnt down in the riots of 1780 . . . The rooms at that time were small and dirty; and those prisoners even who could afford to pay the highest rents, were unable to obtain more than a single room, which served them for both eating and sleeping." Prisoners often messed together, "taking their meals alternately at each other's rooms," a "turn-up bedstead" being "buttoned against the whitewashed wall, to make the better room for a table around which they were sitting." And, according to him, there was a great "laxity of moral sentiment" in the prison. But young Stephens was fortunate indeed for, as he goes on to recall, "among the fellow Prisoners with whom my Father was acquainted were three or four literary characters, from whom I can remember to have received particular attention, out of his presence, and the load of books, etc. with a view to the cultivation of my taste. Among them was Christopher Smart the Poet." He further says, "I have mentioned Smart, and Jackson, and Main, and Thompson, because they all took a particular interest in the dawn of my understanding, if I may judge by their professions or their conduct, for they were very kind to me.[33] The Revd. William F. Jackson was an Irish revolutionary and William Thompson was a portrait painter; Main, a Scotsman, had been a prominent bookseller and publisher of Boston, Massachusetts. Smart did not become brutalized in prison as so many did and as it would have been so very easy for him to do; not only did he find compatible friends in men like Stephens and those around him, but he also went out of his way to be kind to young James, lending him books and guiding his dawning understanding. Not only did he hymn the praises of charity in his poetry; he practiced it even at a time when selfishness might be expected. Fanny Burney records of him at this time that in "a letter he sent my father not long before his death, to ask his assistance for a fellow sufferer and good offices for him in that charity over which he presides, he made use of an expression which pleased me much, 'that he had himself assisted him, *according to his willing poverty.*' "[34] His poverty was real; not too long before his death he wrote to a Reverend Mr. Jackson, almost surely his fellow prisoner, "Being upon the recovery from a fit of illness, and *having nothing to eat*, I beg you to lend me *two or three shillings*, which (God willing) I will return, with many thanks, in two or three days."[35]

That Smart should have had to turn to somebody other than one of his old friends for so small a sum suggests that he had been forgotten by them. London was full of men with whom Smart had lived in terms of great intimacy; many of them had had occasion to enjoy his hospitality. Dr. James Nares the musician was such a one; Smart had once invited him to dine, writing the charming *Epistle to Dr. Nares* in lieu of a note. Nares was in a position to call attention to Smart's distress, as his brother Justice George Nares and others were trying to establish a Society for the Discharge and Relief of Persons imprisoned for small Debts. That Smart should have suffered extreme need at a time when there was an organized movement afoot, partly guided by the brother of one of his friends, to alleviate such suffering as his is ironic. Yet nobody came forward to help him. Some may have thought him dead; the newspapers and periodicals were so full of Wilkes and his running battle with the government that Smart's name did not so much as appear in the columns of domestic intelligence when he was arrested, tried, and sentenced. Lord Mansfield, before whom he appeared when tried, did nothing for him. Dr. Johnson, the indignities and hardships of his own Grub-Street career many years behind him, had long ago washed his hands of him. Garrick and Murphy made no move to help him; Bonnell Thornton had died in 1768. The many friends and acquaintances who had subscribed to his works gave no sign of awareness of his existence. His brother-in-law, Thomas Carnan, printed his *Hymns for the Amusement of Children*, announced in the *Public Advertiser* on December 27, 1770, but without Smart's name as author. Whatever he gained from the sale of this little book could not have been enough to make any great difference in his way of living in the Rules. And the dedication to His Royal Highness Prince Frederick, Bishop of Osnaburgh, if it was intended to start a move for royal clemency, failed to achieve any effect. The Prince, who was little more than five years old, was being tutored by the Reverend Dr. Markham and Mr. Cyril Jackson; the former had subscribed to the *Psalms* and the latter was the son of Dr. Cyril Jackson, a contemporary of Smart's at Cambridge. Possibly Smart had gained permission to dedicate the *Hymns* to Prince Frederick through the good offices of one or both of these men. With the publication of these *Hymns*, written largely during his confinement, Smart was heard no more as a poet. Some months before they were published, however, he wrote a four-line poem "to the wife of Mr. Emanuel Da Costa, then clerk and librarian to the Royal Society."*

*"A.S.N." sent the poem for inclusion in the August, 1818, *Gentleman's*

It is a slight, complimentary, piece of verse, whose sole interest may be in the second line,

> O' Fam'd at once to charm the ear and sight.
> Thou emblem of all conjugal delight,
> See Flora greets thee with her fragrant powers,
> A groupe of Virtues claims a wreath of Flowers.

Doubtless presented with a bunch of flowers, it expressed Smart's bitterness at having been separated from his own wife years ago. But it is at the same time a brief resurgence of the poet of happier years who could readily turn his hand to a graceful compliment.

Although Smart dedicated his *Hymns* to a child and wrote them for children, they are more than mere hack work, tossed off with speed and indifference. They were written when Smart was in prison and despairing of rescue. Into these poems, some of them of a bare simplicity and naiveté that have few equals in literature of merit anywhere, Smart brought together for a last time some of the major themes of his poetry. The very titles of some of the thirty-six hymns in the collection are a recapitulation of many of his preoccupations as a man and poet. While hymns on charity, gratitude, generosity, and praise would be expected to have a part in such a collection, it would by no means be inevitable to find others on learning and on "good-nature to animals." Hymn XVIII, "Prayer," begins with a line, "Pray without ceasing (says the Saint)," that is in itself a record of Smart's most memorable trait. And Hymn XXV, "Mirth," showing anew the love for flowers that is a recurring characteristic of his poetry, is a good example of the artless quality of these little poems.

I

> If you are merry sing away,
>   And touch the organs sweet;
> This is the Lord's triumphant day,
> Ye children in the gall'ries gay,
>   Shout from each goodly seat.

Magazine stating that it "was addressed, in 1758, to the wife," etc. Since Da Costa did not become clerk to the Royal Society until 1763 and since he was in the King's Bench Prison when Smart was there, the poem is probably of this latter period, particularly since it is followed in the *Gentleman's Magazine* by the unexplained date June 7, 1770, at which time Smart and Da Costa were fellow prisoners.

II

It shall be May to-morrow's morn,
   A field then let us run,
And deck us in the blooming thorn,
Soon as the cock begins to warn,
   And long before the sun.

III

I give the praise to Christ alone,
   My pinks already shew;
And my streak'd roses fully blown,
The sweetness of the Lord make known,
   And to his glory grow.

IV

Ye little prattlers that repair
   For cowslips in the mead,
Of those exulting colts beware,
But blythe security is there,
   Where skipping lambkins feed.

V

With white and crimson laughs the sky,
   With birds the hedge-rows ring;
To give the praise to God most high,
And all the sulky fiends defy,
   Is a most joyful thing.[36]

Others of the hymns are not so simple and surely proved too much for the children for whom they were bought. The first stanza of "Generosity" probably gave some difficulty.

That vast communicative mind,
That form'd the world and human kind,
   And saw that all was right;
Or was thyself, or came from Thee,
Stupendous generosity,
   Above all lustre bright.

And the whole of "Learning," with the expression in its third stanza of Smart's preference for the classics over science,

Humanity's a charming thing,
And every science of the ring,
   Good is the classic lore.

261

must have caused little brows to knot in perplexity.

Even the youngest who could read responded to Hymns XXXII and XXXIII with their woodcuts, the first of a raven in a tree and the second a child on a hobby-horse. "Against Despair, Old Ralph in the Wood" makes even the hymn on "Mirth" appear a piece of brittle sophistication by comparison.

I

A Raven once an Acorn took
    From Bashan's tallest stoutest tree;
He hid it by a limpid brook
    And liv'd another oak to see.

II

Thus Melancholy buries Hope,
    Which Providence keeps still alive,
And bids us with afflictions cope,
    And all anxiety survive.

The following hymn, "To Saturday," is equally primitive.

I

Now's the time for mirth and play,
Saturday's an holiday;
Praise to heav'n unceasing yield,
I've found a lark's nest in the field.

II

A Lark's nest, then your play-mate begs
You'd spare herself and speckled eggs;
Soon she shall ascend and sing
Your praises to th' eternal King.

Almost twenty years earlier, in 1751, Smart had written a "Morning Hymn, For all Little good Boys and Girls, Which is also proper for People of riper Years" for Newbery's *Lilliputian Magazine*.[37] Although written for a magazine which went so far as to list the names of all the little Masters and Misses who subscribed to it, the poem is one of a series intended not only for the young in years, but for those "of riper years" as well. It was to the young in heart that Smart addressed himself in his poetry, from his earliest efforts to his last.

But at the heart of the hymns of 1770 is the trinity of virtues he had celebrated in the greater part of the poetry he had written, especially after his release from confinement in 1763. Praise, charity, and above all, gratitude: these are what he preached and these are what he practiced. He described a cat in Hymn XII as "purring gratitude" and wrote of the Lord, "he himself, 'tis clear,/ Is also gratitude" in Hymn XXI. Charity he invoked,

> O Queen of virtues, whose sweet pow'r
> Does o'er the first perfections tow'r,
> Sustaining in the arms of love,
> All want below, all weal above.

praise he defined,

> Tho' conscience void of all offence,
>   Is man's divinest praise,
> A godly heart-felt innocence,
> Which does at first by grace commence,
>   By supplication stays

and gratitude he elevated, as he had before, to highest place.

I

> I upon the first creation
>   Clap'd my wings with loud applause,
> Cherub of the highest station,
>   Praising, blessing, without pause.

II

> I in Eden's bloomy bowers
>   Was the heav'nly gardner's pride,
> Sweet of sweets, and flow'r of flowers,
>   With the scented tinctures dy'd.

III

> Hear, ye little children, hear me,
>   I am God's delightful voice;
> They who sweetly still revere me,
>   Still shall make the wisest choice.

IV

> Hear me not like Adam trembling,
>   When I walk'd in Eden's grove;
> And the host of heav'n assembling,
>   From the spot the traitor drove.

263

V

Hear me rather as the lover
    Of mankind, restor'd and free;
By the word ye shall recover
    More than that ye lost by Me.

VI

I'm the Phoenix of the singers,
    That in upper Eden dwell;
Hearing me Euphrates lingers,
    And my wondrous tale I tell.

VII

'Tis the story of the Graces,
    Mercies without end or sum;
And the sketches and the traces
    Of ten thousand more to come.

VIII

List, my children, list within you,
    Dread not ye the tempter's rod;
Christ our gratitude shall win you,
    Wean'd from earth, and led to God.

Whatever the children who read these hymns thought—and the little book went into three editions in five years, proof that it was at least bought—Smart had the private solace that came from writing them at a time when he needed spiritual comfort most.

In this last published work, albeit written for children, Smart consciously or unconsciously repeated those mannerisms or peculiar features of his poetry which had characterized the poems written during and after the period spent in the madhouse. Here again is the pervasive alliteration, the alliterative doublets, alliterative and non-alliterative triplets, and the old possessive form in "Christ his." Here, too, are some of the identical old or unusual words remarked in his earlier religious poetry. At one juncture, and quite unexpectedly, there is a brief but charming avowal of his pride in the English, an old theme in his work; in Hymn XIV, to "Loveliness," he begins,

Good-nature is thy sterling name
Yet loveliness is English too.

Elsewhere he echoes and helps to make understandable lines in *Jubilate Agno*, for when he writes in *Hymn* XIX, on "Patience," that "Job, son of Issachar, at length/ Proves Patience is the child of Strength" he is quite arbitrarily identifying Job, the son of Issachar, with Job of the land of Uz, the exemplar of patience.* In *Jubilate Agno* he associated Issachar with strength (B2, 612), and earlier, at B2, 405, he had written, "For JOB was the son of Issachar and patience is the child of strength!" All of his later religious poetry from *Jubilate Agno* through these *Hymns For the Amusement of Children*, although to a far lesser extent in the Parables than in any other body of this poetry of proportionate length, is of a piece.

On May 22, 1771, twelve inmates of the King's Bench Prison sat as a jury and found that Christopher Smart "upon the Twentieth day of May Instant died a Natural Death within the Rules of the Prison."[38] Christopher Hunter stated that his uncle died "of a disorder in his liver" (p. xxvii), a statement that need not be, as it has been, interpreted as cirrhosis, with the implication that Smart's intemperance finally killed him.[39] Smart was buried in the since destroyed Church of St. Gregory by St. Paul on the 26th of May.[40] His epitaph may fittingly be supplied by Fanny Burney.

> But now I speak of authors, let me pay the small tribute of regret and concern due to the memory of poor Mr. Smart, who died lately in the King's Bench Prison; a man by nature endowed with talents, wit, and vivacity, in an eminent degree; and whose unhappy loss of his senses was a public as well as private misfortune. I never knew him in his glory, but ever respected him in his *decline*, from the fine proofs he had left of his better day, and from the account I have heard of his youth from my father, who was then his intimate companion; as, of late years, he has been his most active and generous friend, having raised a kind of fund for his relief, though he was ever in distress. His intellects, so cruelly impaired, I doubt not, affected his whole conduct.[41]

His nephew, Christopher Hunter, wrote to a friend soon after Smart's death, "I trust he is now at peace; it was not his portion here."

* His warrant for identifying Issachar with strength comes from Genesis, 49:14, "Issachar is a strong ass, crouching down between two burdens."

Appendix A
Smart's Confinements For Madness

At one point in *Jubilate Agno* Smart writes "Let Shetherboznai rejoice with Turners. End of Lent 1761. No. 5" (C, 56). The end of Lent in 1761 was March 21, the very day upon which he wrote the line marking that event.[1] "No. 5" may mean, in the absence of any other explanation, that Smart was marking the fifth time that he had seen the end of Lent while in confinement. This would mean that his first confinement occurred some time before April 9, 1757, the end of Lent for that year, and that he was out of that confinement before the end of Lent. Now, as Smart's admission to St. Luke's Hospital was on May 6, 1757, he must have been confined privately for a month or more before this, a procedure entirely in accordance with eighteenth-century practice in these cases. Mrs. Piozzi speaks of when "poor Smart . . . was first obliged to be put in private lodgings," and Blackstone corroborates the legality of confinement in the house of a relative or friend, adding that "when the disorder is grown permanent, and the circumstances of the party will bear such additional expense, it is thought proper to apply to the royal authority to warrant a lasting confinement."[2] Since efforts to get Smart admitted to St. Luke's Hospital began at least as early as March 18, 1757, when the petition and certificates for his admission were read and approved, and since when he was admitted it was from the parish of St. Gregory's by St. Paul's where Newbery had his business, he almost surely had been under his father-in-law's care for some time before the petition was sent in. Lent ended on March 25, 1758; Smart was still in St. Luke's. By April 14, 1759, the end of Lent, Smart had been out of St. Luke's for eleven months, had been at liberty for a while, and then had been confined for a third and final time—in Mr. Potter's madhouse in Bethnal Green where he remained until January 30 or 31, 1763. Thus he would have seen the end of Lent for the years 1759, 1760, and 1761 at Potter's; for 1758 in St. Luke's Hospital; and for 1757 in private lodgings, almost surely with Newbery. On June 17, 1760, Smart wrote in *Jubilate Agno*, "For Y is young—the Lord direct me in the better way going on in the Fifth year of my jeopardy June ye 17th. N.S. 1760. God be gracious to Dr YOUNG" (B2, 560), in this fashion recording his entry into the fifth year of his confinement. From this it is evident that he himself put the time of his first confinement at approximately, if not exactly, June 17, 1756. Lent in 1756 ended on April 17, and by the evidence of line C 56 it is clear that Smart was not then confined. His original contributions to the *Universal Visiter*, contracted for in November, 1755, but with publication of the first number actually taking place on February 2, 1756, began to fall off in April and May, giving further reason to accept a date around June 17, 1756, as the very day he entered his first confinement.

Contemporary references, mainly Fanny Burney's, speak of Smart's two confinements, but there is no need to suppose this a contradiction of the argument that Smart was actually confined three times, since his first confinement was with Newbery and doubtless an intermittent one with periods of liberty. The family would naturally have taken pains to keep the whole matter as quiet as they could. And when the *Critical Review* in its April, 1756, number remarked, referring to Smart, that it waged no war with Bedlam, Smart's disorder may have been manifesting itself already, or the critic may simply have been unnecessarily cruel. Mrs. LeNoir speaks of her three-year-old sister's presentiment of their father's madness being realized "soon after" the nightmare occurred; this would have had to be in early May of 1756 at the very earliest, as Marianne was born on May 3, 1753. What Mrs. LeNoir meant by "soon after" is not clear. If she meant only a few weeks or months, then her statement that her father returned to confinement no more is mistaken, for he entered St. Luke's in 1757, a fact she does not mention. If she means one or two years, and writing in 1831, at the age of seventy-seven, this is more probable, then the confinement in Mr. Potter's establishment followed the year at St. Luke's. In 1756 Mrs. LeNoir was only two years old and it is extremely doubtful that she would have at all remembered even visiting her father in confinement, let alone any details of the visit. Her anecdotes and statements are almost surely correct in their general details; it is when she particularizes dates and ages of people that her memory is not completely to be trusted.[3]

When Garrick gave his benefit performance for Smart the latter was mourned in the poems written on that occasion as one who had lost his reason, and he was said in one public announcement of the benefit to have been in confinement when the performance took place on February 3, 1759. On January 17, 1759, the *Public Advertiser* had announced the performance for January 26 and had described Smart as a "Gentleman, well known in the Literary World, who is at present under very unhappy Circumstances." Smart was, then, mad or thought mad and almost surely in confinement at least as early as the first days of January. Certain lines in *Jubilate Agno* are dated by Smart himself and aid in a conjectural reconstruction of the day upon which or near which he entered the madhouse. In section B1 of the poem he blesses "the thirteenth of August" in three successive lines (49–51), the first that bear dates in the extant part of the poem, immediately after having written in the preceding three lines that he had "made over" his "inheritance" to his mother in consideration of her infirmities, age, and poverty. Smart wrote one, two, or three lines or pairs of lines a day in the *Jubilate*; if he wrote one line or pair a day, and the poem is presumed to have been undertaken immediately or within a few days of when he entered the madhouse, the date of his confinement would emerge as July 14, 1758. At this time, beginning on May 19, 1758, his friends were trying to get him admitted to the incurable ward at St. Luke's and he was probably not therefore in a madhouse, having been released two months earlier from the hospital. If Smart wrote three lines or pairs of lines a day, March 11, 1759, would be the day upon which he entered the madhouse and began *Jubilate Agno*; this would seem to contradict his being in confinement on February 3, 1759, when the benefit was performed on his behalf. If, as seems most likely, he averaged two lines or pairs of lines each day, the date of the beginning of his last confinement would be January 4, 1759, a date which accords with all the available evidence. Smart's *Epistle to John Sherratt, Esq.*, published soon after he left Potter's madhouse, contains the lines,

> Well nigh sev'n years had fill'd their tale,
> From Winter's urn to Autumn's scale,
> And found no friend to grief and *Smart*,
> Like Thee and Her, thy sweeter part

which, if interpreted literally, means that for almost seven years, from January 20 ("Winter's urn") to September 23 ("Autumn's scale") he had been friendless. Hence, from January, 1756, when the first number of the *Universal Visiter* was being prepared for publication—it appeared on the second of February—to September, 1762, when John Sherratt and his wife, assisted by others, began those efforts which were to culminate in Smart's release some four or five months later, he felt that he had been deserted by all his friends. He did not look upon the public charity of the benefit performance in 1759 as a kindness. Since "Autumn's scale" does not refer to the end of Smart's confinement, which took place on January 30 or 31, 1763, "Winter's urn" does not mark the beginning of that confinement.

Appendix B
Smart and Mrs. Midnight on the Stage

While there is no doubt in my mind that Smart took the role of Mrs. Mary Midnight on the public stage in the years that he was at liberty, it is nevertheless a fact that during the time of his confinement in St. Luke's Hospital a Mother Midnight continued to appear on the stage in various entertainments. Starting with June 15, 1757, and including performances in the rest of the month of that year, the extant playbills and notices in newspapers show some thirty-five appearances of these entertainments under the names Medley Concert, Medley Concert and Auction, Impromptu Faragolio, Miss Midnight's Medley Concert, and New Medley Concert. On January 6, 1758, there was a performance of the New Medley Concert; on February 4, 7, and 9 Miss Midnight's Medley Concert was performed. Smart was released on May 11, 1758; on May 15 and June 1 and 18 of that year there were performances of the Old Woman's Oratory. In how many, if any, of these performances before May 15, 1758, Smart took a part cannot be known with certainty. Mrs. Midnight is listed as one of the actors in the three performances in August, 1757, as well as on September 2 and 28. Since Smart, as I have said, was almost surely the original stage Mother Midnight, the persistence of that name in the fourteen performances in 1757 may be explained in two ways. Either Smart, in the curable wing of St. Luke's, was allowed outside the hospital on occasions, which is most unlikely because of the hospital rules, or some other performer impersonated Mother Midnight on the nights she appeared in this period. Theophilus Cibber became the director of these entertainments starting December 24, 1757, and continued to direct or have a part in them until up to about 1759, at which time they ceased for a year. But Cibber was not Mother Midnight in these performances, for extant playbills list his name for certain parts of the Medley Concerts or Medley Concerts and Auctions at the same time that they list Miss Midnight and Mother Midnight. Mother Midnight is down for "Handel's Water Music" on August 11, 1757, and for the same with a "Preamble on Kettle Drums" on August 31. So too, for September 2 and 5, but on September 8 the "Water Music with a Preamble on the Kettle Drums" is by Woodbridge. The fact that the Water Music, "with a Preamble on the Kettle Drums" was part of the program for the fifth performance of the Old Woman's Oratory on January 7, 1752, and that it was thought necessary to distinguish between Mother Midnight and Woodbridge makes it somewhat more probable that Smart was resurrecting part of his old repertory for his scattered appearances, some of them with Cibber. On September 12 Mother Midnight reappears and Woodbridge's name is dropped, and the former also performs the Water Music for September 28 and October 3 and 5. Handel's Water Music, without the later addition of the Kettle Drums, was a feature of the third Old Woman's Oratory and continued a staple item with and without the Preamble.

Similarly, there is the even stronger possibility that Smart was allowed some periods of accompanied liberty while in Potter's madhouse after he had spent about a year there, for there was a revival of Mrs. Midnight's Concert and Oratory at the Haymarket on February 14, 1760. "Orations by Mrs. Midnight" as well as a "Rhapsody on the Death of a late Noble Commander by Mrs. Midnight" made up part of the bill; among the other performers' names was that of a Miss Gaudry. There was the further information that "Miss Midnight had no concern in the management of a performance lately exhibited at the Haymarket under the above mentioned name, but was only there as a performer"; evidently somebody was trying to capitalize on the Midnight pseudonym.[1] Less than a month later Londoners read in a playbill of a benefit for Mr. Gaudry and Mrs. Midnight for the last time in that theatrical season. The benefit was to take place at the Haymarket on March 6 at which time Mrs. Midnight's Concert and Oratory was to be put on "as it was originally perform'd in the Year 1754." In the first part Mrs. Midnight was to attempt the original prologue and then, after a Scotch Song by Mr. Lauder, there would be an "ORATION, by Madam MID-NIGHT her own Self." Mr. Gaudry was to sing a new cantata composed by himself in Part II. "By particular *Desire*, Mrs. MID-NIGHT will speak an EPILOGUE, riding on an ASS," thus bringing Part III to an end. To the full program of these three parts, only a fraction of which have been mentioned, was added a musical entertainment called *Britannia's Triumph* and other items, including an "EPILOGUE of THANKS; written, and to be spoken by Mrs. MIDNIGHT." Every care was taken to duplicate the kind of programs put on in 1754. In an "N.B." Mrs. Midnight and Mr. Gaudry expressed their humble hope that they would be "honour'd with the Presence of the Ladies and Gentlemen for this Night only, as they are determin'd no Care shall be wanting to render the Performance thoroughly agreeable." Tickets could be had of Mrs. Midnight "at Mr. *Collingwood's*, Glazier, in *Coventry-Court*," as well as "of Mr. Gaudry" and elsewhere.[2] On September 8, 1760, again at the Haymarket, there was a concert in which, the advertisement announces, "will be introduced the Original Orations for (this night only) by Mrs. Midnight . . . *Prologue* by Mrs. Midnight." Mrs. Midnight was also to give her "Advice to the Critics, with a specimen of ancient and modern acting." *Britannia's Triumph* was on the bill and Mr. Gaudry was to offer a "Rhapsody on the Death of General Wolfe." This was another benefit performance for Mrs. Midnight and Mr. Gaudry; the former hoped "the Ladies" would "favour her."[3] *Mother Midnight's Orations; and other Select Pieces; as they were spoken at the Oratory in the Hay-Market, London,* published in January, 1763, and edited anonymously but commonly accepted as of Smart's compilation, contains the epilogue to *Britannia's Triumph*; an epilogue spoken by "Mrs. Midnight's Daughter, riding upon an ass;" and "A Specimen of Modern Acting." Also included was *The Gifts: A Dramatic Interlude,* As it was intended to be performed At the THEATRE in the Hay-Market, *London.* Set to Music By Mr. JOSEPH GAUDRY." This interlude, of which there is no other mention elsewhere, further identifying Mr. Gaudry of the March 6, 1760, benefit performance, was written shortly after the accession of George the III, for the first speech, spoken by Liberty, reads

> Tho' late *Britannia* for thy favour'd Son,
> Thy godlike GEORGE, in Tears of Blood we mourn'd,

> These Sorrows now shall soften and subside,
> Since in his blooming Heir his Virtues all,
> With Equal Lustre glow.

Toward the end of the interlude two lines give evidence that the performance was to have taken place before the actual coronation of George III on September 22, 1761,

> Each active Patriot for the Day prepares;
> When *Britain's* Monarch shall receive his Crown.

Since the King had set the date of his coronation by a royal proclamation of July 8, *The Gifts* was written between that date and September 22. Although the interlude was not performed, Mrs. Midnight did deliver a Loyal Oration, reprinted in the same collection, in which she spoke of "that late awful Solemnity, the Coronation of our good and gracious King" and of the wedding of George III. Possibly a performer other than Smart took the part of Mrs. Midnight in 1760 and 1761, speaking prologues and epilogues written by Smart, delivering the "Loyal Oration" and others, probably taking part in *Britannia's Triumph*, and maybe even preparing to perform in *The Gifts*. Yet the playbill for the March 6, 1760, benefit with its insistence that Mrs. Midnight "her own self" would deliver an oration as part of a program "as originally perform'd in the Year 1754" gives strong reason to believe that Smart was permitted to leave the madhouse for the purpose of donning the costume of an old woman and entertaining the public from the stage of the theater in the Haymarket. By February, 1760, when the first mention of the revival of the authentic Old Woman's Oratory occurred Smart had been in Potter's madhouse for just over a year and had probably won the confidence of his keeper. Had he proved intractable during his first year Newbery could have had him committed to the incurable ward at St. Luke's Hospital on April 7, 1760, when he came up for readmission.[4] That he did not do so not only speaks well for him but also suggests that Smart had so improved under Potter's care and regimen that he was not thought incurable. At least two poems that he wrote in 1761 were accepted for publication, further evidence of his recovery.[5]

APPENDIX C

BOOKS*

in use at *Cambridge* about the year 1730,
for *Arithmetic, Algebra, Geometry,*
Physics, Mechanics, and *Hydrostatics.*

Acta Eruditorum (Lipsiae) 1686, 1690, '91, '94, '95.
Acta Philosophica.

Bacon, F. (Trin.), Historia de Ventis. Lug. Bat., 1638; Lond. 1672.
———— Sylva Sylvarum, 1627, ed. 9, 1670.
Bartholin, Casp. nepos (Copenhagen) Physicks. Lond. 1703.
Bentley, Ri. (Joh. & Trin.) Boyle Lectures. Lond. 1693.
Bernoulli, Jac. (Basle, Heidelb.) de Gravitate Aetheris. Amst. 1683.
Boerhaave, Herm. (Leyden) Chymistry (Shaw) 4to. Lond. 1626.
Boyle, Ro. (*Oxon.*) History of Cold. Lond. 1665, 1685.
———— Physico-Mechan. Experim. *Oxon.* 1660. Contin^d, 1669; Lond. 1682.
———— Principles of Nat. Bodies. Lond. 1674.
———— Sceptical Chymist. *Oxon.* 1661, 1680.
———— Works (abridged by Shaw) 3 vols. 4to. 1725.
Bradley, Ri. (Camb.) on Gardening. Lond. 1626.
Browne, Peter (*T. C. D.*) Procedure of the Understanding. Lond. 1728.
Burgundiae Scholae Philosophia. 2 vols. 4to. Nürnb. 1682, Paris 1684, '7.
Burnet, T. (Clare & Chr.) to Keill in Appendix to his own Theory. Lond. 1698.
———— Theory of the Earth. Lond. 1681—9.

Cartesius, Réné (La Flèche) Principia. Amst. 1644, &c.
Castellus, Bened. (Montp.) de motu aquae. ital. Rom. 1628. english, Lond. 1661.
Caswell, J. (*Wadh.*) Trigonometry. Lond. fol. 1685.
Chambers, Ephr. Dictionary (sub vocibus *Air, Barometer, Circulation of Sap,*
   Deluge, Dissolution, Diving Bell, Elasticity, Electricity, Fire, Fluid, Fossil,
   Gravity, Matter, Perpetual Motion, Pump, Sound, Syphon, Tarantula, Thun-
   der, Vegetation) fol. 1728.
Cheyne, G. (Edinb.) Philos. Princip. Lond. 1715.
Clarke, S. (Caius) Letters to Dodwell. Lond. 1706.
———— Letters between him and Leibnitz. Lond. 1717.
Clericus, Jean (Geneva) Physica. Cantab. 1700, 1705.

De Chales (Challes), Cl. Fr. Milliet (Turin) Cursus Mathematicus, fol. 4 vols.
   Lyons 1690.
—————————— Euclid. *Oxon.* 1685, 1704, &c.
De la Hire, Philip. (Paris) Conic Sections. Paris, 1655, 1685.
De Lanis, Fr. Tert. (S. J.) Magist. Nat. & Art. Brescia 1684, 1692.
De la Pryme, Abr. (Joh.) in Philos. Transactions.
De l'Hôpital, Marquis, G. F. A. (Paris) Conics. London, 4to. 1723.
Derham, W. (*Trin.*) Letters. (Ray's.) Lond. 1718.
Desaguliers, J. Theo. (*Ch. Ch.*) transl. of Marriotte's Hydrostatics. 1738.
Descartes, see Cartesius.
De Witt, J. Conics. Amst. 1659.

Euclid, cura D. Gregory. fol. *Oxon.* 1703. Gr. and Lat.

Friend (or Freind), J. (*Ch. Ch.*) Praelect. Chem. *Oxon.* 1704, 1709, et alibi.

* From Christopher Wordsworth, *Scholae Academicae* (Cambridge, 1877).

Gassendi, Pierre (Aix & Paris) Philos. Lond. 1658.
Gordon, Patrick (?T. C. D.) Account of Trade Winds. ?Geography Anatomized 1693, 1716.
's Gravesande, W. Ja. (Leyden) Philos. Newton. Lond. 1720.
————— Physic. Elem. Math. Lug. Bat. 1720.
Green, Ro. (Clare) Principles of Nat. Philosophy. (Solid Geom.) Camb. 1712. ibid. 1727.
————— Princ. Philos. of Expansive and Contractive Forces.

Hales, Steph. (C. C. C.) Vegetable Staticks. Lond. 1727.
Hammond's Algebra.
Harriott, T. (*S. Mary Hall*) Artis Analyticae Praxis. Lond. 1631.
Harris, J. (S. John's) Lexicon Technicum (sub vocibus *Deluge, Hydrostaticks, Perpetual Motion, Spring, Thunder, Vegetation*) 1708.
Hawksbee, F. (F. R. S.) Phys. Mechan. Experiments. Lond. 1709, 1719.
Helmont, J. Bapt. van (Louvain) Opera.
Hooke, R. (*Ch. Ch.*) Micrographia (Elzevir 1648). Lond. 1665, 1671.
————— Posthumous Works. Lond. 1705.
Huet, P. D. (Caen) Censura Phil. Cartes, 1689, Paris 1694.
Huyghens, Chr. (Lugd.) Opera Posthuma. Lug. Bat. 1703.

Jones, W. (F. R. S.) Abridgement of Philos, Transact.
————— Analysis per Quantitatum Series, Fluxiones ac Differentias. 4to. Lond. 1711.
————— Synopsis Palmariorum Matheseos. Lond. 1706.

Keill, Jo. (*Balliol*) Epist. de Legibus Attractionis. *Oxon.* 1715; 4to. Lug. Bat. 1725.
————— Examination of Burnet's Theory of the Earth. *Oxon.* 1698.
————— Introd. ad Phys. Lect. (1701, 1705, 1726) . *Oxon.* 1715.
Kersey, J. Algebra. Lond. 1673–4, 1725.

Law, Edm. (Joh., Chr., Pet.) Translation of King's Origin of Evil. 1732.
Le Clerc, see Clericus.
Le Grand, Ant. (*Douay & Oxon.*) de Carentia Sensus in Brutis. Lond. 1675.
————— Instit. Philos. 1694.
Leibnitz, Godf. W. (Leipzig) and Clarke's Controversial Papers (1717).
Lister, Mart. (Joh. & *Oxon.*) Account of Trade-winds. (? 1683.)
Locke, J. (*Ch. Ch.*) Essay on the Human Understanding. Lond. 1690, &c.
Lowthrop, J. Abridgement of Philos. Transact. Lond. 1716.
Lucretius de Rerum Natura I. (Creech *Oxon.* 1695. Maittaire 1713.)

Maclaurin, Colin (Glasg. & Aberd.) Geometra Organica, sive Descriptio Curvarum, Universalis. Lond. 1720. 4to. (Algebra 1742).
Malebranche, Nic. (Sorbonne) Search after Truth. Lond. 1720.
Marriotte, Edm., see Desaguliers.
Michelotti Pet. Ant. de Separ. Fluidorum. 4to. Venice 1721.
Milnes, Ja. (? M.D. Camb., M.A. *Oxon.*) Conic Sections. *Oxon.* 1702, 1723.
Miscellanea Curiosa (Halley, Molyneux, Wallis, Woodward, &c.). Franc. and Leips. 1670–97.
Musschenbroeck, Pet. van (Leyden) de Cohaerentia Corporum.
————————— Elem. Physico.-Math. Lugd. Bat. 1729.
————————— Phys. Experim. de Magnete.

Newton, Is. (Trin.) Algebra.
————————— Arithmetica Num. and Specios. Probl.
————————— Optice. Lond. 1704.
————————— Principia Mathem. (1687) ed. 2, Camb. 1713. ed. 3, 1726.
Newtonianae Philosophiae Institut. 12mo.
Nieuwentyt, Bern. Religious Philosopher (a translation, J. Chamberlayne, *Trin.* —Lond. 1718–19, 1730.)

APPENDIX C

Ode, Jac. Phil. Nat. Principia. Traject. ad Rhen. 1727.
Oughtred, W. (King's). Clavis Mathem. Lond. 1631. *Oxon.* 1652, &c.; Transl. Halley, 1694.
Ozanam, Jacques. Cursus Mathem. Paris 1693, 1712.

Pardie, Geom. 1701.
Pell, J. (Trin.). Idea of Mathematics. 1650.
Pemberton, H. (Leyden). View of Newton. Lond. 1728.
Philosophical Conversations.
————————— Transactions.
Polenus, J. (Padua) de Motu Aquae. 4to. Patav. 1717.

Quincy, J. Dispensatory. Lond. 1718; ed. 7, 1730.

Ray, J. (Cath., Trin.). Physico-Theol. Discourses. Lond. 1692, 1693, 1717, 1721.
Reflections on Learning (by T. Baker, Joh.) 1699, 1700, &c.
Rohault, Jacques. Physica (S. Clarke); ed. 4, 1718.

[Saunderson, Nic. (Chr.). Algebra (posthumous), 4to. Camb. 1740.]
Simpson, T. Algebra. Lond. 1737, 1746.
Simson, Ro. (Glasg.). Conics. 4to. Edin. 1735.
Stillingfleet, E. (Joh.). Origines Sacrae. Lond. 4to. 1662, fol. 1709.
Sturmius, J. Chr. (Altdorf). Auctarium.
————— Colleg. Experiment. siue Curios. 1672. 4to. Nürnb. 1675—85.

Tacquet, Andr. *S. J.* (Antwerp). Euclid (W. Whiston); ed. 3, Cantab, 1722.
Torricellius, Evang. De Motu projectil.

Varenius, Bern. Geographia (Newton) Camb. 1681; (Jurin) Camb. 1712, 1714.

Wallis, J. (Emman., Qu.; *Savil. Prof.*). Logic. *Oxon.* 1687, 1729.
————— Op. Mathemat. fol. 1699.
Ward, Seth (Sid. & *Trin.*) Idea Trigonom. In usum juvent. 4to. *Oxon.* 1654.
Watts, Isaac. Logic. Lond. 1725.
Wedelius, G. Wolfg. Theoria Saporum. Jen. 1703.
Wells, E. (? *Ch. Ch.*) Arithmetick, 1713. Lond. 1726.
————— Geography. *Oxon.* 1701; ed. 4, 1726.
————— Trigonometry. Lond. 1714.
Whiston, W. (Clare). Praelect. Phys. Mathem. Cant. 1710.
————— Theory of the Earth. Camb. 1737.
Wilkins, J. (*New Inn, Magd. H., Wadh.*). Mathem. Magick. Lond. 1648, 1691.
Wingate, Edm. Arithmetick. Lond. 1630, 1726.
Wolf, Christian., in Elementis Math. Mechanica. Genev. 1732.
Woodward, J. (Lambeth). Theory of the Earth. Lond. 1695, 1723.
Worster, Ben. Princip. Nat. Philos. Lond. 1722, 1730.

A list of Books in use at Cambridge
about the year 1730
for Optics and Astronomy.

Acta Eruditorum Lipsiae. anno 1683.

Bentley, Ri. (Trin.) Boyle Lectures, Serm. VII. Lond. 1693.
Boyle, Ro. (*Oxon.*) Works, abridged by Shaw. 1725.
Bullialdus, Ismael (Boulliau) De Lineis Spiralibus, Paris, 1657.
Burgundiae Philosophia. (Cf. p. 79 supra.)
Burnet, T. (Clare and Chr.) Theory of the Earth. Lond. 1681—9.

Cartesius, Renat. (La Fleche) Dioptricks.
—— Meteor.
—— Principia. Amst. 1644.
Chambers, Ephr. Dict. (sub vocibus *Halo, Light, Moon, Parhelion, Rainbow.*) 1728.
Clarke, S. (Caius) Demonstration of Sir I. Newton's Philos.
Clericus, J. (Geneva) Physica. Cantab. 1700, 1705.

De Chales, C. F. M. (*Soc. Jesu,* Turin) Cursus Mathem. Lyons, 1690.
Derham, W. (Trin.) Astro-Theol. Lond. 1714, 1726.
Domekins, G. Peter. Phil. Newton. Lond. 1730.

Fabri, Honorat. (Rome) II. de Homine. Paris, 1666.
Flamsteed, J. (Jes.) 1672—1713.

Gassendi, P. (Aix and Paris) Astron. 1702.
's Gravesande, W. J. (Leyden) Physico-Math. Lug. Bat. 1720.
Gregory, Dav. (Edinb., *Oxon*) Astron. folio *Oxon.* 1702. engl. Lond. 1715.
—— Catoptricae et Dioptricae Sphericae Elementa. Oxon. 1695. (Lond. 1705, 1715, 1735.)

Harris, J. (S. John's) Astron. Dial. (ed. 3. 1795.)
Hooke, R. (Ch. Ch.) Posthumous Works. 1705.
Huyghens, Christian. Discursus de Causis Gravitat. Lug. Bat. 1724—8.
—— Opusc. Posthuma. Lug. Bat. 1703.
—— Planetary Worlds, or Cosmotheoros. Hagae. 1698. Lond. 1699.

Johnson, T. (King's, Magd.) Quaestiones (Opticae pp. 27, 28).
———————— (Astronomicae pp. 32, 33) Camb. 1732; ed. 3. 1741.

Keill, John (*Balliol*) Examination of Theorists on the Earth. Oxon. 1698.
—— Introd. ad Astron. Oxon. 1715.

Lowthorp, J. (Joh.) Abridgement of Philos. Transactions, 3 vols. 4to. Lond. 1716.

Malebranche, Nic. (Sorbonne) Search after Truth. (1674), Transl. T. Taylor. Lond. 1720.
Miscellanea Curiosa (Halley, Molyneux, &c.)
Molyneux, W. (F. R. S.) Dioptricks. 4to. Lond. 1692.
—— in Misc. Curiosa, II. 263.
Musschenbroeck, P. van. (Leyden) Elem. Physico-Math.

Newton, Is. (Trin.) Lectiones Opticae, Opticks, 4to. Lond. 1704.
—— Optice. lat. ed. S. Clarke. Lond. 1706, 1728.
—— Principia Math. Lond. 1687. Camb. 1713.

Ode, Ja. Phil. Nat. Principia. Traject. ad Rhen. 1727.

Pemberton, H. (Leyden, Gresham Coll., F. R. S.) View of Newton. Lond. 1728.
Philosophical Conversations.
———— Transactions.

Riccioli, Giov. Bapt. (Parma) Almagestum Novum. Bologna 1651–69.
Rizzett, Giov. de Luminis affectionibus, or the present State of the Republik of Letters.
(Rizzett, Giov.) a Confutation of.
Rohault, Jac. Physica. ed. 4. (by S. Clarke) 1718.
Rowning, J. (Magd.) Opticks.

Smith, R. (Trin.) Opticks, Camb. 1728, 1738.

NOTES

Tacquet, Andr. *(Soc. Jesu,* Antwerp) Catoptricks (1669).

Wallis, J. (Emm. Qu. *Savil.)* Opera Mathemat. Oxon. 1687—99.
Whiston, W. (Clare) Praelectiones Astronom., Camb. 1707.
———————————— Physico-Mathem., Camb. 1710.
———————— New Theory of the Earth. Lond. 1696, 1725.
Worster, Ben. Princip. Philos. Lond. 1730.

Notes to Chapter I

1. Information from the Snotterton estate papers at Raby Castle. John Smart is identified as Peter's brother in letters of the latter quoted in Christopher Hunter's *An Illustration of Mr. Daniel Neal's History of the Puritans* (Durham, 1736), pp. 158 and 160.
2. Biographical details on Vane and Smart are from the *DNB.*
3. Indentures of Jan. 16 and 17, 1707, and March 7 and 8, 1722, in P.R.O. C11/2482/34., dated October 25, 1743.
4. Somerset House, vol. Richmond, fol. 179.
5. E. Hughes, *North Country Life in the Eighteenth Century: the Northeast, 1700–1750* (London, 1952), p. 74.
6. W. H. D. Longstaffe, *History and Antiquities of the Parish of Darlington* (London, 1909) , p. 183.
7. Editor, *The Poems of the late Christopher Smart,* 2 vols. (Reading, 1791) , I, vi, hereafter referred to as Hunter. Unidentified quotations having to do with Smart's life are from this source.
8. Edward Hasted, *The History and Topographical Survey of Kent* (Canterbury, 1778—99), II, 241.
9. Letter to Cuthbert Sharp preserved in Sharp MS 28 in the Durham Cathedral Chapter Library. I quote from p. 1 of this third in a series of three letters from Mrs. LeNoir to Sharp. The letters are dated July 13 and 30 and August 22, 1831.
10. Since the Webbs were ancestors of Thackeray the novelist, there exists some relationship, however distant, between him and Smart.
11. See below, pp. 250—1 for the full text of the letter.
12. Edward Hasted, *The History and Topographical Survey of the County of Kent,* 2nd ed. (Canterbury, 1797—1801), V, 45—6.
13. Kent County Archives, catalogue mark U36 T1401.
14. Hasted, *Kent,* 1st ed., IV, 383-4, 385, and 390.
15. Hasted, *Kent,* IV, 261, *passim* and Benjamin Martin, *Natural History of England* (London, 1759), I, 187.
16. See James Boswell, *The Life of Samuel Johnson,* ed. by G. B. Hill, revised by L. F. Powell (Oxford, 1934—50), I, 99—100 (hereafter *Life)* and *Schola Regia Cantuariensis: A History of Canterbury School,* by C. E. Woodruff and H. J. Cape (London, 1908), p. 173.
17. Quotations from Smart's poems are from the first editions unless otherwise indicated.
18. Bodleian Library MS, *E. H. Barker's Correspondence, Vol. III* (1832-38). fol. 245 ff. The same anecdote, with minor verbal variations, appears in a letter to Sharp, August 22, 1831, p. 5.
19. *Letters,* ed. E. Hughes, *Surtees Society Publications,* 165 (Durham, 1956), p. 65.
20. Quoted in Hughes, *North Country Life,* (1952), p. 363.
21. *Letters,* p. 61.
22. *Letters,* ed. R. W. Chapman (Oxford, 1952), I, 339.
23. *Letters,* pp. 166 and 193.
24. Quoted in William Hutchinson, *The History and Antiquities of the County Palatine of Durham* (Newcastle-on-Tyne, 1785—94), III, 267.
25. Dean Cowper's *Letters,* pp. 109, 113, and 116.

26. *Memoirs of the Last Ten Years of the Reign of George the Second* (London, 1822), I, 101.

27. *Letters*, p. 153.

28. See note 13, p. 277. The same anecdote occurs in Mrs. LeNoir's letter to Sharp of August 22, 1831, p. 4.

29. See note 13, p. 277. The anecdote is repeated in the letter to Sharp of August 22, 1831, pp. 4–5.

30. *Historical MSS Commission*, Egmont, III, 308.

31. *Letters*, pp. 153–4 and 183.

32. *Six North Country Diaries*, ed. J. C. Hodgson, *Surtees Society Publications*, 118 (Durham, 1910), p. 212.

33. D. A. Winstanley, *The University of Cambridge in the Eighteenth Century* (Cambridge, 1922), pp. 17–18 and the Yale edition of *Horace Walpole's Correspondence*, IX, 104, n. 12–letter to George Montagu, May 15, 1750.

34. H. E. Busteed, *Echoes From Old Calcutta* (London, 1908), pp. 124, 162, and 161.

35. Mrs. LeNoir to Sharp, August 22, 1831, p. 2.

36. Quoted in *Durham School Register*, ed. T. H. Burbidge (Cambridge, 1940), 3rd ed., p. 5.

37. Hughes, *North Country Life*, p. 363.

38. Hutchinson, *History of Durham*, II, 275–6.

Notes to Chapter II

1. *Correspondence*, edited by Paget Toynbee and Leonard Whibley (Oxford, 1935), p. 3.

2. K. β. "Scholarships," p. 42 in Pembroke College Library Treasury and Aubrey Attwater, *Pembroke College Cambridge, A Short History* (Cambridge, 1936), p. 96.

3. Boswell, *Life*, I, 76.

4. K. β., "Scholarships," p. 42.

5. *The Two First Parts of His Life* (London, 1756), pp. 9–10 and 18.

6. *Pembroke College Annual Gazette*, No. 6, June, 1932, pp. 23–4. Scobell's sizar was billed for £2. 5s. 5d. for the same term.

7. *British Education* (London, 1756), p. 17.

8. B. β. 6, "Pembroke College Register," p. 66.

9. Translated by Mr. Nicholas Cox, in 1964 a third-year student at Pembroke College.

10. M. α. 4, "Treasury Accounts, 1729–1750."

11. *Correspondence*, p. 233.

12. B. β. 6, "Pembroke College Register," pp. 113 and 119.

13. See *A Book of Cambridge Verse*, ed. by E. E. Kellett (Cambridge, 1911), p. 416. Trinity College accounts for 1744–46 record expenses for a trough and chain "for the eagle."

14. *Aeneid*, vi, 501–2 and *Satires*, II, ii, 79; Loeb translation.

15. See Gray's *Correspondence*, p. 291, and Roger Lonsdale, *Dr. Charles Burney* (Oxford, 1965), p. 25.

16. M. α. 4, "Treasury Accounts, 1729–1750."

17. From Pembroke College MS. B. β. 6, pp. 95 and 97, quoted in part in Ainsworth and Noyes, *Christopher Smart*, p. 21.

18. *Correspondence*, pp. 291–2.

19. C. H. Cooper, *Annals of Cambridge* (Cambridge, 1895), III, 530. See my "Christopher Smart and the Problem of Ordination in the Eighteenth Century," *Church Quarterly Review*, January–March, 1966.

20. "University-Audit Accounts, 1741–1786."

21. M. α. 4, "Treasury Accounts, 1729–1750."

22. Brittain, *Poems by Christopher Smart*, p. 287 finds what he considers heretical doctrine in Smart's *Hymns and Spiritual Songs*. But see Karina Side, "Christopher Smart's Heresy," *MLN*, LXIX (1954), 316–19.

NOTES

23. Pembroke College MS B. β. 6., p. 132.
24. Harvard College Library Collection.
25. BM Add MS 48345, pp. 46–8.
26. In James Osborn Collection, Yale University.
27. Puttock and Simpson sales catalogue, June 3, 1878, lot 267: $\frac{1}{2}$p. 4 to.
28. Quoted by Edmund Gosse in *TLS*, May 27, 1926, p. 355.
29. Collection of Donald and Mary Hyde.
30. Collection of Donald and Mary Hyde. Christie sale catalogue, July 23, 1856, lot 572: C. Smart to Dodsley, Pembroke Hall, Cambridge, January 12, 1747–8, records the existence of one more letter in this correspondence.
31. *Correspondence*, pp. 318 and 323–4.
32. *Correspondence*, pp. 273–5.
33. Liber Absentiae, F.$_\alpha$.
34. "Bursar's Accounts" and "Receipts of the Bursar", M. $_\alpha$. 2 and 3; "Treasury Accounts, 1729–1750," M. $_\alpha$. 4; and "Liber Absentiae," F. $_\alpha$.
35. B.β. 6, "Pembroke College Register."

Notes to Chapter III

1. Berg Collection of New York Public Library, Diary Manuscript, Box VIII letter of October 29, 1792, and Mrs. LeNoir to Sharp, letter of August 22, 1831, pp. 1 and 9.
2. Also involved in the transaction was a Mr. Collet, undoubtedly Richard Collet who led the band at Vauxhall. Manuscript in the Hyde Collection.
3. Jessié Foot, *Life of Arthur Murphy* (London, 1811), p. 51.
4. Letter to Sharp, August 22, 1831, pp. 1 and 9.
5. B. β, "Pembroke College Register," pp. 166 and 167.
6. The entire text is available in Brittain, *Poems by Christopher Smart*, pp. 234–35.
7. See Cambridge University Audit Book, 1741–86. The sums Smart got were, in order, £10.2.8$\frac{1}{4}$; £10.2.7; £9.18.9$\frac{1}{2}$; £10.7.6$\frac{1}{2}$; and £9.17.1.
8. See Brittain, *Poems by Christopher Smart*, pp. 54–5. Smart and Wilkes might, hence, have been acquainted as early as 1750.
9. Possibly George Russell of St. Mary's Hall who took his A.B. in 1750. The Yale University Library has Russell's copy with a manuscript note in his hand identifying certain pieces as his own and others as communicated by him.
10. See *The Midwife*, II, 25–6 and 48. Sedgly wrote for the *Westminster Journal*, then edited by Rolt, and probably then Smart through him.
11. The St. Alban's Lodge No. 2, which met at the Black Bear Inn in Cambridge, was granted a warrant on March 31, 1749. See John Lane, *Masonic Records, 1717–1886* (London, 1886), p. 56. Since a candidate for admission into the Freemasons had to be at least twenty-five years old, Smart could have joined at any time after April 11, 1747.
12. Gray's *Correspondence*, p. 260.
13. See Roland Botting in *English Literary History*, IX (1942), 286–7.
14. Manuscript in the Hyde Collection. He may also have been getting ready to borrow money again from Tyers in July by puffing the "Ridotto al Fresco" at Vauxhall in *The Student* for June, 1751.
15. The rest of the song may be seen in *The Midwife*, III, 60–1 or in *The General Magazine* for December, 1751.
16. Quoted in *The London Stage, 1660–1800, Part 4: 1747–1776*, ed. by G. W. Stone, Jr. (Carbondale, Ill., 1962), p. 302.
17. Letter to Sharp, August 22, 1831, p. 9.
18. *London Stage, Part 4*, ed. Stone, pp. lxxx, 355, 374, 433, 422, and 438.
19. See Botting, *Christopher Smart in London*, p. 29, n. 70, for a description of the animal comedians.
20. Quoted in Yale *Walpole Correspondence*, IX, 131, n. 6.
21. This is the year date given in her obituary in the *Reading Mercury* for May 22, 1809.

22. Quoted in Ainsworth and Noyes, *Christopher Smart*, p. 74.
23. Letter of August 22, 1831, p. 3.
24. See *Notes and Queries*, CCIII (1958), 441–2.
25. See Botting, *Christopher Smart in London*, p. 34 for further details.
26. VIII (January, 1753), 78–9. See also *The March of the Lion, or The Conclusion of the War between Dunce and the Dunces written with all the blackguardism of Justice Bobadil, all the politeness of the Inspector, all the wit of the fool, and all the smartness of Mary Midnight* (1752).
27. See Botting in *JEGP*, XLIII (1944), 56 for the Latin original. No other example of Smart's Latin epistolary style exists.
28. My reasons for connecting Smart with these are set forth in the *Bulletin of the New York Public Library*, LXIV (1960), 147–58. Since numbers 1 and 2 of *The Muses Banquet* were announced as published in the same newspaper of November 16, 1751, the collection must have come out periodically in numbers and then have been bound and edited for publication in 1753.
29. The claims for Smart's authorship are mine; see the *Bulletin of the New York Public Library*, LXI (1957), 373–82.
30. Translated from BM Add MSS 14936 by Mr. Nicholas Cox, third-year undergraduate of Pembroke College in 1964.
31. *The London Stage, 1600–1800, Part 4*, p. 450.
32. See my *New Essays of Arthur Murphy* (East Lansing, 1963), pp. 1–16 for the identification of Murphy as author of *The Entertainer*.
33. *Temple Bar*, CXXX (1904), 534–40.
34. *Gentleman's Magazine*, LIV (December, 1784), 907.
35. Arthur Newbery, *The Records of the House of Newbery*, (Derby and London, 1911), p. 13.
36. It was not printed until 1758, see below p. 121.
37. See *Bulletin of the New York Public Library*, LXIV (1960), 147–58.
38. The poem is actually lines 61–66 and 81–4 of Terentianus Maurus' preface to his *De Litteris Syllabis Pedibus et Metris*, a grammatical and metrical study of Horace written entirely in verse.
39. There are particularly full notes on the *Art of Poetry*, with Smart quoting Hurd very often and referring to Rymer, Francis, and Dacier.
40. See below, pp. 195–96 for the full text of the letter.
41. *Life*, II, 345.
42. "On receiving, from his most ingenious Friend Mr. Christopher Smart, No. I of a periodical pamphlet, entitled the Universal Visiter." James Osborn Collection of Yale University.
43. See Stuart Pigott in *TLS*, June 13, 1929, p. 474, for fuller details of the contract.
44. See below, p. 196.
45. See Roland Botting, "Johnson, Smart, and the *Universal Visiter*," *Modern Philology*, XXXVI (1939), 196 and my *New Essays by Arthur Murphy* (1963), 179–84.
46. See *The Library*, 4th ser. XVIII (1937), 212–214 and 5th ser., X (1955), 203–205 and *Modern Philology*, XXXVI (1939), 293–300. The total number of pages in the *Universal Visiter* dwindled from 54 in the January issue to 38 for December. Some space was taken up by musical settings by William Boyce, Samuel Howard, Joseph Baildon, and I. C. Smith for various songs printed.
47. His remark on metrics in the *Universal Visiter* occur on pp. 9, 73–4, and 128.
48. Percy Fitzgerald, *Life of David Garrick* (London, 1868), I, 284.
49. See Roger Lonsdale in *RES*, N.S., XII (1961), 403.
50. Brittain, *Poems by Christopher Smart*, p. 28, is authority for this statement, giving the date as April 28 and the newspaper as the *Daily Advertiser*, but although no such announcement appears in that newspaper for that date, Brittain's year date and quotation from the newspaper need not be questioned.
51. See *RES*, N.S., X (1959), 38–44 for the identification of the *Critical's* reviewers.

NOTES

52. *Life*, II, 345.
53. *Thraliana*, ed. K. C. Balderston (Oxford, 1942), p. 176.
54. *British Synonymy* (London, 1794) II, 3—5.
55. *Thraliana*, ed. K. C. Balderston, 2nd ed., (Oxford, 1951), p. 728.
56. *Life*, I, 397.
57. *A Continuation of . . . Whitefield's Journal* (London, 1739), pp. 97—98.
58. W. Russell Brain, "Christopher Smart: The Flea that Became an Eagle," *Medical Bookman and Historian*, II, no. 7 (1948), 295—300.
59. See *The London Stage, Part 4*, I, ccxxviii.
60. Letter of July 13, 1831, p. 217.
61. A. Hazen, *Samuel Johnson's Prefaces & Dedications* (New Haven, 1937), p. 217, n. 2. At the earlier date he was already in Potter's madhouse, although his help with the edition would have antedated publication of the first volume.

Notes to Chapter IV

1. Letter to Sharp, July 13, 1831, p. 217.
2. K. G. Burton, *The Early Newspaper Press in Berkshire, 1723–1855* (Reading, 1954), p. 109.
3. Letter to Sharp, August 22, 1831, p. 2.
4. Letter to Sharp, July 13, 1831, p. 218.
5. See above, p. 115.
6. Pp. 340–41. First-hand reports of life in private madhouses are to be had in *The Adventures of Alexander the Corrector* (London, 1754) by Alexander Cruden.
7. *Life*, I, 397.
8. *Life*, II, 374.
9. *Life*, I, 377n.
10. See J. P. Emery, *Arthur Murphy* (Philadelphia, 1946), p. 84.
11. *Letters of Samuel Johnson*, ed. R. W. Chapman (Oxford, 1952), III, 271–2. See *Johnson Newsletter*, XXIV, No. 1 (1964), 10–11, for the date of the letter.
12. Letter of August 22, 1831, p. 7.
13. F. B. Falkiner, *A Pedigree, with Personal Sketches, of the Falconers of Mount Falcon* (Dublin, 1894), p. 20.
14. *Alumni Dublinenses*.
15. Letter to Sharp, July, 1831, p. 219.
16. Letter to Sharp, August 22, 1831, p. 9.
17. See below, p. 252.
18. See Appendix A.
19. *Jubilate Agno* was first edited by W. F. Stead (London, 1939) and subsequently by W. H. Bond (Cambridge, Mass., 1954); the former has much annotation while the latter reproduces the poem in the order in which it was written. See pp. 16–19 of Bond's edition, whose designation for the various parts of the manuscript I use throughout, for the history and description of the holograph manuscript.
20. See Appendix B.
21. See above, pp. 48—52.
22. See above, p. 45.
23. See the London *Daily Advertiser* for June 27, 1753.
24. St. Luke's Hospital Committee Minute Book, July 26, 1751, to November 24, 1758.
25. See my article in *Modern Language Notes*, LXXI (1956) 179–182, where Smart's reading in the periodicals is discussed more fully.
26. She was evidently known to Smart's friend Murphy; see Jessé Foot, *Life of Arthur Murphy* (London, 1811), p. 138.
27. Among the books or authors readily identifiable are Bishop Bayly's *Practice of Piety* (D,43), Ovid (B1,204), Locke (B2,650), Pliny (D,111), Ascham (D,53), Evelyn (D,111), Ennius (B1,74 Let), Cicero (B2,386), Homer (B2,633), Virgil

(D.84), the *Palatine Anthology* (B1,82), *Twelfth Night* (B1,189), and *Paradise Lost* (B2,373).

28. See Christopher Devlin, *Poor Kit Smart* (London, 1961), pp. 108–110 for further examples.

29. London (1713), p. 233n.

30. See B1, 222 through B1, 295.

31. Smart quoted an excerpt from the latter work in *The Midwife* (I,246) and was probably further interested in it because Plot takes occasion to attack the Freemasons.

32. The claims for these are made, respectively, in Albert Kuhn, "Christopher Smart: The Poet as Patriot of the Lord," *ELH*, XXX (1963) 121–36; K. M. Rogers, "The Pillars of the Lord: Some Sources of *A Song to David*," *PQ*, XL (1961), 525–34; Stead, ed. *Rejoice in the Lamb*, pp. 37–40 and *passim*; and my "Christopher Smart, Free and Accepted Mason," *JEGP*, LIV (1955), 664–69.

33. See Appendix C for two lists of scientific works in use in Cambridge around 1730.

34. Translated from the French by Samuel Humphreys in 1733 and going to a tenth edition by 1766, it was a popular work in seven volumes.

35. Fourth ed. (1763), V, 267.

36. B2,347. See William Whiston, *A Plain and Familiar Introduction to the Newtonian Philosophy* (London, 1754), p. 161.

37. As quoted in Robert Smith, *A Compleat System of Opticks in Four Books* (Cambridge, 1738), p. 74.

38. See D. J. Greene, "Smart, Berkeley, the Scientists and the Poets," *JHI*, XIV, (1953), 327–52.

39. See note 37 above.

40. 1712, p. 29; Chapters iii–vi are largely an attack on Newtonian science.

41. Luke, 16:21.

42. K. A. McKenzie, *Christopher Smart: sa vie et ses oeuvres* (Paris, 1925), p. 98.

43. See my article "The Probable Time of Composition of Christopher Smart's *Song to David, Psalms,* and *Hymns* and *Spiritual Songs*," *JEGP*, LV (1956), 41–57 for the tables of parallels.

44. These range from D,148, to D,221, but are concentrated in lines 199, 203, 208, 217, 220, and 221.

45. See above, pp. 105–106, for Smart's opinion of Lowth's lectures.

46. A, 44, 50, 71.

47. B, 150–2.

48. See above, p. 142.

Notes to Chapter V

1. See *The Early Diary of Frances Burney*, ed. A. R. Ellis (London, 1907), I, xlv and 116n.

2. Lady Caroline Cowper had married Henry Seymour, Esq., in 1753. She was the niece of gossipy Spencer Cowper, Dean of Durham and enemy to Harry Vane.

3. See Appendix B, p. 271.

4. See Appendix B, 271–72.

5. See below, p. 196.

6. See below, p. 181.

7. Gray's *Correspondence*, p. 802.

8. *Letters of James Boswell*, ed. C. B. Tinker (Oxford 1924), I, 39.

9. Translated, 1734–1741, IV, 532.

10. See R. D. Havens, "The Structure of Smart's *Song to David*," *RES*, XIV (1938), 178–82 and Brittain, *Poems of Christopher Smart*, pp. 292–310. The latter is by far the best analysis of the *Song* so far written although at times it is overly ingenious.

NOTES

11. J. R. Tutin, ed. *A Song to David* (London, 1898), pp. 47–8 lists many of the "Scripture References" in the *Song* but overlooks that quoted in this paragraph.

12. Stanza 44 continues to pose difficulties.

13. Compare stanzas 15 and 16 of the *Hymn to the Supreme Being*.

14. See A. J. Kuhn in *ELH*, XXX (1963), 121–36, on this theme of Smart's poetry.

15. XXIX (September, 1763), 227.

16. XVI (July, 1763), 72; See Botting, *Christopher Smart in London*, p. 46, for the full text of Smart's accusation against the *Critical*.

17. Gray's *Correspondence*, pp. 801–04.

18. See Charles Petersdorff, *A Practical and Elementary Abridgement of the Cases Argued and Determined* (London, 1829), XII, 394—6.

19. XVI (November, 1763), 395.

20. See Benjamin Nangle, *The Monthly Review, First Series, 1749–1789* (Oxford, 1934), for identification of the reviewers.

21. XXIX (November, 1763), 398.

22. John Forster, *Life of Goldsmith*, (London, 1854), I, 167–68.

23. *Correspondence of Thomas Percy & Edmond Malone*, ed. A. Tillotson (Baton Rouge, Louisiana, 1944), p. 38.

24. Sotheby & Co. catalog, item 531, April 22, 1958.

25. BM Add MSS. 48800 gives the number for 1752; the receipt is in the Pembroke College Library copy of the Psalms.

26. See above, p. 11 for the poem on the lilies.

27. Col. Hall was probably the Lt. Col. Hall of the 37th Regiment who died at Minorca on December 18, 1763.

28. The manuscript is in the Pembroke College Library copy of the Psalms.

29. Nangle, *Monthly Review, First Series*, 1934, p. 25.

30. See Karina Williamson, "Christopher Smart's *Hymns & Spiritual Songs*," *PQ*, XXXVIII (1959), 414.

31. XX (September, 1765), 210—11.

32. XXXIII (September, 1765), 240–1. The tone suggests Langhorne as the reviewer.

33. See Brittain, *Poems by Christopher Smart*, pp. 179–81 for examples of this.

34. See Susie Tucker in *Notes and Queries*, CCIII (November, 1958), 468—70, whence I derive these and some following examples.

35. George Wither's in 1623 and Thomas Ken's in 1721.

36. *Transactions, The American Lodge of Research, Free and Accepted Masons*, V, No. 3 (April, 1951–January, 1952), 366–7.

37. See *London Magazine*, 1747, p. 145 for the original song and tune.

38. See John Lane, *Masonic Records, 1717–1886* (London, 1886), pp. 4 and 23.

Notes to Chapter VI

1. This and the following letters to Panton are taken from Cecil Price, "Six Letters by Christopher Smart," *RES*, N.S., VIII (1957), 144—8.

2. Quoted in Devlin, *Poor Kit Smart*, p. 170.

3. *Posthumous Letters From Various Celebrated Men; Addressed to Francis Colman, and George Colman, the Elder* (London, 1820), p. 90.

4. *Calendar of Home Office Papers of the Reign of George III, 1766-1769*, p. 109.

5. Hunter, p. xxii, is the sole authority for the granting of the pension; no official record has come to light despite diligent search.

6. XIX, 21–3; Loeb translation.

7. *Life*, III, 356.

8. XVIII (January, 1758), 45–52.

9. Bk. iv, Ode 13; numbered 12 by Smart in his translation.

10. Here and in what follows I quote from Francis's 2nd edition, 1747.

11. Text from MS in Pembroke College Library. Norman Callan, ed. *Collected Poems* (1949), reads inaccurately, "There remains," in the last stanza.

12. Brittain, *Poems by Christopher Smart*, reprints two of the epistles. Smart's translation of the sixth satire of the second book is an admirable example of his handling of dialogue.

13. Charles Welsh, *A Bookseller of the Last Century* (London, 1885), p. 166.

14. Harvard College Library Collection.

15. XXXVIII (May, 1768), 409.

16. Sir Thomas Robinson was for a time director of entertainment in Ranelagh Gardens and was fond of books, music, and the fine arts in general. (*DNB*)

17. *Early Diary*, ed. A. R. Ellis (London, 1907), I, 28 and 66.

18. 3 vol., (London, 1832), I, 205.

19. See *Notes and Queries*, CXCIX (1949), 321–4 and CCII (1957), 71–3, on the date and details of this ode. The most recent discussion of the whole vexed question is in Roger Lonsdale, *Dr. Charles Burney* (Oxford, 1965), pp. 485–90.

20. See above, p. 68.

21. Walter Arnold, *The Life and Death of the Sublime Society of Beef Steaks* (London, 1871); for Havard, see *Boswell's London Journal* (London, 1950), p. 52, and for Thornton, see Walter Besant, *Westminster* (London, 1895), p. 329.

22. Quoted in Brittain, *Poems by Christopher Smart*, pp. 51–2.

23. See W. H. Bond in *TLS*, April 10, 1953, p. 237 for additional information about a related transaction.

24. See Devlin, *Poor Kit Smart*, pp. 178–181 for fuller details.

25. Quoted in Devlin, *Poor Kit Smart*, p. 182.

26. See C. E. Whiting, *Nathaniel Lord Crewe, Bishop of Durham, (1674–1721)* London, 1940.

27. W. H. D. Longstaffe, *The History and Antiquities of the Parish of Darlington in the Bishopric of Durham* (London, 1909), p. 255n.

28. Quoted in Brittain, *Poems by Christopher Smart*, pp. 53–4.

29. See W. H. Bond in *TLS*, April 10, 1953, p. 237, some of whose legal terminology I have borrowed.

30. Quoted in Roger Lonsdale, *Dr. Charles Burney* (Oxford, 1965), p. 69.

31. John Noorthouck, *A New History of London* (London, 1773), pp. 681 and 682.

32. *Oxford Magazine*, V (1770), 122–6 and 186–9; VI (1771), 50–1 and 64–5.

33. *The Memoirs of James Stephens*, ed. by M. M. Bevington (London, 1954); my quotations are scattered through pp. 89-99.

34. *Early Diary*, I, 133.

35. *Gentleman's Magazine*, XLIX (July, 1779), 339.

36. All quotations are from the facsimile reprint of the third edition, 1775, edited by Edmund Blunden (Oxford, 1947).

37. See Botting, *ELH*, IX (1942), 286–7 for this Hymn.

38. Quoted by W. H. Bond in *TLS*, April 10, 1953, p. 237.

39. Ainsworth and Noyes, *Christopher Smart*, p. 141.

40. Chester MS. 48, 336, Burials, in the College of Heralds.

41. *Early Diary*, I, 133.

Notes to Appendix A

1. See *Harvard Library Bulletin*, X (Spring, 1956), 201–7, for the dating of lines in *Jubilate Agno*.

2. Quoted in *Johnsonian Miscellanies*, ed. G. B. Hill (Oxford, 1897), I, 320 and n.2.

3. See above, p. 17 where she confuses the ages of the young Harry Vane and Peggy Smart.

Notes to Appendix B

1. *The London Stage*, ed. Stone, p. 774.

NOTES

2. Bodleian Library, Douce Prints, a. 49.
3. *The London Stage*, ed. Stone, p. 806.
4. See above, p. 113.
5. See above, p. 166.

INDEX

I have not indexed Appendix C for obvious reasons and I have included only a few entries from the notes. Names of modern scholars cited or quoted are also omitted. Some entries, those under Cambridge University and Pembroke College, for example, are selective rather than inclusive; I give references only to what I consider important rather than record every appearance of Cambridge University or Pembroke College. I have not, as a further example, seen any need to encumber the index with an entry for London, although there are entries for a few places in that city. But the entries for persons are complete. I have attached short identifying tags, chiefly for the obscurer names in the index; what will be obscure to one may not be to another, although I doubt many readers would recognize any large number of Smart's fellow students or the subscribers to his poems and Psalms. References to Colleges are to those in Cambridge unless otherwise indicated. Numbers in italics point to the most important and extended discussions of a particular work or person. S=Smart; subs.=subscriber.

INDEX

Baildon, Joseph, composer, 201, 280

Baker, Thomas, of Pembroke College, 139

Ball, Dr. John, *Modern Practice of Physic*, 115-16

Banks, Mr., Cambridge tailor, 234

Barnard, Lady, wife to Christopher Vane, 4

Barnes, Rev. G. W., subs. to S's Psalms, 86n

Barrowby, Dr. William, member of Beef Steaks Society, 250-1

Barry, Spranger, actor, 73

Barwell, Mrs., S's landlady, 167, 190, 249

Bathurst, Charles, bookseller, 51, 63

Battie, Dr. William, treats the insane, 30, 113, 114-15, 118, 123, 132, 203

Bayle, Pierre, *General Dictionary*, 172

Bayly, Lewis, Bishop of Bangor, *The Practice of Piety*, 281

Bazire, John, associated with S's father, 4

Beard, John, singer, 202, 250

Beaumont, Francis, 42

Bedford Coffee-House, 107, 251

Bedford, John, of Pembroke College, 27

Bedford, John, Jr., of Pembroke College, 42, 43, 45

Behn, Mrs. Aphra, 23

Benbow, John, naval hero, 217

Bennet, James, friend of S, 141

Bennet, Kitty, S writes poem to, 141

Bentham, Joseph, printer to Cambridge University, 50

Bentley, Dr. Richard, 199

Berg, George, composer, 201

Berkeley, George, Bishop of Cloyne, *Essay on Vision*, 154-5

Bess, resident of Canonbury House, 86n, 137

Bethlem Hospital (or Bedlam), 110, 111, 113-14

Bible, 109, 130, 147, 155, 158, 162, 168, 170, 172, 176, 191-2, 208, 213, 214, 220, 240, 245, 265 and n

Bill, John, of Christ's College, 139

Birch, Thomas, miscellaneous writer, 102n

Bird, Mr., subs. to S's Psalms, 203

Blackstone, Sir William, 266

Blackwell, Samuel, subs. to S's Psalms, 203

Blake, Robert, naval hero, 217

Blyth, Mr., collects subscriptions for S's Psalms, 186

Book of Common Prayer, 147, 155, 208, 209, 211, 216

Booth, Justice of the Peace, neighbor of S's, 87

Boswell, James, 104, 111, 116, 126, 169-70, 233

Bourdaloue, Père Louis, 42

Bowes, George, of Durham, subs. to 1752 vol., 82

Boyce, Dr. William, composer, 26, 61, 82, 91, 185, 201, 202, 204, 221, 280

Bridges, Brook, of Sidney Sussex College, 140

Bright, James, brings suit against S, 250

Britannia's Triumph, 271-2

British Magazine, or Monthly Repository, 190, 193

Brown, James, of Pembroke College, 30-1, 40-1, 43, 202

Brown, Dr. John, writer, 69

Burchell, Miss, singer, 73

Burney, Charles, 35, 38, 44, 48, 59, 60, 61, 62, 70, 70n, 82, 96, 105, 108, 112, 125, 141, 145, 166, 201, 202, 244, 250, 256

Burney, Fanny, 48, 61, 244, 249-50, 255, 258, 265, 267

Burslem, James, of Pembroke College, 27, 28

Butler, Samuel, *Hudibras*, 31

Byng, George, Viscount Torrington, naval hero, 217

Caesar, Julius, 9, 22

INDEX

Covent Garden Journal Extraordinary, 92

Cowley, Abraham, 228

Cowper, Lady Caroline (later Seymour), S dedicates work to her, 282

Cowper, Dean Spencer, Dean of Durham, 13, 14-15, 16, 18, 282

Cowper, William, the poet, 123, 155, 202

Cox, Nicholas, translates two Latin poems by S, 278, 280

Cranfield, Lionel, 1st Duke of Dorset and Earl of Middlesex, 83

Craven, Lord, scholarship, 30, 31-2, 193

Crewe, Nathaniel, third Baron Crewe of Stene, 253

Critical Review, 110, 111, 119, 169, 174, 183, 187-8, 189, 191, 194, 199-200, 202, 204-5, 208, 231-3, 246, 247-8, 267, 280, 283

Crockatt, James, bookseller, 209

Cromwell, Oliver, 163

Crossinge, Richard, of Pembroke College, 57

Cruden, Alexander, *The Adventures of Alexander the Corrector*, 281

Cumberland, Richard, the dramatist, subs. to S's Psalms, 202

Cutting, Leonard, of Pembroke College, 138, 139

Dacier, André, French critic and translator, 240, 280

Da Costa, Emanuel, S's fellow prisoner, 259, and n

Daily Advertiser, 77, 88, 99, 164, 280, 281

Daily Gazetteer, 91

Dalrymple, Sir David, friend of Boswell, 169

Dalton, John, his alteration of *Comus*, 52

Dalton, Richard, friend of S, 196, 203

David, King of Israel, 29, 65, 160, 168, *171-5*, 176-7

Davies, Thomas, actor and bookseller, 104

Delany, Patrick, *Historical Account of the Life and Reign of David*, 42, 171, 172

Delap, John, of Magdalene College, 140

Delaval, Edward Hussey, of Pembroke College, 83, 227

Delaval, Sir Francis Blake, patron of S, 73, 74, 83, 107, 226-7

Delaval, John Blake, patron of S, 43, 73, 74, 83, 187

Delaval, Master John Hussey, S dedicates work to, 199

Demosthenes, 22, 42

Denham, Sir John, 229

DeQuincy, Thomas, 242n

Derham, William, physico-theologist, 147

Derrick, Samuel, reviewer for *Critical Review*, 111

Desaguliers, J. T., *Mathematical Elements of Natural Philosophy*, 152

Dionysius, of Halicarnassus, 229

Dixon, John, mezzotint engraver, 248, 249

Dodd, Dr. William, editor of *Christian Magazine*, 102n, 166, 202, 209

Dodsley, James, bookseller, 195, 198

Dodsley, Robert, bookseller, 46, 50-3, 54, 59, 63, 198, 278

Dongworth, Richard, S's master at Durham School, 19-20, 22, 24, 82, 137, 146

Donne, John, 217

Dorsett, Michael, of Pembroke College, 27, 28, 43

Dowse, J., bookseller, 94

Drake, Sir Francis, 16th century naval hero, 217

Draper, Mrs., S writes poem on, 193

Draper, General William, military hero, 139, 181, 193

Drury Lane Journal, 92

Dryden, John, 49, 250

INDEX

Gaudry, Joseph, composer and singer, 167, 270, 271

Gay, John, 96, 199

Gazetteer and London Daily Advertiser, 122

The geese stript of their quills, 92

General Advertiser, 73n, 92, 200

General Evening Post, 51

General Magazine, 279

General Review, or Impartial Register, 84

Gentleman's Magazine, 21, 35, 36, 49, 54, 58, 60, 63, 74, 75, 76, 81, 89, 92-3, 96, 100, 101, 110, 119n, 121, 124, 128, 144, 174, 189, 248, 259n, 284

George II, King of England, 52, 57, 172, 174

George III, King of England, 143, 218, 271-2

George, Prince, later George III, King of England, 73, 95

Gesner, Conrad, *Historiae Animalium*, 148

Gilder, —, musician, 221

Gli Amanti Gelosi, or the Birth of Harlequin, 79

Goldsmith, Oliver, 55, 59, 60, 120, 189-90

Gordon, John, actor in S's play, 184, 202

Gosling, Francis, recommends S to St. Luke's Hospital, 112, 114

Grainger, Dr. James, reviewer for *Monthly Review*, 66, 202; *The Sugar Cane*, 66

Granier, Mr., actor-dancer, 141

Gratulatio Academiae Cantabrigiensis, 52, 56-7

Gravesande, William, scientific writer, 152

Gray, Thomas, 23-4, 24, 25, 26, 28, 30, 31, 36-7, 43-4, 51, 52, 53, 53-4, 119, 133, 139, 151, 170, 184, 202, 210; *Ode on a Distant Prospect of Eton College*, 52

Green, Dr. John, Bishop of Lincoln, *The Academic*, 150

Green, Robert, *Principles of Natural Philosophy*, 152, 155

Griffiths, Ralph, editor of *Monthly Review*, 89, 188, 200, 231, 246

Grotius, Hugo, 43

Gudius, Gottlob Friedrich, German writer, 199

Guido, Italian painter of Siena, 187

Gulston, Francis, of Pembroke College, 139, 203

Guthrie, William, miscellaneous writer, 59

Gyll, Thomas, diarist, 20

Gyraldus, Lilius, 50

Halford, Richard, of Pembroke College, 139

Hall, Colonel, S writes poem for, 193, 283

Hall, Thomas, "the young giant," 133

Hallett, Benjamin, child musician, 78

Hamer, Lady, friend of S, 248

Handel, George Frederick, 60, 146, 270

Harborne, William, witness to *Universal Visiter* contract, 105

Harrison, William, S's school fellow in Durham, 82

Havard, William, actor, 82, 107, 118, 202, 251, 284

Hawkesworth, Mrs. 196

Hawkesworth, John, 61, 96, 102, 103-4, 105, 167-8, 195-6, 197, 198, 200, 202, 223, 233, 240, 243

Hayman, Francis, painter, 60, 61n, 81, 202, 250

Heartley, George, of Christ's College, 139

Hengist and Horsa, story of, 85

Henley, "Orator" John, 24, 75, 76-7, 91

Hesiod, 22

Higgs, John, of Trinity College, 139

Hill, Aaron, Merope, 118

Hill, John, miscellaneous writer, 71, 88-91, 107, 189; *The Impertinent*,

INDEX

La Bruyère, Jean de, 52

La Fontaine, Jean de, 42

Ladies Magazine, 70

Lambert, George, member of Beef Steaks Society, 251n

Langdon, William, naval hero, 217

Langhorne, John, reviewer, for *Monthly Review*, 168-9, 170, 194-5, 188-9, 200, 202, 281

Langton, Bennet, subs. to Merrick's Psalms, 203

La Roche, Deodata, acts in amateur *Othello*, 74

La Roche, Elizabeth, acts in amateur *Othello*, 74

Lauder, —, singer, 78, 271

Laurence, Mr., bookseller, 186

Lawman, —, "the mad attorney," 53

Leach, Dryden, bookseller, 200, 226, 254-5

Legard, Sir Digby, subs. to 1752 vol., 83, 144, 203

LeNoir, Elizabeth. *See* Smart, Elizabeth

Leroche, Miss, S's "fellow traveler from Calais," 100

A Letter to Dr. Samuel Chandler, 173

The Life of David, or the History of the Man after God's own Heart, 172-3, 174

Lilliputian Magazine, 75, 262

Livy, 22, 240

Lloyd, Robert, editor of *St. James's Magazine*, 141, 166, 202, 224

Lloyd's Evening Post, 118

Locke, John, 42, 281

Lockman, John, poetaster and friend of S, 82, 104; poem on S's benefit, 119

Lodge, Ralph, subs. to S's Psalms, 203

London Chronicle, 246

London Gazette, 143

London Magazine, 8, 47, 53, 54, 55, 58, 71, 283

Long, Dr. Roger, Master of Pembroke College, 30, 31, 45, 53, 82, 138, 202

Long, Samuel, composer, 201

Lowe, Thomas, singer, 73, 82, 202

Lowth, Dr. Robert, Bishop of London, 69, 166, 196, 204, 214, 282; *Praelectiones de Sacra Poesi Hebraeorum*, or *Lectures On Hebrew Poetry*, 105-6, 159, 197, 214

Lucretius, 55, 83

Lyne, Richard, of King's College, 139, 184

Lyttleton, George, 1st Baron Lyttleton, 52

MacDonald, —, keeps madhouse, 123

Macklin, Charles, actor, 73, 107

McMahon's, Mr., Dublin base for Anna Maria Smart, 126

Maidstone, 6-9, 21

Main, —, bookseller, 258

Mallet, David, *Alfred*, a masque, 73

Mapletoff, Robert, of Pembroke College, 45

The March of the Lion, 280

Markham, William, Bishop of Chester, 259

Marsh, Richard, S's schoolmate at Durham, 139

Marsham, Maidstone family, 8

Marsham, Honorable Miss, subs. to 1752 vol., 82

Martial Review, or General History of the Late War, 189

Martin, Benjamin, scientific writer, 59

Mason, John, of Maidstone, subs. to 1752 vol., 82

Mason, William, 52, 53, 57, 69, 119, 139, 169, 184, 185, 201, 202, 210, 215, 224-5, 226, 244, 254, 255; *Musaeus*, 52

Masters, Mary, *Familiar Letters and Poems on Several Occasions*, 102

Mawley, Joseph, of Vauxhall, 82

Maurus, Terentianus, *De Litteris Syllabis Pedibus et Metris*, 280

INDEX

Maxwell, Francis Kelly, of Pembroke College, 203

May, Samuel, of Pembroke College, 31, 36, 43

Medicina Gymnastica, 43

Medway river, 10-11

Mendez, Moses, subs. to 1752 vol., 82

Merrick, James, poet, 54, 144, 192, 200, 203-5, 208, 209, 215

Miller, Philip, *Gardener's Dictionary*, 148

Milton, John, 42, 63; *Comus*, 52; *Il Penseroso*, 49, 50, 83, 205; *L'Allegro*, 49, 50, 83, 205; *Paradise Lost*, 282; *Samson Agonistes*, 183

Monson, George, Anne Vane's 2nd husband, 18, 19

Monson, Mrs. George. *See* Vane, Anne

Montagu, George, friend of Horace Walpole, 80, 278

Montagu, Mary, confined at St. Luke's, 112

Monthly Review, 44, 66, 89, 92, 96, 108, 110, 168-9, 174, 182-3, 186, 188-9, 191, 194-5, 202, 204-5, 231, 233-4, 246-7

Moore, Edward, fabulist, 96, 199

Morgan, Mr., of Westminster, subs. to 1752 vol., 83

Morgan, Elizabeth, confined at St. Luke's, 112, 113

Morning Herald (London), 77

Mother Midnight's Oratory, 75-81, 90, 92-3, 98-9, 101, 119, 139, 141, 167, 221, 239, 250, 269-72

Murphy, Arthur, 61, 70, 83, 91, 105, 107, 111, 125, 132, 202, 251, 254, 259, 281; *The Apprentice*, 107-8; *The Entertainer*, 99, 280; *Gray's Inn Journal*, 93, 94, 100, 110, 120; *Hilliad*, notes to, 91; poem on S's benefit, 118

Murray, William, 1st Earl of Mansfield, 32, 83, 227, 255, 257, 259

The Museum, or Literary and Historical Register, 46, 51, 54, 58, 198

Musgrave, Edward, of Pembroke College, 139

Nares, Dr. James, composer, 197, 201, 259

Nares, Justice George, 259

Nares, Robert, philologist, 198

Neale, James, of Pembroke College, 27

Nelson, Robert, 215, 216; *Companion for the Fasts and Festivals of the Church of England*, 215-16

Nepos, Cornelius, 9

Newbery, Francis, son of the bookseller, 243, 250

Newbery, John, S's father-in-law, *59-60*, 62, 63, 67, 68n, 69, 70, 70n, 72, 75, 75n, 77, 81, 82, 86, 87, 90, 93, 94, 98, 99, 100, 101, 102, 104, 105, 108, 109, 111, 112, 114, 119, *120-1*, 122, 127, 129, 132, 133, 166, 174, 189, 192, 195, 200, 209, 230, 243, 250, 254, 262, 266, 267

Newbery, Mary, daughter of the publisher, 86n

Newbery, Mary, wife of the publisher, 86, 255

Newcastle, Thomas Pelham-Holles, 1st Duke of, 15-16

Newcome, Henry (?), English divine, 42

Newton, Sir Isaac, 43, 136, 150, 153-5

Nieuwentyt, Bernard, *The Religious Philosopher*, 152

Noell, —, entertainer in S's Oratory, 78

Noorthouck, John, *New History of London*, 114-172

Oates, Titus, 163

O'Brien, William, actor, 118

Ode to February . . . Attempted in the manner of Mr. S———t, 96

Orpheus, 171

Ovid, 9, 22; *Metamorphoses*, 229, 230, 232; *Tristia*, 165

294

INDEX

INDEX

125-8, 135-6, 155, 192, 201, 243, 251

Smart, Christopher, General

baptized, 5; lives in Shipbourne, 6; family coat of arms, 7; school in Maidstone, 9, 12; early life in East Barming, 10-13; flora and fauna of Kent, 10-12; love for Medway River, 10-11; love of flowers, 10-12; a gardener, 11-12; not withdrawn as child, 12; anecdotes of, 12-13, 87, 127-8; goes to Durham, 13; social life in Durham, 14; early use of cordials, 16, 117; school vacations at Raby Castle, 16-18; in love with Anne Vane, 17-19; allowed 40 pounds annually by Duchess of Cleveland, 19; early poems, 20-21; studies in Durham Grammar School, 21-2; leaves Durham, 22; admitted to Pembroke College, 24; Leonard Addison, his tutor, 24-6, 29-30; becomes Watts Scholar, 26; his studies at Cambridge, 27, 31; his coevals at Cambridge, 27-8; his wit, 28; his friends, 28-9, 139-40; opposes Master of Pembroke, 31; writes Tripos verses, 31; wins Craven Scholarship, 31; corresponds with Alexander Pope, 32-3; writes College Jubilee ode, 33-4; writes ode on his B.A. degree, 34; poem on confined eagle, 34; early trips to London, 35-6; poem published in *GM*, 35-6; elected Fellow, 36; his College offices, 36, 42, 44-6, 57; views of the University, 38-42; becomes Master of Arts, 42; his reading at Pembroke, 42-3; arrested for debt, 43-4, 222, 223, 255-6; his extravagance, 44; preaches before Mayor of Cambridge, 45; speech on martyrdom of Charles I, 45; becomes catechist, 45-6; leaves Cambridge, 46, 57-8; in love with Harriot Pratt, 46-9; friendship with Charles Bur-

ney, 35, 48-9; critic of poetry, 49-50, 227-9; correspondence with Dodsley, 50-3; proposes collection of poems, 51; his energetic nature, 53; his comedy *A Trip to Cambridge*, 53-4; publication of various poems, 54-7; writes for *Gratulatio*, 56-7; arrives in London, 58-9; and Newbery, 59-60, 120-1; London friends, 60-2; described, 61; self-described, 61; and the Seatonian prize poems, 62-7, 74, 94, 100, 102, 111, 144, 175, 177, 209; themes of his poetry, 64, 155-6, 175, 216-17, 229, 262-3; aspects of his poetry, 66-7, 157-8, 177, 178, 212-15, 242, 264; pseudonyms, 68-9, 70; writes for *The Student*, 68-71; resurrects old poems, 69; Mrs. Midnight's Oratory, 70, 75-81, 269-72; literary quarrel with Kenrick, 71-2; and Freemasonry, 73, 81, 150, 170, 279, 282; amateur *Othello*, 73-4; publishes collection of poems, 81-6; his subscribers, 81-3, 167, 183-4, 186, 190-1, 200-3, 222; his patriotism, 84, 98, 106, 107, 182; marries, 86-7; birth of his children, 87; loses Fellowship, 88; quarrel with Hill, 88-91; criticizes his own poetry, 91; illness (or madness), 94, 100, 109-19; poetry in *GM*, 96; his fables, 96-8; burlesque rhymes, 93, 98; writes letter for Murphy's periodical, 99; his extravagance, 100, 245; projects collection of tales and fables, 100-1, 104; meets Johnson, 101; introduces Tyers to Johnson, 101; visited by Hawkesworth, 103-4, 195-6; edits the *Universal Visiter*, 104-7; praises Lowth's work, 105-6; on the English language, 106; preoccupation with metrics, 107 and n., 240-1; defends Burney, 108; teaches Latin in madhouse, 116; benefit for, 118-19; 267-8; where-

INDEX

West, Richard, Gray's friend, 23, 30
Westminster Club, 40
Westminster Journal, 279
Wharton, Henry, English divine, 42
Wharton, Thomas, Gray's friend, 25, 31, 37, 43, 44, 53, 82
Wheeler, Theophilus, of Christ's College, 10, 29, 33, 81
Whisson, Stephen, of Trinity College, 140
Whiston, William, scientific writer, 98
Whitefield, Rev. George, 26, 117
Whitehead, William, friend of S, 32, 52, 54, 57, 82-3, 140, 164, 202
Wilcox, Dr. John, Master of Clare Hall, 144
Wilkes, John, 68, 164, 250, 251, 252, 259, 279
Wilkinson, Charles, of Pembroke College, 139
William III, King of England, 3
William Augustus, 5th Duke of Cumberland, 125

Willock, Mr., takes subscriptions for S's Psalms, 186
Wilmot, Justice —, examines "mad-woman," 124
Wither, George, 283
Wolfe, General James, 271
Wood, Thomas, composer, 201
Woodbridge, —, musician, 270
Worgan, Thomas, composer, 73, 82, 191
The World Displayed, 121
Worlidge, Thomas, painter, 55, 81, 202
Woty, William, friend of S, 118, 166, 202
Wynn, Dr. friend of Panton, 226

Xenophon, 42

Yates, Richard, actor, 118
Young, Arthur, editor of the *Universal Museum*, 190
Young, Edward, 202

Zerubabel, 147